Recipient of Grace

Continued

Choice-Relationships-Circles of Influence

DONALD L. SCOTT

Brigadier General, US Army, Retired

FROM HUNNEWELL, MO TO WASHINGTON, DC AND BEYOND

Recipient of Grace
Continued

Choice-Relationships-Circles of Influence

DONALD L. SCOTT

Brigadier General, US Army, Retired

FROM HUNNEWELL, MO TO WASHINGTON, DC AND BEYOND

SCRIPTOR HOUSE
THE EPITOME OF GREATNESS

Scriptor House LLC
2810 N Church St Wilmington, Delaware, 19802
www.scriptorhouse.com
Phone: +1302-205-2043

Published by Scriptor House LLC
Paperback ISBN:979-8-88692-026-0
eBook ISBN: 979-8-88692-027-7
Hardback ISBN: 979-8-88692-145-8

Contents

FOREWORD

The Library of Congress is America's oldest federal cultural institution; the world's largest collection of human knowledge in almost all languages and formats; the main research support of the

U.S. Congress, and the largest record anywhere of the diverse cultural and intellectual creativity of the American people. It is an asset of growing importance to the United States in an increasingly knowledge- dependent world.

Anyone responsible for directing this one-of-a-kind provider of free public service has a staff with a wide variety of scholarly and technical skills. It was agreat good fortune, for the Library-and for me individually as the 13th Librarian of Congress-to have General Don Scott as our dedicated and effective Deputy Librarian of Congress during an important decade in the Library's history.

During the preceding decade, my first as the Librarian, I had relied mainly on acting deputies from the existing staff. We improved the cataloging and security of the Library's traditional collections on Capitol Hill, launched a large-scale online National Digital Library, bringing unique American treasures from the Library's collections for education and inspiration to Americans everywhere. We began working with Congress to plan massive new preservation facilities for paper-based collections in Fort Meade, Maryland, and for audio- visual materials in Culpeper, Virginia.

As I approached the second decade of my service as Librarian, we clearly needed a more permanent Deputy Librarian who could become the Library's first Chief Operating Officer. I launched a nation-wide search, and was fortunate to find Don Scott, who had the stature and experience to take the lead in coordinating and managing the widening range of all our disparate operations. He brought to the Library high-level executive experience within the Army and subsequently in Atlanta and with AmeriCorps. He gave us a fresh outside perspective and a strong ethic of dedication to public service on behalf of a patriotic mission.

Don Scott helped the Library to share his active belief in Facilitative Leadership. He ran meetings of the Library's Executive

Committee-pointing towards decisions rather than simply recycling issues for more meetings. At the same time, he himself not only interacted with other groups and individuals, but arranged to train almost all levels of Library management in this process. As I write these words in the late spring of 2014, I am myself engaged in year-long consultations with various levels of management and staff to produce a Library of Congress Futures Program.

One of the great privileges of working at the Library of Congress is the quality and dedication of a variegated staff from whom one can learn something new each day at work. It was a personal pleasure to have been able to work in close partnership with a General who made such a contribution to the human -as well as administrative-life of this institution. He supported fairness in hiring, staff development, and life-long learning within the Library-just as we are now promoting life-long learning in America more generally.

Characteristically, Don is still serving the nation even in retirement on the Board of the Library's Archive of American Folklore. He is an active supporter of the Library's two major oral history projects, both mandated by the Congress: interviews with American military veterans of foreign wars and with participants in the Civil Rights movement. His continued life-long devotion to his wife, family and the local community that nurtured and supported him are as admirable as his service to the nation.

Marjorie and I and many others here will always remember Don and Betty with appreciation and affection. We admire their vitality and good humor. We share their enduring hope for a better and even more inclusive America-and their belief in God's providence and promise for all of us.

James H. Billington

20 June 2014

PREFACE

Welcome to the continuation of my life story Recipient of Grace Continued. The initial story, Recipient of Grace was published in April 2015 and did not contain a preface. The purpose of the Preface is to tell you the reason for the continuation of my life story. There have been so many changes in my life and the world since the 2015 publication that I felt compelled to record my thoughts, concerns and share my insights with readers interested in the continuation of my life journey. The three areas of greatest impact to me are the deaths of six influential people in my life, the rise of racism and threat to democracy in America and the importance of retaining Historical Places like New Philadelphia, IL (National Historic Site) Historical Black Colleges and Lincoln University (MO) specifically, as a foundational learning experience towards inclusion, equality and belonging in America. Each of these concerns involve the choices we make as humans and Americans and the relationships we form to meet our needs, aspirations, and goals; therefore, this is the reason for the continuation of my life story. And the second purpose of this Preface is to inform you that the Dedication, Foreword, Acknowledgments, and Introduction in the 2015 edition have not been changed; also, no changes have been made to My Retirement Years and My Governing Values in the back of this continuation. I added an After Word to summarize my thoughts and life lessons and to challenge you to examine your thoughts and contributions you are making in your choices and relationships as a human of American cultural persuasion. With that as the reason for including a Preface in *Recipient of Grace Continued,* I could thank you for purchasing the book place a period here and let you start from the beginning. However, my intuition is that those who read the 2015 edition may want or need a glimpse of what's in the three new chapters before deciding to purchase Recipient of Grace Continued. This overview is included in the Preface just for you.

- **Chapter Twenty-Seven: The Power of Choice and Relationships**

Every human, regardless of nationality or era lived has had to make choices and form relationships to achieve life's needs, aspirations or goals. In my reflections of how choice and chance put humans together for sundried reasons my thoughts revealed that God is the originator of choice and relationships and that these gifts result in either our pleasure or pain in our lives. I share my life story, the choices I and others made for me and how relationships helped or hindered me achieving my needs, aspirations or goals. My intent in this chapter is for you to reflect on your story- your choices made to seek your needs, aspirations and goals and your relationships as you read my story and evaluate applying my suggested lessons learned to your life. This is a chapter that uses our past to make better choices and maintain mutually productive relationships to meet our needs, aspirations and goals now and moving forward.

** Much of what I offer as lessons learned about relationships conforms with the axioms of Choice Theory founded by William Glasser, MD and is taught at the institute that bears his name at wglasserinc@gmail.com. However, my insights about choice and relationships came from my parents and family,   selected teachers from K-12 and selected college professors, and from friends and especially from the six individuals who died after the publication of *Recipient of Grace* in 2015. They are the inspiration for deciding to continue my life story, and their identity and significance are highlighted below:

- **Lieutenant General Andrew** "Andy" Chambers, friend and mentor, died 2017 and was instrumental in my development as an army officer, husband, father and Kappa Alpha Psi fraternity brother. We first met in 1977 and he and wife, Rita adopted us into their family as that time and the family relationship continues. Throughout our 40-year relationship he modeled trust and used his influence to help those he believed to be good stewards of soldiers and the welfare of their families. Highly regarded by senior army leaders, the famous First Cavalry Division and its Commanding General conducted a formal farewell review at his Internment ceremony at Arlington National Cemetery. He is prominently mentioned in Chapters 12, 14, 16 and 18.

- **Charlene Scott Robinson**, 4th older sister and mentor, died April 2018 and was a mentor, friend and counselor throughout my life until her death. Fondly called, Sister Chuck, she was 15 years my senior and shared care provider duties for me with my mother and sister number five during my early development years. She was the most spiritually devout of the seven of us and always had a kind word and hope no matter the difficulty of persons or circumstances. She was my last sibling to die and throughout our 80-year relationship her counsel and trust in me bolstered my self-confidence.

- **Dr. James H. Billington**, friend and mentor, died 2018 and was my supervisor for 10 years, the longest serving boss in my 45 year career. Dr Billington trusted me with full authority to manage the day-to-day operations of the Library of Congress from 1996-2006. His wisdom, courage and tenacity in the preservation of knowledge in all formats for the use of congress and the American people inspired me to learn and follow his example. I am grateful for his friendship and for writing the Foreword in *Recipient of Grace*.

- **Betty Jean Forte Scott**, wife of 57 years, friend, mother of my sons and trusted partner, died April 13, 2019. Betty was instrumental in all aspects of my life choices to meet our, needs, aspirations and goals in our adult life, I didn't realize how much I relied on her judgement and influence until her death. She modeled candor, love, trust and loyalty with those in her circle of relationships and influence. Betty is mentioned throughout the first twenty-six chapters.

- **Merrill Edward LaVern Scott** (Mel) youngest son, fraternity brother and friend died March 2021. Mel's death has been difficult to accept because of his sudden heart failure that ended his fruitful 57 years of accomplishments as husband, father, son, friend and Federal Aviation Authority in Labor Management Relations. He entered into a comprehensive relationship with God, resisted alcoholism through Alcohol Anonymous, restored relationships with his children and found martial bliss with Gailya McElroy Scott in the five years before his sudden death. Mel was my go-to editor in *Recipient of Grace* and is mentioned in the acknowledgement and throughout the first Twenty-Six Chapters.

- **General Colin Powell**, mentor and advocate, died 2022. He and wife Alma, a friend and mentor to Betty, used their influence to nurture and open opportunities in both our military and post military career. They are mentioned in Chapter Thirteen.

  - **Chapter-Twenty-Eight: Different Perspectives and Shared Goals.**

This Chapter shares my discovery and concerns that my perspective on the self-evident truths in the Declaration of Independence has evolved from a black view of victimization to a humanitarian view of using personal influence and power to encourage and enforce equal application of the law based upon the belief that all men (individuals) are created equal and endowed by their creator with the inalienable rights of life, liberty and the pursuit of happiness. The success of the Civil Rights movement and collaborative efforts of black Civil Rights leaders and white elected and appointed leaders in the mid 1940s to the 1970s and beyond produced the greatest application of equality under the US Constitution and the ideals of the Declaration of Independence. In this chapter I acknowledge that some white Americans have recognized the inhumanity of denying opportunities of life, liberty and the pursuit of happiness to individuals on the basis of race and collaborated with black leaders to pass and enforce laws that provided equal rights and opportunities for black and people of color as promised in the Declaration of Independence and the amended US Constitution. It is from this view of American's struggle with equality for black and people of color that I review my life experiences of the 1940s to the present to examine if racism is the reason for the political divide in the Donald Trump, Make America Great Again (MAGA) era of the Twenty First Century. I explain the circumstance of grief over my late wife's death in 2019 that compelled me to reflect on the limitations racial segregation had on our pursuit of our God given rights, and on the opportunities the enforcement of equal rights laws that helped us achieve some of our goals and aspirations previously denied under the laws of racial segregation. That reflection came during 2020 when Trump was using his office to encourage the rights of white nationalists to protest against their rights to discriminate on the basis of the superiority of the white race, and urging predominantly white audiences to support the slogan, Make America Great Again, a euphemism, suggesting that America was great when racial segregation protected the dominance of white supremacy in all aspects of governance and opportunity in America. My alarm and outrage over what I determined was his effort to undue the equal rights achieved in the 1960s Civil Rights era compelled me to imagine a return to the era of white autocracy under Trump should he be reelected to a second term as President, and resulted in my book, *American Racism and What You Can Do About It,* published in 2020. One of my main purposes in the book was to urge white voters to not vote for Trump if they desired an America ruled by democracy because in my view, Trump wanted to rule by autocracy and return the country back to a practice of the denial of equal rights to those who opposed his view of equal justice and equal rights. I don't know how effective my message was to white readers but fortunately, President Biden won the Presidential election; but unfortunately, Trump received nearly fifty percent of the white vote and captured the Republican Party. Trump's MAGA influence continues to dominate and divide mostly white Americans who explain their support of Trump on the basis of economic, social, educational or border security policies; masking, in my view, their support for his embrace of white supremacy and a return to a form of autocracy that resembles past segregation policies on the basis of race and political views. I expect some readers will disagree with my charge of racism by Republicans and the MAGA faithful, therefore, I use the tensions of America's past experience with accepting racial integration in education, housing and employment in the Civil Rights struggles of the 1950s-1970s to identify how racism was justified and resisted. I also highlight the white elected and black civil rights leaders who modeled humanitarian like behavior to defeat former racist and white power advocates of that era. The actions and example of Harry Truman, Thurgood Marshall, J Waites Waring and Earl Warren teach us the what, why, and how racism was defeated. These men were shaped by the racist policies of their day and had the courage to enforce change against the force of opposition by people who looked like themselves.

Different perspectives and shared goals is a call for every American and especially those old enough to vote to make a conscious choice to identify with what it means to be an American and examine the role that race, gender and economic factors play in your acceptance of the self-evident truths of life, liberty, and the pursuit of happiness. This is a call to get involved!

- **Chapter Twenty-Nine: New Philadelphia, Illinois and Lincoln University Missouri -Black Repositories of Freedom Essential to Understanding the Meaning of American Exceptionalism**

I share my unabashed admiration for the African American founders and their white allies of these two historic sites that continue to highlight the true meaning of American Exceptionalism; overcoming obstacles of legal restrictions by race, gender or servitude to deny individuals in America their rights to life, liberty and the pursuit of happiness. I learned about New Philadelphia since the publication of Recipient of Grace in 2015 and share the fascinating story of founder "Free Frank" McWorter, the first American of African descent to platte a town in America. Free Frank born into and enslaved by his father-owner purchased the freedom of himself, his wife, children and some of his grandchildren before his death in 1854. The original land is now a National Park site near Barry, IL. The story is inspiring and highlights the importance of family, freedom, faith and friends in the pursuit of life, liberty and shared happiness.

Lincoln University Missouri, my alma mater, founded by former Missouri slaves and Union Soldiers of the 62nd and 65th Colored Infantry and their white officer is also a fascinating story. These men overcame the legal restrictions imposed on black Americans to establish the only Historical Black College founded by black civil war veterans and their white officer. While many know Lincoln as the "School Too Good to Die" because of integration of white students in 1954 few are aware of the threats to retain its status as a Historical Black College over the years of its existence. This repository of the American struggle is alive and thriving because of leaders working with allies to keep the Soldiers Dream alive. I am "Mighty Proud of Lincoln" and privileged to highlight the men and women whose efforts are essential knowledge for future struggles that may threaten Lincoln's status as a Historical Black College.

This concludes the overview of the three new chapters and Afterword that inspired *Recipient of Grace Continued.* Enjoy the read from wherever you start and thanks for your interest in my life's journey. I hope you find something useful to enrich your life choices and relatonships. Please share your insights or comments at www.DonScott.org. Thanks.

All The Best,
Donald Scott

Racial Identity and Birth Are No Predictors of Humanity and Worth

This self-inspired rhyme surprised my concluding thoughts for you to ponder as you nurture the choices and relationships of your life.

Betty

DEDICATION

To Betty, my toughest critic, loyal wife, loving mother to Jeffrey and MEL, and doting grandmother to Taylor, Desiree, Gina, and Summer. Your loving kindness speaks louder than your candor, and your unstinting generosity is acclaimed by all who know you. Mine is you!

This book is the product of four years effort and much help and encouragement from family and friends. This may be my first and last literary publication and the only opportunity to use this format to thank those who made this opportunity possible.

Betty Scott is always at the top of my list because of her enduring love and support of my efforts no matter how weird or wrongheaded she thinks they might be. Her edits, suggestions, and belief in me added clarity to my thoughts and fueled my resolve to get this done. And when I needed help to speed up the prose in telling the episodes of my life in the 1970s, our son MEL lent his impressive editing skills to get the job done. Sentences that are clear, concise, and interesting are his contributions.

Joel and Faye Dant, my brother and sister cousins, my sister Charlene "Chuck" Robinson, friends Jack Windom, Ruth and Robert Newton, Charles Wartts, Dr. "Tony" Holland, Rae Par Moore, and Kate Becker made up my go-to team. When I needed extra eyes to proof my drafts, Joel and Faye gladly obliged; sister "Chuck" always provided answers for dates and special family events; Ruth and Robert, Lincoln Alums, introduced me to the editing services of Lincolnite Charles Wartts, who exceeded expectations and became a friend; Jack Windom, a Lincolnite and lifelong friend, was always available to listen and provide wise counsel; Dr. "Tony" Holland, Lincoln University Professor Emeritus, always shared his vast knowledge of African American history and publishing options; Rae Par Moore and Kate Becker, from my AmeriCorps National Civilian Community Corps (NCCC) experience, gave me excellent suggestions and helped with that chapter. Rae, one of my public affairs specialists at NCCC, also helped to edit parts of my life story.

Old soldiers never die, and general officers never lie. I am thankful for the oral histories of Buffalo Soldiers, Floyd Brown (deceased) and Harold Cole, Las Vegas Buffalo Soldiers Chapter, and general officers Andy Chambers (Lieutenant General), Harry Brooks (Major General); Julius Becton (Lieutenant General), and Jim McCall (Lieutenant General). Their illustrious military experience and achievements informed my understanding of our shared experience as Americans of African descent.

No matter how far I roam, Hunnnewell and Hannibal, MO, is always home, and Mary Lou Montgomery, editor, Hannibal Courier Post, honored me by publishing parts of my story during the 2014 Black History month feature in the newspaper.

Dr. James Billington, Librarian of Congress, and one of the most influential people in my life, took the time to write a foreword for my book. I am humbled by his gesture and grateful for his friendship and encouragement for me to finish this book.

As much as I appreciate the help from family, friends, and colleagues, I alone am responsible for the contents of this story.

INTRODUCTION

If you can't say something good about somebody, don't say anything.

> —William "Eddie" Scott,
> May 17, 1886–May 9, 1971.

A trick untried is hard to justify.

> —Amanda Beatrice "BeAt" Dant Scott,
> October 22, 1896–July 17, 1985

Recipient of Grace is a recollection of my life story guided by the sayings of my parents as I recalled events and circumstances from my early years in northeastern Missouri until my retirement from the Library of Congress, January 1, 2007. My dad's quote above, needs no interpretation, but my mother's use of the phrase, "A trick untried is hard to justify" would often come after hearing me or one of my siblings speculate about what our lives would be like if we didn't live in Hunnewell or if we had lots of money. My interpretation of her phrase is that there is no profit in second-guessing what your life choices would be if you had been born into a different set of circumstances because you can never be sure of what the outcome might be. I am humbled, amazed, and thankful that my story justifies my pursuit of the American dream.

I initially wrote my life story for my multiracial grandchildren: Taylor, Desiree, Gina, and Summer. I wanted them to know about my parents' background and the historical setting of my accomplishments as an African American born and reared in Hunnewell, a racially segregated town in northeastern MO, with the unwavering help from their grandmother, Betty. But the more I reflected on the historical period in which my life challenges unfolded, the more I recognized that the racial tensions that led to the passage of the civil rights laws—notably the 1948 executive order that ended discrimination in the military and the 1954 supreme court decision that ended discrimination in public schools—not only shaped my values but also created the changes that made my accomplishments possible. For that reason, I believe that my life story is a product of the "American Dream" and allows my grandchildren and the general reader to examine America's past through the prism of my journey as a poor black kid from Hunnewell, MO. The list of my accomplishments were unimaginable during the 1950s: the first of six siblings to graduate from college, enter the US Army with a commission as a second lieutenant, and retire at the rank of brigadier general, reenter civilian life as the chief operating officer, City of Atlanta, GA, be appointed by President Bill Clinton as founding director, AmeriCorps National Civilian Community Corps (NCCC), and, on the recommendation of Gen. Colin Powell and the competitive ranking of a national search firm, become the deputy librarian and chief operating officer, Library of Congress, Washington, DC. With all these accomplishments on my resume, I was tempted to choose a title that credited my success to a good work ethic, tenacity, and luck. But then one day while out for a walk, a powerful thought struck me . . . Even with luck, tenacity, and a good work ethic, grace was the force that had rewarded me with unimaginable success.

I chose Recipient of Grace as the title because of the grand orchestration of people, events, and outcomes that are the centerpiece of my life story. I also expanded my audience because I believe that the "American Dream" is what it is because of grace, the nation and individuals struggling against the odds to establish "one nation under God with liberty and justice for all" despite the laws and behaviors to the contrary. Some present-day Americans, my grandchildren included, may not see evidence that they can reach their goals because of efforts to restrict their guaranteed freedoms under the US Constitution. Keep the faith. As I discuss in the section "My Early Years," black Americans in 1954 saw little evidence that we could excel beyond becoming a teacher or preacher in an all-black school or church, working as farm or factory laborers, or joining the army and becoming a sergeant. The restrictive laws changed, attitudes slowly adjusted to support the laws, and my life unfolded as related in my story.

As I was reflecting on my past and writing my life story, I was mindful that readers who didn't share similar experiences and events could have difficulty understanding the time, place, and settings of events that shaped my life. I hope that my efforts to simplify commonly used terms or phrases to share my experiences will assist your understanding of the issues raised in the episodes of my life. Disappointment, rejection, anger as well as challenges, change, and celebration were issues at the center of my working life as they are likely to be in your life. For that reason, I include insights at the end of each part of the book that I believe may be helpful to you. I conclude my story with "Retirement Years" to bare my soul and urge you to promote, protect, and defend the battle sites where our ancestors fought and died to help America become the nation her founders described in the Declaration of Independence and the amended Constitution guarantees for current and future generations of Americans.

Gratefully, my choices of a career, a wife, and a set of spiritual beliefs brought me thus far and, with God's grace, will carry me through the experience of death. My hope is that my sons', Jeffrey and MEL, and grandchildren's, Taylor, Desiree, Gina, and Summer, life choices will bring them happiness through their respective life journeys. I pray that everyone reading my memoir will find the right combination of life choices that work for them.

CHAPTER ONE

My Early Years: Family, School and Segregation

The dominant influences in my early life were my family, schoolteachers, and the racial segregation mandates that were the law of the land at that time. Both my mother's and father's families were born into slavery in Missouri and lived within the limitations of racial segregation all their lives. Attending "colored" schools, worshipping in "colored" churches, and confining social activities to interactions with family and friends were the norm mandated by the separation of the black and white races in the state of Missouri. While racial mandates influenced how and where I went to school, my preparation for the life challenges ahead was cultivated by caring teachers, family members, and an employer who did not allow rigid racial codes to interfere with his generosity in sharing his knowledge.

The culture of racial segregation is difficult, perhaps even impossible to convey to those who have never experienced it. However, my task in this chapter is to attempt to explain, both psychologically and physically, the pain and fear of being denied access to public places. I'm speaking of such indignities as having to enter public places through side or backdoors marked "colored entrance," being bussed to school to maintain racial segregation, and enduring the humiliation of having to bury your loved ones in the most undesirable section of the local cemetery. All these and more were the hurdles confronting us in our determined efforts to make the best of our potential as human beings.

Three Rooms for Seven People

I was the youngest of seven children, born in a three-room house in

Hunnewell, MO, on February 8, 1938. My parents, Amanda Beatrice Dant Scott (1896–1985) and William Edward Scott (1886–1971), gave birth to four other children in that same three-room house. These were my brother, Edward (1931–2009), and three of my five sisters, including Frances (1921–1993), Mary (1928–2011), and Charlene, born in 1925. My sister Edith, also known as "Sis" (1916–2007), and Essie Lee (1917–1979) were born on a farm outside of Hunnewell. For about five years, all seven of us lived in our little three- room house—and during Christmas, Mother's Day, and the Fourth of July, that number would double.

The Shadow of Slavery

Both of my grandfathers were born into slavery. Charley Dant, my maternal grandfather, was born in Marion County, MO, in 1857, and Henry Scott, my paternal grandfather, was born in Monroe County, MO, the same year. Here they met and married my grandmothers, Mary Fields Dant and Matilda Green Scott, respectively. Both sides of the family were subjected to the formidable challenges of the Reconstruction era and the intense application of racial segregation policies that followed. Henry Dant, born in 1840—Charlie Dant's father and my great-grandfather—lived to be 105 years old, and the narrative of his life as a slave was recorded via The Federal Writer's Project initiated by President Franklin D. Roosevelt. His historical chronicle is still stored today at the Library of Congress in Washington, DC.

My mother was the fifth of twelve children that included nine girls and three boys and came from a very close-knit family. I had lots of aunts, five of whom had no children but who were avid cheerleaders for me and their other nieces and nephews. It so happened that my aunts had the knack of making each of their nephews and nieces think that they were special in their world. Their love and acceptance were not based upon how smart you were, though they applauded good grades, or on how good an athlete you were, though they bragged on the accomplishments of those who were good athletes, or on how good- looking you were, though they raved over lighter-skinned babies and straight hair. They loved us simply because we were one of them.

In stark contrast to my mother's family, my father was an only child. His mother, my grandmother Matilda, lived in Hunnewell and was cared for by my dad until her death, which occurred around 1950. My father had many cousins who lived nearby, but we didn't start visiting them until he purchased a car in 1948. Most of his cousins lived so deep in the country that the road usually ended at their front doors.

My dad worked as a section laborer on the Chicago, Burlington, and Quincy Railroad, taking care of the tracks between Monroe City and Shelbina. He made a decent wage, which included retirement benefits and railroad travel privileges. Although we were poor in material possessions, we always had plenty of food to eat and adequate clothing to wear. Such admirable feats required ingenuity, skill, and hard work. For instance, my mother made shirts for me and my brother and dresses for my sisters out of flour sack material.

Another case in point is that my dad had a two-acre plot of land that we called "the little farm," where he raised hogs and chickens for food, kept a cow for milk, and grew corn, wheat, or soybeans for profit. Meanwhile, my mother planted a garden to provide vegetables for the dinner table as well as for canning. Hog killing time took place between Thanksgiving and Christmas and was always a festive occasion. I didn't have to go to school on that day; instead, I helped with the many tasks necessary to butcher and prepare the meat for preservation. My uncles, cousins, neighbors, and their wives helped us with the various tasks and in return received a share of the meat. What we lacked in money was more than made up in food because our family ate very well.

I was eleven years old in 1948 when my dad purchased our first family car. My brother Edward, who was eighteen at the time, was the only member of the family who could drive. According to my dad, he bought the 1939 Chevy for us so that we would have a way to go places without having to rely on others for travel outside of Hunnewell.

Hunnewell During My Time

Hunnewell is located along Highway 36 (now Highway 72), the east–west route that runs through the northern part of the state from Hannibal to Kansas City. During my early years, the town's population of 412 residents included only 30 Negroes (adults and children) and served as a primary means of economic support for the farmers of Shelby and Monroe counties.

The town boasted two banks and two grocery stores, one which sold general merchandise and another which specialized in poultry. It also included a drug store, a doctor's office, the telephone office, a hardware store, and a local newspaper and post office. There were three white churches: Christian, Methodist, and Catholic. The "colored" Mount Zion Baptist Church held services on the first and third Sundays. In addition, the bus and train stations were the principal means of transportation to and from Hunnewell. The white public school taught grades one through twelve, and the one-room "colored" school, located on the church grounds, taught grades one through eight. The school closed, however, before I became old enough to attend.

School Bussing to Maintain Racial Segregation

Like all Missouri towns, racial segregation laws required separation of blacks in public places and especially in schools. Hunnewell's school for "colored" students closed in 1944, and for my first eight years of schooling, I was bussed round-trip fourteen miles each day to Monroe City's Washington Colored School. This was a three-room building constructed exclusively for Negro children in 1937 by the Works Progress Administration (WPA), a federally sponsored program established under President Franklin D. Roosevelt. One room housed grades one through four, other grades five through eight, and the third room housed grades nine through twelve.

Mrs. Batsell, who commuted thirty-four miles round-trip from Shelbina on the train every day, taught me grades one through four. I commend her to this day for making me think I could learn anything she put in front of me. This "can-do" attitude has served me well throughout my adult life. There were about thirty students in the four grades, with each class averaging about seven students. Mrs. Batsell more than fulfilled her challenging teaching duties by using a system of rotation. This allowed her to move from one class to another by assigning lessons to be completed silently during her absence.

There were five students who started the first grade with me. They were Harold Russell, Renzo Smith, Tommy Talton, Edna White, and Roy Williams. Mrs. Batsell required students to recite lessons and do their math problems on the chalkboard in front of the combined class. Even though the other three classes were given study assignments to complete silently, she often called on a lower-grade student to help a higher-grade student with math or reading. Tommy was the smartest among us and was the first to be called upon.

For special recitations like the Gettysburg Address or to perform lead roles in school plays, she would hold auditions. Quite often I succeeded in winning the lead role or was selected to do the recitation. She was also a disciplinarian and emphasized good posture for all of us. She zeroed in on me for walking with my shoulders stooped forward and would sometimes whack me across my back with her yardstick. Though her technique may seem harsh by today's standards, it helped me to correct my posture.

In all fairness, Mrs. Batsell didn't always resort to her yardstick for maintaining classroom decorum. She also employed other disciplinary measures like assigning you to stand in a corner of the room or forbidding you from participating in extracurricular activities. Nevertheless, she did not tolerate disruptive behavior in her classroom and did not hesitate to spank a guilty student's open palm with a ruler as punishment. But she quickly got over being displeased with bad behavior, and she never talked down to us or mistreated us. By the end of the school day, all was forgiven, and she would routinely stand at the door while we lined up to kiss her on the cheek.

During recess, she would attempt to level the playing field by rotating the selection of team captains, whose job was to pick the players for competing softball teams. This technique had the advantage of letting each student know how their peers rated their abilities. Harold, Renzo, and I were usually the first to be picked, regardless of who was selected as team captain.

However, a very special and cherished memory of Mrs. Batsell's influence on my development came when I was in the eighth grade. I was selected to represent Washington Colored School by competing in a vocal contest at Douglass High School in Hannibal. Although she was not my teacher at the time, Mrs. Batsell became my voice coach and rigorously rehearsed me for the contest. She even wrote notes for me to take home to my mother with instructions on preparing an egg white and lemon mixture for me to imbibe before bedtime. She also mentally prepared me to overcome my fear of singing before a large crowd by coaching me to look just above the heads of the crowd. She instructed me to start in the middle and then move your eyes to the right and slowly back to the left. This savvy maneuver made it appear as though I was maintaining good eye contact throughout the performance.

The contest represented a significant and memorable event for me because of the prominence Douglass High School and the city of Hannibal itself enjoyed among black families and students in the surrounding towns. It was also huge because one of my mother's four sisters, Aunt Ella Bell, taught high school at Douglass. My mother also had a brother who lived in Hannibal, and all family members in the area were expected to come hear me sing.

To top it off, my sister Frances from Chicago sent me a brand-new pair of blue suede shoes (which were considered very fashionable at the time), and my aunt Eloise gave me a dapper pin-striped suit that looked almost new for the event. On the big day of the contest, dressed in my finest duds and with a generous amount of Murray's hair pomade to slick my parted hair to my scalp, I executed Mrs. Batsell's instructions to the letter and won first place for my spirited rendition of "Standing in the Safety Zone," a gospel standard. Of course, Mrs. Batsell was ecstatic. Moreover, Mr. Majors, who was the principal at Washington Colored, was overjoyed to win a contest at Douglass. I'm sure I don't need to tell you that I was simply relieved that the competition was finally over.

The Church and the Cemetery

The "colored" Baptist Church, where I was baptized at the age of twelve or thirteen, continued to operate in Hunnewell into the mid- 1980s. My dad was a deacon, who provided our community with a strong role model of what a good deacon was supposed to do. He did not drink or curse and was kind to neighbors and strangers alike. My mother attended church every Sunday and insisted that all her children attend as well.

My grandmother Matilda was also a devout member of the church. She attended Baptist conventions and housed visiting preachers and other churchgoing folks who needed a place to stay. At that time, there were no hotels, motels, or indoor dining at restaurants for "colored" people. She had a good voice, and I remember that she used to sing a gospel song called "Packing Up Getting Ready to Go" every Sunday that we had church. Grandma "Tillie's" earthly journey ended in 1951, and she was buried next to Grandpa Henry in the "colored section" of Godfrey Cemetery. My mother and father and three sisters (Edith, Essie, and Mary) were all buried in that section as well, which is located in the back of the cemetery near the railroad tracks.

Church services were always held on the first and third Sundays at our church. The pastor for most of my years in Hunnewell was Reverend Pearl from Quincy, IL. He and Mrs. Pearl had two daughters, Jackie and Helena, both about my age. There were usually no more than fifteen people in the congregation at one time. Reverend Pearl always extended the invitation to join church at the end of his sermon, even though the only persons in attendance who did not belong to the church were Jackie, Helena, and me. When we were about thirteen years old, Jackie and Helena finally joined, leaving me behind. Reverend Pearl continued to open the doors for membership until my mother hunched me in the side and said, "You might as well go on up there because he won't stop until you join." Shortly thereafter, the three of us were baptized in a pond near LaGrange.

Family, Work, and Self-Awareness

My playtime in Hunnewell ended when I was about eleven or twelve years of age. Up to that time, I spent my summers playing ball, riding bikes, and slipping off to the forbidden swimming hole, a pond near my grandmother's house on the west end of town. My mother insisted that all able-bodied members of the family should get a job. My oldest sister, Edith, was the single exception. She was born with partial paralysis that affected her vocal cords and her dexterity.

My older brother worked as a truck driver for C. J. Horn's Grocery and Poultry House, while my youngest sister worked as a domestic worker for C. J. Horn's son and business partner. Finally, I started mowing C. J. Horn's lawn under the demanding eye of Mrs. Uri Horn. She was a stickler for thoroughness and would settle for nothing less than perfection. I didn't like working for her but learned that if I wanted to be paid for mowing her yard, I had to meet her standards.

The Korean War

My brother Edward, a true role model for me, was drafted in May 1952. He was soon after inducted into the US Army and sent to fight in the Korean War. His absence from our family placed a great burden on us because he was the driver and caretaker of the family car. "Sonny," as he was then called, had taught Mary, our youngest sister, and me how to drive the car even though I was underage. But neither of us knew how to maintain the aging thirteen-year-old car. From watching my brother, I knew how to check the oil and change a flat tire, and between me and Mary, we kept the car running during his absence.

Even though my dad couldn't drive, he helped out by getting his driver's license just so I could drive legally while he accompanied me in the car. Fortunately, no driver's test was required in order for parents to obtain a license in Hunnewell and other rural areas in the early 1950s. My brother's absence was felt when it came to driving in particular, but it was also a great worry for our mother in general. She tried hard not to let her emotions show, but Christmas and Mother's Day celebrations were especially tough for her. I had never seen my mother cry until I walked in the kitchen one Christmas during the time that Edward was in Korea. She was stirring flour in a bowl, tears running down her cheeks. I asked her what was wrong. "I was just thinking about 'Son' and hoping that he is safe over there," she said. I gave her a hug and felt sad for her and for my brother's absence.

Working in the Hay Fields

In the summer of 1951, I was thirteen years old and growing taller and stronger. Consequently, I was hired by Joe Gill to work in the hay fields. Joe had a two-man operation consisting of him and Moose, a hired hand, who received room and board in exchange for his labor. Joe owned a couple of big trucks and a combine and contracted with local farmers to harvest their hay and grain crops. I was initially hired to walk the hay field beside the truck and lift the forty- to fifty-pound bales onto the truck bed.

It didn't take long for Joe to discover that I couldn't keep up with the moving truck, so he put me on the bed of the truck to stack bales and help with the loading. I wasn't strong enough or tall enough to throw the bales eight feet high, so Joe moved me to the job of driving the truck. From then on, he and Moose did the lifting and loading while I drove the truck, a job that I actually liked doing. Joe was a fair-minded man, and in his home, he did not abide by the custom of having a separate table for me to eat. However, the rest of the farmers did observe the custom and set a separate table for me. This humiliating custom was not to my liking, but I didn't protest. However, because of my youth and lack of experience, I placed myself in an awkward position that later compelled me to protest the way I was addressed and treated.

During that summer, I had learned to do the "hambone," a rhythmic sound made by alternately slapping your thighs, your chest, and making a popping sound by smacking your open palm across your mouth. I learned this from my nephew and proudly demonstrated my rhythmic abilities to Joe and Moose. They thought it was great and began calling me "Hambone" and asking me to perform the spectacle at each farmer's house where we were served dinner. However, their comments and laughter gradually began to make me feel like I was playing the role of a black clown. I asked Joe to stop calling me Hambone, and I removed the skit from my repertoire. I also stopped eating watermelon for the same reason. I realized that I had to be careful not to portray myself in a negative light around white people and to insist on being called by my given or last name. My truck-driving days for Joe came to an end that summer because of a more exciting and lucrative job offer to work at the Monroe City newspaper office.

A Bold Move: Working in the Print Shop

Bob Wright, my nephew, eighteen months older than me, walked boldly into the Monroe City News office where no black person had ever been employed. He approached the owner and told him that he needed an apprentice who knew how to melt lead for reuse in the linotype machine, set type for ads, and operate a printing press and that he was just the guy to do all of that. Bill Nolen, the owner, hired him on the spot.

Bob's mother, Essie (1916–1979), was married to a Methodist minister, and Bob was the oldest of their eight children. Rev. Samuel Wright, his father, had been reassigned to a small church in Coffee Ville, KS, but did not want to relocate his family there. So, the family initially sent Bob and Rose, their oldest daughter, to live with the reverend's family in Detroit. It was there that Bob learned his printing skills from his uncle who owned a small print shop. Essie and the other six children lived in Hunnewell, and the children were bussed to Washington Colored School in Monroe City for six months or so. After school was out in Detroit, Bob and Rose returned to their mother in Hunnewell, where Bob became the first Negro to work in the local print shop.

When "Rev" was given yet another assignment and the family was preparing to move to Lexington, KY, Bob convinced Bill Nolen that he needed to train someone to continue his tasks. He therefore introduced me as the right person who could quickly learn the job. I was hired on the spot and kept the job through weekends and summers all during high school, as well as through my first year of college.

The print shop experience was also an educational advantage for me. In addition to learning a trade, I was also learning about the history of Monroe and Shelby County residents. This was the case because one of my responsibilities was to search the archives for the twenty to forty years ago column that appeared in each edition of the weekly newspaper. I also began to notice the double standard of the racial segregation laws and their lack of enforcement when I was with white employees from the newspaper office. I was served at the soda counter in the drug store with no objections from any person who came in the store. However, when eating at the local bus station, the only restaurant that served hot meals, I was required to eat in the kitchen where a small table was set for "colored" customers. My dad's cousin, Imogene, was the cook and served me as many helpings as I could eat, with dessert thrown in free of charge.

Bill Nolen died shortly after I started working at the newspaper, and his sister, Berta Lee Nolen, took over the operation of the paper. She and the journeymen printers, Rex Durr and Oliver Blosser, generously shared their knowledge with me and taught me how to set type from the California Job Case and how to do make-up ads as well as run the presses, including the big cylinder press that produced the weekly newspaper. I also discovered that printers' conversations and small talk centered on current events and humorous stories. The print shop environment was a welcome refuge that afforded me a brief respite from the hard realities of racial segregation practices that I had experienced working in the hay fields.

Seventy Miles Round-Trip to Douglass High School

I attended Douglass High School for three years, and for the first two years, I rode the bus seventy miles round-trip every school day. The bus, which also transported Shelbyville and Shelbina kids, picked me up in Hunnewell at about 6:45 a.m. From Hunnewell we proceeded east on Highway 36 to the "K" Road, which we took for about five miles in order to pick up the Mayfield kids, then we would backtrack to Highway 36 and continue east to Monroe City's Washington Colored School. There the bus would drop off the Mayfield family, pick up about eight black students and continue east to Hannibal and Douglass School, arriving about 8:20 a.m. The return trip was equally circuitous and monotonous.

Douglass High: Regional Center of Education and Social Activity

Douglass was the educational and social hub of activity for black kids within a seventy-mile radius of Hannibal. In addition to the black kids on my bus route west of Hannibal, black kids from LaGrange, Canton, Palmyra, New London, and Frankford were bussed to Douglass in order to maintain racial segregation. The school was founded shortly after the Civil War and initially employed white teachers. However, black parents of that era petitioned for black teachers, and the school gradually hired a group of well-educated instructors that set high standards in academic as well as athletic programs.

A notable figure, Blanche Kelso, one of the early principals, was elected as the first African American US senator from the state of Mississippi during Reconstruction. Moreover, I take special pride in pointing out that Aunt Ella Bell Hobbs, my mother's sister, taught home economics and often served as assistant principal at the school.

My years at Douglass were not remarkable from the standpoint of athletic or academic achievement. My grades were average, and I participated in the band, the choir, and theatrical plays. But it was only possible for me to attend events on such special occasions by staying overnight with one of my aunts.

Douglass School had a remarkable reputation for preparing "colored" children for the world of work or for higher education. Most, if not all high school teachers, including my aunt Ella Bell, held Bachelor of Arts or science degrees from accredited colleges and universities.

Our high school teachers never allowed themselves the luxury of excuses for having to make do with secondhand laboratory equipment, books, or furniture from the white schools. Instead, they raised the bar by demanding high achievement and even perfection from their students. Opportunities for extracurricular development were also available. I joined the Boy Scouts but dropped out because of the difficulty of staying after school to make the meetings and complete the projects.

As a teenager, one of the most rewarding aspects of attending Douglass High was the social contacts with kids from Hannibal and surrounding communities. My association with these students only came about as an unintended benefit of racial segregation, which meant that they were bussed to Douglass to comply with Missouri state mandates. My parents were very generous to me in this regard by trusting me with the family car for social activities during my junior year, a privilege which meant the world to me. Their only stipulation was that I could only take Renzo with me and that I had to be home by the time I said I would.

During my third year at Douglass, I was transported to school by Mr. Chambers, a white man who commuted to Hannibal daily because of his job at one of the factories there. He picked me up in front of my house at about 7:15 a.m., and we made no stops until he dropped me off in front of Aunt Eloise's house. We usually arrived in Hannibal before school started, so I walked the rest of the way from there. On the other hand, I usually arrived back home by 4:30 p.m., a half hour ahead of the bus. I thoroughly enjoyed the door-to-door service.

To this day, I do not know why the Hunnewell School Board couldn't or wouldn't pay for me to ride the school bus. Neither do I know if Mr. Chambers was paid by the school board or my father, but I expect that my dad was involved in the arrangement. Mr. Chambers was such a kind person that he probably would not have taken the money if offered. However, the close bond of friendship with my Douglass School classmates was shaken when state officials announced that our class would be integrated into the white high schools in our communities at the beginning of the 1955 school year.

Opportunity to Excel: Integration of Monroe City High School

The 1954 supreme court decision to desegregate all public schools

had the greatest impact on my life up to that time. The Missouri School Board's announcement to integrate northeastern Missouri schools caught everyone by surprise. I remember my dad's reaction when we learned that I would be integrating Monroe City High School in 1955. He sat me down and cautioned me to be very careful around white girls when I went to school in Monroe City. He said words to the effect that "if you get in trouble in that way, I won't be able to get you out."

I knew exactly what he meant. I had already heard stories about how Negro men in Monroe City had been physically threatened for making alleged overtures to white women. Such occurrences were part of the folklore handed down from centuries of slavery and racial segregation in Marion, Monroe, and Shelby counties. My dad was a very calm and even-tempered man and was not known to lecture my brother, sisters, or my mother on any topic. Rather it was his quiet manner and solemn tone of voice that convinced me of the seriousness of his concern about my behavior as one of the first young "colored" men to integrate an all- white high school. By contrast, my mother was prone to lecture us, but not this time. "You better listen to your daddy," she said simply.

Basketball Recruitment Visit

In the summer of 1955, two unknown white men appeared at our front door looking for me. They turned out to be Coach Billy Key, head basketball coach at Monroe City High, and Mr. Joe Burditt, father of one of the school's star players. After introducing themselves, they asked if I was interested in playing basketball for the team. By that time, I had grown to about 6'2" inches tall and weighed about 160 pounds. In addition to my height, their interest had been piqued by the fact that I had attended Douglass High School, a school with a well-earned reputation for producing good basketball players. A little taken aback, I confessed that I had never played basketball at Douglass, but that I was interested.

We had a basketball hoop that my brother had put up after he returned from Korea, and coach asked if I would demonstrate my shooting ability. I rose to the challenge and took pleasure in dazzling him with my accuracy by making shots from the familiar places I had practiced over the years. I could hit almost every shot from the end of the clothesline, from the bare spot in front of the damson tree, and from the center of the yard. It was like taking candy from a baby.

My aim was deadly accurate from those spots, especially with nobody guarding me or attempting to block my shot. The coach and Mr. Burditt appeared to be impressed and said they would return with Jerry, a solid ballplayer, and a few others in a couple of days. They returned one weekend shortly after and took me to the outdoor court behind the closed Hunnewell High school building, where the coach pitted me against Jerry for some -one-on- one competition. It didn't take long to see that Jerry was clearly more accurate in his shot making than me. However, my rebounding ability was clearly evident, and the coach appeared satisfied and urged me to come out for the team.

My Monroe City High School Adventures

The first day of school was a big event for everyone. All the white students formed a corridor along the walkway and silently watched us enter the schoolhouse door. Renzo, Roy, Edna, and I, four of the five who started first grade together at Washington Colored School, entered Monroe City High as graduating seniors. I don't recall what events occurred that first morning, but I do remember our first English or Speech class with Mrs. Mitchell. She attempted to find out how much we "colored" students knew about sentence structure by writing a sentence on the chalkboard and having us to diagram it. I'm proud to say that Mrs. Batsell's teaching approach at Washington Colored School served us well as we took turns identifying the parts of the sentence down to its last object. Then our new teacher went from sentence construction to comments about speech and diction. I have forgotten to whom she was responding when she said, "Class, what is it that the old darkie minister said?" She paused momentarily before answering her own question. "Don't try to be what you ain't, be what you is!" She broke out in a loud laugh. To their credit, most of the white students did not laugh, and we "colored" students sat silent and embarrassed. Mrs. Mitchell resumed talking as if she had never uttered the racial slur.

I made the basketball team and was welcomed by most players on the team. Those who were not happy did not let their feelings show out of fear of arousing Coach Key's anger. The coach was a tough taskmaster and equal dispenser of pain for any who failed to comply with his instructions. He taught me the fundamentals of playing the position of center and forward. He put me in during the very first game, during the middle of the second quarter, and told me to show him what I could do. My first shooting attempt wildly missed the basket, but the crowd cheered as if it had gone through the net. My rebounding strength was dominant as most of our opponents were three inches shorter than I was. Obviously pleased with my performance, the coach placed me on the starting roster after the first game. The team had a 30-1 win/loss record by the time I was hospitalized with an appendicitis attack near the end of the season. The team made the state tournament for the first time in the school's history and ended up with a 31-3 season record.

I also sang in the choral ensemble and was selected by Mrs. Rice Maupin,

the music teacher, to represent the school in a musical contest at Kirksville State Teachers College (now Truman State University). This time around I didn't go through any lengthy preparations like I did at Washington Colored but won second place in the boy's solo category singing a song entitled "Shoes."

The only titillating gossip during that first year at Monroe City High was about the crush one of the popular girls, who happened to be white, had on me. She attempted to engage me in conversation at every opportunity, and even though I liked her, my parents' warning was stronger than my curiosity. I avoided her like a rabbit hiding from a hound.

The school year ended without serious racial incidents, and all four black students were among Monroe City's 1956 graduating class. The four of us were placed side by side in the class graduating picture, which, I think, meant that we were seen more as a group rather than as individuals. I graduated with excellent grades and was awarded a $25.00 award by the Kiwanis Club for best citizenship.

College Expectations without a Plan

I continued working at the print shop during the summer but was informed by Ms. Nolen that she would not be able to hire me as a full- time employee. She, therefore, advised me to go to college. Although her advice was definitely in line with my parents' hopes for me, they informed me that they had no money to pay my tuition and expenses. I had thought about college on my own but had not made the necessary inquiries or preparations to enter a college. Renzo had decided that he would go to Michigan and work with his brother who was a tractor trailer driver hauling goods across the USA.

Most of my former Douglass High classmates joined one of the military branches of service, but that option never entered my mind. I also gave no serious thought to going to live with my brother or one of my sisters who lived in Chicago. Strangely, it seemed like everybody in my family expected me to go to college, but no one, including me, was taking steps to get me there. In the meantime, I was content in my knowledge that I had a job at the print shop until the end of summer and that I would cross the bridge to my future only when I was forced to make a decision. Then providence stepped in because I'm convinced that somebody's prayers were answered, probably those of my parents. Out of the blue, my brother-in-law, Rev. Samuel Ross Wright, commonly referred to as "Rev," called to tell my parents that he was passing through Hunnewell to take Bob, his oldest son, to Lincoln University and that they should pack my bags since he would drop me off at Lincoln as well.

Faith Takes Me to Lincoln University

When Rev called to say that he would take me along with his oldest son, Bob, to Lincoln University, located in the state capitol at Jefferson City, MO, we only had a couple of days' notice to get my few things clean and packed. There was no discussion among my parents and me as to who was going to pay for my college expenses or how much it would cost or even whether I could even meet the entrance requirements. We had faith that Rev would make it all happen because he had a solid record of living by faith. He had married my sister Essie when they were still in high school, graduated as salutatorian of his class, enrolled and completed Lincoln University, all while pastoring a small church and providing for his wife and son. He then went on to complete his seminary training, attended the University of Chicago, and was raising a growing family of eight children on faith and his pastor's salary.

Rev arrived in front of our house on the designated day with his spirits high, which was his usual state of mind. His car had only a fourth of a tank of gas to travel the 130 miles to Jefferson City, but that fact did not seem to concern him. On the trip to Lincoln, Rev was singing songs about Kappa Alpha Psi Fraternity and assured us that he would get us enrolled and that he expected us to pledge "ole Kappa." Upon arrival, Rev visited with Dean Hoard, a former classmate and fraternity brother, and the dean of students at the university. When he reported back to me and Bob, he announced that Bob was to be enrolled on a track scholarship. As for me, Rev said I could enroll and work at the LU Print Shop and also try out for a basketball scholarship. Now, for the question of how Rev got us to Jeff City on a quarter of a tank of gas, I have sometimes speculated that the gas hand was not functioning properly. And yet when looking back on all the other mountains that had crumbled when confronted by Rev's faith, I decided to rank getting us to Lincoln as one among Rev's many little miracles.

Bob was a legitimate track star, having won and set a new Indiana State record in the half-mile event. Meanwhile, I opted to work in the print shop and arranged with the university business manager to have my wages applied against my tuition, room, and board. However, I did have to come up with $150.00 that my dad borrowed from the Hunnewell Bank. Russell Yancey, the bank president, required Dad to put up the deed to our house as security for the loan. I thought putting the house up as security for a $150.00 loan was excessive, but Dad did not question the requirement as he signed the loan.

CHAPTER TWO

Lincoln University: Finding a Career Path

Lincoln University was founded in 1866 by former slaves who served in the Sixty-Second and Sixty-Fifth US Colored Infantries. Having been slaves in Missouri, the founders and their white officers established Lincoln to educate black residents like me, "Rev," Aunt Ella Bell, and hundreds of out-of-state blacks who desired a quality education.

Administrators and professors at Lincoln specialized in helping students earn a quality college education through work-study programs. Both my nephew Bob and niece Rose Wright participated in the work- study program. I worked in the university print shop during all four of my years at Lincoln and also worked part time in the university cafeteria washing dishes. The university withheld most of my salary to pay tuition and board as I had requested. Enrollment in Advanced ROTC was a major source of my discretionary money as the monthly stipend was $27.50; this was an enormous amount of money at the time. My mom sent $5.00 about every other week, which was enough to buy me a meal ticket, an act of love and sacrifice which I always appreciated. At the end of four years, I owed the university $800 but was successful in securing a student loan to pay off the debt.

Black Cultural Awareness

For me, Lincoln was a place to learn about black cultural practices in music, dance, and social interaction. The majority of students was from St Louis and Kansas City and infused the campus with their brand of popular slang, dance, blues, and jazz. Those from Chicago, New York, Pennsylvania, and the states of Oklahoma and Texas added to the smorgasbord of style, dress, and culture of the campus. The campus population of about two thousand students was large enough to have a range of black cultural diversity and small enough to know just about every student on campus.

I made up for lost time with regard to many of my social deficits at Lincoln and learned to strategically position my interests so as to align myself with the personalities that influenced campus politics and opinions. Printing the campus newspaper, The Clarion, kept me in touch with the news and the news makers. Students majoring in journalism wrote the stories and provided the layout to the Graphic Arts Department for publication. My close relationships with journalism majors Ronald Powell (deceased) John J. Johnson III (JJ) and Joe Guyton led to lifelong friendships.

Kappa Alpha Psi Fraternity

My grades were average at Lincoln with the exception of the semester I completed the pledge-ship program to become a member of Kappa Alpha Psi Fraternity. My nephew Bob had made Kappa the semester before me and was instrumental in encouraging me to complete the pledge program so I could be like him and "Rev." I had all but decided to forgo being a Kappa member when Bob, and several others with whom I had pledged, won me over. Subsequently, I was elected as captain of my pledge line, and between pledging, my job at the print shop, and classes, I almost flunked out of college.

The result was that I was placed on probation. When I arrived home for the Christmas break, my mother, having received notification of my probation, asked what happened to my grades. I explained that my grades were poor because of the fraternity, work, and all the other commitments I was attempting to keep up. "Well, I guess you did the best you could," she said. I promised her that I would do better and get myself off academic probation. My renewed efforts succeeded in bringing my grade point average back up to a "C," and I came to fully appreciate being a member of

Kappa Alpha Psi Fraternity. I enjoyed the fraternity's popularity and recognized that the ordeal helped to prepare me for both life and career challenges which would require me to withstand the pressures imposed by others, handle the criticism of teammates, and help in achieving a common goal.

ROTC: Pathway to Excellence

ROTC was the activity that I most excelled in at Lincoln. I made the drill team as a freshman and was selected as a squad leader the first year. By the second semester of my sophomore year, I was selected to be the drill team commander, a position I held until my senior year. I enjoyed the challenge of teaching drill team members precision and unison in executing marching and manual of arms movements. I also liked the high standards and immaculate dress requirements in wearing the uniform and performing before crowds during LU Homecoming parades and at competitive drill events.

My strongest criticism as drill team commander came from students who were army veterans. Lloyd Mallory, a vet from Palmyra, MO, was particularly helpful. His and others feedback was always useful because in my view they had been there, done that, and had earned credibility as soldiers in the real army. My most rewarding moment as drill team commander was the presentation of a commemorative coin awarded to me by members of the drill team at the end of my command tour. The inscription read, "To our leader, friend, and classmate. Honor to you—Honor Guard." I still have the coin and cherish the memories of those who both nourished and supported my leadership.

I also excelled at ROTC summer camp at Fort Riley, KS, in the summer of 1959. I was designated a distinguished military student by the ROTC instructors who conducted and evaluated the training camp. This was especially significant to me because I was not among Lincoln ROTC students who had received the designation from Lieutenant Colonel Johnson, our professor of military science (PMS) at Lincoln.

The competition at Fort Riley included students from predominantly white

Midwest colleges and universities who hailed from the states of Minnesota, Nebraska, Missouri, Kansas, Iowa, Illinois, and Arkansas. My company first sergeant, Master Sergeant Humble of the University of Minnesota, was a tough evaluator and rated me among the top cadets in the company. Therefore, I completed the camp with a new sense of self-confidence and awareness. I also gained a deeper appreciation of the economic gap separating me and the students from major universities I had met at camp. Several of my platoon mates attended DePaul University, and one of them—a white cadet whose name I believe was Ray Sydlo— offered to drop me off at my house in Hunnewell since he had to pass through on his way to Chicago. There were six of us laughing and enjoying our freedom from the rigors of ROTC summer camp, while Ray drove us to our homes in his 1958 Chevrolet convertible. I sensed that Ray knew nothing about my world at Lincoln and that his world at DePaul was as foreign to me as mine was to him. Yet we were able to bridge our worlds at ROTC summer camp.

Not in the Statistics

I graduated from Lincoln in the summer of 1960 as the proud holder of a bachelor of arts degree and as a distinguished military graduate with a commission as a second lieutenant, Infantry, US Army. When I went to get Dr. Cyrus ("Butch") Taylor's signature to certify that I had met the degree requirements, he took my papers from me and in a good-natured manner commented, "You know you are not even supposed to be here." Dr. Taylor went on to explain that he had read a report that said the probability of Negro children from poor families and small towns going to college was zero. I was unaware of the statistic and hurriedly asked him to sign my certification papers.

After signing and handing them back to me, he asked his customary rhetorical question, "Where are you going?"

"To the register's office to turn in my certification," I answered, even

though I was fully aware that his question was intended to provoke deeper thought regarding my purpose in life. For four years, I, like many other students who majored in subjects under Dr. Taylor's purview, had grown accustomed to passing him on our way to class and hearing him ask, "Where are you going?" Of course, his question was quickly followed by his standard response: "If you don't know where you are going, you will never get there." I only knew that I was graduating from Lincoln University and was scheduled to enter the US Army as a second lieutenant in January 1960.

My combined graduation and commissioning ceremony was a major event for me and my family. My mother, my youngest sister, Mary, and two of my aunts came to witness the ceremony. My dad stayed at home to be with my oldest sister. Their very presence let me know how proud they were of my accomplishments. Neither of my parents were comfortable finding words to express their love for us, nor were they comfortable in unfamiliar surroundings. Their presence at both my graduation from Monroe City High School and from Lincoln University spoke volumes about their love for me and of how proud they were of my accomplishments. As for me, I was proud to be a college graduate but needed to find a job until I could enter the army in January 1961.

Looking for a Job

The euphoria of being the first in my family to graduate from college did not last long. I needed a job to tide me over until my

January 1961 reporting date to the US Army. I was not inclined to look for work in Monroe City or the Hannibal area because there were no promising job opportunities to fit my skills or degree qualifications. In fact, black printers with graphic arts degrees were usually limited to either teaching the trade in a vocational educational school or working as an apprentice in a union printing shop in cities with large black populations. Most job opportunities were located in northern cities, with opportunities in the south confined to black-owned newspapers or printing shops. I was not interested in going south or in teaching at a vocational education institution. My thought was that I could probably find a job in a print shop either in Kansas City or Chicago until my entry date into the army. I knew from my apprentice experience at the Monroe City News that printing positions were filled by word of mouth. Being a member of the Printers Union, which I was not, was also a big advantage. Mr. Lucius Jones, a printing instructor at Lincoln, was a union member in good standing and agreed to help those of us who were graduating to find a job. He opened the door for me and Charles Lawson, a fellow graphic arts graduate and a newly minted second lieutenant, by contacting his friend at the Minneapolis Star Tribune.

North to Minnesota

Mr. Jones gave us a good recommendation, and we decided to strike out for Minnesota. Lawson had a cool set of wheels, a 1956 Ford Sport Victoria, and I had a high level of confidence that we would be hired. Jones was a journeyman printer, well connected in the trade, and we were billed as his protégés. Plus, I had work experience as an apprentice albeit in a small town nonunion shop. As we rode north through the cornfields of Iowa, I was excited over the prospect of seeing the bright lights of Minneapolis and St Paul. Our thoughts and conversation during the trip mainly centered on our job needs of the moment, as well as our expectations of being hired by the Minneapolis Star Tribune. We arrived in Minneapolis and were fortunate enough to secure a room from a black family on a daily rental basis. Back then, it was a common practice for black folks travelling south in particular to stay with black families because white motels and hotels would not rent to black travelers. Although the state of Minnesota was known to provide public accommodations to black people, we chose to stay with a black family because of limited money.

Early the next morning, we met with Mr. Jones's contact person, filled out employment applications, and did not have to wait long for an answer. Some time that afternoon, we were informed that because of our pending military commitment, the company would not hire us, preferring instead to hire someone who would be willing to complete an apprentice program leading to proficiency as a journeyman. It was a disappointing decision, and neither of us had a fallback position. Lawson decided he would go to Michigan to search for a job with the Ford Motor Company, a place he had worked before. I had no interest in going to Michigan but asked to be dropped off in Chicago, where my brother and two sisters lived.

East to Chicago

When we arrived at my sister Frances's house, I called my mother and learned that I had received a notice from the army asking if I wanted to move my entry date forward to September 24, 1960. I was so happy about the news that everyone in the room thought I had won the lottery. I asked my mother for the army contact number before sharing the news with Lawson, who immediately requested the number so he too could ask that his entry date be moved up. I confirmed my new entry date the very next day, and Lawson moved on to Michigan where I believe he received his confirmation within a week or two.

Even though I was relieved to be going into the army soon, I still needed a job. My brother came to the rescue and got me hired on at E. A. Clammage Window Company where he worked. My job there was to break cracked or irregular glass into small pieces for recycling. I was the highest qualified window breaker in the industry! Edward was very proud to introduce me as his younger brother who was a college grad and a second lieutenant in the US Army. My brother's boss and fellow workers had a good time joking about the lieutenant and college graduate who was having a tough time breaking glass correctly. I didn't mind their good time at my expense because they also proudly introduced me as the second lieutenant with the college degree. I felt more like a celebrity than the lowly employee that I was because I did more visiting with other employees than I did breaking glass.

The two months I spent with my brother in Chicago during July and August of 1960 were filled with good times and lots of male bonding with my brother and his interesting set of friends. All of them had migrated from the south, moving north to Chicago to escape a harsh racial environment and limited job opportunities in places like Arkansas and Mississippi. Most of them were married or had significant others and worked at the window company. Every day presented a new drama for the married guys. My brother and I were single and went to a different hangout on the south side of Chicago almost every night. The married guys would try to hang out with us but would invariably get locked out of their apartments or suffer some similar act of punishment inflicted upon them by their other half.

We eventually moved from my sister Frances's apartment into our own apartment on Greenwood Avenue, where we could enjoy the freedom of coming and going as we pleased. Another perk was that we didn't have to keep everything so neat and orderly the way we did at Frances's place. The summer passed quickly as I prepared to leave for my training at Fort Benning, GA, where I planned to heed my brother's advice to listen to the sergeants because they knew what was going on. He had made sergeant during the Korean War and believed that sergeants ran the army while the lieutenants were learning to be officers. I collected a lot of fond memories from that summer. At the same time, I looked forward to my training, but really had no idea of what I was about to encounter.

Insight on My Early Years

I have reserved this segment of my memoirs to share my thoughts on the most significant human development tools that shaped my life, character, and beliefs during my formative years. Caring parents and teachers, preparation, champions of equal opportunity, and faith are the universal tools that shape the lives of young people regardless of the era, circumstances of birth, or economic conditions. Time, circumstance, and chance happen to all human beings; the human reproductive process does not allow us to choose the time, gender, race, nationality, or economic standards of our parents or of the country we are born into. But once we are here, caring parents and teachers can help us make the best of our circumstances.

My parents and teachers, along with the champions of equality and people of faith, nurtured me through World War II, desegregation of the military, the integration of public schools, the Korean War, and the beginning of the Civil Rights Movement. Those national and international events impacted my life and the lives of millions throughout America. I am inspired to highlight the role they played in my life because their model can be adapted to the circumstances and conditions of youth born into twenty-first century America.

There is no substitute for a parent's love and sacrifice in order to nurture and encourage the talents of their children. Both my mother's and father's parents were born during slavery or during the Reconstruction period that came after the Civil War. The circumstances of their birth as African Americans severely limited their opportunity to develop their skills, knowledge, and abilities. The impact of segregation meant accepting the limitations of social and economic development for themselves and their children. Even so, they were the children of caring parents and acted on the belief that education was the key to defeating racism and ending racial segregation.

My mother completed the eighth grade and was an avid reader of newspapers, cookbooks, and the Bible. My father attended one year of schooling, could sign his name, add and subtract mentally, but could not read or write. They carried forward the desire instilled in them by their parents to see that we got more education than they did. In the late 1930s, my dad was the only African American resident to attend a Hunnewell school board meeting to petition for a "Colored School" to educate his children. Because of the priority my parents placed on education, my brother and four sisters completed high school, and all members of my family expected that I would not only graduate from high school but would also go to college. As a consequence, all my parents' grandchildren attended college and most graduated, extending the view that education is the best pathway to defeat racism and avoid poverty.

The togetherness of the Dants, my mother's family, continues and now includes the Scotts (my dad), Wrights (my sister Essie's husband, Sam), and Trotts (Sam's mother's side of her family). I planted the seed to combine our DSWT connections into one biannual reunion to honor the legacy of our ancestors. My sister Charlene Scott Robinson's son, Command Sergeant Major (CSM) Howard Robinson, and nieces Sonja Scott Woods and Beverly Wright Granata lead the planning for this great biannual event. Education continues to be our dominant priority in the development of DSWT children.

My parents and grandparents made the best of their circumstances,

bought houses to raise their children and land to grow crops and gardens, and expected that their children would do the same for their children. Therefore, all of us purchased our own homes and cared for our children except Mary and Sis, who never married and remained in the family home until their deaths.

My parents' attitude toward racial segregation and whites was to abide by the laws and treat white people as they would want to be treated. Rube Dowell, my dad's boss, and his family were the only white friends who regularly socialized in our home. The few who did not abide by the golden rule in their dealings with us were confronted by my mother who did not believe in turning the other cheek. My dad was an optimist, and long before the Supreme Court ruled on the desegregation of public schools, he firmly believed that change for the better was inevitable. I could tell by his measured tones in cautioning me to watch my behavior around white girls at Monroe City High School that he saw the potential for violence. It was this insight on my father's part that prompted his warning to me to avoid placing myself in a position to inflame such emotions.

My mother was more of a realist; she was not as trusting as my dad. She was the disciplinarian in our family and developed the power to control our behavior with a look that meant cease what you are thinking about doing. I knew that my mother would be the one I had to answer to if I got into trouble, and I did not relish the tongue-lashing she was capable of dishing out. She also exhorted us to believe in ourselves and not to act as if anyone else was better than we were. They were a good team and made joint decisions affecting our desires and aspirations.

I learned to shortcut their decision-making process by going to my dad and saying, "Momma said it was okay for me to do xyz if it was okay with you." The response was always favorable. I knew they cared because their whole lives were a sacrifice for us. They deferred buying material things for themselves so that we could have decent clothes or money to buy lunch or pay school fees. Their parental caring, like their religious faith, was expressed in deeds and not in words.

My parents' faith in God was manifested in a God of love who loved them and wanted them to love others. Neither of them talked about their faith, quoted scripture, or attempted to push their faith on us, other family members, or their friends. I think their greatest test of faith came when my oldest sister was born with a handicap. She was unable to develop her motor skills so she could not walk normally, feed or dress herself, or use her vocal cords to speak. The doctor did not expect her to live past the age of ten, yet my parents integrated her into our family to the extent that they taught her to do as much for herself as she could and taught us to assist her with what she couldn't do.

Through their care, love, and faith, Sis lived to reach her nineties, was never hospitalized, and never admitted to an assisted living facility. I attribute her long life and generally stable condition to the care she received from my parents, my youngest sister, Mary, and our collective prayers for her total well- being. During the final months before her death, my sister called me with her concerns about the fact that Sis was not eating and not responding in her usual manner. Mary asked me whether she should take her to the hospital. I knew she would not be able to communicate with the hospital staff and that the unfamiliar environment would be frightening to her, so I told my sister to call a nurse to come to the house and take her vital signs.

While waiting for a response, I prayed that the God who made her and who had sustained her in life would continue to provide for her needs until He was ready to bring her home. The nurse reported that her systems were shutting down, that she was not in any pain, and that there was no need to take her to the hospital. Additionally, Heather, a granddaughter of Rube, my dad's boss, and a practical nursing assistant, volunteered to stay with Mary and comfort Sis until her death. Our collective prayers were answered, and I attribute her living well beyond her tenth birth date to the unshakeable faith of my parents and their belief in the power of a loving God. I also believe that their faith came through private meditation and in my dad's case, by listening to the word as delivered by preachers. Nonetheless, in both cases their faith was manifest by their deeds. They shared, gave more than they received, treated their neighbors with love and respect, and did their best to prepare us for more opportunities than they had.

My home training was augmented by teachers and others outside of my home that I label as champions of equality. Mrs. Batsell, Bill and Berta Lee Nolen, Coach Key, and Ms. Maupin stand out in my mind as persons who looked past skin color and provided opportunities for me without regard to color, status, or gender. I brought readiness to learn and courage to try, and they inspired me to meet their expectations. On the national level, the champions of equality who opened doors that significantly improved my opportunities for success were: President Harry Truman (who desegregated the military in 1948), Civil Rights Attorney and Supreme Court Justice Thurgood Marshall, Chief Justice Earl Warren, and President Dwight D. Eisenhower, who played a major role in ending racial segregation in public schools in 1954.

I would also add to my list the names of Brooklyn Dodgers' manager Branch Rickey and Jackie Robinson, who together integrated major league baseball in 1948. The above champions of equality opened doors that reached all the way to Hunnewell. I was ten years old when Jackie Robinson broke into the major leagues. Shortly after, some white kids came to my house to invite me to play baseball. When choosing sides and positions, Charles Grubb, who was an avid baseball fan, yelled out, "Donnie is on our team and plays second base because that's Jackie Robinson's position." I have often wondered if I would have been invited to play with those kids if Jackie had not broken into major league ball. There is absolutely no doubt in my mind that the integration of Monroe City High School and my opportunity to meet Coach Key and Ms. Maupin would not have happened without the 1954 supreme court decision to desegregate public schools. I am also certain that desegregation of public schools in Missouri ushered in a challenge to the survival of Lincoln University and other historical black colleges in the southern states.

The former slaves and soldiers of the Sixty-Second and Sixty-Fifth Colored Infantries who founded Lincoln University also merit being called champions of equality. Their efforts made it possible for me and thousands of African Americans to earn college degrees, develop skills, and receive commissions denied to us by "white only" universities in the state of Missouri and other southern states. Lincoln University professors and teachers prepared us to excel in competitive job markets with full knowledge that our race and ethnicity would be hurdles in our path to success in segregated America. They amassed an unmatched record in teaching and preparing capable students to meet high academic standards, despite the fact that most were denied access to the best educational and developmental resources at the high school level.

LU faculty and administrators also created job opportunities for many like me to pay tuition through work-study programs in order to complete our college degree requirements. Lincoln and other historically black colleges clearly exceeded the purposes they were created to serve during the era of racial segregation. The 1954 supreme court decision also forced Lincoln and other state-supported colleges to open enrollment to all and compete for students on a statewide or national basis. Lincoln, like most, still carries the designation of a historical black college but has become a majority white commuter college. The great tragedy of Lincoln as a commuter college is the loss of purpose and faculty attuned to educating students with average intelligence, little or no money, and who have been deprived of a strong educational foundation at the high school level. Sadly, Lincoln and most historically black colleges, in my opinion, no longer merit being called champions of equality.

The common ground that defines my champions of equality was their ability to advocate the principles of justice and equality for all in the face of a strong vocal minority who championed the status quo of racial segregation. A sad fact in America's history is that the "silent majority" will tolerate inequality and injustice until a person with conviction, passion, and courage rises in their midst to address the wrong. My story is possible only because my champions embraced and acted on their convictions and on the ideals framed in the Declaration of Independence and the amended American Constitution.

Time, circumstance, preparation, and chance continue to bring young people into the world dependent upon someone to help them to be successful in life. Caring parents and teachers, champions of equality, and the cultivation of faith in a God that loves unconditionally—and wants us to love each other— hold out to them a strong chance for success. This combination of human development tools helped me to succeed during the tests of war, economic disasters, and social unrest during my early years. It is still my firm belief that the aforementioned tools represent the best hope of those who would embrace and employ them to help our young people achieve success in the twenty-first century.

W.E. SCOTT FAMILY: Right to Left 1ˢᵗ row: Mary V. Scott, Aug 3, 1928-; Charlene (Chuck)m June 9, -; 2ⁿᵈ row, William (Eddie), May 1886-May 1971; Edith Mae, May 2, 1915 - Nov 28, 2007; Essie Lee, Oct 20, 1916 - 1979; Lola Frances, April 6, 1919 - 1987; Samuel Ross Wright (Brother-in-law): 3ʳᵈ Row, Amanda Beatrice Oct 18, 1898 - July 1985; Edward Orlando, June 6, 1931 - Oct 2008; Donald LaVern, Feb 8, 1938 --.

W. E. Scott Family picture in front of my birth home, Hunnewell, MO, circa 1959.

Kneeling right to left: Mary, August 1931– December 2010 and Charlene, June 1925–

Standing front row: William Edward "Eddie" May 1886– May 1971; Edith "Sis," May 1915–November 2007; Essie Lee, October 1916–January 1979; Lola Francis, April 1919– 1993; Samuel Ross Wright, January 1915–April 1989.

Standing back row: Amanda Beatrice, October 1898– July 1985; Edward Orlando, June 1931–October 2008; and Donald LaVern, February 1938

CHAPTER THREE

In Search of the "Real Army"

Throughout my advanced ROTC years at Lincoln University, I was always told by my instructors that "this is not the real army." I readily accepted that statement as a fact since we were on a college campus. However, as I was packing my few possessions and preparing to depart Hunnewell for Fort Benning, I was excited because I knew that I was finally going to the "real army."

The Train to Georgia and Fort Benning

I met up with my friend Lawson in Saint Louis, and we boarded a train to Columbus, GA, home of the US Army Infantry School at Fort Benning. We were outfitted in our tan uniforms, usually reserved for "dress" occasions, and our shoes were shined to a high gloss. Our US insignia was also polished to a high shine and pinned to the lapel of our coats, which prominently displayed our shiny new second lieutenant bars on the shoulder. We had been told by our college ROTC instructors that the uniform would ease the hassle of a black officer traveling through the south. We boarded the train in St Louis and were able to choose our seats but were told by the conductor that the train would stop in Cairo, IL. At that junction, we would be required to move to the "colored" or so-called Jim Crow car.

Cairo was the dividing line between the northern and southern states, also known as the Mason–Dixon Line. When we arrived in Columbus and got off the train, I unwittingly followed the white passengers walking into the train station when I suddenly became aware that I was on the "white" side of the room. I quickly moved from the "white only" section and stood on the "colored" side of the room. Then someone informed us that we would have to take a cab marked "For Colored Only" to Fort Benning. We didn't do much talking on the way to the base, but the ordeal with the signs and "white only" lines made an impact on us. I was glad to see the base, but by that time, my enthusiasm for seeing the sights had waned. I was no longer interested in seeing what the city of Columbus looked like.

Infantry Officer: Gateway to the Real Army

Integration into the student company to which we were assigned went smoothly, with no signs of racial segregation. My class was made up of over two hundred second lieutenants who had been commissioned within the Infantry Branch. Most held commissions from West Point, and the remainders were from colleges and universities throughout the United States that offered Army ROTC. The purpose of the basic course to which we had been assigned was to familiarize us with the basic tools needed to perform our duties as officers in the units that we would be assigned to after graduation.

As part of our entry-level orientation, we were informed about the local segregation practices for black soldiers and officers off base and advised that racially integrated groups of soldiers would not be served in off-post establishments. The Officers' Clubs were integrated, and students were encouraged to use them. In spite of the discriminatory practices of off-post clubs, the black clubs were well known for their hospitality to second lieutenants looking to have a good time while stationed at Fort Benning. For that reason, many black officers from historically black colleges had a high wash-out rate and were cautioned about the dangers of partying too much.

Two Lincoln graduates in the class just ahead of mine had washed out and were still in town undergoing "out processing." There was also a rumor in the air that hinted that race had something to do with their failure to make the grade. Early in the class cycle, I was getting my boots spit shined by one of the black shoe shine guys who asked me how many blacks were in my class. I told him there were ten of us. "All yaw ain't gonna make it," he asserted as if the matter was a foregone conclusion.

Assignments for quarters or "billets" for student officers were made alphabetically by last name. We were also assigned a roster number for the posting of grades. The course was structured so that a test was given after each major block of instruction in tactics, map reading, weapons, and small unit administration subjects. And to successfully complete the course, a student officer had to attain a total score of 800 out of 1,000 points. Scores were posted after each test, and I made a point to keep a record of my scores. I made a firm decision that I would not party or buy a car until I reached the magic 800 point total. I hit that number with about three weeks to go, confirmed it with my advisor, and immediately started partying.

My first stop was at the used-car dealers who paid no attention to the local practice of racial segregation. In fact, they rolled out the welcome mat for all student officers. Choose any car on the lot, they said. No money down and no payment until January, they cajoled us (and this was in November), an offer too tempting to pass up. A long white 1959 Bonneville with fuel injection and red interior caught my eye, and I drove it off the lot that day. I made the rounds of every club in Columbus and Phoenix City, AL, and even visited Talladega College (about two hundred miles round-trip) a couple of times.

From Partying to Praying

The day before graduation, a list was published for student officers who had been pegged to see "the colonel," and my assigned number was on the list. I worried that I was going to be washed out, so I double- checked my total point score and confirmed that I had over 825 points. Then I worried that they had raised the total needed to graduate, and I didn't get the word. I prayed like never before.

That evening, I drove my car down to a parking spot overlooking the Chattahoochee River and prayed that I would graduate. As I was praying, tears rolled down my cheeks, and I could hear the refrain of "Just as I am without one plea and that Christ died for me." I stayed there a long time, but when I left, I was at peace and felt that everything would be all right.

The next day, I reported to the colonel—and only then did he reveal the reason why I was standing before him. He said that even though I had enough points to graduate, I had failed all the tests given during the past three weeks. He asked me to explain why. I took a deep breath, stood as straight as I could, and told him about the car and the partying. He counseled me that a good officer never takes anything for granted, and he thought I had the potential to become a good officer.

I thanked God for answering my prayers and graduated with my class. I drastically cut back on partying during my attendance at Airborne School, attended church a couple of times, and departed Fort Benning with a set of airborne wings pinned to my chest and second lieutenant bars on my shoulders. I headed for my next assignment at Fort Leonard Wood, MO, fully expecting once again that I would find the "real army."

Fort Leonard Wood: Teaching and Learning the Basics

Fort Leonard Wood is located in a scarcely populated part of southwestern Missouri close to the Ozarks. During the 1960s, the largest town was Waynesville, a city that rigorously enforced racial segregation practices. When it came to bars, clubs, and public facilities, you could easily believe that you were still in Columbus, GA. I was not thrilled over the assignment, but it was close to family and friends in Hunnewell, Jefferson City, and at Lincoln University. These fringe benefits provided me with some consolation. I spent Christmas 1960 with my parents in Hunnewell, and although not happy about my assignment, I looked forward to being a part of the "real army."

Basic Infantry Training

I reported to headquarters, second training regiment, and was assigned to E Company, Second Battalion as the company training officer. Capt. Willis G. Powell, commanding officer, welcomed me to the company and explained my duties. In a nutshell, I was to accompany the troops at training 24/7 as well as perform a host of other duties: mail officer, mess officer, pay officer, vector control officer (bug control), and supply officer. Captain Powell and I were the only officers in the company. I later learned that he received his commission through Officer Candidate School (OCS) and served in combat in Korea. He was careful not to fraternize with noncommissioned officers (NCOs) and made certain that our conversation was strictly about military matters. He monitored my performance by checking for my presence at early morning chow, served promptly at 5:30 a.m. He also monitored me during night training exercises (which included a midnight change of guard duties) and during severe weather— ice and snow in winter and excessive heat in summer.

The NCOs ran basic training; it was a well-oiled machine. I remembered my brother's good advice and did not interfere with their assigned responsibilities. They, in turn, made sure that I knew how to brief Captain Powell when he showed up to check on my performance, the status of training, and the welfare of the troops. Once my first basic training class was successfully completed, Powell stopped the early morning chow visits and late night change of guard checks. I think he knew that I had gotten his message. I always expected him to appear at the most uncomfortable times and during the most severe weather conditions, so I made sure I was present on such occasions.

From "Colored" Officer to Army Officer

My first officer efficiency report was a most memorable event given what Captain Powell said about me and for what I learned from it subsequently. Powell called me into his office, motioned me to have a seat by the side of his desk, and explained that he was required to rate my performance. He began by stating that I was the best "colored officer" he had ever had the privilege to command and that he had rated me higher than the others. He pointed to the middle block and showed me the "x" he had placed to indicate where he had placed me on the rating scale. He went on to explain what a good job I had done and urged me to keep up the good work.

I left his office feeling like I had been given a good evaluation, although I interpreted his comments to mean that I was better than the other "colored officers" he had rated although I had no idea how many. However, I speculated that I was considered average in comparison to my white peers.

Major Lister, the battalion commander, saw me a few weeks later and asked how Powell and I were getting along. I said fine. At that point, Major Lister told me that he had reviewed the performance report Powell had given me and had sent it back for his correction. He then proceeded to instruct me on the army's policy toward the evaluation of its officers. "You are not to be evaluated on the basis of your race, but on the basis of your performance," he said adamantly. Furthermore, he expected that Powell would call me in to discuss the rating and that I should listen to him.

Sure enough, Powell called me in and said that after thinking about what a fine job that I had done, he had decided to change my rating to above average. He showed me where he had marked the above average block and allowed me to read his comments. His final report dropped the reference to my color and now asserted that I was "one of the best officers" he had had the privilege to command. I thanked him and said nothing about Major Lister's counsel. I later learned that Major Lister was a native of Jefferson City, the home of Lincoln University, and that he had grown up not too far from Lincoln's campus. Whether this prompted his intervention, I do not know. I do know that Powell was from the south and Lister was from the border state of Missouri, and both were probably in the army when President Harry Truman desegregated the military in 1948. I vaguely recall that there was a post-wide meeting for all career officers that reinforced the army's commitment to implementing the Truman doctrine. I simply concluded that Major Lister was committed to practicing what the army preached, and Captain Powell was not.

My next company commander was Capt. "Hoss" Kessler, a pilot on ground duty and a delightful man to be around. He was a jovial, good-natured officer who empowered me to keep "the snakes out of the swamp" and continue running the company. He called every one "Hoss" whether officer or NCO and mingled easily with the troops without damaging his effectiveness. He and his wife had me over for dinner several times. During the middle of the month, he would joke about remembering the days when he was a poor lieutenant with a big car like mine and no money to buy gas. At the end of his commentary, he would pull out a wad of money, peel of a $20 bill, and tell me to "go fill that thing up" and come back bright eyed and bushy tailed, all compliments of flight pay.

Mentoring by a "Colonel" in Master Sergeant's Stripes

After leaving Captain Kessler, I was reassigned to be the officer in charge of marksmanship or the record range, so called because of the record range's paramount importance in the accurate tabulation of trainee scores. Each company competed for the highest number of experts, sharpshooters, and marksmen at the end of the training cycle. Master Sergeant Hare had been the noncommissioned officer in charge (NCOIC) of the range forever and minced no words about how he ran the range and would keep me out of trouble. I found out how well respected he was when Brigadier General Dodge, the assistant post commander, visited the range. As his sedan was approaching with the one-star plate displayed in the center of the grill, the spotter sergeant ran into the range shack and told MSG Hare that the general was coming. Hare said to me, "Lieutenant, that's your job to go report to him."

I had never reported to a general before and was excited to have the opportunity. I grabbed my clipboard with all the pertinent training data and trotted out to give my spiel. Standing at attention and holding my salute in front of the general, I only got out the word "sir" before the general waved me off and asked for MSG Hare. They greeted each other with a handshake and stood by the car conversing casually for the duration of his visit. I later learned from Hare that he himself had been a full colonel but had accepted a reduction in grade to master sergeant so that he could retire as an officer. After the Korean War, the army forced officers with less than twenty years of service to be separated from the officer corps in order to meet reduced strength levels. Officers like Hare, who had prior enlisted service, could revert back to their enlisted rank, continue to serve until they reached twenty years, and retire at their highest grade earned. Hare had gone through the Alcoholics Anonymous Twelve-Step Program and had a wealth of knowledge about life and the pursuit of success. He mentored me more than anyone at Fort Leonard Wood. A favorite saying of his was that there were only two reasons that people don't get what they want out of life: "They don't want it bad enough or they are not willing to pay the price." At the time, I didn't know what I wanted out of life so I was content to wait for my promotion to first lieutenant and whatever else came next.

Promotion to First Lieutenant and Company Commander

I was selected to command E Company, Fifth Training Battalion early in 1962, about two months before my promotion to first lieutenant. The Fifth Battalion was called "the black battalion" because the battalion commander and two of the five company commanders were black, including the one I was replacing. I considered myself well prepared, having served under two seasoned company commanders and having been mentored by the experienced NCOs I had supervised. I felt ready for the challenge of a company command post. Plus, I thought I could teach basic marching maneuvers, the manual of arms, and physical training as well as the NCOs—and better than most officers.

When I took command, President Kennedy had been in office for more than a year, and many of his policies hastened the racial integration that Truman had started in 1948. I was really impressed with Kennedy's statements about serving the country and equal opportunity, but my first sergeant was not enthusiastic about the changes and took every opportunity to let me know that the army was still reporting manpower by race. He took particular delight in explaining that the army's morning report still divided officers, NCOs, and soldiers by race. He dampened my enthusiasm by pointing to the officer section and showing me that Lieutenant Condon, my assistant training officer, was the only white officer in the company. He went further to point out that I was listed as the only Negro officer on the company's morning report. President Truman's desegregation policy had not yet materialized.

The Military Draft, Manpower, and Racial Harmony on Post

My troops were a cross-section of America and represented every race and socioeconomic status of the population. The draft was not popular nor was it perfectly administered in the country, but it insured that military manpower needs were met from a cross-section of the male population in the country. Racial problems were at a minimum on army posts, where soldiers of all races got together at the clubs and canteens to enjoy letting off steam after their third week of training. I had great rapport with the troops and genuinely cared about their welfare and success. This became apparent when I experienced a racial discrimination incident which was witnessed by some of my troops. However, it was because of this incident that I learned that my troops, regardless of color, respected me as their

company commander.

Off-Post Racial Discrimination and Embarrassment

One weekend, my troops had been granted passes, and I was dressed in civilian clothes. I stopped at an off-post gas station and restaurant to get fuel and a sandwich. I gassed up, went inside and paid for it, and then walked into the adjoining restaurant to order a hamburger for takeout. The place was full of trainees in uniform, many of whom recognized me and excitedly invited me to join them at the counter. But before I reached the counter, the waiter made a point to loudly state that they didn't serve "colored" and that I could go around to the back and order a takeout sandwich.

Embarrassed as I was, I did not acknowledge the waiter's instructions and walked up to those who recognized me to ask if they were enjoying their weekend pass. A few attempted to apologize for the awkward moment, but I attempted to gain the upper hand by acknowledging their concerns and exiting the place with as much dignity as I could muster. That experience taught me to stay in character 24/7. From that moment on, I made a conscious attempt to stay in character as company commander when dealing with the troops or NCOs under my command—at all times and under all circumstances. The majority of my NCOs were black and competent but were not as well bonded together as the ones in my previous company. My mess sergeant, a Mexican American, was married to an African American woman, and they often wound up in my office for counseling. I also had a supply sergeant who needed close supervision in accounting for company property. He had the reputation of being a willing trader but not a smart one. He would make a generous swap for scarce items of supply and accept an even swap for easy to get items. Fortunately, I was able to manage all the problems of command and keep the company competitive despite the daily problems that surfaced without warning.

CHAPTER FOUR

Time Out for Marriage: A New Perspective

My chance meeting with Betty Forte in the spring of 1961 was the beginning of a mutually deep personal relationship, one that resulted in our marriage in March of 1962. Betty and I had known each other since the ninth grade at Douglass High School. We had always been friends but had never dated in high school or at Lincoln, where we both enrolled in 1956. She had always had a steady boyfriend until she married Charles Lawson, whom I knew and spoke about earlier in this reflection.

Their marriage produced a son and ended in divorce in late 1960. Betty and I were opposites from the standpoint of dating and steady relationships. I had dated every girl who lived on her block in high school but managed to maintain a steady relationship during my senior year at Lincoln that ended when I left for the army. However, I was not in a serious relationship when I saw her in the spring of 1961.

I was in Hannibal for a family gathering, either Mother's Day or the Fourth of July. The occasion took place at my aunt's house, which happened to be on the same street where Betty and her son were living with her parents. I was driving by her parents' house one day, saw her in the backyard, and stopped to say hello because I had not seen her in a good while. She was wearing a white blouse and a pair of shorts and had her hair done up in a way that perfectly framed her face. Suddenly, I felt like I was seeing her for the first time in my life. As I was driving away, I succumbed to an uncharacteristic impulse and told her that I was going to marry her someday. I had never made such a statement to any woman and drove away feeling good about what I had said.

We dated throughout the rest of 1961 and ended the year with an intimate weekend in St Louis, where we talked about the possibility of marriage. I was in no hurry to curtail my freedom but knew that she was a class act and that I couldn't find a better woman to marry.

I returned her to Hannibal and went back to take care of my troops at Fort Leonard Wood. In early 1962, about the same time I was taking command of E Company, Betty attempted to call but couldn't reach me by phone. It was a weekend, and I was flying in an army plane piloted by a friend. He was a captain who was flying to Ohio to see his estranged wife and their children. I was tagging along for company and morale support while he mounted an attempt to persuade his wife to rejoin him at Fort Leonard Wood.

Not being able to reach me, Betty called my mother to inquire. My mom didn't know where I was but promised Betty that she would give her a call as soon as she had contacted me. When I called my mom, I knew from the sound of her voice that she knew Betty was pregnant and that I had to call Betty and arrange a marriage date sooner rather than later. Betty confirmed that she thought she was pregnant, and we agreed to get married on March 3, 1962. We purchased the rings. I arranged for the wedding to be held in the Second Training Brigade Chapel and for Capt. Roland Thompson, brigade chaplain, to conduct the wedding.

Lt. Joe Lewis, my friend and roommate, agreed to be my best man. Capt. Johnnie Brooks, a friend and mentor from my Second Battalion days, and his wife, Ernestine, arranged to let us stay with them a couple of days after our weekend "honeymoon" in St Louis. With all the arrangements completed on my end, Betty's parents brought her, her sister, and my mother to participate in and witness the ceremony. Chaplain Thompson briefed me on the significance of the marriage vows and attempted to keep me calm before the ceremony. Joe, Chaplain Thompson, and I were in our blue dress uniforms. The ceremony went off without a hitch, and we were pronounced man and wife surrounded by the approving smiles and eyes of our parents and others in attendance.

Betty returned to Hannibal to work, and I continued to command my company. She was making more money than I was, but I felt it was my responsibility to provide for our housing and homemaking needs. I made arrangements for on post housing, traded in the Bonneville for a 1962 Tempest, and purchased three rooms of furniture for our quarters (without consulting Betty) so that everything would be in order when Betty arrived. When the time came, the three of us—Betty, Lloyd, and me—moved into our assigned quarters located at 53 Jadwin Drive. It was there in a three-bedroom house that we began our life together as a military family.

Husband, Father, and Family Considerations

Other than attending Lincoln University in Jefferson City, Betty had not lived outside of Hannibal. We were both surprised at how well she, and later Lloyd, adjusted to living on an army post. She had been on the honor role in high school, had an engaging personality, and made friends easily. She immediately made friends with Jeannette Cofield, recently married to Lt. Amos Cofield of the Third Training Regiment, and a neighbor in our assigned housing area.

Jeannette helped Betty to make drapes out of sheets and pleating tape. They also shared trips together to the commissary and—when money allowed—to the Laundromat. My new wife confided her embarrassment to me about going through the checkout line and not having enough money to pay for the selected items. Then, even worse, she had to decide which ones to take back while the line behind her grew longer and longer. She quickly learned never to go to the commissary without a check in order to avoid being embarrassed.

Going to the commissary with $15 was bad enough, but the fact that she had to wash our clothes in the bathtub was really hard since she was pregnant. To save money, I ate most of my meals in my company mess hall. One day she decided to surprise me by preparing a home- cooked meal of pork chops and pork and beans served on a paper plate. When I attempted to cut the pork chops, the chops flew one way and the beans slid into my lap. For the next forty years, she never again served me dinner on a paper plate! (However, during the past seven years of retirement, meals have been served on whatever is available.)

Lloyd quickly adjusted to having another daddy in his life. He called his two grandfathers Daddy Merrill and Daddy Albert, and his biological father Daddy Charles, so I became Daddy Scott. Lloyd made a lot of friends and learned to ride his bike and to take the military post bus anywhere he wanted to go in the neighborhood despite the fact that he was only five years old.

Betty's first experience with the officers' wives' coffee affair was quite memorable. Before we were married, I had heard some of my officer friends' wives talk about the importance of the junior officers' wives deferring to the colonel's wife on matters of social etiquette. Therefore, I was quite anxious to hear what Betty had to say about her first meeting. When I asked how it went, she related that she was sitting next to this distinguished-looking lady who engaged her in conversation about how she liked the military. She replied that she had not been in it long enough to decide. About that time, the waitress at the club asked Betty what she would like to drink, and she replied that she would like a Coke. The waitress replied that they only had coffee or tea at that time of morning. Overhearing the waitress's reply, the lady sitting next to Betty told the waitress, "You heard what she said! She said she wanted a Coke, and while you are at it, bring me a scotch and water." I was even more curious and asked her the name of the distinguished lady. When she told me Hartline (Colonel Hartline, the regimental commander's wife), I nearly choked!

CHAPTER FIVE

Joining the Counter Intelligence Corps

My two-year obligation was coming to a close in September 1962, and I had to decide whether to stay in the army or get out. Since I was newly married and I liked the military, I accepted an extension of active duty as a voluntary reservist. My training company was performing well, and I was looking for something else to do other than the repetitive cycles of basic training.

President John F. Kennedy's dynamic influence penetrated the army, and doors began opening for black officers. I was approached by the Fort Leonard Wood Special Agent in charge of the Counter Intelligence Corps Office and informed of the search for black officers to become special agents. It sounded interesting and exciting, especially the part about wearing civilian clothes and carrying a special badge and credentials to identify the holder as a special agent of the Army's Counter Intelligence Corps. I passed both the test and interview and received orders in July to attend the fifteen-week Intelligence Research Officers Course at Fort Holabird, MD.

Going over my company's accounts as I prepared to leave for my new assignment, I learned what a poor trader my supply sergeant truly was. His ineptitude nearly cost me $800 due to a shortage of rifle rods when I changed command. Fortunately, my good angel was looking out for me, and the battalion supply sergeant balanced out the shortage— probably because of the past "generosity" of my supply sergeant. I received an above-average performance rating from Captain Vego, my battalion commander; however, every positive attribute was offset by a shortcoming.

Betty and I ran into a few challenges in vacating the quarters we had occupied on post. Clearing the quarters with the Post

Housing Office provided some humor as well as taught us some valuable lessons about preparing for and passing the inspection. Being short on money, we had done our own cleaning of the house and yard. Passing the inside inspection was no problem, but the yard had some leaves trapped in the well below the ground floor windows.

Dressed in my best-tailored khaki uniform, I jumped down in the well, got down on my hands and knees, and started raking out the leaves with my hands. I didn't see the humor, but my new wife thought it a hilarious sight to see a lieutenant on his hands and knees and a sergeant holding a clipboard with the authority to pass or fail him. We passed, and I drove Betty and Lloyd to Hannibal, where they would stay with her parents while I was at Fort Holabird.

The Intelligence Research Officer's Course

Fort Holabird, MD, located outside Baltimore, was the home of army intelligence activities before the Army Intelligence Branch came into existence. Counter intelligence, area intelligence, and combat intelligence were the main subjects taught at the post. The Intelligence Research Officer Course specialized in counter intelligence (covert intelligence gathering activities) and was even a step farther away from the "real army" than the basic Infantry training I had just left behind. Like me, my fellow classmates had all been recruited from other branches of the army and assigned to the Counter Intelligence Corps. Unlike me, most had majored in pre-law or political science in college. The instructors were experienced special agents with service in counter intelligence duty dating back to World War II. At that time, however, they worked in the Office of Strategic Services, the forerunner of the Central Intelligence Agency.

Course Content and Colorful Instructors

Course content focused heavily on the constitutional rights of US citizens, security clearance procedures, personnel security interviews and investigations, surveillance techniques, and the threat of the Communist Party to military security. Major Mo Murray (an African American) and Major Tarbutton were two of the best and most impressive instructors teaching the course. Both had experienced undercover assignments in the Communist Party of the United States of America (CPUSA), and both were masters at telling stories to get their points across. Tarbutton taught about the essential questions for conducting personnel security interviews and used the acronym LIDMC to help us memorize that it meant loyalty, integrity, discretion, morals, and character.

He would offer great personal examples of situations where one or more of these attributes could have tripped him up. Even though listed as number three, discretion trumped all others in the intelligence agent's tool kit. With good teachers like Tarbutton and Murray, I passed all tests and received above-average evaluations in the conduct of personnel security interviews and surveillance techniques. It was no easy feat for an African American to blend into the crowd of predominantly white male workers in business suits on Dundalk Avenue downtown. Even more challenging was the fact that it was common knowledge at the time that a black man wearing a business suit downtown was on surveillance training from Fort Holabird.

The Birth of My First Son

On September 24, midway through the course, Betty called to tell me that we had a healthy eight-pound boy. She also wanted to know what I wanted to name him. I thought about naming him after me, but I opted instead to name him after a big named movie actor. I had always admired Jeff Chandler and the role he played as

Cochise in the film Broken Arrow. In addition, the name Jeff signified polish and glitter for me because all my instructors at Lincoln used to idolize a former student named Jeff for his determination and will to succeed.

For that reason, I chose Jeffrey as his first name and Jerome as his middle name. Jerome was my mother's second oldest brother. He was known and respected for his fist fighting ability, which cost him his life at an early age. Betty kept me updated on Jeffrey's progress weekly. I had to use a pay phone outside of the Officers' Club to call her. Once during our weekly call, a group of partiers were passing by. One of the women opened the door of the phone booth and yelled something like, "Come on, honey, let's go party." Trying to explain a drunken woman yelling into a phone booth to a wife hundreds of miles away is an impossible task. The phone line went dead, and it took me three days to reconnect with Betty. From then on, I made sure no one could open the phone booth door when I was talking to her or getting updates on our son.

Civil Rights Movement: A Common Topic among Classmates

As much as I enjoyed learning about the subject matter of the Counter Intelligence Corps, I found the background and views of the Civil Rights Movement among fellow student officers more interesting. Most had little previous association with black Americans in civilian life and were curious about my thoughts about the Civil Rights marches and other activities. The recruiting activities of the CPUSA were one of the topics that provoked the most questions about blacks as possible targets. Many southern white officers believed that outside agitators were stirring up the "coloreds" and were the cause of the trouble in the south. As the only black officer in my class, I was often asked my views and answered that I knew no one who was a member or who had been approached by the CPUSA.

Major Mo Murray was the expert and answered most of the questions to the apparent satisfaction of the majority of the class. The conversations in the classroom were always civil, guarded, and impersonal. Outside of the classroom and during extracurricular sports activities, the subject of race became personal and uncomfortable for me and one of my classmates.

Bill Simpson and I got off to a rocky start playing touch football against each other. His "touch" was closer to a "tackle," and I reacted in kind. We eventually got to know each other better, and he explained that he had never socialized with a "colored" as an equal and was always taught at home that they were not equal. He informed me that his family had a lot of "colored" folks working for them, treated them fair, but never socialized with them. He said he regarded me as an equal and wanted to introduce me to his mother and father when they came up for graduation. However, he also confessed that he was afraid of how they would react to him having me as a friend. I spared him the agony by saying I understood but that I had to leave right after graduation to go see my wife and firstborn son whom I'd never had the pleasure of meeting.

Chicago and the Quasi Army Structure of the 113th Military Intelligence Group

I reported to the 113th Military Intelligence Corps Detachment at Chicago, IL, and was assigned to a field office at their headquarters on Bryn Mawr Avenue. Betty and Baby Jeff accompanied me while Lloyd stayed with his grandparents to help ease our financial burden. Meanwhile, the three of us moved in with my sister Charlene and her husband until I found an apartment.

I don't recall how or who assisted me, but I found an apartment across from Fifth Army Headquarters on Lake Shore Drive. The logistical problems were significant for our family since we only had one car, very little money, and my commute to Bryn Mawr

Avenue was about one hour each way. Betty was pregnant again but found a job at the Campbell Soup Company on Chicago's west side. This meant that she had to endure quite an ordeal to get to and from work. She had to catch a bus to my sister Charlene's apartment to drop off Jeff, catch another bus to Campbell Soup, and reverse the trip to get home each day. The odd thing about my commute was that the Fifth Army Field Office (FAFO) of the 113th was housed at Fifth Army HQ, right next door to our apartment!

Badge Number 6774: My Identification and Mission

My job as a special agent was to assure that individuals were cleared for access to classified information; I verified employment, checked their background for law enforcement violations and credit references for their reliability, and interviewed character references to determine their loyalty, integrity, discretion morals, and character. I was assigned a 1962 green Plymouth Valiant with US Government plates, wore civilian clothes, and assigned a geographical area of operation. The car could not be used for personal transportation, ruling out that option as a resolution to my commuter problems. I vaguely recall North Avenue as my southern boundary, Addison Road as the western boundary, and Devon Road as my northern boundary. I verified employment and interviewed the persons listed as references of candidates who lived or worked within my area of operations. One night a week was set aside to meet with those who preferred to be interviewed at their homes after work, which added an additional strain on our family.

The Chain of Command

Everyone wore civilian clothes and was called "Mr." except the commander and his executive officer. Since I was familiar with the chain of command and where I fit into the hierarchy, it didn't take me long to identify officers, NCOs, and enlisted members. Lt. Col.

Claude Patrick, commander of the 113th, was referred to as the colonel, and Maj. Billy Buchannan, executive officer, was called major. The rest of us were simply addressed as "Mr." or special agent. Since the insignia of rank in the army I was familiar with identified where you fit in the hierarchy, I needed to know what "Mr." was senior in rank to me. My orientation as a new agent was accelerated after Betty and I were invited to the commander's house for dinner as part of his welcome program for newly assigned officers and their wives.

The Influence of the Commander's Wife

I had been working at Bryn Mawr for about two months when I received an invitation for me and Betty to have dinner at Colonel Patrick's home in Deerfield. I had met with him briefly when I reported in and was impressed by his professional bearing and the quality and cut of the suits he wore. He was a lawyer and carried himself as a man of culture. On the night of our dinner, we parked our small Pontiac Tempest in his spacious driveway. I was not surprised that he lived in a large Tudor house in an upper-class neighborhood.

We were graciously received and welcomed by the Colonel and Mrs. Patrick. Sometime during the evening, Mrs. Patrick asked Betty about where we were living and how she liked living in Chicago. When Betty finished telling her about our commuting problems—mine to get from Fifth Army to Bryn Mawr Avenue and hers to my sister's house for babysitting and then catching another bus to her job—Mrs. Patrick was alarmed. Her view was that Betty should not have to endure such hardship, and she promptly told the colonel that he needed to fix the problem.

We had a very pleasant evening with the couple and left their home feeling that Mrs. Patrick really cared about our situation. Several weeks after our dinner visit, I was reassigned as Fifth Army Special Agent. I didn't know what happened to the agent who had been in the job forever and did not ask. We never overlapped, so I learned about my new job assignment from my secretary, Ms. Vickers, and a black lieutenant named John Webster, who had been assigned to the job before my arrival. Ross Guinta and another special agent were my two hotshot field agents who helped to keep our office caseload current.

My Credibility Challenged in Chicago's Gold Coast Neighborhood

Even as the special agent in charge, I continued to work routine investigation cases. In this regard, I will share two work-related experiences as typical examples of how I was viewed and accepted as a black agent. The first of these took place in Chicago's affluent Gold Coast neighborhood and the second during an encounter with a top executive at Sears and Roebuck.

I had to interview a character reference whose residence was in Chicago's Gold Coast area located along Lake Shore Drive. Realizing that I was going to an area where Gold Coast residents were not accustomed to having an African American ring their doorbell at 7:00 p.m., I decided to take special care in verifying my identity by presenting my badge and credential as a special agent of the US Army up front.

I arrived at the prestigious-looking house promptly at 7:00 p.m. and was standing at the front door facing what appeared to be a Tiffany-stained glass window. After I rang the doorbell, a woman peeked through the window and asked what I wanted. I told her I had an appointment to interview Mr. _ and asked if he was home. She ignored my question and inquired about the purpose of the interview. I gave her the full spiel, including holding up my credentials for her to see through the glass door—bad mistake! She cracked the door, took my credentials, closed the door, and departed the room. I had just violated rule number one: "Never Ever Let Your Credentials or Badge out of Your Hands"! I stood there for what seemed like an eternity, wondering if she had gone to get her husband or to call the police. Finally, she came back with her husband after about ten or fifteen minutes.

He opened the door, invited me in, and handed me back my credentials. Rule number two was to conduct the interview with only the designated character reference. I gently explained the need to interview him privately; however, the woman blurted out that she knew the person in question as well as her husband and that any questions about his character would be answered by them both. Moreover, she wanted to know what authority I had to ask about their friend in the first place. I went through my spiel once again, and since her husband did not ask her to leave, I decided to break rule number two and went on to conduct a joint interview. The man thanked me for my patience and apologized for my being held at the front door due to the protestations of his wife. Nothing in our role-playing interviews at Fort Holabird had prepared me for a skeptical, uncooperative, and questioning spouse.

Button-Popping Interview at Sears Chicago Headquarters

Another unforgettable experience as a special agent was an interview I conducted with a Sears and Roebuck executive at the Sears Tower in downtown Chicago. He was listed as a character reference for a friend who was currently undergoing screening for a security clearance. The interview was scheduled for 11:00 a.m., and I expected that I would be done and on my way by 11:30. To keep from being late, I parked in an alley near the Sears Tower, which made for a short walk to the building. Upon my arrival at the reception area, I was quickly ushered into a large spacious office overlooking the Chicago River as it flowed into Lake Michigan.

The receptionist ushered me into the executive's office where he warmly welcomed me, very impressed that I was conducting the interview for his friend's security clearance. I completed the interview and was preparing to leave when the executive invited me to have lunch. I declined, stating that I had to head across town for another interview. However, as I reached out to shake his hand, a button on my aging suit coat popped off.

Meanwhile, the executive politely picked it up and handed it to me. Embarrassed, I put it in my pocket and thanked him for picking up my button. He then said he was headed out to lunch and would walk me to the elevator. While waiting for the elevator, he complimented me on how well I had conducted the interview. But as I was putting on my overcoat, another button popped off. I picked up the button and made a feeble attempt to say something funny, but he had changed the subject and went on to compliment me for serving our country.

I hurried back to my car parked in the alley, looking back to make sure the executive was not following me. I got in and pulled out my brown paper sack lunch and felt sorry for myself. I shared the button- popping incident with Betty when I got home, and we both had a good laugh. We also agreed that we would buy me a couple of new suits. The new suits came from Robert Halls, a cheap but well-known clothier on the south side of Chicago and added a financial strain to the budget which had gotten even tighter with the arrival of our new son.

The Birth of Merrill Edward LaVern (MEL) Scott

I was present for every kick and movement during Betty's pregnancy with our youngest son. He was born August 18, 1963 at Chicago Lying-in Hospital.

He was premature and had to remain in the hospital for a couple of weeks before the doctor would let us take him home. The army paid all the hospital expenses, except for the $25 I had to borrow before they would release him to us. Betty insisted that she did not want to have another child, so when asked what to name him, I picked "Merrill," her father's first name. For good measure, I tacked on "Edward," my father's middle name, and "LaVern," my middle name. Merrill Edward LaVern (MEL) was called "brother baby" by Jeffrey, and the nickname was adopted by us during the first three years of his life.

The Move to Fort Sheridan and Commute to Fifth Army Chicago

Job wise, we moved from Twin Towers to Fifth Army Headquarters at Fort Sheridan, IL, where I rode a chartered bus with other officers who worked at Fifth Army. I had the distinction of being the only black officer and the only officer who wore civilian clothes on the bus. I may have been the only lieutenant, as most were captains, majors, lieutenant colonels, and colonels.

Early into my commute, one of the lieutenant colonels asked what I did and why I was wearing civilian clothes. He was the loudest officer on the bus, always joking, laughing, and being the funny guy. When I explained that I was a special agent and showed him my credentials, he loudly proclaimed that my cover was blown and that I had to be an officer and a lieutenant because the bus was only for commissioned officers. He then proceeded to hold court and asked me what rank I hoped to achieve in the army. When I said full colonel, he broke up laughing, repeated what I said for others to hear, and loudly stated in the middle of his guffaws: "Son, they don't make 'em your color." I had seen a black full colonel on the steps of the Pentagon when I visited there from Fort Holabird, so I knew that they had at least one my color.

Challenged Efficiency Report Opens Door to New Assignment

I was reassigned from FAFO back to the 113th Headquarters as an adjudicator under Kenneth Roth and Don Fox, a GS 12 Civilian.

I commuted in a carpool with Major Buchannan and three other officers. Actually, I had not given much thought to my next assignment until Roth gave me my annual performance evaluation.

He had checked the average block for me but used glowing words about the great job I had done as Special Agent in Charge (SAIC) at FAFO. I asked him why he had rated me as average, and he stammered that he had never seen a perfect officer and had, to date, never rated any officer above average. Several weeks later I learned that he had given Gene Epperly, a white officer, an above-average performance evaluation. When I confronted Roth with the information, he turned red as a beet, acknowledged that Gene was getting out of the army, and was trying to persuade him to stay in. Roth then agreed to change my rating to above average. He also suggested that I should apply for language school and request to be trained as an area intelligence specialist, which would qualify me to conduct covert intelligence operations.

He went out of his way to have Don Fox, who had already been accepted to language school, talk to me about the application process. Don helped me complete the application and knew the approval authority at the Pentagon, and my application came back approved for the forty-seven-week Vietnamese Language Course at the Defense Language Institute, West Coast Branch at Monterey, CA. Furthermore, approval for the course was linked to a follow-up assignment to the 441st Military Intelligence, Special Action Force Asia, and First Special Forces Group on Okinawa. Two rough winters in Chicago made accepting orders to move to sunny Monterey, CA, an easy choice. Betty was as excited as I was to be heading to California. Our little family had grown, and I traded the Pontiac Tempest for a nine-passenger Ford station wagon.

CHAPTER SIX

Moving West and Learning the Vietnamese Language

Don Fox and I agreed to convoy to Monterey and left right afterNew Year's Day 1965. Betty and the boys stayed with her parents and would fly out once I was offered housing. Our drive out was uneventful until we began climbing the high mountainous terrain. The scenery changed from desolate brown desert to lush green valleys. However, at the base of the valley, the station wagon conked out, and I had to have it towed to Monterey.

I had quite a few things to do before classes started, but applying for on-post housing at Fort Ord was my highest priority. Then there was the car issue which was also paramount. As it turned out, the station wagon needed a new engine, and the car dealer had a restored 1949 Mercedes four-door sedan that caught my eye. Its low mileage, sliding sunroof, and jet-black color seemed to fit the exotic surrounding of Monterey and Carmel, CA. So, I bought it!

I reconnected with Renzo, my best friend, and now a first lieutenant stationed at Fort Ord, conducting basic training. Because of my study schedule, he probably spent more time with Betty and the boys than I did. In fact, my classes had started when housing was assigned and on the very day that Betty and the boys—Lloyd, Jeffrey, and Mel—arrived at the airport. Renzo picked them up from the airport and took them to our new home. It was a beautiful three-bedroom ranch-style house with a view of the lights along the Monterey Bay Peninsula at night.

Small Class, Total Immersion, and Long Study Periods

The most remarkable experience from language school was the teaching method and the diverse backgrounds of the five students in my class. Of the four officers and one NCO in the course, four were West Point graduates. The lone NCO, Staff Sergeant Paxton, was a black belt in karate, held a high rating in Aikido, and was a very studious bachelor. The West Point men were Capt. Bill McCaffrey, Lt. Dennis Culp, and Lt. Ron Tomlinson. Each of us was assigned a Vietnamese name and could only speak Vietnamese to each other and our teachers in the classroom. Our teachers were a Vietnamese married couple fluent in English as well as their native language.

The class day was four hours long, and each day began with each of us

having to recite the assigned dialogue (a conversation between two Vietnamese people). The vocabulary used in the dialogue increased in complexity of sentence structure, meaning, and pronouncement of the phrases with each passing week. The conversations covered relationships with family and friends, shopping and restaurants, work and entertainment, and military topics covering weapons, training, tactics, logistics, first aid, and administration. This was the most intense studying I had ever done, and it caused me to stay up late into the night to master the dialogue, vocabulary, and diction for each day's assignment.

A Glimpse into the "Real Army"

Associating with the West Point graduates was educational and interesting. All the officers were Infantry and had had assignments in the "real army" since graduating from Infantry Officer Basic Course at Fort Benning. Each had completed Special Forces training and was being assigned to the First

Special Forces Group and Special Action Force Asia (SAF Asia) at Okinawa. Our common connection was Okinawa and SAF Asia. They knew nothing about the 441st Military Intelligence Detachment and thought of me as being associated with "a cloak and dagger" outfit.

Happy Hour Turns into an Expensive Evening

Capt. Bill McCaffrey and I carpooled to school, and our wives got to be good friends. Bill introduced me to Pete Dawkins, the Heisman Trophy winner, Rhodes Scholar, and West Point graduate. We started a routine of going to the Officers' Club for happy hour on Fridays to break the monotony of the study routine. My wife, Betty, and Bill's wife, Nancy, decided to put the kids in a nursery and join us for the fun, frolic, and dinner. Bill's reaction was one of great joy as well as surprise; mine was surprise and concern about how I was going to pay the bill for dinner and get the kids out of the nursery! Thankfully, the Officers' Club honored the signature of officers like me that allowed us to pay for fun, frolic, and dinner on payday at the end of the month. The lesson taught me to drive my own car on Fridays or check in with Betty before going to happy hour!

Course Completion and Okinawa: The Army's Moving Magic

With my language course successfully completed, Betty and the boys once again went to live with her parents until I could get housing at Okinawa.

I was not at all sure about how the transportation was going to work. Betty and the boys would have to return to Hannibal until housing was available and then from Hannibal to Okinawa. Meanwhile, our household goods would be placed in storage for thirty months since the army provided furniture and housing on the island. But how the army planned to get me, Betty, the boys, the car, and other essential items to Okinawa by the requested date was a mystery to me. Thankfully, I completed the paperwork while the transportation officer and Betty did the rest.

Once on the island of Okinawa, I reported to the 441st MI Detachment,

was assigned to the Counter Intelligence Section, and got on the list for on- post housing. The uniform for CI agents was fatigues with "US" pinned on the lapels and no rank insignia. The CI and Area Intelligence Section (AI) also wore civilian clothes when off the island. The commanding officer and members of the Combat Intelligence Section wore their rank insignia whether on or off island.

It was amusing because officers were assigned military housing by rank, belonged to the Officers' Club, and had friends and college classmates in Special Forces and other SAF ASIA units that knew our rank.

Capt. Homer Pickens was my boss and provided me with the most knowledgeable orientation on my duties and the role of SAF ASIA. The 441st MID was the intelligence arm of First Special Forces Group (airborne), the parent organization of the military organization designed to combat warfare being waged by hostile forces in the Pacific and Southwest Asia theater. Many of SAF ASIA's duties were related to Thailand, and I was immediately sent on temporary duty (TDY) assignment to learn my counter intelligence duties.

However, before departing, Captain Pickens gave me a thorough briefing on how he rated officer performance. His explanation was so detailed that he provided a sheet of paper listing all the desired outcomes for each task that an officer had to accomplish to earn a top-block rating. He also told me that I could not receive a top block because I would not be able to complete the full cycle of assigned tasks before his departure. Pickens sent me TDY with Maj. Robert Cox, executive officer of the detachment, to learn our CI role in Thailand. I learned that the major had a no-nonsense reputation as a CI operative. He was very precise in his instructions about using surveillance techniques, avoiding the use of classified information in public conversations, and silently sweeping hotel rooms for hidden microphones or listening devices upon entering the room. He was cross-trained in both covert and overt intelligence operations. James Bond movies were the rage in the orient at the time, and I was a little more than impressed with "REC," which was his initials and trademark signature on notes and documents.

Thai Counter Intelligence Contacts

We wore civilian clothes in Thailand, and our primary contact was the CI office in the Joint United States Military Assistance and Advisory Group (JUSMAAG) located at the US Embassy. The SAIC of that office was Capt. Rayford Tapley, an African American, whom I learned was a graduate of Tuskegee University. Our primary purpose in Thailand was to assist "Mr." Tapley's office in finding who was responsible for smuggling US military weapons from Vietnam through Cambodia into Thailand.

Our job was to conduct low-level listening operations at bars frequented by soldiers on rest and relaxation (R&R) from Vietnam. Cox took me to the designated bars and showed me where to sit for the best vantage point in the room, what to drink, how to develop a cover identity, and how long to stay in a bar. We developed a lead from a soldier on leave from Vietnam who reported that he had been approached to smuggle weapons out of Vietnam. The soldier said he was instructed to travel to a seaside resort in Pattaya, where he would be given final instructions and paid for agreeing to smuggle the weapons. Three of us placed him under surveillance and followed discreetly every place the soldier went, except into the commode, where according to the soldier, his contact pointed a weapon and warned of fatal consequences if he reneged on the deal. The soldier came out of the bathroom ashen in color and frightened out of his wits. He related what had happened inside the bathroom and asked where we were. I was in the bathroom and saw the soldier go into the commode stall and close the door. He and I were the only two people, I can say for certain, present in the bathroom. The soldier asked to return to his unit in Vietnam, and we arranged for him to do so immediately. Following the incident, I concluded that the spy business was for James Bond and that it was safer doing personnel security interviews than trying to catch a real or imagined smuggler.

The other important lesson "REC" taught me was where and how to shop for Thai gems and jewelry. Cox had excellent contacts with "Johnny" of Johnny's Gems, a popular jewelry store in Bangkok. He introduced me to "Johnny" as his trusted point of contact in Thailand, and "Johnny" extended me the privilege of purchasing whatever I wanted and sending him a check for the amount when I returned to Okinawa. This contact would prove advantageous to my career aspirations on a future trip to Bangkok.

I remained in Thailand for sixty days, working with Tapley and getting to know his wife, Mercilee, and their family. I would later meet and become good friends with her family who lived in Tuskegee. I returned to Okinawa in time to take possession of our housing quarters just before Betty and the boys arrived.

Betty and the Boys Arrive

We were assigned a three-bedroom house in Kashaba Terrace. In the meantime, I was receiving jump pay and was promoted to the rank of captain, and Betty landed a job at the Post Engineers. We had more money than ever before and employed a "sew girl," a maid, and a yardman. We also reconnected with Joe Guyton, as well as Mary and Lewis Hefner, Lincoln University alums, who were also assigned to SAF ASIA. New friends were many, but Bill and Jackie Miller became lifelong friends. Bill was a member of my unit, and I had the privilege of being the sponsor who met and helped his family settle into their quarters while Bill was on temporary duty off island.

Captain Middleton, or "Middy" as we called him, was also a member of my section and a great golf player. Middy was a popular golfing partner to several senior officers during mandatory outings. I must confess that I was a little resentful until I received an assignment to escort a senior officer to Thailand because of my in-country counter intelligence connections.

Escort Duty: Unexpected Career Assistance

Captain Pickens was reassigned and rated me above average on my performance evaluation report. Capt. Dick Post became the chief of the Counter Intelligence Section, and I continued conducting classified security inspections on units that made up SAF ASIA and First Special Forces.

An unexpected opportunity came my way when Col. "Flash" Gordon, G2, US Army Ryuku Islands (USARIS), requested an escort officer to accompany him to Thailand on an official visit. I believe the commanding officer at the time was Maj. Fred Aydelette, and it was he who recommended me for the assignment because of my study under Major Cox. It was also an unusual request because the G2 was not in SAF ASIA or First Special Forces Chain of command. Nonetheless, as the senior intelligence officer on Okinawa, his authority was not questioned.

Colonel Gordon provided a list of places he wanted to visit and assigned me to coordinate his itinerary and plan all travel arrangements to and within Bangkok. He and I had never met until we arrived at the airport, and I briefed him on his itinerary. I had done my homework well, even checking his background, and knew that he was a West Point graduate. He was very formal in manner and direct in conversation. He grilled me on flight times, stops at the Philippines and Saigon, names and titles of officials he would meet in Thailand, and the safety of the hotel I had selected for him during our visit.

He relaxed a little after being briefed on each detail of the journey as well as what was to happen at each port of call. Halfway through the visit he was completely comfortable with me and his itinerary. As impressed as he was with his reception by JUSMAAG and Captain Tapley's office, the welcome he received from the hotel manager and from "Johnny" of Johnny's Gems clinched his high regard for my coordinating abilities.

On the flight back to Okinawa, he asked about my background and what my aspirations were in the army. I told him about my being commissioned as a distinguished military graduate from Lincoln University and being turned down for a regular army commission. He listened intently and urged me to reapply and to send the application through his office. Wasting no time, I completed the application, requested a regular army commission in the newly formed Military Intelligence Branch, and sent it through Colonel Gordon. Ninety days later, I had a favorable response. Military Intelligence Branch had exceeded authorization for regular army captains but informed me that the Infantry Branch would grant me a regular army commission if I wanted it. A regular army commission would provide me with protection against a forced reduction in officers, an advantage I lacked as a reserve officer. After conferring with Betty, my chain of command, and Colonel Gordon, I gladly accepted the offer.

Regular Army: Unexpected Assignments and Leadership Challenges

I was immediately reassigned from the 441st MID to the 97th Civil Affairs Detachment to keep their respective officer allocations current. The MI had no authorizations for Infantry captains, but the 97th Civil Affairs Group had a vacancy, and I was assigned there. Then bizarre things started to unfold for me within First Special Forces Group because of my branch transfer back to the Infantry.

Green Berets: Contested A-Team Commander Assignment

The First Special Forces Group assigned me to a "B" Team to deploy to Thailand and train Thai Infantry units for Vietnam. I thought the fact that I was now wearing the Infantry insignia, wearing the Green Beret, and had basic training experience was good reason to include me as a member of the team. It was not true. Maj. Ralph Weekly, B-Team commander, discovered after our arrival in Thailand that I was not a graduate of the Special Forces School and therefore could not command the "A" Team that I was slotted to command. He called back to Okinawa for resolution and was told to use me as an assistant "A" Team commander.

When told that I would be an assistant to Capt. Bill Sylvester, I strongly objected while pointing out that there was no "assistant A-Team commander" on the Table of Organization in Special Forces and that I was senior in rank to Bill and would go back to Okinawa rather than accept that arrangement. Major Weekly assigned me as the A-Team commander and Bill as my assistant. I was comfortable in the position because of my previous experience as a basic training company commander and due to my familiarity with Thai customs. I led all team meetings and directed our training assignments with the Thai Infantry School. In conclusion, Captain Sylvester and I maintained a professional relationship and worked through the tensions posed by the presence of two strong personalities sharing one leadership position.

Promotion to Major: Change of Orders from Vietnam to Fort Benning

When I returned to Okinawa to the Ninety-Seventh Civil Affairs, I had about three months to the end of my tour. However, I was greeted by good news with unexpected consequences. I was promoted to the rank of major and notified that I would be assigned to Vietnam at the end of my tour. Staff Sergeant Bailey, the administrative NCO at Ninety-Seventh Civil Affairs, suggested that I ask Colonel Parks, the commander, and the Ninety-Seventh to write a letter on my behalf requesting that I attend the Infantry Officer Advanced Course and defer assignment to Vietnam until its completion. He even prepared a draft letter for me through Colonel Parks explaining that my attendance at the Infantry Advanced Course would better prepare me to perform duties as an Infantry officer in Vietnam. Colonel Parks signed the letter and called Infantry Branch, and my orders were amended.

We left Okinawa for Fort Benning, GA, in order for me to attend the thirty-six-week Infantry Officer Advanced Course. In the thirty months that we had been on Okinawa, a lot had changed in the United States. However, as we would soon discover, a lot had remained the same. During our time on Okinawa, we had communicated with our family through letters and tapes. The boys had grown a lot. Lloyd was ten years old and in the fourth grade, while Jeff and MEL were six and five, respectively, and ready to start first grade and kindergarten.

It would now become necessary for them to attend school in the south. Betty had not travelled to the south and was a little apprehensive about motel accommodations in Tennessee, Kentucky, and Mississippi, states that we would have to pass through on our way from Missouri to Georgia. The assassination of

Martin Luther King Jr. in 1968 was still vivid in the minds of most Americans. Strained relations between blacks and whites, especially in the south where we were headed, were the order of the day. In addition, because of the Vietnam War, Columbus and Fort Benning, GA, were experiencing an influx of officers needing housing, and we were adding to that population. Therefore, our arrival in Georgia at this time coincided with a point of heightened tensions on several fronts.

CHAPTER SEVEN

Off-Post Housing Discrimination in Columbus, GA

We arrived in Columbus and went through the usual procedures of getting settled, including finding a temporary place to stay, checking out the schools and looking for housing. We found temporary quarters at the Camellia Motel and Apartments, a popular and overcrowded motel outside the gate at Fort Benning. On-post housing was maxed out, and the housing referral office sent me along with hundreds of other officers off post to seek housing rentals in the Columbus area.

When I arrived at the approved real-estate rental office, a long line had formed, and I fell in behind a white major to await my turn at the counter. He and I struck up a conversation about our previous and current assignments.

As we talked, the line inched forward, and my anxiety increased with each step. The major reached the counter and stated that he needed a three-bedroom house with at least two baths. Meanwhile, the agent casually handed him three sets of keys, allowing him to choose the house that best met his requirements.

When I reached the counter, the agent asked about my housing needs while simultaneously attempting to sneak another book on top of the one she had just used. I replied that my housing needs were the same as the major she had just given three sets of keys, and since he could only live in one of the houses, I would wait for his return and choose from the other two. The agent stammered and went to get an older man who minced no words in telling me that they had a limited number of houses for "colored" officers and that I could go look at them if I wanted.

I repeated my offer to wait for the white major to return and then I would choose from the two remaining houses. At this point, the man angrily told me that this was Columbus, GA, and that Mr. McNamara (secretary of defense at the time) did not run things down here in Georgia, and the only housing available to me was in the "colored section." I left the office feeling angry, hurt, and determined to report this encounter to somebody who could do something about it.

The Commanding General's Swift Response

I headed straight for the commanding general's office to report the discrimination. My anger intensified as I drove back to the post. My thoughts ranged from the anger over not being able to provide a decent place to live for my wife and sons to the blatant inequality boldly announced by the agent with no fear of consequences. In his mind, no power on earth or in heaven could stop him from discriminating on the basis of race! This thought process on my part led to even more dismal thoughts about the meaning of my commission as an officer in the US Armed Forces.

I walked into the command suite and stated that I wanted to see the commanding general about a racial discrimination incident I had just experienced downtown. The chief of staff came out to see me, took me into his office, and asked me to relate what had happened. My emotions were still high, and at the end of relating what had happened, I offered to surrender my newly awarded major's oak leaf insignia of rank if the army allowed a double standard in the rental of off-post housing to black officers. The colonel, who was very compassionate about my situation and emotions, called the post housing officer and sent me to his office for a resolution.

The post housing manager found a three-bedroom apartment on post for our family to move into. I was really thrilled at the quick response in taking care of our needs, but even more gratified when the Assistant Commandant Brigadier General Sidney Berry addressed our entire class over the off-post housing discrimination incident. I was proud to be a member of the US Army that day and felt privileged to witness the general's remarks that the army would not accept discrimination among its soldiers on- or off-post. However, when he asked for a show of hands from black officers who had been discriminated against in off- post housing, my hand was the only hand raised in the air. I knew for certain that another black major had accepted a house in the "colored section" of Columbus. I later asked why he did not raise his hand, and he replied that he was okay with the house he had rented and did not want to cause any trouble. He was from the south.

The Infantry Officer Advance Course was a valuable experience and taught me many of the tools of ground combat operations that would help me get through my assignment in Vietnam. We renewed our friendship with Renzo and his wife, Brenda, and also with Jack Windom and his wife, Charlotte. Jack was a Lincoln University classmate and a brilliant chemical officer teaching the employment of tactical nuclear weapons at the Infantry School.

We also added a small miniature poodle to our family. We named him Toussaint L'Ouverture and nearly loved him to death. Jeff and MEL broke his little legs twice using him as a ball, tossing him back and forth to each other. Neither admitted who dropped him, but the veterinarian warned us that one more injury and he would have him taken away from us. We left Georgia with "Tous" riding in his special place in the middle ledge of the back window, heading for Shilling Manor, Salina, KS, and Vietnam.

Next Assignment: Vietnam and "The Real Army"

Betty chose to stay at Shilling Manor, a home for waiting wives and children of service men as well as women assigned to Vietnam. The manor was a closed air force base renovated for waiting wives. She learned about it and a couple of other places through a story printed in the Army Times. I was surprised by her choice to live so far away from our family in Missouri but felt good about the security and accommodations my family would have living on a military base. I left them at Shilling Manor, and the face of my youngest son waving goodbye to me at the Salina Airport was etched in my memory as I departed for Vietnam.

Insights on First Eight Years of Military Life

In chronicling my first eight years in the military, I have attempted to provide what I believe to be worthwhile reflections on marriage, career challenges, and the need for mentors. The political landscape in the year 1960 supported segregation laws that limited and—in the cases of southern states— denied African Americans equal access to jobs, housing, and education. And although in 1948 President Harry Truman signed an executive order ending racial segregation in the military, twelve years later when I entered the army, black Americans were still limited in their access to assignments leading to higher rank. As evidenced by Truman, the political views of politicians mattered then, and it matters now.

Politics Matter

Soldiers should not be politically active when on active duty, so I kept my political views to myself for the thirty years, eight months, and seventeen days that comprised my military career. I am profoundly grateful to the men and women who championed equal rights for minorities and women in America and especially for those of us who served in the military. Eleanor Roosevelt, Mary McCloud Bethune, Harry Truman, John Kennedy, Lyndon Johnson, and Martin Luther King Jr. lead my list of champions for civil rights and equal opportunity. Their individual efforts, during their time, made the challenges more tolerable in my time. Likewise, their collective efforts enabled the armed forces to become the undisputed leader in equal opportunity for minorities and women.

In the early 1960s, racial prejudice often wore NCO stripes and officers' bars and gave cover to those who did not embrace President Truman's policy to desegregate the armed forces. Fortunately, the NCOs and officers who supported desegregation policies and used their influence to help deserving minorities and women take advantage of available opportunities, outnumbered those who did not. My journey during these eight years may have taken a different turn had I not had a helpful Major Lister, Lieutenant Colonel Patrick, Col. "Flash" Gordon, Staff Sergeant Bailey, Colonel Parks, chief of staff at Benning, or Brig. Gen. Sid Berry, assistant commandant. I also learned that it is necessary for a soldier to stand up for himself when he is the target of racial discrimination. To turn a blind eye, rationalize away, or accept the humiliation of being discriminated against is, in my mind, being a traitor to the victories won by the champions of racial justice and equal opportunity.

African Americans must constantly be vigilant against any assault on the victories won for minorities and women in the twentieth century by the champions of equal rights. Many African Americans who are enjoying the fruits of a college education, a good job, a six-figure salary, and a robust 401K don't see the need to worry about a resurgence of wholesale racial discrimination. My advice: think about race and rights as you do about life and death; young men and women in the prime of life don't think about dying but buy a life insurance policy just in case they do!

Minorities living the American dream don't think about being discriminated against but should be vigilant and protect the laws that made it possible for their entry into mainstream America. An influential politician who supports those hard-won laws and policies is the best insurance to protect civil rights and equal opportunities for all Americans. To soldiers in uniform: do not get involved in local, state, or national politics but have the courage to confront racial injustice or policies that discriminate against you, your family members, or other soldiers or their family members.

"The Real Army"

The "real army" is where the majority of West Point graduates are assigned. That was true in 1960, and I believe will always be true. The heart and soul of the army are the men and women who fill the ranks of its major tactical elements: corps, divisions, brigades or regiments, battalions, companies, and platoons. West Point graduates are educated and groomed to lead these tactical levels of command, and their assignments reflect that practice. My assignment to provide soldiers with basic military training was out of the mainstream.

The sergeants and officers I met at Fort Leonard Wood were survivors from the Korean War. Most of the officers at the rank of captain and above received their commissions from OCS—enlisted men or women selected to complete a rigorous training course in order to become a commissioned officer. Others were promoted to the rank of commissioned officers because of their heroics on the battlefield in Korea. Many of the sergeants in the grade of E6 or above had been officers in the Korean War; however, in order to retire as an officer, they were willing to accept a reduction in their enlisted grade. The only West Point graduate I knew was Col. Franklin Hartline, second training brigade commander. My guess is that Brigadier General Dodge, assistant post commander, was also a West Point graduate.

At Fort Leonard Wood, majors or captains commanded training battalions, and captains or lieutenants commanded basic training companies. All of us were in a voluntary reserve officer status, and most captains and majors were nearing retirement. Morale among the basic training cadre, officers, and enlisted men was not particularly high. A common complaint of the sergeants was that Leonard Wood was not the "real army." Career counseling was not part of my commander's job description, and I received more mentoring from a riffed colonel/master sergeant than I did from any of my company commanders.

My tours of duty in the Counter Intelligence Corps were totally outside of the mainstream. The officers, with few exceptions, were voluntary reservists on active duty and focused on career paths in the army that could lead to high-level civilian intelligence jobs after retirement. I had a strong desire to be in the mainstream of the army.

On Marriage: Choice, Chance, and Change

Choice, chance, and change happen to all and continue to be a significant factor in my life experiences. Choice is the dominant one among the three life-shaping factors because we are given the power to choose our reaction, no matter the consequences, to circumstances involving chance or change. My romantic interest in Betty began with a chance meeting that sparked a flame within me that led to intimacy and resulted in our choice to get married.

As a matter of chance, I saw her in her parents' backyard as I was driving by one day. And yet this seeming "accident" may have been God's intervention in our lives camouflaged as chance. After fifty years of marriage, I choose to believe that our meeting was preordained by our creator. It was meant to be. During those early years, the army expected army wives to meet many volunteer and social obligations as an extension of their husbands. Betty met or exceeded these expectations in spite of the challenges presented by working outside of the home. And she did so without jeopardizing her standing within the wives hierarchy while at the same time enhancing my career. Chance, choice, and change are unchanging factors of life. Making good choices trumps chance and change any day of the week—and especially on Sundays.

Career Moves

Accepting the branch detail to the Counter Intelligence Corps led to my application and acceptance of a regular army commission, which returned me to the Infantry Branch. That decision carried risk as well as the potential for rewards. Rewards increase with efforts to acquire and use one's knowledge, skills, and abilities to complete assigned tasks and to work collaboratively with coworkers and supervisors. Influential people may be watching and may choose to help open doors of opportunity. This axiom proved to be true in the cases of Major Lister, Lieutenant Colonel Patrick, Colonel Parks, Staff Sergeant Bailey, the Fort Benning chief of staff, and Brig. Gen. Sid Berry, who acted in my best interest and without expectation of personal gain or reward. This is the best kind of help that can be given or received.

Confrontation

Constructive responses to real or perceived injustice are good for preserving self-worth and self-respect. Confrontation was not a task that I enjoyed, but I learned the necessity of asking my supervisor to tell me what tasks I had to perform in order to receive a top-block performance report. Capt. Homer Pickens taught me this lesson by telling me his expectations of my performance in order to award me a top-block evaluation. His explanation was clear, comprehensive, and fell within my job description. I did not receive a top block from him because he departed the command before I had the opportunity to perform some of the cyclical tasks required of me. For this reason, I had no problem accepting his evaluation.

CHAPTER EIGHT

Vietnam and the Real Army

The civilian 707 jetliner departed for Vietnam from Travis Air Force Base, CA, full to the max with soldiers. The flight attendants tried to lift our spirits with good-natured comments about the tropical weather that awaited us, but we were too preoccupied with our own thoughts. My seatmate was a Maj. Jim Adams from Phoenix City, AL, across the river from Columbus and Fort Benning, Georgia, and was on his second tour. I was on my first tour, eager to learn what he could tell me about Vietnam. We chatted easily, and I learned that we both were headed to the replacement center at Cam Ran Bay. We talked about our past assignments, our families, where they were living during our absence, and how much we would miss them during the year-long tour. At one point in our conversation, Jim surprised me by saying that he didn't think that he would make it back alive. I was startled by his statement, so I asked him why he felt that way, and he said that it was just a feeling he had. We didn't dwell on the subject and changed to topics of mutual interest. Between naps, meals, and small talk, we landed at Cam Ran Bay, and our unknown journey in sunny Vietnam in the fall of 1969 began.

The replacement center at Camranh Bay was a beehive of activity, with officers and enlisted soldiers "processing out" to return to the USA and our group "processing in" to learn our unit of assignment in Vietnam for the next year. However, since we arrived at night, our group had to wait until morning to learn our unit assignment. We and the outgoing guys were bunked in a building near the Officers' Club and shared a few drinks at the club. The outgoing guys were joyful, full of hope for life at home, and eagerly shared their bad experiences— experiences they were happy to be leaving behind.

Many of their complaints were leveled against the Fourth Infantry Division and its area of operation in the jungles of the Central Highlands. The more they drank, the harsher their word picture of service with the division. Their laundry list of complaints were voiced in tandem and included: rainy weather, thick jungle terrain, poor supply lines, widespread cases of trench foot, being wet for extended periods, going without rations and potable water at times, and having limited cover via air strikes during enemy contact. The not- so-subtle warning was to do anything to keep from being assigned to the Fourth Infantry Division. I had read or heard most of their complaints before, thanked them for the drinks, and went to bed anxious about my assignment.

The next morning during processing, both Jim and I, along with hundreds of other officers and soldiers, were assigned, of course, to the Fourth Infantry Division. Shortly after the announcement, we were loaded onto C130 cargo planes and flown north to Pleiku; from there, we were bussed to Camp Enari, home of the Fourth Infantry Division Headquarters in Vietnam.

Camp Enari looked like a sprawling military post with rows of prefabricated buildings (quanson huts) erected on concrete blocks laid out in grids. The camp was surrounded by jungle on three sides and a huge mountain on the other side. The Americans called it "Dragon Mountain," but the Vietnamese called it "Nui Ba Den" or "Black Mountain." The Vietnamese name coincided with the mountain's color, but to the Americans, its shape looked like a Dragon. Surprisingly, I felt at ease as we passed through the gate and headed toward a row of buildings with trucks and buses coming and going. We stopped and a cheerful sergeant greeted us. He directed us off the bus and welcomed us to the Fourth Division In-Processing Center. It was the end of the line for those of us assigned to division headquarters and units collocated at Camp Enari and transition point for those assigned to divisional units located at bases in the surrounding jungle. All of us "newbees" had to receive a three-day orientation briefing before reporting to work.

Because of my past experience in counter intelligence, I was assigned to the Intelligence Staff (G2). I was happy with the assignment but explained to the assignment officer that I needed a job as an Infantry battalion operations officer (S3) or as an executive officer (XO) of an Infantry battalion to establish my credibility as an Infantry officer. He told me that those positions were filled by nomination from the division personnel officer (G1) and approved by the battalion commander. He suggested that over the next six months, I needed to build a good reputation in the intelligence job, get a good recommendation from the G2, and make a good impression on a battalion commander in need of an S3 or XO. I accepted his suggestion and was on my way to check in with the G2 office when I saw Jim Adams coming out of the G1's office. He had a worried look on his face and told me that he had been assigned to the G5 as the division's psychological operations officer (PSYOPS). I asked why he was worried about it, and he explained that he didn't know anything about PSYOPS and knew that the job entailed travel throughout the division's area of operation to work with Vietnamese province and military officials. He replayed his fears to me about being killed in Vietnam; he felt that the travel involved in the assignment represented an omen of his worst fears.

Although I didn't know anything about "PSYOPS" either, I offered to trade assignments with him to relieve him of his fears and because I thought it would be more exciting than sticking pins on a map in the G2's office. We both went into tell the G1 that we wanted to switch jobs because I was more qualified to do the job than Jim. The fact that I spoke Vietnamese and had Special Forces experience working with indigenous people won me the assignment.

The G1 switched our assignments, and even though I knew that the G2 position was a better pathway for me to establish my credibility as an Infantry major, I felt that I made the right decision. With my assignment settled, I, along with about three hundred other newbees, attended our last orientation class on the subject of observing the customs and courtesies of the Vietnamese people.

Ironically, the major giving the class announced that he was giving an abbreviated version of the topic because the division PSYOPS officer completed his tour and had returned to the United States. He didn't know that I was in the audience and had been assigned to the job. However, the very next week, I was standing before the newbees telling them the importance of winning the hearts and minds of the Vietnamese people. I quickly learned that the weekly orientation briefings were only one of many functions I had to complete as the division's PSYOPS expert.

My learning curve was steep, and my class room and teachers were the principal staff officers in the nightly commanding general's briefing room and fellow majors "in the know" at the nightly gossip sessions in the barracks. As I prepared to start my new job, my thoughts turned to the realization that I didn't know a soul in the division commanded by Maj. Gen. Donn R. Pepke and was finally in the real army for the first time in my career. I reported to my boss, Lt. Col. Jim Marini, the division civil-military operations officer (G5). He was an armor officer, newly appointed to the position, and welcomed me warmly as he told me up front that he didn't know anything about PSYOPS. He handed me some files left by my predecessor and told me that I had no staff, would brief PSYOPS activities at the nightly division commander's briefing s and that I had a week to get up to speed before my first nightly update briefing. I quickly read the files and the army's Field Manual on Psychological

Operations to learn that my duty was to

- advise the division staff on the use of leaflet drops, loud speakers, artillery and air strikes to weaken and induce the enemy to defect to the government of South Vietnamese or give up the fight and to inform villagers of the health and welfare provided by our US forces on behalf of the South Vietnamese Government.

- manage the division's "Cheiu Hoi" program. This program entailed the use of North Vietnamese and Viet Cong Soldiers defectors to work with US Army combat units as advisors on enemy tactics and techniques. They were dubiously called, "Kit Carson Scouts." The division was authorized one hundred scouts, and I was responsible for keeping track of their placement and status.
- orient new soldiers on the importance of maintaining a good relationship with the local populace—the Vietnamese and Montagnards, indigenous tribes, people—through observance and practice of their customs and courtesies.
-

My means of waging psychological warfare was an assigned jeep with a Kit Carson Scout driver to visit villagers and tribes and the use of the commanding general's U6 fixed wing plane to drop leaflets and make loud speaker announcements. For the heavy persuaders like artillery delivery of bombs or leaflet-filled projectiles, I coordinated with the appropriate division staff officer. According to the manual, I could use these assets singularly or all together, in which case it was called a PSYOPS campaign.

I was an observer the first week I attended the commanding general's nightly update briefing. These briefings reminded me of a nightly television news broadcast. The principal staff officers were the news anchors covering a set format of topics that informed the general of

- the battles engaged or ongoing
- causalities inflicted or received
- the number of enemy and US soldiers killed
- equipment destroyed or captured
- enemy supplies and weapons captured or destroyed
- sightings of large numbers of enemy and their direction of travel

These topics were briefed by principal staff officers who had successfully commanded battalions in those areas (Pleiku, Kontum, or Ankhe) or were selected to be on the staff because of their potential to command one of the general's combat battalions. Two of the selected briefers, Lieutenant Colonel Prilliman, operations officer (G3), and Lieutenant Colonel Stevenson, personnel officer (G1), had successfully encountered and handled the topics in the areas covered as battalion commanders. The stakes were high for both former and future commanders on staff; those who had commanded and received a great evaluation report were certain to get promoted to colonel and attend the war college, and those like my boss, Marini, were certain to command a battalion if they impressed the general and the chief of staff with their performance on the staff. Col. Gordon Duquemin, the division chief of staff, had successfully commanded a brigade in one of those areas and was the direct boss of the principal staff and Pepke's go-to guy for day-to-day operations. The "Duke," as he was affectionately referred to outside of earshot, quickly volunteered to follow up on questions or issues that were not answered to General Pepke's satisfaction. Prillman appeared to be the dominant personality among the briefers and the one most likely to lighten the mood with a humorous comment in between the often ominous nature of the briefing topics. Officers in the rank of major attended the briefings as assistants to the principal staff and often briefed the details of troop movements and minor operations. I was impressed by the cautious informality of the presenters as they informed General Pepke, with a pleasant look but no-nonsense demeanor, of the significant activities in the division's area of operation. That was my introduction to the personalities and war zone news presented at the nightly six o'clock follies.

My introduction to office politics at division headquarters began my first night in the building that housed the majors who worked at the division staff. Todd Poch, secretary of the general's personal staff who worked under the

"Duke," and Jerry Patten, assistant personnel officer under Lieutenant Colonel Stevenson, invited newcomers to Poch's room for a meet-and-greet opportunity. Jim and I, the only newcomers, attended and over wine and cheese learned the latest rumors of who's about to get fired, promoted, or was on the hot seat. We were also politely grilled about our background, assignment expectations, and given an open invitation to attend the nightly gathering either in Poch's or in Patten's room after dinner in the troop mess hall. Both Todd and Jerry dined in the commanding general's mess with the principal staff officers. Between the two, they knew or professed to know everything that was going on in the division was the only African American major on the staff when Maj. Sam Ebbsen arrived about a month after me, and neither Jerry nor Todd knew his ethnicity. I didn't know either until he and I spent most evenings after work getting to know each other and talking about our families and ancestral roots. Sam was a New Yorker, of Virgin Island ancestry, and his multiracial features didn't fit any choices given for race or ethnicity on the personnel form. Sam was assigned as the headquarters commandant, meaning he was responsible for all the administrative and logistical functions to support the general's staff. He was determined to become a battalion operations officer or executive officer and did not socialize much with the headquarters clique. He did an excellent job as commandant and secured a job as battalion S3 after about three months in the division staff. After Sam left, Patten asked me if he was African American. I said that he was a Virgin Islander from New York and appeared to be proud of his ancestry.

I learned that other than myself, there were only two other African American officers in the division. One was a major serving as a logistical officer (S4) in one of the brigades, and the other was also a major who served as battalion executive officer, First Battalion Thirty-Fifth Infantry. Both were in units located on Camp Enari, and the rumor mill touted that the brigade S4 was well thought of by the division commander. Nothing was said about the other major, whom I knew as a fellow student at Fort Benning, and I assumed that he was doing well in his position. I wanted to do well in my position and learned from the well-connected majors that their bosses regarded PSYOPS as a necessary function and that I could use the position to make myself known to battalion commanders to land a job as their deputy or operations officer. From the first week on, I performed tasks described in the PSYOPS manual with the villagers, ethnic tribes, and Vietnamese officials in an effort to let the general and staff know that I was on the team.

My first couple of reports during the commanding general's nightly briefings proved to be a significant learning experience about how little interest the commanding general and the primary staff paid to the information presented by Lieutenant Colonel Marini (G5), Major Coyne (civil affairs), and me. We were the last presenters, and the body language of the general—and especially the majors who acted as presenters for the other staff sections— appeared disinterested and in a hurry to go to dinner. I took note of the reaction and kept looking for ways to connect PSYOPS to the actions that got the general's attention at his six o'clock briefings.

My chance came when General Pepke, frustrated that the major highway between Pleiku and Ankhe required the full-time assignment of his only cavalry squadron to prevent the enemy from placing land mines on it, exploded and told his staff to find a better way to keep the highway open. Shaken over the general's directive and abrupt departure from the briefing room, the G3 and G2 huddled to find a solution. I immediately suggested to Marini that I could do a PSYOPS campaign to enlist the help of the ethnic tribes who lived along the highway to tell us the enemy-staging areas and locations of the mines placed on the highways. Armed with that information, we could use artillery or helicopter gunships against the enemy's efforts. Marini took my suggestion to the G3 and G2, who agreed to me presenting the plan to the general.

On the night of my briefing, I actually believed that the plan would work and enthusiastically used maps and pictures of tribes along the route to support my plan. My brief highlighted the fact that the key element of my campaign was to enlist the Montagnard Tribes to report their sightings of enemy or enemy sympathizers who were planting mines along the main supply route. To that end, I would provide the location of sightings to the G2 and G3, who in turn would coordinate an ambush or direct artillery strikes against the suspected locations. I emphasized my excellent rapport with the Montagnards, showed a miniature wood carving of General Pepke's helicopter they had produced, and announced that the campaign had been coordinated and approved by the G3, G2, and Lieutenant Colonel Marini. General Pepke grunted his okay as the principal staff looked on in amusement, and my fellow majors snickered.

For about ten consecutive days, the G2 reported a decrease in mining activity. The doubters started to take notice. Moreover, the ambush sites coincided with the locations given to me by the Montagnards and the general started to take notice. The highway mining incidents decreased to two or three, and General Pepke released the division cavalry squadron to perform their normal reconnaissance missions.

General Pepke awarded me the Bronze Star Medal for Achievement, and with the "Duke" by his side grinning like a proud papa, I felt like a member of the team. The recognition and award served to enhance my standing with the principal staff—and especially among the clique of majors at headquarters. And the timing could not have been better.

I was enjoying my status but still wanted to burnish my credentials as an Infantry major by being an XO or S3 of an Infantry battalion. About a month after my successful PSYOPS campaign, my opportunity came in the form of a report presented at the general's nightly update briefing. One of the Infantry battalions at Camp Enari was going through a major incidence of disorder between black and white troops and the battalion XO was fired for failure to maintain good order and discipline. The "Duke" quickly asserted that the situation was under control and that he would keep an eye on it. I didn't know at the time that the XO was the black major that I knew from Fort Benning Career Course. Later that evening, I was summoned to the "Duke's" office and told that he was sending me down to take over as the XO of the First Battalion, Thirty-Fifth Infantry and to restore order and discipline.

I was happy but also concerned that the change in my position from division headquarters to an Infantry battalion would cause Betty concern for my safety. In the letter I wrote her that night, I told her about my new job and explained that I would still be at Camp Enari and that she should not worry over my safety. I also explained that I had made the decision to take the risks associated with being an Infantry officer by taking the difficult jobs in combat rather than working in the relative safety of staff jobs. I dropped the letter in the mailbox, packed my duffel bag, and tried to sleep while wondering what kind of mess I would find in the battalion.

Battalion Executive Officer

I checked into Third Brigade Headquarters and was briefed by the executive officer on the situation at the First Battalion, Thirty-Fifth Infantry (Cacti Green). From the military police report the XO used to brief me, I learned that the former XO was fired because he had allowed black enlisted soldiers to take over the unit's recreational room and NCO's lounge in order to establish them as all black clubs. The report also stated that the blacks were running the battalion.

The XO had been shipped out, and Captain Close, the battalion headquarters company commander, was the senior officer in charge of the battalion's support operations at Camp Enari. Lt. Col. Cliff High, battalion commander, was at the battalion's forward operating base in the jungle, was informed of the problems, had relieved the XO, and was expecting a call from me over the battalion's field radio network. I did a quick in processing at brigade headquarters and was driven to the battalion headquarters by a brigade driver.

When I walked into the battalion headquarters building, Captain Close, an African American officer and headquarters company commander, reported his identity and relayed that the battalion commander wanted me to call him as soon as I arrived at the headquarters. Over the field radio, Lieutenant Colonel High welcomed me under difficult circumstances and told me that he had granted me full authority to use the powers under the Uniform Code of Military Justice, that he and the Bn S3 had their hands full fighting the enemy, that he was counting on me to restore order and discipline in the battalion's rear area at Camp Enari, and that I needed to helicopter out to brief him when I had everything under control. I gave him a reassuring "willco," which means I understand your order and will comply. Although Lieutenant Colonel High and I knew nothing about each other, I instinctively liked him; his tone of voice was conversational but also authoritative. When I turned my attention to Captain Close and the problems at hand, I had no doubts about my authority to fix whatever they were.

Captain Close took me to my office and began briefing me on the events that led to the black soldiers feeling empowered by the former XO to take over the dayroom and NCO lounge. He also confided that he believed the white sergeant major from Alabama contributed to the black soldiers feelings of being discriminated against by placing them on "shit" details and leaving white soldiers off of the disdainful duties. At that point in his briefing, I told Close to bring in the sergeant major so that I could get both of their perspectives on the causes and solutions to restore order among the troops in the battalion rear. With both present, Close essentially told the same story about the blacks taking over and their complaints against the sergeant major's roster duties. The sergeant major countered that his assignment of roster duties was even handed before the former XO told him not to put brothers on latrine cleaning or picking up cigarette butts off the ground duties. He also volunteered that even though the XO undermined his authority, he tried to be fair in assignment of roster duties. I announced that this was a new day and that I expected the sergeant major and captain to perform their duties without regard to race or ethnicity and asked if there were other pressing issues that were a barrier to restoring the chain of command and responsiveness to orders.

The sergeant major told me that three black soldiers, allegedly the ring leaders of other blacks who had taken over the dayrooms, would not perform roster duties or stand in the mandatory morning and evening formations; all three were on UCMJ suspended sentences for violating orders and/or disorderly conduct. Captain Close also told me that individual weapons and ammunition were not being returned to the arms room when soldiers came in from the field and no one in the chain of command knew the whereabouts of the weapons; rumors were flying that there would be a race war if the brothers were treated unfairly. By now it was about 4:00 p.m. (1600 hours), and I wanted all weapons and ammunition locked in the arms room before nightfall and the troops to know that I was enforcing all battalion policies without regard to race or rank.

I ordered a mandatory formation for all troops in the rear, except those on perimeter security, vacated the suspended sentence of the three ring leaders, directed Captain Close to call the military police to take the three ring leaders into custody, established a curfew after the evening meal, and directed a weapons and ammunition search immediately following the mandatory formation.

The sergeant major formed the troops and turned the formation over to Captain Close, who in turn saluted and reported to me that all were present or accounted for. As I looked over the formation, I noticed three black soldiers standing in the rear of the formation, hands in their pockets, no headgear and talking to each other. I began by telling the troops that I was the new XO and announced the curfew, weapons search, and other policies for the use of the recreation room (dayroom) and NCO club. I could see a few black troops in formation keep glancing behind to see what the three ring leaders were doing. About midway through my announcements, the military police arrived, and Captain Close directed them to the ring leaders, and all eyes turned to see what was happening. The MPs put the three ring leaders in handcuffs, placed them in the back of their jeeps, and hauled them to the division's confinement facility. I continued with my announcements and concluded that any soldier with a complaint could come see me.

We secured all weapons and ammunition in the arms room; there were no incidents that night, and I lifted the curfew the next night. I flew out and briefed Lieutenant Colonel High the next day, reported actions taken to restore order, and received his approval and encouragement to keep up the good work. He also charged me to fix the resupply system of pushing requested clothing and comfort items out to the companies in the field as the company commanders had complained that the system, which was a major responsibility of the XO, was not responsive to their needs. I made notes of his directions and promised to get it fixed, and before returning to the rear, Lieutenant Colonel High told me that the First and Second Battalions of the Thirty-Fifth Infantry would probably be deactivated and its colors shipped back to the United States in early 1970. The information was not for release to the troops but was for alerting me of the heavy workload of disposing of the battalion's equipment if and when the order was received.

I returned to Camp Enari and focused the battalion S4 (logistics officer), the cooks, Captain Close, and the sergeant major on taking care of the resupply requests of the field soldiers before they ate or went to bed. I also continued to closely monitor the racial makeup of the sergeant major's roster details and his supervision of soldiers carrying out those duties. Remembering my early experience as a second lieutenant, I showed up early in the morning, late at night, or at the hottest part of the day to make certain resupply and roster duties were being done properly. Lieutenant Colonel High commended me on the responsiveness of resupply operations for the troops in the "bush," and soldiers in the battalion rear stopped complaining about the makeup of roster details. We kept a close watch on weapons and ammunition turn-in from troops returning to the rear for out processing, and I had no major disciplinary incidents during the remainder of my time as XO in the Catci Green. However, the Cacti Second Battalion, Thirty-fifth Infantry, was another story.

Appointed to Investigate an Attempted Murder

Shortly after defusing the racial tensions in Cacti Green, I was appointed to conduct a formal investigation of an attempted murder in Cacti Blue. The two battalions were located in adjacent blocks of buildings, which made it easy for me to visit the site and interview the soldiers involved and members of their chain of command. The MP report of the incident alleged that three black soldiers (one died in the incident) reportedly attempted to kill two white soldiers with a fragmentation grenade. My job was to determine what happened and the effectiveness of the battalion's chain of command.

I interviewed and obtained sworn statements from the remaining two black soldiers and other eyewitnesses. Based on the interviews and sworn statements, here is what happened . . .

A black soldier whose tour of duty had ended was out processing to return to the United States and was missing some government-issued items. He and the supply sergeant got into an argument over the missing items, and the black soldier threatened to kill the white supply sergeant. Later that evening, the black soldier with the help of two other black soldiers decided to "frag" the supply sergeant, that is, throw a live hand grenade at him so as to cause severe bodily harm or death. The three black soldiers were high on marijuana, and under the cover of darkness, they crept up to the back of the supply room building, and while kneeling on the outside of the building, one of the three black soldiers attempted to push a grenade through a hole in the wall smaller than the grenade. The soldier became so focused on pushing it through the hole that he released the grenade's handle, causing it to explode. As a result, he was beheaded by the grenade explosion. The white sergeant and his white assistant inside the supply room were unharmed, and the surviving two other black soldiers sustained only minor cuts and bruises.

When I interviewed the white battalion executive officer and the black sergeant major, both claimed no knowledge of the threats or of the incident that led to the grenade incident. They also claimed no knowledge of racial tensions or marijuana use among the troops in their battalion. However, both white and black soldiers said that name- calling and racial slurs were frequently exchanged, and when reported to the XO or sergeant major, nothing was done about it. The soldiers interviewed also said that marijuana was easy to buy and used by many when they returned from the "bush" (jungle and combat operations). I easily concluded that racial tensions, easy access to drugs and alcohol, and an inept chain of command created volatile environment in the battalion's rear area, an environment that resulted in a soldier's death.

Before completing my report, I made a special visit with the XO and sergeant major to report my findings and conclusions. I knew they could be damaging to their careers so wanted to give them advance notice before I forwarded the report to the commanding general. They each stuck to their story and insisted that they were unaware of racial problems, the argument that led to the incident and easy access to drugs and alcohol prior to the incident and death of the black soldier. Both gave me a list of actions they were taking to address the issues, and I included them in my report.

After interviews were completed, I found that the three black soldiers did attempt to kill the two white soldiers, that a volatile racial climate existed in the battalion rear, and that the chain of command was derelict in their duties. I sent my report through brigade headquarters to the commanding general and learned about a week later that the executive officer and sergeant major were relieved of their duties. This was around the end of December, and the official draw down of troops was made public. The Third Brigade Headquarters and two battalions, the First and Second Battalions of the Thirty-Fifth Infantry, were to be deactivated and the colors returned to the United States.

The timing of the announcement could not have been better timed as I was scheduled to meet Betty for R&R in Hawaii in January 1970, my six- month tour break in Vietnam. Based on my talks with Lieutenant Colonel High, I assumed that I would help phase out the battalion's equipment as the XO and then be reassigned to another job. At any rate, when the time came, I met Betty in Hawaii for more relaxation than rest for the wonderful week we spent in Hawaii. My first week back in Vietnam from R&R was full of surprises.

Lieutenant Colonel High told me that his S3 (operations officer) would phase out the battalion's equipment and that the division G1 (personnel officer) wanted to see me as soon as I returned from R&R. I hurried to the G1's office and was offered my choice of operation officer (S3) jobs that was or was coming open. Lieutenant Colonel Stevenson (G1) told me that General Pepke approved my assignment to the position of my choice because of my stellar accomplishments in assignments since I had been in the division. I was surprised, elated, and eager to get started. I asked which of the battalions the best was, and without hesitation, he said the First Battalion, Fourteenth Infantry. He added that it was probably the best battalion in the division because the commander was strict and knew his business. Lieutenant Colonel Stevenson wished me well and told me to get my gear and report to Lieutenant Colonel Simko.

Simko's Welcome

I was excited about the opportunity to become the operations officer of the First Battalion Fourteenth Infantry (Golden Dragons) and immediately got a taste of Simko's direct and to-the-point communication style. He told me that he did not think that I was as good as the commanding general thought because all my accomplishments were in either staff jobs or a second-rate Infantry battalion. He went on to tell me that he had a captain as his S3 (operations officer), doing a great job, and that he would remain in the position while I spent a week "humping the bush" (carrying an M16 and a 50-lb rucksack like an enlisted soldier) with each of his line companies to learn how they operated. My feelings went from elation to incredulous, but I held my emotions in check because I wanted the job. He told me that the battalion, which had been under the Third Brigade (Pleiku), was being transferred to the First Brigade (Ankhe) and suggested that I get to know the company commanders whom I would be "humping" with for the next three weeks.

For the next few days, I got to know Captains Wheeler, Bowman, and Treadgill, company commanders, who were busy making sure that their soldiers had serviceable equipment before moving back to the "bush." They suggested that I be a part of their command group, that is, the radioman, medic, and themselves. From this small group, I learned how to pack my rucksack (backpack), tips of survival in the jungle, and especially the importance of keeping my P38 (can opener for C ration cans) on my key chain with my identification tags around my neck. While learning these important tips, I was trying to control my resentment of having to be a rifleman when I had successfully been a basic training company commander, Special Forces "A" team commander, Infantry career course graduate with the rank of major, a battalion XO and had the recommendation of the division commander. The thought occurred to me several times that maybe the black soldiers I sent to jail knew racism when they saw it, but I balanced my resentment with the notion of racism or not, the fact that I was now in the position to show that I was willing to go the extra mile to get the job; once in the position, I could show that I would excel while in job. My feelings were somewhat put at ease when I was included in Lieutenant Colonel Simko's commanders call the night before moving out to resume combat operations to brief them on the order of march and other essentials of information if we made contact with the enemy. He specifically instructed them to take care of me and share their operating procedures in advance of my assuming the S3 (operations officer) duties. I learned that the commanders called him by his radio call sign, "Dragon" even during face-to- face conversation.

I was with the lead company on the morning we marched out of Camp Enari, loaded down with combat gear, carrying a Colt Automatic Rifle (CAR15) and walking single file in the middle of the company formation, and felt great to be a part of a unit with high morale. The company commanders were seasoned and exceptionally well qualified. Wheeler and Bowman entered the army as privates and earned commissions through OCS, and Treadgill earned his at West Point; they also demonstrated concern for my safety and welfare as well as respect for my rank.

The company commanders reported directly to the "Dragon" but regularly communicated through the battalion operations officer on routine matters. The commanders kept me close to their command centers so they could keep me informed of reports they received from their platoons about enemy sightings or contact before they reported the same to the battalion operations center. In this manner, the company commanders shared their likes and dislikes about reporting requirements imposed on them from the operations center. I began to understand how my observation of their operations was useful in my preparation to assume the role of operations officer.

After about three or four days with the first company, I resolved in my mind that I would make it a point to encourage my host company commander to share with me that I could do as the operations officer to make their jobs easier and better. I gained valuable insight from each of the company commanders, mentally catalogued their strong points in style, leadership, and decision-making, and digested their dislikes about the operations of the tactical operations center (TOC) that I would soon take over. After about three or four days with each company, I radioed the TOC that I was returning to assume the role as the battalion operations officer. I purposefully avoided asking the "Dragon" for permission because I had accomplished what he wanted me to learn in half the time he prescribed.

I caught a helicopter ride back to the "TOC," landed, and walked into the Operations Center, where I told the captain (S3) that I was taking over and that he could get on the chopper, return to the rear, and begin preparation to return to the United States. He wanted to know if the "Dragon" had approved of me taking over and him leaving, and I said, "Don't worry, I will let him know. The chopper is waiting, and you'd better get on it." He had his bagged packed, grabbed it, and in a low run, jumped on the chopper.

I had briefly met the crew that manned the TOC and announced that I was now the S3 and needed an update on the company locations. The operations sergeant, who had a heavy German accent, asked if the Dragon knew I was taking over, and I told him to get me briefed up, continue to do his job, and I would do mine. Midway through his update and encrypted radio message from our new First Brigade operations center was received, providing the battalion a new mission. The operations sergeant said the Dragon wanted to see all new missions before the S3 so that he could give directions to the company commanders and the TOC staff. I told him to give me the message, call the Dragon, and tell him that we had a new mission and I would brief him when he arrived.

I immediately analyzed the mission and came up with recommended options for the commander to make decision and using all that I learned from the Fort Benning Infantry career course prepared a quick briefing for the Dragon, who was on his helicopter returning to the TOC from doing an air reconnaissance.

My first test as S3: when the Dragon's chopper landed, I met him and told him that I had analyzed the mission and was prepared to give him the options for conducting the attack. He asked where is the S3, and I said, "Sir, I am your S3. I sent the captain back to meet his DEROS (date oversea tour ends), and I have a briefing for you." He said okay, so I found a spot outside of the TOC to get away from the noise from the radio traffic and placed the map on the ground, and we both squatted as I began to tell him the mission. Brigade intelligence report had reliable information that the enemy had a cache of weapons and supplies at a known location, and our mission was to seize or destroy the weapons and supplies. I laid out the options available to accomplish the task and recommended the one I thought best; Bowman's company, accompanied by helicopter gunships, conducted an air assault to seize and destroy the weapons at the grid coordinate. When I finished, the Dragon fired a series of questions: Why Bowman's company? What happens if the enemy attacks? Do we have close air support? Without hesitation I answered each question to his satisfaction. He took a brief pause from looking at the map, looked at me, and said, "Okay, S3, let's go with it. I'll be in the air with Bowman's company." I confirmed the plan with the company commanders and was thankful that the Dragon approved the plan but more importantly, that he had made me live with the company commanders for my orientation with the battalion.

At the designated time for pickup (I think it was 2:00 p.m./1400 hours), the helicopters arrived and began picking up Bowman's company; the Dragon and his pilot was hovering in his two-seater Light Observation Helicopter (LOH), and I was at the TOC monitoring the radio. Everything was going according to plan until

Bowman radioed with an emergency request for a medical evacuation (medevac) chopper and announced that the Dragon's helicopter had crashed near his pickup point. I relayed the request to medevac and gave a spot report to brigade, so the brigade commander knew what was going on. The medevac was on site within in minutes, and Bowman radioed again and reported that the Dragon was dead, his body airlifted out, and his helicopter pilot was flown to the field hospital with what appeared to be minor injuries. We were all stunned momentarily over the news but continued to make the necessary notifications of the Dragon's death while monitoring the conduct of Bowman's air assault mission. I got a helicopter and went to the crash site to talk to Bowman before he lifted off to continue his assault mission. Bowman, unflappable, told me that the Dragon's chopper was attempting to land at his pickup zone when the rear tail rotor blade struck a tree and plummeted to the ground, impacting on the side where the Dragon was seated. The pilot, with minor injuries, had told Bowman that he did not want to land at the site but was overruled by the Dragon.

Col. Harold Yow, First Brigade commander, whom I had never met, arrived in the midst of all that was happening and wanted an update. He landed near the crash site, and as soon as his helicopter touched ground, Yow jumped off and walked briskly toward me and the group huddled at the crash site. From the markings on his helicopter, I recognized that he was the brigade commander and made a beeline to meet him. I reported and was midway describing how the crash happened when another helicopter approached and was landing near Colonel Yow's. Yow said it was probably the battalion XO whom he had told to come out so he could decide which of us would assume command of the battalion until he could get a replacement for the Dragon and told me to continue with the update on the crash and assault mission. When I finished the briefing, Yow took me and the battalion XO aside and asked, "Which one of you is senior in rank?" Each of us reeled off our dates of rank, and the XO was my senior, but Yow immediately stated that the XO would continue doing his job and that I would be in command of the battalion until he could get us a new battalion commander. The XO and I voiced our support of each other's role during the interim period without a lieutenant colonel as battalion commander. Yow's departing comment was that the battalion had a lot going on, told me to continue on with the assault mission, and said, "Call if you need me." The assault mission resulted in capturing and destroying a small cache of weapons and no casualties. The battalion continued its search- and-destroy mission in Bindinh Providence under my command for about ten days until the arrival of our new battalion commander.

Passing the Reins to the New Commander

I was eager to pass the command to Lt. Col. Bob Nailor, and the company commanders were anxious to know what kind of man would now be exercising authority over them. The only information about him came from him when he arrived at the forward operating TOC in Bindinh Providence. His most recent assignment had been at the pentagon, and his last troop assignment had been during the Korean War (about eighteen years since his last assignment over soldiers). When notified that his orders to Vietnam had been moved up because of the unexpected battalion command vacancy caused by Lieutenant Colonel Simko's death, he only had the chance for a short orientation on air mobility tactics at Fort Benning. I told him my assignment history with emphasis on my knowledge of the battalion's operations, the strength of the company commanders, and shared what little I knew about Colonel Yow's command philosophy and leadership style. We hit it off from the start. The battalion was still conducting search-and-destroy missions and encountered light enemy contact so there were no crisis situations requiring Nailor to make tactical decisions. His first week was spent visiting and meeting the company commanders while they continued their search-and-destroy missions. Colonel Yow visited our TOC every day and had a fifteen- to thirty-minute private conversation with him or took him for an aerial reconnaissance of the brigade's operational area. The two appeared to get along well.

About the third week of April 1970, all the battalions (about one thousand and eight hundred soldiers) of the First Brigade were ordered to brigade headquarters in Ankhe for a classified briefing. Colonel Yow assembled all the battalion commanders and S3s (operations officers) in a well-appointed briefing room and told us that the brigade would lead the Fourth Infantry Division to conduct an attack inside of Cambodia to destroy known North Vietnamese army supply depots and to prevent enemy forces from moving supplies into Vietnam. Yow orchestrated a masterful and dramatic presentation as he opened the briefing with the announcement that all information was classified as the attack was to be a surprise ordered by President Richard Nixon and involve all US combat units from southern (Saigon) to northern (Quang Tin Province) South Vietnam. His G2 (intelligence officer) showed a large map of the known and suspected supply depots and known and suspected North Vietnamese Regimental size enemy units locations along the length of Cambodian side of the border with South Vietnam.

The mention of North Vietnamese regulars in regimental strength (four hundred to six hundred soldiers) was enough to elicit an audible gasp from several people in the room. Yow concluded the dramatic briefing with a forceful presentation of a Gorge Patton like order of how and who would lead the brigade's attack. In commanding voice and a synchronized strike of his briefing pointer, he announced each battalion's objective; ours (First Battalion, Fourteenth Infantry) was on top of the known location of the North Vietnamese regiment. My "pucker factor" was high, and all eyes were riveted on the map. He emphasized that all units would have to be on the ground in Cambodia by a time certain (I think it was 1800 hours/6:00 p.m. Vietnam time) and that the initial attack would be without long-range artillery support, but that once the landing zone was secure, the Fourth Division's artillery battalion would set up their guns and provide fire support inside Cambodia. However, helicopter gunships and air force fighter jets would support the initial assault. We were all nervous about being out of field artillery range during the initial landing but accepted the helicopter gunships and air force jets as the best available for the risky landing. Yow passed the briefing to his S3 to provide the details of getting the battalions to the staging area at Plei Djreng, a former Special Forces base near the Cambodian border, and provide the details of mounting the operation from Plei Djreng. There was no loitering or small talk among the battalion commanders after the meeting as we were anxious to brief our company commanders about the operation.

Lieutenant Colonel Nailor and I departed the briefing, assembled the company commanders, and gave them the details of the attack. Two companies and the heavy mortar platoon would be airlifted from Plei Djreng and conduct an air assault near the NVA location and secure the landing zone, for the arrival of the third company and the battalion's TOC; once assembled, the battalion would attack the location to kill the NVA and to capture or destroy the weapons and supplies. The company commanders were mainly concerned with the lack of artillery support and resupply of ammunition. We assured them that their concerns would be taken care of, and they went off to brief their platoon leaders.

The Cambodian Invasion

The battalion was trucked to Plei Djreng, set up a defensive perimeter, and spent the night waiting for the big lift to Cambodia. On the morning of April 30, 1970, the brigade's lead battalion lifted off and headed for their objective. The flight time from the pickup point to the objective was about thirty to forty-five minutes, and factoring in round- trip and refueling, ninety minutes was the planning interval between having enough helicopters to make the trip.

The two companies and the mortar platoon of the Golden Dragons (First Battalion, Fourteenth Infantry) were lined up along the runway by 1000 hours (10:00 a.m.), and the mood of the soldiers was upbeat and created sort of a festive atmosphere. I was manning the jeep-mounted radio/the Tacital Operations Center and in contact with our company commanders, First Brigade TOC, and the helicopter airlift coordinator. At about 1400 hours/2:00 p.m., the unmistakable sound of helicopter rotor blade whop against the air was heard at about the same time the lead chopper pilot came up on the battalion TOC radio and reported that he was in bound with a flight of eighty helicopters. When I looked in the sky and saw the single line of helicopters descending toward the landing strip, it looked like a long snake in the air, and it was the most helicopters the battalion had ever been allocated for an airmobile operation probably in the division's history. From touchdown to lift off took less than thirty minutes for Lieutenant Colonel Nailor and the first wave of the Golden Dragons to be airborne and headed toward our objective in Cambodia. The First Brigade's TOC radio was close enough to mine that I could hear the traffic from other units attempting to take their objectives in Cambodia. One in particular got my and the soldiers' attention waiting along the runway and those passing on their way to other destinations. The commander of the division's cavalry squadron, screening the border and engaging enemy targets near the objectives, was giving a lively account of his troubles. His call sign was "Black Jack 6," and his running commentary went something like this: "This is Black Jack 6, and I am taking rounds from my target area—ok, I got that one, but I've got a couple bullet holes in the front. Am losing altitude and on my way back to my location, Black Jack out." All of us around my radio went silent as well. About thirty minutes later, the now familiar voice came back on the brigade radio with, "This is Black Jack 6. I am back in the air with a new ship and engaging targets along the route." As soon as the troops heard Black Jack 6's voice cracked over the radio, a yell erupted and troops were shouting,

"Yea, Black Jack!" It was an exciting moment interrupted by the tension created by "Dragon 6" (Lieutenant Colonel Nailor's) radio transmission to me as "Dragon 19." Dragon 6 said that the battalion was taking fire from their landing zone and that fuel was running low and he was turning back to the pickup point in Plei Djreng. I asked about casualties, and there were none, and for clarity, I repeated his message to be certain I understood him to say he was aborting the mission and returning, and he said, "Roger" (that is correct) and ended the transmission. I relayed the message to First Brigade, and within minutes, Colonel Yow and General Walker, the new fourth division commander, came rolling up to my location, jumped out of their jeeps, and asked what was going on. I relayed the message, and Yow angrily said to get him on the radio. When Dragon 6 answered, Yow grabbed the handset and yelled, "What in the hell is going on?" Nailor explained that they were taking fire from the landing zone and emphasized that the helicopters were running low on fuel and it would soon be dark as the reasons he aborted the attack. Yow continued to yell his disapproval and told him to go back and complete his mission and that he would be fired if he came back to the pickup point. Nailor's transmission went silent, and General Walker said to Yow, "Let's wait to hear what he has to say when he gets on the ground in a couple of minutes."

Nailor's helicopter landed, and he made a beeline toward my location but was intercepted by Yow and General Walker about midway. They huddled, and I could hear Yow continue to yell at Nailor but could not make out what he was saying. When the yelling ceased after about fifteen minutes, the three came over to my location, and Nailor told me to get the company commanders together for an update; Yow grabbed the handset on his jeep radio, contacted one of his other battalion commanders, briefly explained why Nailor aborted the mission, and asked if he thought his battalion could get in before nightfall. The battalion commander said, "Yes, sir" and within minutes was loaded on choppers and headed for Cambodia. General Walker was observing and conferring with Yow. Lieutenant Colonel Nailor briefed his commanders on his decision to abort the mission and told us to be prepared to make the insertion into Cambodia the next day. The company commanders appeared relieved and had little else to say other than to thank him for not putting them in a difficult situation. I, too, was glad that Nailor didn't put the battalion in a bad situation but knew that Yow was thoroughly hacked with him.

Later that evening around dusk, reports came over the radio that the battalion Yow sent to take our objective had a couple of officers killed and several NCOs and enlisted men killed or wounded and feared that they were surrounded by enemy. Air Force C130 airplanes dropped flares around them throughout the night, and helicopter gunships and air force fighter jets were also on station during the night.

The next morning, we were lifted into Cambodia unopposed by enemy activity and operated there for about a week without causalities. There was clear evidence that enemy troops had been in the area and recently vacated their positions, probably because of the massive US troop invasion. After about a week, we were airlifted back to the Vietnam side of the border to conduct search-and-destroy operations from a firebase hastily vacated by a battalion of the 101st Airborne Division.

The firebase was littered with discarded ration boxes, trash, and empty C-ration cans scattered over the ground. We landed on the firebase; Lieutenant Colonel Nailor approved my recommendation to leave one company to secure the TOC, set up perimeter security, and to pick up the litter left by the previous battalion. The other two companies conducted search operations for enemy troops that might have slipped across the Cambodian border into Vietnam. The security company commander was rushing to get the perimeter setup, clear fields of fire, and establish listening posts for early warning before darkness and nightfall arrived. Sometime that afternoon, Colonel Yow radioed Lieutenant Colonel Nailor and told him that General Walker had flown over the firebase, and it looked like a garbage dump and wanted all the trash and debris gone before darkness. Nailor ordered the company commanders to stop what they were doing to get all soldiers and clean up the trash before night fall. The company commander assigned to secure the perimeter complained about the order to clean up because he was worried about security of the firebase and the safety of his soldiers. I went to Nailor and told him that we did not have security established and that cleaning up the firebase was a much lower priority. He was firm; I argued for security, and he told me that he knew that he was not in good graces with General Walker and Colonel Yow and he was not going to let them down. The firebase got cleaned up before dark, and the listening posts didn't get established until dusk.

That night or early morning the next day, all hell broke loose; machine- gun fire and rocket-propelled grenades exploded inside our perimeter, and I couldn't raise anyone on the radio to find out what was happening. I radioed the brigade TOC that we were under attack and would provide details when known. I grabbed my CAR15 to leave the bunker to find out what was happening, but I was ordered not to because anyone moving was a target either for the enemy or for friendly fire. When the smoke cleared, we had two soldiers dead and several wounded. I blamed myself for the dead and wounded because I gave in to Nailor's demands for cleaning up the firebase over establishing perimeter security. Looking at those two young soldiers being placed in body bags triggered my outrage, and I told Nailor that I should have disobeyed his order and that he, Colonel Yow, and General Walker had their priorities out of place. Nailor told me to go cool off and to give a detailed report to the brigade TOC. Early that morning, Colonel Yow and General Walker arrived to survey the damage, and as their helicopters were touching down, Nailor told me to go check the perimeter positions and that he would brief them on the attack. I did as instructed and knew that Nailor was protecting me from delivering my anger over misplaced priorities to Colonel Yow and General Walker. For the next week, there was very little enemy activity.

Nailor was doing a recon in his LOH and called in an artillery strike on enemy soldiers moving a herd of water buffaloes. I was at the TOC, heard the request for artillery, and checked the map coordinates. The target was out of the battalions area of operation, so I issued a check fire (don't shoot) order; then I asked him to describe the uniforms of targeted enemy soldiers. Nailor responded that they were not wearing uniforms, but he surmised that they were probably supplying enemy soldiers wearing uniforms. I reminded him of the rules of engagement and cancelled the artillery fire request. Shortly after that incident, the battalion was ordered back to brigade headquarters at Ankhe for a one- week stand-down (rest and resupply). Much like the surprise before the Cambodia invasion, this was an unexpected but welcomed break in the routine of search-and-destroy operations.

The battalion had just landed and was in the process of getting settled in temporary barracks. Nailor and I had started to unpack dirty clothes when a runner knocked on the door of the small two-room building we were sharing and told Nailor that Colonel Yow wanted to see him immediately. Nailor departed quickly and was gone for less than thirty minutes. When he returned, he looked dazed and immediately started putting his clothes back in his duffel bag. I asked what was going on, and as he continued to pack, he said that he had been fired and that a helicopter was waiting to take him to Pleiku. He thanked me for supporting him and told me to tell the company commanders that he was sorry he couldn't personally tell them what a great job they had done but he had to hurry to catch the helicopter. Now I was stunned and followed him out the door toward the waiting helicopter. Just before he boarded the helicopter, I asked if I was still the battalion XO; he yelled back that Colonel Yow didn't say anything about me. I saluted, said good-bye, and headed straight to Colonel Yow's office. When I arrived at Yow's office, I introduced myself to Yow's secretary and asked to speak with him. He agreed to see me so I entered his office, and I asked if I would be replaced as the battalion S3 (operations officer) since Lieutenant Colonel Nailor had been fired. Yow told me to have a seat, which I did. He explained that I would not be replaced and that he was counting on me again to hold the battalion together. He volunteered that Nailor was not providing the leadership that the battalion deserved and that he was bringing in a highly effective and experienced lieutenant colonel to command the battalion. He expected the new commander to report within a couple of days before we resumed combat operations. I left Yow's office secure in my position but still a little uneasy over Nailor's sudden departure. When I got back to my hut, I assembled the company commanders and operations staff and told them Nailor had been relieved and that our new commander would arrive in a couple of days. The company commanders and staff were shocked and wanted to know if Nailor's decision to abort the attack in Cambodia was the reason for his firing. I told them that Yow had acted because they deserved better leadership. They appeared to be bolstered by the statement that Yow wanted them to have better leadership and affirmed that they would continue to give me and the new commander 100 percent. I think we all knew that Nailor's decision to abort the attack in Cambodia was behind his firing, but nothing would be gained by talking about it.

Quinn's Arrival

Lt. Col. John Quinn arrived the latter part of May 1970, a couple of days before we left the brigade area to resume combat operations. He was on his third tour to Vietnam, had an easy manner of communicating, and told me that he would probably not make any changes until he understood the battalion's strengths and weaknesses. The logistical support staff and the battalion XO increasingly sought my approval, and the company commanders also looked to me for command decisions. Lieutenant Colonel

Quinn spent his first couple of weeks visiting the company commanders, the battalion XO, and Colonel Yow and listening to transmissions over the TOC radio where I spent most of my time responding to the various requests for approval.

About his second week, he changed from observer to commander. One afternoon, several company commanders complained to me over the radio about not getting requested supply items. I responded by chewing out the battalion S4 (supply officer) for not getting requested items to the company commanders and threatened to fire the S4 if supplies didn't get delivered as requested. Truth be told . . . I did not have the authority to fire him. Notwithstanding, when I finished my tirade against the S4, Lieutenant Colonel Quinn, who had listened to the conversation from inside the TOC, said, "Come on out here, S3, and cool off a little bit." I followed him out of the TOC, he sat down on the ground, and he motioned for me to have a seat on the ground beside him. He said, "For the past couple of weeks, I have been watching you run this battalion, and you have been doing a great job. However, now I am going to lighten your workload. All you have to do from now on is be the S3 and I'll be the battalion commander and help you get supplies delivered on time and a few other things that I noticed are not working well."

Quinn got us on the same sheet of music, and I learned the finer points of professionalism from his coaching and leadership. While we continued to perform search-and-destroy combat missions, he also upgraded the soldiers with the latest and best available sleeping bags, other comfort items, and hot food delivered to the troops at least once a week. He also discovered that our 4.2 mortars were not accurately firing the mortar rounds because the tubes had been fired so much that the ridges inside of the tubes were worn out. Of course, we got the tubes rebored just in time. Several days before the end of my tour, enemy mortar rounds began dropping inside of our perimeter, and our mortar platoon was able to effectively return their fire before the enemy could cause casualties.

I was within a month of completing my tour of duty in Vietnam and started to wonder about my next assignment. One afternoon, the brigade S3 called for a meeting of the battalion S3s to review operational plans. While in my helicopter on the way to his location, I heard over the radio that one of the other S3's helicopters had been shot down on the way to the meeting. When I arrived at the brigade TOC, Maj. Glenn Mallory, the brigade S3, asked me if I was on the list to attend the Command and General Staff College (CGSC). I had no idea what he was talking about and said, "No, why?"

He said, because if (named the major) was killed in the helicopter crash, there would be an opening on the CGSC list because he was on it. Mallory laughed and went on with the meeting. Fortunately, (named the major) survived the crash and as far as I know attended the CGSC class. When I returned to the battalion, I asked Lieutenant Colonel Quinn about CGSC, and he explained the selection process and its importance to professional development and promotion. He also told me that he was preparing my evaluation report and that he was recommending me for CGSC, early promotion to lieutenant colonel, and command of an Infantry battalion. I was elated but still did not know my next assignment and had no means of contacting my assignment officer in Washington, DC from the heart of the jungle in Vietnam.

Several nights later, on a clear moonlit night in the heart of the jungle, I was getting ready to get into my sleeping bag when one of the radio telephone operators on duty came and told me that my wife was calling me on our tactical radio. Bewildered, I hustled to the TOC and grabbed the handset, and sure enough it was a Military Auxiliary Radio System (MARS) operator who had found the battalion's radio frequency and patched Betty into our frequency from our home telephone in Salina, KS. At the end of our statement or question, we had to say "over," and the conversation was less than ten minutes. Betty managed to tell me that I was being assigned to Tuskegee University to teach ROTC. She had gotten the information from a friend who had seen the reassignment orders and told her. I couldn't believe that Betty could get in touch with me in the jungle, but my assignment officer couldn't . . . funny. I told Lieutenant Colonel Quinn about the miraculous call and my projected assignment. He said that he would speak to Colonel Yow and thought that my assignment should be at the pentagon or teaching at the Infantry School.

About a week before leaving Vietnam, I had confirmation of orders to Tuskegee. Colonel Yow came to our firebase and told me that he had heard that General Mildren, whom he knew, was being promoted to three stars and was looking for a black officer to be his aide. I had no idea what an aide would have to do and asked Yow if he knew. He basically said, "You do whatever he wants you to do," and added that my wife would also be expected to do whatever Mrs. Mildren wanted her to do. He also volunteered that Mildren was a tough taskmaster and offered to recommend me for the job. I thought about it for a brief second and decided to stick with Tuskegee ROTC.

The week of my return to the United States I was scheduled to leave the firebase on a Friday to out process through Pleiku. I think it was on a Monday or Tuesday when enemy mortar rounds started falling inside our perimeter, and we all ducked for cover. When the mortar rounds stopped, Quinn told me to get on the next helicopter and go home to see my family. We said our farewells, and when the next helicopter landed, I did a low run and jumped on it, and as the pilot was lifting off the ground, enemy mortar rounds again started dropping inside our perimeter toward the helicopter pad. We made it to Pleiku safely, and I reversed the route that brought me to Vietnam by way of Camranh Bay, Saigon, and then the great USA.

The flight from Saigon to the USA was loaded with a cheerful bunch of soldiers. I was very happy to be returning home but couldn't help remembering that Maj. Jim Adams, my seatmate on the flight over to Vietnam a year earlier, did not make it back alive. Jim was killed in a jeep accident in May 1970, true to his premonition that he would not make it back. I don't recall my seatmate or our conversation on the return flight home but do recall that I was anxious to see my family and get on with the next chapter in our lives.

So much had happened in my Vietnam tour that I had no time to reflect on finding the real army and the experiences that shaped my perspective and career. Adjusting from the Vietnam military firebase experience to the antimilitary environment on the all-black campus and town of Tuskegee Institute, AL, in the fall of 1970 had its own challenges and frustrations.

CHAPTER NINE

My Tuskegee Odyssey

My return home celebration from Vietnam was cut short by malaria and a hospital stay at Fort Riley, KS, and having to hastily arrange for our household goods to be placed in storage while we found a house in Tuskegee, AL, my new duty location. This was in August 1970, and we wanted to enroll our sons in school so they wouldn't fall behind in their classes. My task was made more difficult because the only information available was the orders that assigned me to Tuskegee Reserve Officers Training Corps (ROTC) program as the assistant professor of military science, Tuskegee Institute, my reporting date, a telephone number, and the statement that no military housing would be available and that Fort Benning, GA, was the nearest military base that I could ship my furniture, receive medical support, and use the commissary (buy food) and the post exchange (PX) clothing, furniture, and miscellaneous items. Since I had not heard from anyone in my new assignment, I called my new boss, Lt. Col. "Bob" Everett, the PMS, at Tuskegee Institute. When I spoke to him, I heard the unwelcomed information that he had only recently learned that I was being assigned. He told me that he hadn't contacted me earlier because he did not know how to contact me. He went on to tell me that decent housing in Tuskegee was scarce; the public school system was inferior, and private schools had a long waiting list and that he needed me before the fall semester started in three weeks. That was the beginning of my rude awakening about the army and my status as a career officer and the defining role of race in Tuskegee and Macon County and the limits of my patience with double standards.

Betty and I dropped off the boys with our parents in Hunnewell and Hannibal, MO, had a short visit with family, and then headed south with some trepidation to find housing in Tuskegee, AL. We both remembered our unpleasant experience finding suitable nonmilitary housing in Columbus, GA, a year earlier and did not want a repeat experience in Tuskegee, AL. We knew that the town of Tuskegee, and the college that bore its name, was predominantly all black, but we had no idea about the availability of suitable housing. Even though we had the option to separate with me going to Tuskegee alone and Betty and the kids staying in Kansas, we had ruled out being separated as a family.

. . One year in Vietnam was enough.

When I arrived in Tuskegee, a small town of approximately two thousand people in 1970, the town square divided the black and white enterprises. The whites owned the businesses in the square and lived north of Main Street while Tuskegee University, John Andrews Hospital, and the Veterans Administration Hospital were managed by blacks and employed the black residents who lived south of the square. The signs pointed me to the campus, and I stopped the first person I saw on campus to find out where the ROTC department was located. I was directed to what was described as one of the oldest wooden buildings on the campus painted pink with a sign that would read "Phelps" Hall. I walked into the pink building, found and introduced myself to Lieutenant Colonel Everrete, and shared information that my wife was with me and that we left our sons with their grandparents while we looked for housing. He met Betty, said that he and his wife would have us over to their house for dinner, and told me that the only suitable temporary place to stay and dine was "Dorothy Hall," the campus guesthouse. He was an air defense artillery officer with a precisely trimmed thin mustache, grinned easily, and quickly added that Dorothy Hall was not air-conditioned. We checked into Dorothy Hall late in the afternoon and was greeted with the sweltering heat that the large ceiling fan labored to pull the hot air from the screened windows back out through the screened doors.

We got settled and found our way to Lieutenant Colonel Everett's beautifully constructed, pleasantly furnished, and comfortably air- conditioned rented home. He and his wife, Mae, were gracious hosts and shared observations about the community, schools, and their nearly four-year tour at Tuskegee. He was close to twenty years in the army, had not been to Vietnam, and was expecting to receive orders within the next year. I shared my brief ten-year military experiences, emphasizing my past year Vietnam tour and separation and desire to find suitable housing quickly so that we could get the boys settled before school started. They offered little encouragement; they shared that they had had to wait an extended period to rent their current home and how difficult it was for newcomers to be accepted by the "Tuskegee power elite." The power elite in Tuskegee consisted of the college deans, medical doctors, and senior hospital administrators. Everett offered to do everything he could do to help us and offered that he thought our best hope was to rent a campus-owned house. The house he mentioned was being vacated by a professor who had taken a position at another university. Mae offered to help Betty get the boys into the university-run private school, and Everett promised to introduce me to the administrator over campus housing.

Betty started the task of getting our sons enrolled, and I was introduced to Wright Lassiter, business manager over the college's property. Wright was very cordial, a member of the US Army Reserve unit at Tuskegee, and when told of our housing needs, he said that we might be in luck. There was a university house on the campus, next to Dr. Luther Foster's house, president of the university. The house was scheduled to become vacant within the next month, and he would put our name on the list. At last, I felt some relief about our housing situation. Meanwhile, Betty was still meeting the "right" people to get our sons enrolled in the elementary school ran by the university, the "Children's House." We felt confident enough that both of our needs would fall into place by the time school started that year that I planned to pick up the boys in

Missouri and bring them to their new home in Alabama. However, until that time came, I focused on learning my new job as the assistant professor of military science.

My first assignment as the assistant professor was to teach the freshmen an introductory course about the role of the US Army in the defense of America. Tuskegee at that time required all enrolling male freshmen to take two years of ROTC with the aim of attracting some with interest and leadership potential to complete the next two years and earn a commission in the US Army as a second lieutenant. This was a time of antimilitary sentiment across the country and particularly among students at many colleges and universities that hosted ROTC. Everret told me that Tuskegee had a long history of support at the university and only had a few students who advocated against ROTC being offered on the campus. He also stressed the importance of preparing Tuskegee ROTC students to do well at the five-week summer camp conducted at Fort Bragg, NC, for ROTC third-year students from all universities and colleges in the southeastern United States. He emphasized his belief that Tuskegee ROTC students didn't do well at the camp because most were unaccustomed to interacting on an equal basis with whites and the five-week camp was an intimidating experience.

As an aside, Everett mentioned the vast inequality of Tuskegee's ROTC facilities as compared to southern white universities facilities, most notably Auburn University's facilities, just fifteen miles down the road from Tuskegee. I inquired if the two schools had any kind of joint training to help students bridge the lack of familiarity between the races; he said no because of the long- standing policy of racial segregation in the south. I thought it strange that we were teaching students to lead racially diverse army soldiers but still operating racially segregated colleges and universities in the south, but I didn't push the issue with my new boss. He taught the graduating seniors, and Captains John Metz and

Rod Hargo taught sophomores and juniors, respectively, and I was assigned to teach the freshmen. I think both John and Rod had been to Vietnam, and both appeared to be very knowledgeable officers who had adjusted to the limits of racial segregation imposed on army ROTC instructors teaching at southern universities and colleges. I reviewed my lesson plans and prepared to teach about two hundred incoming male students two hours a day from Mondays through Thursdays. During this time, Betty had managed to get our sons enrolled in

Children's House. Lassiter was still optimistic that we could take possession of the campus house around mid-September, and Dorothy Hall could provide us an extra room for the boys until we moved into the house. I made a marathon round-trip drive to Missouri to get the boys, and we settled into the cramped quarters of Dorothy Hall.

Two weeks into the start of the school year, I checked with Lassiter on the campus house and learned that it was still not available. I explained to Lassiter the difficulty we were having living in cramped quarters without cooking facilities and a long list of other inconveniences and asked again when the house would be available. He paused and finally revealed that the professor had actually left the area several weeks prior, but he had left all his furniture behind inside the house. I exploded and demanded to know why the university couldn't remove the furniture so that my family could move in to the house. Wright began his answer by explaining the courtesies extended to faculty members, and I immediately went ballistic and asked to see his boss. He told me that President Luther Foster was his boss but to give him another week to see if he could get the house vacated and ready for us to move in. I was in no mood to listen to what I considered to be a delay tactic, so I stormed out of Wright's office and into Lieutenant Colonel Everett's office. I told Everett that the house had been vacant for weeks and that my family was prevented from moving in because the previous tenant, the professor, had left his furniture behind in the house. I was visibly upset. Everett then asked me to calm down and not to rock the boat. He went on to say how important it was for the army to maintain good relations with the university and that he had worked really hard to build a good working relationship with the campus and the community.

I couldn't believe my commanding officer was telling me to be calm while my family was living out of suitcases and without a kitchen when a house could have been available weeks prior. I prefaced my disbelief of Everett's reaction on my behalf with "sir" and told him that I was going to see President Foster since he did not see the need to act on my behalf. I left his office and headed straight for the president's office, introduced myself to his secretary, Ms. Punch, and explained that I wanted to see the president about a housing problem that I thought he could resolve. I explained the situation to Ms. Punch, and she politely listened and then informed me that President Foster was not in the office but that she would give him the message when he returned. I left the office feeling that she knew I was angry over the housing issue. I also got the impression that President Foster was in his office, but Ms. Punch chose not to get him directly involved with the housing issue.

The next day, Wright Lassiter called and told me that we could move into the house in two weeks. I contacted the Fort Benning Transportation Office to arrange delivery of our furniture and provided the date and address for delivery. As a part of the delivery contract, the clerk stressed that if for any reason the delivery could not be received, that I would have to pay for the return of the goods to the warehouse and storage fees. I went to see Lassiter to emphasize the importance of the house being available on the date and time promised and was reassured that the house would be ready to move in. Betty was relieved to know that the days of cramped quarters and laundry mats were coming to a close and in anticipation of having our own house, purchased a new washer and dryer for delivery on the same date as our furniture delivery. With the promise of that important issue being settled, I decided to visit Auburn University to see how their ROTC facilities compared with Tuskegee's.

I found a roster of officers assigned to ROTC at Auburn University and recognized Maj. Ron Tumlinson's name and was pretty sure that he and I had attended language school and served on Okinawa together. My initial plan was to observe the ROTC buildings from the outside, but since I knew Ron, I would make a surprise call on him and see what the inside of the buildings looked like. I made the fifteen-minute trip, pulled up in front of a large well-kept brick building with a concrete sign announcing "Army ROTC," parked my car, and entered the building. I entered the personnel office, and I was greeted by a sergeant. The look of surprise on his face was noticeable. He asked if he could help me. I asked to see Major Tumlinson; he immediately scampered off to tell Ron had a visitor. Ron came out to greet me, and the first words out of his mouth were, "Ong. Coo (Mr. Ku, my Vietnamese name at language school), what are you doing here?" I sensed that Ron's surprise and question had more to do with me, a black army major, being at Auburn than his surprise to see a former classmate, so influenced by mischief; I told him that I was reporting in as a newly assigned ROTC instructor. Ron said, "The colonel is going to shit a brick . . . Nobody told us you were coming." I immediately smiled and told him that I had recently reported in at Tuskegee Institute and decided to come see how Auburn's ROTC facilities compared to those at Tuskegee. He relaxed and invited me into his office for a cup of coffee. We caught each other up on our most recent assignments and discussed our ROTC assignments. Ron, a West Point graduate and Infantry officer, told me that he was assigned ROTC duty at Auburn in conjunction with completing a master's degree. I shared how I learned of my assignment to Tuskegee and could only assume that my assignment was based on me being black and the army agreeing to cooperate with the racial segregation policy to keep ROTC on college campuses in the south racially segregated. Ron was sympathetic to my views and told me that the subject had been discussed among Auburn ROTC officers and they were told that the president of Auburn was adamantly opposed to accepting black officers on the ROTC staff. I suggested that our two campuses think about conducting joint training exercises to prepare our students for their ROTC summer camp, and Ron agreed to work the idea on his end. I left feeling that I had gotten something positive from my visit to Auburn despite my feeling of being crapped on by the racially motivated assignment to Tuskegee University. I made the short drive back to Tuskegee weighing the pros and cons of complaining to Infantry Branch about the army's policy of using race as a criterion to staff ROTC on southern college campuses and universities. I was still mulling it over in my mind as I drove into the ROTC parking lot at Phelps Hall, compared the wooden building to the handsome brick building at Auburn. I debated talking to Lieutenant Colonel Everett about my visit to Auburn or about complaining to Infantry Branch about making assignments based on race but decided to keep my thoughts to myself. Everett accepted the status quo and would probably advise me to do the same.

The day finally arrived for us to take possession of the house, and Betty and I were excited to be moving into a house that we could call home. I got a call early that morning from transportation office to meet the delivery truck in front of the house between 2:00 p.m. and 3:00 p.m. I was leery of Lassiter's promises so I drove to the house and looked through the windows; I could see that the furniture had not been removed. I was livid. I called Lassiter's office; then I drove to his office, and with each attempt to contact him, his secretary said that he stepped out and would tell him that I was looking for him when he returned. By the time I returned to the house, both the furniture and Sears appliance delivery trucks were there and the drivers anxious to unload their deliveries. I explained why I couldn't get in the house, and realizing that I would have to pay if the furniture delivery truck returned to the warehouse, I asked if one of the delivery drivers had a hammer. One was promptly placed in my hand. I broke one of the window panes in the front door, reached in, unlocked the door, and asked if they would help me stack the previous owner's furniture in one of the back rooms. I suspect that my being in my army uniform influenced their decision to be helpful, and we quickly melded into a team. While we were stacking and unloading, Lassiter came striding up to the house with his big apologetic grin and after my brief outpouring of disappointment, joined the stacking and unloading efforts. Even the previous owner showed up with a U-Haul before we completed stacking his furniture. He took his stuff out the backdoor as we used the front door to bring in and hastily arrange our stuff. We spent weeks cleaning and rearranging furniture.

The "furniture event" is what tipped the scales and pushed me to call the Infantry Branch and complain about the inequity of using race as a criterion for ROTC assignments in the southern states. Fueled by a seemingly clear cause, I telephoned the Infantry Branch in Washington, DC and spoke to a personnel officer about the manner in which I was notified of my assignment to Tuskegee. We also discussed the hardships of our reception at Tuskegee and the inequity of using race as a criterion to assign black officers to southern colleges and universities. The personnel officer was not at all sympathetic to my complaints. He said that my record showed potential to educate students to become officers through the ROTC program and emphasized that the decision to assign officers on the basis of race to southern colleges and universities was way above his and my pay grade. His parting words were for me to use my talents to help and stop complaining. It was not really what I wanted to hear, but it at least made me think that I was doing what I could to address the issues affecting me and other black soldiers.

The next eight months ushered in a series of changes and events that added to the unusual experience of my Tuskegee ROTC assignment. Lieutenant Colonel Everett and Captains Hargo and

Metz were reassigned to other posts, and they were replaced by Lieutenant Colonel Seabrook, Captains Corley and Radcliff, and Maj. Harold Williams. I assumed the leadership role during the four-month lag between Everret and Seabrook and followed through on the implementation of a joint training project between Tuskegee and Auburn

ROTC students. This was a "first" in the history of the two racially segregated universities, and it succeeded in bridging the racial separation gap and helped students from both campuses better adjust to their leadership roles in racially integrated units at ROTC summer camp at Fort Bragg, NC.

After Seabrook's arrival, I had another "first," at least a first for Macon County, AL. Unwittingly serving as the army survivor assistance officer (SAO), I helped the family of soldier killed in Vietnam with burial arrangements for a white family from Notasulga, AL. Sometime in the summer 1971, Lieutenant Colonel Seabrook called me into his office and told me that he had received a call from ROTC headquarters in Atlanta, GA. He informed me that they wanted the Tuskegee ROTC department to appoint a Survivor Assistance Officer (SAO). Most notably, the SAO was the individual who completed administrative duties and details and conducted burial arrangements for fallen soldiers. In this case, a soldier from Macon County had been recently killed in Vietnam. Seabrook told me that although I had conducted the most recent SAO assignment, he was assigning me as the SAO for the Macon County soldier because the other officers in the ROTC detachment were new. Seabrook assumed that the family I would be calling on to deliver the news was black. Boy was he so wrong. He, and apparently others, made the assumption of race because he was told that Auburn University ROTC had been assigned to designate an SAO to do the death notification, but after realizing that the family lived in Macon County, headquarters shifted the SAO duties to Tuskegee ROTC. I too agreed with Seabrook's assumption because at the time Macon County residents were about 90 percent black. I immediately called the family and explained my assigned duties and that I was on my way to assist them with the burial of their son, Ronald.

The family lived in a rural part of the county just outside the city limits of the town of Notasulga. The town was about 80 percent white at that time. On the drive there, my thoughts reflected on my last SAO assignment where the deceased soldier's wife refused to believe that her husband had been killed and she collapsed in despair. I wasn't prepared for that reaction then, so I mentally prepared myself to handle whatever reaction the family members might direct toward me on this assignment. However, my thoughts shifted when I reached the family's mailbox and turned on to the dirt road leading to the house. I noticed a lot of cars parked on both sides of the road. As I drove closer to the house, I saw men out front, all white, and the look on their faces registered surprise as they watched me, a black soldier, drive up and park. My anxiety shifted from dealing with emotions of sadness to the reality of the emotions of racial prejudice. I was in my army green uniform with necktie and ribbons. I parked the car and got out. One of the men asked me what I wanted and questioned why I was there. I explained that I was assigned by the army to help the family with burial arrangements for the fallen soldier. I asked to speak with the soldier's parents. At that point, one of the other white men asked what happened to the white officer that was there previously. Before I could answer, a small lady came out of the house and asked who I was and motioned me to come over to her. I approached her and told her who I was. I explained why I was there and then asked to see the soldier's parents. She identified herself as the mother. Based on the stares from the men outside, I was compelled to offer that I would arrange for a white officer to assist her with her son's arrangements if she desired. The little lady immediately said "no" and explained that in her son's last letter he told her that the only person helping him adjust to Vietnam was a black sergeant. She said if a black man was kind enough to help her son in Vietnam, then she had no problem with a black soldier helping arrange her son's burial. She then introduced me to her husband and other family members and announced for all to hear that I would be helping them make the burial arrangements for her son. There were no more stares, strange looks, or pointed questions.

I requested a burial detail from Fort Benning about seventy miles away, to provide full military honors for the fallen soldier. On the day of the funeral, I arranged to meet the burial detail of fifteen soldiers from Fort Benning outside of the city limits. I wanted to inspect the burial detail before the actual funeral. I had heard that the burial details from Fort Benning were not too sharp. A lieutenant was in charge of the detail, and I ordered him to form the detail for inspection so I could do a walk-through. They passed my inspection and did an excellent job at the burial site. The family thanked me profusely for arranging the honor guard and for my assistance with other administrative requirements. I was glad that the arrangements went well; I closed out my report and returned to my ROTC teaching duties.

About two weeks after the burial, Ms. Evans, our executive secretary, told me that the Alabama State representative, Thomas Reed, was on the phone and wanted to speak to me. I asked what about and she didn't know. Reed introduced himself as the first black state representative of Macon County and related that until a few days ago residents of Notasulga had refused to meet with him because he was black. He told me that he had been invited to hold a meeting in Notasulga and he attributed their change of attitude to the rapport I established with the family in Notasulga. I thanked him for sharing the information with me and was amazed at the far-reaching influence that civility played in race relations in the staunchly segregated Macon County. I was even more amazed by the gifts of gratitude from their vegetable garden the fallen soldier's family delivered to our house throughout the spring and fall of 1971.

During the spring of that year, several events happened to change my attitude about life in general and Tuskegee in particular. My father died in May 1971 after a short illness. He was eighty-three, and he was my rock. Not just my rock, he was the rock of my whole family and the small community of Hunnewell. I felt his loss more than anticipated because for the first time I realized how important he had been in my life. He was a stoic man and did not talk much, but when he did, people listened. He was a cool dude. He worked hard for the railroad; his hands were hard and reflected honest work, and he loved life and he loved me. I remembered thinking after he died that my dad was so important to me and the family that the world should know that "Eddie" Scott of Hunnewell, MO, had died today. I returned to Tuskegee after his funeral thinking of my mortality and my relationships with my wife and sons.

Also, during the spring of 1971, we moved into a much nicer house on Bibb Street, one of the more prestigious neighborhoods in Tuskegee. We were adjusting to the peculiarities of life in Tuskegee. Betty got a job at the Veterans Hospital and made friends with the local populace, and the boys were enrolled in the Children's House and made friends with other kids of their age in the neighborhood. And fortunately, I had become friends with Wright Lassiter and other influential professionals of the university wing of the populace.

My one-year return from Vietnam was marked by my completion of the ROTC summer camp at Fort Bragg, NC, and the start of fall ROTC classes at Tuskegee. Shortly after the fall classes began, I received a call from an Infantry Branch assignment officer alerting me about my second assignment to Vietnam in early 1972. I did not want to go back so soon. I had only been back for a year and wanted to know why I was returning so soon. The assignment officer gave no explanation and told me to expect orders within a month. I told Lieutenant Colonel Seabrook about my alert notification, and he volunteered to call Lt.

Col. John "Shack" McCloud, a friend and classmate from his alma mater, South Carolina State University. He was a senior executive of the Infantry Branch assignments.

When I called McCloud, he unloaded! He told me that I was receiving orders to return to Vietnam because it was my turn to go back and that I could resign my commission or go back, simple as that. I thought, What an ass hole . . . His angry tone of voice surprised and confused me. I had no intention of resigning my commission; I worked too hard and sacrificed too much to do that. I went to Seabrook and asked if McCloud had given him any hint of being angry with me. Seabrook said that McCloud was very cordial and that he was shocked to hear that I was given the ultimatum to go or get out. I then called Lt. Col. John Quinn, my former battalion commander in Vietnam, who was the chief of colonel's assignment in the Infantry Branch, to get his advice on McCloud's reaction to my question.

Quinn wasted no time checking my record and looking into the alert notification. He called and told me that the Infantry Branch officer I had called a year earlier to complain about the racial segregation practices had placed a note in my file labeling me a disgruntled officer. He also told me that he had destroyed the note and that Infantry majors with only one tour in Vietnam were being given a one-year turnaround for a second tour and suggested that I would probably not be there a year because the war was winding down. He invited me to come to Washington, DC as his house guest and visit Infantry Branch so he could introduce me to my assignment officers. I immediately took a flight to DC and was introduced to McCloud by Quinn, who extolled my accomplishments as his S3 (operations officer) in Vietnam and told them to take good care of me when I came back from my second Vietnam tour. McCloud offered no apology for his tone and ultimatum but grinned and gave assurance to Quinn that he was going to look out for me in future assignments. Quinn's influence with my assignment was effective. My return orders to Vietnam had been pushed back to September 1972, allowing me a two-year turnaround and more time with my family.

Betty and the boys decided they wanted to stay in Tuskegee during my tour in Vietnam, and I was completely comfortable with the support they would have from friends in the Tuskegee community. My assignment orders were to First Field Force Headquarters, Nha Trang, South Vietnam, a familiar geographical area to me from my first tour in Vietnam.

CHAPTER TEN

Vietnam Second Time Around Finding My Own Way

The Cam Ran Bay Replacement Center was winding down operations but still in the business of assigning replacements. There were more soldiers going home than coming into Vietnam. Outgoing soldiers were full of rumors of the war winding down, and compared to the hustle and bustle I observed on my arrival in 1969, everything was shrinking: fewer soldiers, smaller US military compounds, and cheerful attitudes of disengagement from Vietnam. Nearly all US combat units had gone from Vietnam, and the Regional Assistance Commands (RAC) had been created to help Vietnamese combat units take over the areas vacated by US and Korean units.

My orders assigned me to First Field Force Vietnam Headquarters in Nha Trang, but since there was no longer an IFFV, I was assigned to the second RAC's forward headquarters in Pleiku, the area formerly the responsibility of the Fourth Infantry Division during my first tour. The routine of loading replacements on C130 Air Craft for transport to Pleiku had not changed, and I boarded the plane with others and deplaned at the familiar site of Pleiku airfield. In processing was different.

I was interviewed by two Infantry majors serving as personnel officers for SRAC forward headquarters commanded by Brig. Gen. Mike Healy. The majors explained that they also supported SRAC Headquarters in Nha Trang directed by Mr. Peter Brownback, a senior USAID officer. They had two open positions for an Infantry major, one as S3 (operations officer) advisor to a Vietnamese brigade in Kontum and the other as assistant operations officer in Nha Trang. They had reviewed my records and told me that pending the approval by General Healy, I would be assigned as an S3 (operations officer) advisor to a Vietnamese combat brigade in Kontum Province. Healy was out and not expected to return until the next day so they suggested that I check into the barracks and meet General Healy the next day. The two majors were very chatty, and I learned that both were Infantry officers, one a graduate of the CGSC and on his first Vietnam tour, and the other major was on his second tour and had been selected for CGSC. I got the impression that both were eager to avoid going to Kontum as an operations officer advisor to the Vietnamese brigade and that I was their ticket to remain at SRAC forward.

Around 1630 (4:30 p.m.), the majors suggested that I should go to the mess hall for the evening meal and that they would meet up with me there. I grabbed my gear, walked out of the building, and asked a driver of a jeep parked in front of the building to take me to the airfield. As luck would have it, a C130 was preparing to take off for Nha Trang, and I flashed a copy of my orders and climbed on board.

On the flight to Nha Trang, I decided that I would report in to SRAC Headquarters there, ask to see Mr. Brownback, and tell him why I wanted to be assigned in Nha Trang. Again, luck was on my side. It was about 1800 hours (6:00 p.m.) when I arrived at the headquarters building in Nha Trang. There were no military personnel present when I entered the reception area and was greeted by a civilian. I told him I had just come from Pleiku and wanted to see Mr. Brownback. He disappeared for a brief moment, returned, and escorted me in to see Mr. Brownback. I told him the process I had completed at Pleiku and shared my observation that the two Infantry majors who interviewed me were more qualified to be the S3 advisor to the Vietnamese brigade in Kontum than I was. He asked why, and I told him because of their selection to attend CGSC, at Fort Leavenworth, KS, and that I had not been selected even though I had a stellar combat record and recommendations from my previous tour in Vietnam. He asked me where I received my commission, about my parents, my immediate family, and my career goals. When I finished my thirty-minute- version answers to his questions, he appeared to be satisfied and told me he was in need of an Infantry major with my military experience. He dialed the phone and asked to speak with General Healy. He explained to Healy that he had just interviewed me to fill his assistant operations officer position and asked if that would cause him a problem. He thanked him, welcomed me on board, and directed his assistant to get me checked into a room. That was my first and last meeting with Mr. Brownback. I reported to Lieutenant Colonel Brookshire and Col. Frank Duggan and never had the opportunity to see or meet with Mr. Brownback.

I shared a room with Maj. Darryl Heinrich, a quartermaster officer with previous experience as an assignment officer in Washington, DC and a penchant for order and neatness in keeping the room clean. Darryl and I became very close friends and worked together as assistant operations officers under the daily supervision of Brookshire and occasional oversight of Duggan. Both gave us complete authority to make decisions and to perform our duties. Our job was to keep abreast of combat operations of Vietnamese and Korean units operating in the provinces around Nha Trang and pass the information to General Healy's headquarters in Pleiku. The Korean forces ceased operations around mid-November and returned to Korea. Their departure made us all a bit uneasy, but the Vietnamese Army proved equal to the task of protecting the populace from enemy forces.

I also directed the coordination of intelligence-gathering operations for the security of US installations in the city of Nha Trang until the Vietnamese Army took over the function around the end of November 1972. Many Vietnamese civilian employees and military officers expressed their fears and concerns over US military leaving the country, believing that the Vietnamese army and political leaders would not be able to defeat the North

Vietnamese Army. One Vietnamese captain who I got to know very well confided to me that he expected to be executed when the North Vietnamese won the war. I never heard from him since that time but often wondered if his prophecy was true.

Rumors of the United States leaving Vietnam gained credibility with each passing day. More units were leaving and more military responsibilities transferred to the Vietnamese. The Christmas holiday came and went, and we continued plotting Vietnamese unit combat operations and sending the information to Pleiku. Every now and then a humorous incident would break the monotony. Brookshire provided one such occasion when he walked into the operations center and announced that he had just received a call from Pleiku wanting to know why we had not sent the boxes. We told him that we would send them when we finished checking the boxes (map coordinates) grouped in a square box and numbered one through however many had been reported that day. About fifteen minutes later, we sent the report electronically and got confirmation of receipt from Pleiku. About an hour later, Brookshire burst into the operations center and demanded to know why we had not sent the "g-d" boxes to Pleiku. In unison, Darrel and I said, "We did." Pointing to the boxes we were packing for shipment to the records holding area, Brookshire, still perplexed, said, "Then what the hell are these boxes still doing here on the floor?" We all laughed after I explained the difference between the boxes on the map and the ones on the floor.

Sometime around mid-January 1973, I received an emergency message from the Red Cross telling me that Betty was in the hospital and I needed to come home to take care of the boys. When I arrived at Tuskegee, Betty was in the hospital with a blood clot in her leg and the boys were being cared for by a friend. Several days after my return home, Betty was released from the hospital and President Nixon announced that America's involvement in the Vietnam was soon coming to an end. The timing could not have been better. I called Infantry Branch assignment, reported that I was home on emergency leave, and asked for instructions in view of the war ending. This time the assignment officer was very helpful and told me that when the end of the war was officially announced that I would be reassigned to Fort Leavenworth, KS, in anticipation of my selection to the CGSC, but I would have to return to Vietnam until the war was officially ended. I was elated over that prospect and asked for reassignment orders to move Betty and the boys to Kansas immediately to keep from having to renew the rental agreement for the house in Tuskegee. That too was approved, and Betty and I flew to Fort Leavenworth to look for housing.

On-post housing at Fort Leavenworth was not available, and we were referred to Boeppler-furnished apartments, where we found a two- bedroom apartment. I signed the papers, paid the deposit, and caught a plane back to Vietnam. Betty handled all the moving arrangements, had our household goods picked up from Tuskegee and put in storage in Kansas, took care of the boys' schooling on both ends, sold my 1971 Volvo, and drove the boys to their new home in Kansas. She probably had accomplished most of those tasks by the time I landed back in Vietnam.

I arrived in time to help finish packing documents and provide input to my performance report covering the period September 1972 to March 1973 in Vietnam. In typical Brookshire fashion, he burst into the operations center and told Darryl and me to prepare our performance report and he would sign them. Not one to get wrapped up in the details, Brookshire did not read the message from the chief of staff of the army providing the typical scores to be awarded officers, by grade, to curb the number of officers receiving an "outstanding" evaluation. Most officers were assumed to be average, and the awarded rating was expected to reflect the averages provided by the army personnel center for each grade; any officer awarded an "outstanding" evaluation by his rating official had to send the report to the first general officer in his rating chain of command.

Darryl and I filled out our performance reports in our room. When we finished, Darryl suggested that we review each other's evaluation to see if we left out anything that should have been included. As soon as I handed mine to Darryl, he exclaimed, "Don, this is terrible. You are setting yourself up to be nonselected for promotions, schools, and other favorable personnel action."

I said, "If you are referring to not giving me an outstanding rating, I read the message and am trying to keep Brookshire and Duggan out of trouble." Darryl's immediate response was to give me a lecture on how the real world in Washington, DC would interpret the chief's message, and after the lecture, he completely rewrote my "outstanding" performance report. When Brookshire looked at our completed performance reports the next day, he complimented us on doing a great job and immediately signed the reports. Colonel Duggan embellished our performance, personal attributes, signed, and sent the report to General Healy. He, too, thanked us for the work we accomplished and wished us well. What started as an uncertain assignment ended with a performance report that elevated my standing in the top 3 percent of Infantry majors.

CHAPTER ELEVEN

Fort Leavenworth, KS: Change and Challenge on All Fronts

Fort Leavenworth, KS, staff was traditionally in full swing conducting the various programs housed at the post, teaching CGSC students, administering US Disciplinary Barracks (penitentiary for military personnel), and performing research projects for the army's Combined Arms Combat Development Activity (CACDA). The CGSC was the main activity on the post as officers in the rank of major were educated to perform command and staff duties at the lieutenant colonel and colonel levels. Approximately eight hundred officers, mostly majors with a few captains and lieutenant colonels, were selected by a board of senior officers to attend the prestigious career-enhancing course. Historically, the number of black officers selected among the eight hundred was less than twenty.

When I arrived from Vietnam in mid-March 1973, someone in the personnel office decided that I would be a good fit as a threats analysis officer and assigned me to CACDA. Although the position required an order of battle intelligence officer, I made no fuss about the assignment, expecting that I would be selected for CGSC within the coming year. So I signed in to my new job and immediately got on the on-post waiting list for housing.

A three-bedroom apartment became available around May because CGSC instructors and students vacated on-post houses and departed for their new assignments. I was really excited when the housing office told me the apartment was on the first floor and our storage room had access to the only window in the basement of the apartments. I made arrangements for our furniture to be moved into the apartment, and on the day of our move, our upstairs neighbor, a lieutenant colonel, introduced himself and told me that he would be moving his stuff into the storage room assigned to me because of the protocol residents of the apartments had agreed to. Not wanting to get off to a bad start with my new neighbor and especially since he was senior in rank to me, I double-checked the apartment and storage allocation drawing provided by housing; certain that the storage area had been assigned to me, I told him that housing had assigned the space to me. He did not disagree and restated the local protocol and his plans to move his stuff into the space. I made no further arguments then, and we continued to get our furniture in the house and set up so that we could have a place to sleep that night. As Betty and I were ready to go to bed, I started thinking about the audacity of the lieutenant colonel taking my assigned storage space and attributed his domineering attitude to him being white and me being black. I was so angry that I started looking for my pistol, and when I found it, I became even angrier because I had no bullets and the pistol was broken. The next morning, I headed straight for the housing office and confirmed that the assigned storage space was mine and that local protocols for the assignment of space were not authorized. When I returned to my apartment, the lieutenant colonel and his family was moving their stuff into my storage area, and I told him that I had just come from the housing office and the space was mine and that the protocol was unauthorized and asked him to please remove his stuff from my area. Without a word to me, he told his sons to start taking their stuff out of my storage area. We did not speak to each other for a couple of months until, unbeknownst to each other, we had volunteered to participate in the post's youth sports program and were paired together to officiate youth basketball games. We never discussed the storage area issue but were civil to each other from then on.

For the ten years America was involved in Vietnam, the CGSC curriculum focused heavily on counterinsurgency warfare and preparing officers in the grade of major for staff and command duties in that brand of warfare in Vietnam and the pentagon. The war's end changed that focus. Army brass sent Lt. Gen. John H.

Cushman as the change agent to shift the focus from counterinsurgency to conventional war fighting aimed at Russia and the then Soviet Union forces. Cushman tackled the change from top to bottom, inside to outside, and required CGSC instructors to simultaneously teach and develop the new curriculum to the CGSC class of 1973–1974. Although not a member of that class, I experienced the turbulence of Cushman's approach to change as it shook up the laid-back ways of all activities on the post.

The general opinion among the approximately twenty or more black officer students in the class of about eight hundred CGSC students was outrage at the amount of homework required by Cushman's new approach. We got to know most of the black officers in the class through social gatherings held at homes of class members because some of off-post restaurants still practiced or discouraged black patronage. Additionally, we shared strong bonds as graduates of historically black colleges and common memberships in black fraternities and sororities. The weekly social gatherings not only provided great food and good drinks but also served as the clearing house to voice our complaints. The most common were the lack of black officers as instructors of the CGSC the staff, the absence of black programs at CGSC, USDB, or on post in recognition of black contribution during black history week, and the lack of racial sensitivity of some of their fellow white classmates. The issues were not part of the CGSC curriculum, and much of the talk centered on how to make Cushman aware of the issues and get them addressed at appropriate topics during the eight-month course of instruction. The bold talk of the brothers at the gathering always vanished by Monday morning classes. Chaplain (Lt. Col.) Paul Easley at the USDB was the activist that got General Cushman's attention about the discontent of black officers during a black history month program for inmates at the USDB. One of the black inmates named Booker gave a dynamic presentation of Martin Luther King's "I have a dream" speech to the inmates and invited guests. General Cushman and a few senior staff officers showed up because Cushman was on his fact finding crusade for change tour. Paul had invited his wife, Sarita, Betty and I to hear Booker's presentation. Booker was terrific in delivery and style; momentarily, he made me forget the massive iron gates that separated us and the inmates from the outside world. Cushman also appeared moved by Booker's presentation. And Paul, wanting to make Cushman aware of the racial complaints of blacks on the post, introduced me as a knowledgeable post resident and prospective CGSC student about the racial climate on the post. Cushman took the handoff and asked my opinion of the racial climate and how to improve it across the post. I shared my views and the common complaints of black officers about the lack of black officer presence and awareness in all major on-post activities. He was interested and suggested that maybe appointing a black officer as a race relations officer and advisor would help resolve the issues. I rejected the notion and strongly emphasized that no staff officer could be an effective change agent and that only he as the commanding general could energize his subordinate commanders to improve race relations on the post. He thanked me for my candor and stated that he wanted every white officer to know what black officers experience as a minority in the army and in America. Meanwhile, I returned to my job in threats analysis and tried to make sense of the stacks of classified documents reporting on the movements of Russian and Soviet Army forces.

My job was to make an array of Russian and Soviet forces positioned, in real time, along the West German border for use by combat development war game branch and active army divisions. The work was tedious and required daily rechecking current intelligence reports for accurate map locations of Soviet and Russian divisions and separate regiments. I gave the effort my best shot and submitted the map overlay to Lieutenant Colonel Spangler, my boss, for approval. He sent it to the big headquarters at Fort Monroe, VA, because he, too, was not an order of battle intelligence officer. The finished product returned with notations to check current intelligence reports because several units had moved since the date I prepared the overlay. From then on, I noted on each overlay that the information was accurate on the date prepared, and

Spangler stopped sending overlays to Fort Monroe for approval. A request from the First Armor Division at Fort Hood, TX, was received for a real-time overlay and briefing of Russian and Soviet Forces locations along a specific geographical area of the West German border. Spangler approved my overlay and sent me and an armor major, Ken Schlosser, to do the briefing. The division was preparing to participate in an annual joint return of US Forces Return to Germany (REFORGER) and wanted the commanders and staff to be briefed on the real-time disposition of Russian and Soviet troops they would engage in the event of actual war.

The exchange between the assistant division commander for Maneuver (ADC-M) and the division's operations officer (G3) during my briefing was the only remarkable event of the trip to Fort Hood. The ADC-M was Brig. Gen. Oliver Dillard, one of the first black officers to make general in the early 1970s, and we were told that Dillard wanted a desk-side briefing in his office after our briefing to the battalion and brigade commanders. I was really excited over the opportunity and especially to meet and brief a black general. The general was very cordial and asked us to wait until the G3 (three grades junior to Dillard) arrived before starting the briefing in his office. We chatted about his alma mater, Tuskegee University, where I had recently taught ROTC and discovered that we had mutual friends in Tuskegee. The G3 arrived and I started the briefing by asking General Dillard how the division would deploy against the threat displayed. Dillard started to answer and was interrupted by the G3 who jumped in and gave the disposition of divisional forces from day one to the end of the exercise. The same pattern of interruption by the G3 continued to the point that I thought he was rude and the general too tolerant of his interruptions.

On our return to Fort Leavenworth, Schlosser raised the issue of the G3's interruptions as unusual, and I questioned if the G3 would have interrupted a white ADC-M. We did not reach a conclusion, but I made a mental note not to allow a subordinate, no matter their ethnicity, to interrupt me when I was answering a question. I chalked the observation up as things to remember and continued to work and wait on the next CGSC selection list.

Army wives use to say that a career army officer's life is governed by "ifs and lists." Meaning that if your name is on a promotion or schools list, the future is bright and the family will probably be uprooted; however, if your name is absent, the future is questionable, and the family better have a backup plan. The CGSC list for school year 1974–1975 was published, and my name was on it. I was happy and relieved. Betty was happy and concerned about uprooting the boys. Lloyd was a star basketball player at Leavenworth High School, enjoyed the recognition, but accepted the notion of moving on; Jeffrey and MEL, in the fourth and third grades, respectively, were happy if their mom was happy. The better news was that we could stay in our on-post apartment while I was a student at the CGSC. After the joy of seeing my name on the list was replaced by the reality that I had another six months to finish my new job as a program management analyst.

Shortly before Lieutenant Colonel Spangler, my boss at threats management, announced his retirement plans, he introduced me to Colonel Hogan, youth activities volunteer director, as the perfect candidate to replace him as the little league baseball commissioner. Hogan thought it such a great idea that he had me transferred to work in his directorate as a program management analyst where I would not have to be away from the post to give threat briefings. I didn't protest the volunteer appointment because it allowed me to make sure my sons were treated fairly in the team selection process. There was so much competition by parents attempting to place their sons on winning teams that my job as commissioner was way more stressful than the threats management officer. But I enjoyed the spirit of the community during the baseball season and especially the opportunity to see the growth and development of our sons. Lloyd was also the first pick desired by coaches in the league, and this was Jeffrey's and MEL's entry into organized little league baseball. The last game of the 1974 summer baseball season ended my status as a staff officer and began my journey as a CGSC student.

A couple of weeks before the class was scheduled to start, I remembered the anxiety about the rigors of CGSC and the underlying racial issues encountered by black CGSC officers in previous classes and determined to pass on the status of issues and concerns to the black officers in the new class before it started. Rumors had it that there were more than forty black officers selected to be in the class. With the help of Chaplain Paul Easley, Maj. Harry Johnson, just recently graduated from CGSC and appointed by Cushman to be the first African American to serve as the chief of police at Fort Leavenworth (Provost Marshall), and a few others, I coordinated the agenda to brief the brothers. The meeting was held off post at the Black Veterans of Foreign Wars building, downtown Leavenworth. The information was spread by word of mouth. We did not want to hold the meeting on post for fear that Cushman or members of the chain of command would not understand our reason for holding a meeting with all black CGSC officers and that they would interpret it as something hostile. Almost all the black officers showed on the day of the meeting; the attendees ranged in rank from captain to lieutenant colonel with mostly majors in between. Jack Windom, my classmate from Lincoln (MO), was the only one that I knew and the rest were from other historically black colleges or sources of commission. I welcomed the attendees, gave the purpose of the gathering, and introduced the presenters and Paul Easley to give a short opening prayer. All were attentive if not a little bit pensive at the start of the meeting. The brothers were informed of the changes Cushman had made in the curriculum—no longer a gentleman's course, meet the standards or get washed out; how the class was divided into work groups—thirty to forty officers from the different branches within the army, other military services, or foreign armies in a work group—we were urged to share experience and contribute to the discussion topics and informed of the progress of racial concerns on the post- Cushman was making progress, appointed Harry Johnson as the first black chief of police (Provost Marshal), and was pushing the staff for more black awareness in post programs. During a brief question- and-answer period, someone raised the question of what do we say about the meeting if asked by someone in the chain of command why we were meeting. I shared that I and the other planners agreed that the meeting was a social gathering of black officers from historically black colleges to renew our common bonds and make new acquaintances and suggested that they could use that answer if asked. The answer satisfied the questioner, and members of the group gave audible agreement with the stated purpose of the meeting. After a few more questions, I closed the program to a loud round of applause, and many appeared reluctant to leave. For most, this was the largest gathering of black officers since our ROTC college days at our respective HBCU, and the atmosphere was convention like in tone and tenor. I felt good about the outcome and thought no more about the meeting until the second week of class when I received a note in my mailbox to see Cushman the commandant with no subject indicated.

I looked at the note in my mailbox and saw the message to go see Cushman, and my mind immediately reviewed all the things that had transpired in the classes I had taken since CGSC started in the first week. I couldn't think of anything that I had done to be called on the carpet for so I headed straight for Cushman's office. His secretary was pleasant and said that the general was expecting me. I knocked on his outer door, stopped in front of his desk, stood at attention, and reported to him as directed. He immediately told me how angry he was over learning that a group of black officers met off post a week before CGSC and what he would have done had he known about it. He said, "If I had known about it, I would have burst into the room and announced that my name is 'Jack' Cushman, and I am the commandant over the CGSC. What is going on here?" When he paused for his breath, I jumped in with, "Sir, as graduates from Historical Black Colleges and Universities (HBCU) where most of us received our commissions as second lieutenants, we had a social meeting. Many of us belong to the same fraternities and share the same culture and the same career goals. Our meeting was no different than army officers who received their commissions from West Point, the Citadel, or Texas A&M universities." I paused thinking I had said enough. The muscles in his face relaxed, and he told me to have a seat. He knew the names of the senior black officers in my class and hinted that he started to call Lt. Col. "Chuck" Murphy, the senior black officer in the class, to explain what the meeting was about until he recalled his and my conversation on racial issues on post when he first arrived. I asked if he would have the same alarm by CGSC officers from West Point (his alma mater), Texas A&M, and the Citadel meeting off post as he did about us HBCU graduates. He admitted that he had never thought about the similarities before and asked that I should not share his reaction about the off- post meeting. We parted on a cordial note, and inwardly shaken, I left his office and drove home to gather my thoughts.

Betty came home on her lunch break, and I swore her to secrecy before sharing my unsettling summons before Cushman about the off- post meeting I had arranged. We both agreed that Cushman probably knew the names of all the brothers who had attended the meeting and that I should tell Harry Johnson about being called in by Cushman to prevent him from being surprised by inquiries or a call from Cushman. Harry was the only person other than Betty that knew about my meeting with Cushman during my year at CGSC.

Many positive changes in race relations at Leavenworth and in the army came during my year at CGSC. Chaplain Paul Easley and other black chaplains frequently preached at the main post chapel services. Paul, the first to speak there, amazed and amused us, by his use of big words like "eschatological" throughout his sermon. I accused him of trying to impress white folks with his vocabulary rather than to save their souls with the use of simple words like "grace." Brig. Gen. Ben Harrison, assistant commandant, frequently visited the Officers' Club and chatted with students, behind the soul music that was newly introduced to the club's entertainment package. Minority speakers and visitors were visible evidence that the army was embracing racial diversity. Newly promoted Brig. Gens. Julius Becton, Art Gregg, and one other visited our class and were given a reception by Cushman, and most memorable of all was the lecture by newly promoted Brig. Gen. "Dick" Cavazos. The first

Hispanic to receive promotion to brigadier general, Cavazos, was a spellbinding speaker who chided himself as the poor man's Audie Murphy; he had won every medal in Korea except the Medal of Honor. He received a thunderous ovation at the end of his talk, and many of us openly expressed our desire to work under his command influence. But the best evidence of change for me was a phone call from Infantry Branch about midway through the course. I was into my fourteenth year of service in the army, comfortable with the knowledge that CGSC completion would secure me twenty years with a good chance for promotion to lieutenant colonel. All of us midcourse CGSC students anxiously expected new assignments and looked for them to be posted on the bulletin board. Infrequently, I would hear a fellow student say that he had received a call from his branch about his next assignment, and I regarded that officer to be an exception and on the fast track. When I answered my home

phone, a female voice asked if I was Major Scott, and answering yes, I heard her say, "Please hold for Lieutenant Colonel Carpenter, Infantry Branch." I took a deep breath and thought, Now what? To my surprise, Carpenter, well known as the lonely end on West Point's winning football team of 1959, said that my performance record had been reviewed and a decision made to manage my career assignments so that my full potential could be realized for the army. He asked if I was agreeable with that, and I told him about the needs of my family: Betty working, good schools for our sons, and preference for remaining in the United States. He said he understood and had only two choice assignments available within Infantry divisions: "Fort Carson, CO, and Fort Lewis, WA, which one do you want?" I asked to talk it over with Betty and get back with him.

We chose Ft Lewis, and the call, the announcement, and the assignment made me feel like the army, and I was on the same page. After graduation from CGSC, we left Fort Leavenworth with Lloyd, Jeff, MEL, and Toussaint (our family poodle) for a new adventure in the Pacific North West. CGSC was a memorable experience. I felt we made a contribution to racial harmony while learning new ideas and career strategies under Cushman's leadership. Best of all, we made new friends for life: George and Rose Hudgens, Jack and Charlotte Windom, and Tom and Sandy Bryant. Betty and I was in high spirits as we embraced the pioneering spirit driving west in a 1956 Nash Rambler.

CGSC Scott Family Portrait

CHAPTER TWELVE

Promises—Assumptions— Surprises

The 1956 Rambler station wagon we purchased for Lloyd, made the two thousand- and five-hundred-mile journey to Fort Lewis, WA, with only a few minor interruptions in our travel. A clutch spring broke near Goodland, KS. And we ran out of gas in the middle of nowhere . . . The gas gauge did not work, and I miscalculated the mileage even after being warned by Betty to refill the tank as we passed by gas stations. Happily some good-hearted people helped us on our way, and we rolled into Fort Lewis full of high spirits and expectations.

We got settled in the guesthouse. The next morning with assignment orders in hand, I reported to the Ninth Division's personnel office (G1) for in processing. Immediately, my expectations were dashed by the assignment officer when he told me that I was being assigned as the training officer in the Department of Plans and Training (DPT). I protested and evoked Lt. Col. Bill Carpenter's authority and insisted that I had to be assigned to the Ninth Infantry Division. Dropping Carpenter's name got me an audience with the lieutenant colonel, the G1 himself. He was straight and to the point. He told me that the commanding general approved assignments in his division— not Lieutenant Colonel Carpenter; in fact, the vacancy Carpenter thought open was already filled by Maj. Ralph Hagler (one of my CGSC classmates) with the commanding general's approval. Unapologetically, he told me that the commanding general approved my assignment as the training officer over the assignment of training areas for the division and all other units of the post. He emphasized that it was an important position and stated that if I accepted it, a better position might be available in the future. Disappointed but acutely aware that I was in a "no win situation" again, I accepted the assignment and reported to my new boss, Col. John Westervelt.

Westervelt greeted me with a hearty welcome. He was happy to receive a CGSC graduate on his staff since he was losing much of his staff to the army's reduction-in-force that was going on at that time. Regardless, due to time constraints, I deferred meeting the rest of the training staff until my return to Fort Lewis. Just before leaving, Westervelt offered to intercede on my behalf if any problems were to arise with getting my family and household relocated to Fort Lewis. I thanked him and then left his office.

We flew back to Missouri and returned with the boys and the dog. Upon our return, we had a short wait for on-post housing but made due with temporary quarters. During our stay in temporary housing, we met Maj. Lew Reeves and his wife, Florence, who extended every courtesy while we were living in the guesthouse. We learned that my diversion from the choice assignment in the Ninth Division was the norm rather than exception at Fort Lewis.

The exception was Maj. Joe Hall, a medical service corps officer, and another of my CGSC classmates was assigned to the Ninth Division medical battalion. Joe was exempt from the whims of the division's personnel assignment officer. Joe and his wife, "Chu," had arrived and purchased a house off post to avoid, as he put it, "the hassles" of losing money by not investing in real estate property. Lew shared his rebuffs at attempting to get into the division; he also shared that the black officer-retired community, though few in number, stuck together and was a resource we could count on. All the retired black officers had retired from Fort Lewis, and John Malloy, a retired lieutenant colonel, and his wife, Glenda, were the people in the know. John was the only retired lieutenant colonel, and the others were majors or below. After our introduction to John and Glenda, we were quickly introduced to the other black retirees as well as to the active army black lieutenant colonels and majors and their families on the post. On Sundays, many of the black officers, enlisted members, and their families, both active and retired, attended the black protestant service at Chapel 9.

Betty quickly got our living quarters set up; the boys were enrolled in school: Lloyd at Clover Park High School, and Jeff and MEL at the Steilacoom Elementary school outside the Fort Lewis back gate. She also landed a job at the Post Engineer Office close to my office in the post-headquarters building.

I was still excited to be a CGSC graduate and vigorously took hold of the reins as the post training officer despite their impending force out of the army. I wanted to make an awkward situation as productive as possible. I instructed my operations assistant, a civilian employee, to arrange a meeting with the officers and enlisted soldiers assigned to the office so that we could get to know each other. With all seven soldiers assembled, I began my upbeat glad-to-be-here speech from my prepared note cards and got as far as saying that I was looking forward to sharing what I had learned as a CGSC graduate to help them achieve their personal goals while accomplishing the mission of the training office. I paused and noticed the expressions on the faces of my subordinates: no smiles, a general lack of enthusiasm, and eyes that conveyed sorrow, gloom, and even anger.

I immediately adjusted my remarks by asking each person to introduce themselves and share their immediate goals. With the exception of the secretary and the MSG, each one of the captains had entered the military as a private, completed officer candidate training, served one or two tours in Vietnam, and was in receipt of a mandatory separation from service notice because of the reduction in officers resulting from the end of the Vietnam War. Their separation dates ranged from as early as two months to the latest of five months. My assistant told a similar story; he had been mandatorily separated from active duty as a captain and had recently been hired as the GS 9 assistant training officer.

After listening to the captains, I readjusted my intended motivational speech and let them know that in view of their separation notices, I understood their concerns for the financial security of their families and themselves. I inquired about the help and time allotted by the army in their job search, and after their various interpretations, I made them a promise: "If you give your undivided attention to your job in DPT, I will add a month to whatever the separation regulation gives you." Their attitudes, interest, and dedication showed in the hard work they accomplished in the time left on active service in the army.

Gen. Volney Warner became the new commanding general of Fort Lewis and the Ninth Infantry Division shortly after my arrival, and his emphasis on managing the training of the Seventy-Fifth Ranger Battalion elevated the importance of my status as the post training officer. The rangers did not belong to the Ninth Infantry Division and fiercely exercised their independence to be trained and evaluated in their unique combat role. General Warner supported their desires and charged my office to coordinate and schedule all training and evaluation requirements for the battalion. With the help of my part- time captains and addition of Maj. Lew Reeves (a black officer in search of a transition position in the Ninth Division), we successfully planned and coordinated the first ever Ranger Army Training and Evaluation Program (ARTEP) in the US Army. Warner was the senior evaluator of their combat readiness and made the airborne jump with them at Douglass Improving Grounds in Utah. Although he broke his foot on the jump, he gave them a successful ARTEP evaluation and was generous in praise for my planning and coordination of the exercise. He assured me a position in the Ninth Division when I was promoted to lieutenant colonel, and Lew Reeves received an assignment as a battalion operations officer (S3) in one of the Ninth Division's Infantry battalions. Colonel Westervelt championed our success as his own and showcased the training office at every opportunity.

The lieutenant colonel's promotion list came out in 1976, and I was among three other majors at Fort Lewis on the list. We all got together and with our wives decided to host a promotion party and reception at the Officers' Club. Our bosses, the generals, and our respective friends were invited. For eight (8) years, I had been a major, and it had started to sound like my first name. I was more than ready to replace it with "lieutenant colonel." General Warner, the post commander, attended the party and wished us well. I didn't mention his promise to help me get a job in the division since I had not yet received the actual promotion.

I was watchful of the lieutenant colonel positions and noted the names of officers available within the division to fill the positions. With Warner's promise, I considered my chances as high to fill one of the positions. The math wasn't complicated since there were only three lieutenant colonel positions within the division. The division commander had discretion to approve and all three positions which were executive officer (XO) positions under each of the three Infantry brigade commanders. I just had to keep doing my job as the post training officer until one of the positions became available.

Lieutenant colonels with more seniority than me were being moved to different positions in anticipation that they would be competitively selected by a board of senior officers in Washington, DC to command an Infantry battalion. Two in that category were assigned as brigade XO positions. Another in that group, Lt. Col. Bob Frix, a helicopter pilot, was assigned as Westervelt's deputy. Bob was amazed at how much I accomplished with the officers assigned to the training section, and we developed a good relationship. We became good friends. Bob knew the odds were not in my favor of getting the brigade XO job without the help of Warner so he too kept close tabs on the only XO position that would become vacant. It was also during this period that I met and became a mentee of the first African American colonel selected to command a brigade level unit at Fort Lewis, Col. Andrew P. Chambers. The story goes like this. I was cutting my lawn one evening in the early spring of 1977 and saw a man dressed in casual running attire jogging past my house. He waved as he went past and then doubled back and ran toward me. He looked like a middle- aged white man whom I did not know so I stopped the mower to find out what he wanted. He was very friendly with a pleasant smile, introduced himself as "Andy" Chambers, and wanted to know how long I had been assigned at Fort Lewis and what my job was. I gave brief answers and asked if he was newly assigned or just on the post temporarily. I nearly chocked when he told me that he was to command the Ninth Infantry Division Support Command and was living in the officers' guest quarters just around the corner from my house. Suddenly realizing I had been talking to a full colonel without addressing him with the full complement of "sir," I quickly rectified my omission and promptly came to attention in front of my lawn mower. As if sensing I was uncertain of his racial identity, he asked how many "brothers" were in command positions and how "we" were being treated. I immediately figured that even if he looked white, his manner and expressions were black, and I liked him. I introduced him to Betty, and she was cooking dinner and invited him to stay and have dinner with us. She had baked a chocolate cake, and late into the evening over dessert and milk (he was not a coffee drinker), I shared my anxiety over the brigade XO position and he shared unpublished news that he believed would change our lives for the better at Fort Lewis. We also discovered that we were Kappa Alpha Psi Fraternity brothers and that knowledge cemented our bond.

Chambers told me that his former boss, Richard Cavazos, was soon to be promoted to major general, and he was to replace General Warner as the post commander. He also knew that Col. H. Norman Schwarzkopf (of Desert Storm fame) was coming to take over the First Brigade and surmised that "Norm" would want to pick his own brigade XO. He knew Schwarzkopf by reputation as a tough exacting commander who was commonly called the "Bear." His size and temperament earned him that nickname, and Chambers's advice was to push Warner to place me in the job before Schwarzkopf took command of the brigade.

My game plan got turned upside down when Schwarzkopf took command about two weeks before the announcement that Warner was being promoted to lieutenant general and reassigned. He would be replaced by Maj. General Cavazos. I hurried to the personnel officer (G1) to see if Warner directed that I would be assigned to the brigade XO position. The G1 said that Schwarzkopf had already chosen an XO from outside the Ninth Division so the position was not available. I went straight to Warner's office.

When I entered Warner's office, I reminded him of his promise to me and relayed what the G1 had told me about the XO position in the First Brigade. Without hesitation, Warner picked up his phone and dialed some numbers. When connected, he said "Norm, I know you have been talking to the G1 about bringing in an XO, but I am sending Don Scott to interview for the job. Don did a great job for me, and I know he will do a great job for you." He hung up the phone and told me to get right on down there and talk to "Norm."

My meeting with Schwarzkopf was short and to the point. He angrily stated that he had given his word to another officer he offered the XO job but would now have to renege on his promise. He was not happy and forcefully stated that he always did what his commanding general wanted and that I would be his XO. He also told me that he "owned" everything in the brigade and that I owned nothing and to stay out of his way. I thanked him for the opportunity and returned to my office. Westervelt was happy that I got the job and wished me well. I cleared out my desk, said my farewell to my training guys, thanked Warner, and started a new chapter at Fort Lewis. It was about eighteen months late, but I finally had a career-enhancing job in the Ninth Infantry Division.

Blasted by the "Bear"

My first opportunity to demonstrate my ability to accomplish the Bear's directives ended in confrontation rather than expected praise. Within the first week of my assignment, he wanted the expeditious discharge he had approved signed so that the troublesome soldier could be processed out of the brigade and the army. He complained that his previous XO had worked on getting the discharge signed for over a month and could not make it happen.

I was confident that this would not be a difficult task because I knew all the post and division staff officers at the headquarters. I started tracking the discharge at the lawyer's office (staff judge advocate). I quickly learned that the discharge packet was legally prepared and awaiting the assistant division commander's (ADC) signature. It had been waiting to be signed for several weeks. I went to the ADC's office, Brig. Gen. Howie Stone, and told his aide that I needed the packet signed. Meanwhile, General Stone heard my voice and asked me to come in and tell him what was going on. After a few pleasantries, he asked me to tell him what the battalion and brigade commander had done to help the soldier adjust to the military. I summarized the case, and Brigadier General Stone signed the discharge packet. Easy work or so, I thought.

The brigade was on a field training exercise, and I made haste to share the good news with Colonel Schwarzkopf, whom I found in the brigade's operations tent. The tent was full with the hum of FM radio traffic going back and forth, officers plotting and reporting unit locations on the map, and the colonel standing in the middle of the tent observing the activity. I decided to report the routine matters at brigade headquarters first sand saved the best for the last. I told him that the discharge papers had been signed, and the soldier was being out processed as we were speaking. The Bear's initial response was to question how I had completed the task so quickly. I talked him through the steps I had taken, but when I told him General Stone had invited me in to explain what efforts had been done to rehabilitate the soldier, the Bear exploded. The area emptied out immediately, with only me and the colonel remaining alone in the tent.

At the mention of General Stone's name, it was as if the colonel's moves were choreographed: his right hand grabbed my left field trouser suspenders and his left arm and finger froze a fraction from my nose, as he yelled, "No one in this brigade talks to generals except me! You understand?"

Totally unprepared and shocked, I reached and grabbed his right hand, pulled it from my suspenders, and said, "Sir, nobody touches me." I had clenched my fist, not knowing what would happen next. Standing face to face, glaring at each other, he suggested that I calm down as we both took a seat and paused for what seemed like an eternity.

Still breathing heavily, he looked over at me and said, "I will fire you." I replied, "I can quit too." He ended the standoff by saying this never happened. I left the tent and returned to the brigade area on post, not sure of my fate as the Bear's XO.

For the next two weeks we did not communicate with each other. I stayed in my office and attended to my duties while he stayed in his office to command the brigade. There was a "wired" communication system that buzzed when he wanted to see one of his four principal staff officers. The number of buzzes coincided with the numerical designation of each of the four principal staff officers, that is, one buzz for the S1 and four for the S4. I could hear the buzzer for the S1 because of the close proximity of our offices, so I was accustomed to hearing the one buzz. One afternoon, I heard five buzzes and did not know it was for me until one of the personnel clerks burst into my office and cried out, "Sir, sir, that is your buzz. You better get in there." I told him, "I have a phone with an intercom, and I don't answer to buzzes. Plus, he has you to summon me when he wants to see me," I added. The next sound I heard was a loud knock on my door, and the Bear in a commanding voice told me to come into his office. I followed behind him and stood at attention as he plopped his six-foot four-inch frame into the chair behind his desk. I waited for him to tell me I was fired. Instead, he told me to have a seat and in a cordial voice and manner said, "Let's start over again." That ended the unfortunate confrontation and was the beginning of a rewarding learning and development experience for me.

Colonel Chambers and General Cavazos helped me stay out of the "Bear's" way while I worked behind the scene to keep the brigade's logistical status among the highest in the division. Chambers coached me through the steps to pass the rigorous inspector general's inspection of the brigades administrative, maintenance, and property records, and we passed with the top rating in the division. Chambers cautioned me to not ever mention to Schwarzkopf that the system I set up to prepare the brigade for inspection came from him. Schwarzkopf was very happy with the results, complimented me on my performance as his XO, and acted as if our earlier confrontation had never happened.

I was Schwarzkopf's XO for a little more than a year and gained a deep respect for his intellect, charm, and candor with those he allowed past his outer persona. I adjusted to his volatile leadership style, and he shared with me the name of the person who had influenced his adoption of that style, Maj. Gen. Willard Latham. He related that he was the recipient of Latham's intimidating leadership style when he served under him in Alaska as his assistant commander of the 172nd Infantry Brigade. I did not know Latham, but it seemed from my observations of Schwarzkopf that he had perfected the style and put his own brand on it. However, in his interactions with his family and during social engagements, he was caring, charming, and considerate—not at all the benevolent dictator he portrayed on the job.

As a newly promoted lieutenant colonel, I was being considered for battalion command by a board of senior officers in Washington.

To better my chances for selection, I asked Schwarzkopf if he would give me a special performance evaluation as his XO. He declined stating that he did not give special performance evaluations. Several weeks later, I was at a post-wide prayer breakfast, and Cavazos asked me if "Norm" was writing a special performance report for me in advance of the battalion command selection board. I related Schwarzkopf's response to my request, and Cavazos told me not to mention that he asked me about the performance report. Schwarzkopf called me into his office a week or so later and asked if I had told Cavazos about his declining to give me a special performance report, and I said, "No, sir, why do you ask?" He said that Cavazos had called and wanted to know if he thought I could command an Infantry battalion. When he said yes, Cavazos replied that his recommendation in a special performance report would be awfully convincing to the members of the battalion command selection board. He just wanted to be sure that I had not mentioned his and my conversation about a special report and to tell me that he was writing the report because Cavazos thought it a good idea. I thanked him for making an exception on my behalf and left his office amazed over Cavazos's insight and influence. Cavazos truly brought out the best in others even when they didn't want to be helpful.

Chambers's prediction that Cavazos would make a change for the better at Fort Lewis became a reality for me and many others looking for selections or promotions. Chambers, Schwarzkopf, and two other colonels under Cavazos command were promoted to brigadier general on the same list; all eligible lieutenant colonels including me were selected to command Infantry battalions and remain under Cavazos in the Ninth Infantry Division.

When Cavazos called to congratulate Schwarzkopf on his selection to brigadier general, everyone in the brigade headquarters rejoiced at his good news because he was in an unusually joyful mood. After calling his wife, Brenda, he told me and the staff about his selection and shared the names of the other colonels on the list with him. When he mentioned that Chambers was also on the list and the only colleague that he really respected, my joy was complete. We celebrated with Andy, his wife, Rita, and their children until the wee hours of the morning. That was the happiest moment of my military career. Andy and Schwarzkopf were both (frocked) authorized to wear the one-star insignia of rank of a brigadier general and immediately reassigned to Hawaii. Both gave me their full colonel insignia (Eagle), and Schwarzkopf also gave me his fullbird dress uniforms as tokens of confidence in my potential. Our families had bonded so closely that both the Chambers's and Schwarzkopf's made us promise to visit them in Hawaii.

I remained XO of the First Brigade for approximately three months after the Bear's departure and had the unique experience of helping the new commander, Col. "Dick" Jarrett, take over the brigade. An Infantry aviator, he was looking for an immediate way to put his stamp on the brigade and wanted to insert some air mobility training into the brigade's training program. He quickly became frustrated, however, because General Cavazos's existing training scheme and policies did not allow for such cyclical deviations. Colonel Jarrett, therefore, relied on me as the link to keeping the brigade's readiness indicators high and as a sounding board for his frustrations. He reinforced what I and many African Americans wanted to see happen: a positive change in the army's command climate for minorities. He often shared with me and Lt. Col. Robert "Steve" Stephens, one of his battalion commanders, his perception that black officers had a better chance of making general than white officers—and that we were "gonna be one." It was obvious to me that both he and his wife in particular expected that "he was gonna be one." When I left to assume command of Third Battalion Forty-Seventh Infantry (Foot Cavalry (Foot Cav)) in the Third Brigade, Jarrett was still trying to figure out how to make a big impression on General Cavazos.

The Foot Cav had the dubious distinction of being at the bottom of all Infantry battalions in the Ninth Division when I assumed command in 1978. My first month in command, the string of bad luck with the Foot Cav, seemed to accelerate on my watch. One of my rifle companies on a training exercise found a decomposing body in an abandoned vehicle in the training area. An investigation ensued, and the military police identified the body as being that of a soldier assigned to one of the other rifle companies in my battalion. Strangely enough, the dead soldier had not been reported as missing or AWOL. As a direct result, Col. Clyde Tate, Third Brigade commander and my boss, lectured me about this being the kind of sloppy administrative work that had given the Foot Cav a bad name. He told me that such negligence hurt the brigade's reputation and demanded that I immediately get on top of things in the battalion.

Within the same week, the second worst incident that could ruin a commander's tour occurred: some weapons were lost or stolen. Capt. Eric Patternoster, the newly assigned commander of Alpha Company, discovered that two M-16 rifles were missing from the arms room and immediately announced that he was conducting a search of all personnel and facilities. I wasted no time in briefing Colonel Tate about the missing weapons and reported the actions we were taking to recover them. Understandably, the colonel was very upset and again reminded me of the poor impression my battalion was having on the brigade and on me as the brigade commander. He then suggested that I should relieve Patternoster from command. I emphasized that Patternoster was a seasoned officer from the Seventy-Fifth Ranger Battalion and like me, had only been in command a week. I added that he was vigorously implementing division, brigade, and battalion procedures to account for the missing weapons and enforcing procedures to prevent future thefts. Moreover, I asserted that this incident had not eroded my confidence in Patternoster's ability to command the company. Tate warned that neither he nor General

Cavazos was lenient or understanding when it came to weapons and personnel accountability. He said,

"Don, you're off to a bad start."

That afternoon, General Cavazos made an unannounced visit to the Third Brigade, picked up Colonel Tate, stopped by my headquarters, picked me up, and instructed his driver to cruise through the brigade and battalion headquarters areas. As we were slowly moving through the area, General Cavazos essentially said, "Don, you have had a rough week. I am confident that you will get to the bottom of all this and get it straightened out. Let me and Clyde know if we can help in any way." He proceeded to ask about my upcoming training cycles and plans and drove back to my headquarters and let me out. As I was climbing out of the back of the jeep, he asked, "How is Betty doing? Give her my best." I heard no more criticism from Colonel Tate about the Foot Cav's past spotty reputation.

I inherited a capable staff and able company commanders from my predecessor. Their common failure was to blame the former commander's policies for the battalion's poor performance on readiness: training, supply and maintenance, and low morale. I borrowed liberally from Schwarzkopf's style and put a stop to that practice immediately. My XO, who was a good guy and very knowledgeable of how Infantry battalions were designed to work, was the first to get the message: "I own everything, and your job is to achieve and maintain readiness standards." On the enlisted side, Stan Harris, my CSM, was a quick learner. He used his humorous persona to keep the NCO chain of responsibilities running smoothly. He and the company's first sergeants were a big help in coaching my young company commanders how to exercise the art of command. Nearly, all were West Point graduates who showed great potential and pulled together to meet and maintain the standards. First Lt. "Bob" Caslen, one of my commanders, went on to reach the rank of lieutenant general and served as the superintendent of West Point.

On the wives' side, Betty continued to work, but efficiently met all volunteer expectations. Betty was expected to be in charge of the wives married to the officers under my command. They were expected to volunteer for military civic functions, that is, thrift shop, Red Cross, coffee and tea gatherings at the club, and so on. Betty was a trailblazer, in that few officers' wives worked during that time and were expected to be an extension of their husbands' command. Colonel Tate's wife, Sadie, kept close watch over the activities of "her wives," and Betty exceeded her expectations.

Colonel Tate became a cheerleader as the battalion's readiness indicators climbed from the bottom to the upper third in the division throughout my tenure in command. He was like a dotting papa over the accomplishments of my young company commanders up until the time he relinquished his command of the Third Brigade. The arrival of my new brigade commander was another coincidence in my life story. Shortly before the end of my battalion command tour, Lt. Col. Bill Carpenter, who assigned me to Fort Lewis, had been promoted and became my new brigade commander. He recognized my potential in battalion command. And despite the initial rocky start at Fort Lewis, I too thought that I was on track to maintain my competitive status as an Infantry officer.

As a soon-to-be successful battalion commander with outstanding performance evaluations, I had no major career worries. After all, the best senior Infantry officers in the army had rated me outstanding, and therefore, I expected an assignment that would lead to being selected to attend one of the Uniformed Services War Colleges and promotion to full-bird colonel. However, Infantry Branch had other priorities for me. The Infantry Branch assignment officer called me in early January 1980 to inform me of my next assignment. I was slotted to be the advisor to the Turkish Army on Infantry battalion readiness issues. "You have got to be joking" was my initial response. The assignment officer was deadly serious and told me that the army needed to send a former battalion commander with an outstanding record and I was it. I attempted to dialogue my way out of the assignment by sharing my immediate family concerns. I told him we had two sons starting their last year in high school next year and I did not want to be out of the country. I asked if there was a possibility for me to be assigned to the Washington, DC area if a general officer requested me to work for him. Cavazos, chief of staff, was nominated to be the chief of congressional liaison, and I felt sure he would help me with the assignment. The assignment officer abruptly stated that he was sending the orders and that I was free to do whatever to try to get them changed. My last words were, "I am not going to Turkey." That is the end of conversation.

Desperate, I called Brigadier General Franklin and told him of my predicament. However, he told that since he had not been confirmed in the position he was unable to make any promises of a job in the congressional liaison's office. I then called a friend at officer personnel center in Washington, Lt. Col. Ernie Harrell, and told him the deal and that I needed help immediately. Ernie, a Tuskegee University grad, told me that his alma mater was in the process of selecting a new PMS and that a black lieutenant colonel had just been nominated to fill the position. He told me to call Dr. Luther Foster, TU president, to ask if I could come back as the PMS. I immediately reached Dr. Foster; he remembered me and said he would be delighted to have me back as the PMS. Dr. Foster asked me what he should do with the nomination packet the army had sent him, and I told him to send it back without comment and he would receive a new one with my name on it. Ernie completed all the coordination for my assignment to Tuskegee within a few days. I heard not another word about Turkey.

I resigned myself to the realization that going back to Tuskegee probably meant that I would retire as a lieutenant colonel. Although the army had recently made the PMS positions at Historical Black Colleges and Universities (HBCUs) a nominative assignment (officers in the top 5 percent of their peers), none had been selected to attend the war college or promoted to full colonel. Betty and I agreed that we would buy a house, our very first, in Montgomery so that Jeffrey and MEL could attend and graduate from the best high school in the area. I would commute to Tuskegee, and she would seek employment in Montgomery. With the assignment issue settled, I devoted my last few months to the Foot Cav and prepared to relinquish command to my successor.

The change of command ceremony was a really big deal for battalion commanders and their families at Fort Lewis. Family, friends, colleagues, and anybody who loved parades showed up to make it a festive occasion. Fort Lewis had been the longest time living in one place, and we had made many close friends; the close-knit group of black retirees showed up in force as visible supporters of our African American efforts to achieve in the military. It was a happy/sad day for me, especially not knowing if this would be my last command of soldiers. The toughest part for me was passing my battalion colors to Bill Carpenter, brigade commander, and him placing the colors into the welcoming grasp of the new battalion commander. It is a meaningful ritual, pleasant to watch as a spectator and an emotional experience as a participant. Betty's part of the ritual was to receive a bouquet of flowers and share in the farewell greetings from friends and colleagues. We got through the event and went to our quarters to finish preparation for our move to Tuskegee.

A sad day was made even sadder when I walked into the house from the change of command ceremony and discovered our dog, Toussaint, lying on the floor and whimpering. Mel and I took him to the veterinarian to see what was going on. The vet examined Tous and said that he had cancer in one of his front legs near his breast. I asked what our options were, and the vet said we could opt to operate or put him to sleep. I asked how much for each, and the vet said $25.00 to put him to sleep and $300.00 to operate. I said,

"Put him to sleep," and Mel grabbed Tous and started sobbing. I told the vet I would get back with him. On the way home, I received a startling revelation from Mel. He was silently holding Tous and told me between sobs, "Dad, you're going to get old one of these days and how would you like it if somebody choose to put you to sleep." I got the message, and Tous was operated on the next day.

We left Fort Lewis for Tuskegee that weekend. Lloyd, a college student at the University of Washington at that time, stayed in Seattle. His staying was another happy/sad moment for me; he was staying for a good reason but would be separated from us by thousands of miles. We all put our best faces on for each other and said our farewells, and the family minus Lloyd headed south for Alabama.

CHAPTER THIRTEEN

Tuskegee, the Second Time Around

In the summer of 1980, Betty and I bought our very first house on what was formerly a cotton plantation on the outskirts of Montgomery . . . The developer named it "Arrow Head" and touted it as the place to live. We joked about using all our savings to buy a house on a plantation that our ancestors would have given anything to get away from. The location was ideal for our primary purposes for being in Montgomery: a good high school (Robert E. Lee) for Jeffrey and Mel, easy access to interstate 80 for my commute to Tuskegee, and a good location to own a home in the event this proved to be my retirement assignment from the army. We wasted no time getting the house settled; Jeff and Mel enrolled in school, and Betty applied for job in the air force civilian personnel system at Maxwell Air Force Base in Montgomery. I hustled to make the orientation for the newly assigned ROTC PMS that was hosted in Atlanta, GA.

I was among four new ROTC PMS reporting to colleges and universities in the southeastern United States. PMS at the University of Alabama, Jackson State College, and Alcorn State College held the rank of full colonel and were in attendance. None of us knew each other but quickly bonded on our new journey. The colonels left no secret that this was their last assignment before retirement, and I made a point to say I was hoping for a promotion but prepared to retire if promotion didn't happen. Personally, I think the army PMS position at Tuskegee warranted the rank of full colonel; the air force ROTC department with the same number of students as the army was headed by a full colonel. Brig. Gen. Carey Hutchinson, our regional commander, warmly welcomed us to the conference and had grand expectations for us improving our various programs. Our orientation topics included enrollment trends on college campuses in our region, explained our recruiting roles on the campus, and the importance of meeting our commissioning goals to retain the program on the host campuses. One other popular topic on the agenda was an "Assertive Leadership Training Workshop." The goal was to help ROTC students lacking strong leader personalities become strong leaders. I thought the training was tailor- made for HBCU ROTC students and planned to incorporate the techniques into Tuskegee's curriculum for ROTC summer camp preparation.

At the conclusion of the orientation, Hutchinson pulled me and the Alcorn's PMS aside and told us that our cadets were among the bottom in performance at ROTC summer camps and at the various army branch schools attended by our new second lieutenants. He charged us to find ways to improve our cadet's performance at both venues. I was familiar with the complaint of poor academic and leadership performance of HBCU cadets and told the general I knew how to correct their performance at both venues. He appeared skeptical and countered by saying that it appeared that my challenge was before me because Tuskegee ROTC students would be at the bottom of all evaluated events at Fort Bragg. I promised to show him my proven plan when he visited Tuskegee in the fall.

Hutchinson was aware that I had completed battalion command, and from his comments about me having three years to turn the program around, I assumed that he also expected that this would be my terminal assignment in the army. Regardless of his assumptions, his message and priorities for me and the Alcorn PMS was crystal clear: improve the performance of our cadets.

Upon returning to Tuskegee, I was happy to see the significant changes to Tuskegee's ROTC facilities in the ten years since I had been assigned there. The old pink building was gone and a brand-new academic building stood in the place of the old wooden structure that was named Phelps Hall. Ms. Ruth Evans, administrative assistant to the PMS, was the only person still working in the ROTC department from my assignment there in

1970. Dr. Foster and many of the deans and department heads were still at the university. Most of our friends from the veteran's administration hospital and the various university departments were still there. We were happy to reconnect with friends and especially Lincoln University alums Delroy and Barbara Gess, and JJ John son; we received a warm welcome from all.

The ROTC staff at Tuskegee was racially integrated; two white and three black officers were the instructors, and five black and one white NCO made up the administrative staff. The army had finally matched practice with its policy in assignments to ROTC duties in the south. White southern universities and colleges were now accepting African American officers as part of their ROTC staff as well as African American students in their ROTC and university programs. However, the stubborn challenges at HBCUs offering ROTC still remained below standard performance at ROTC summer camp and at the army branch schools. As an HBCU graduate and career officer, I juggled the academic, socioeconomic, and racial dynamics to meet or exceed the standards. HBCU students were on the same path with the same challenges and needed a coach to teach them how to meet and excel in the army's competitive environment. I believed that if I did nothing else as a professional army officer, my legacy was to pass on my knowledge to Tuskegee's students commissioned in the army.

My XO had an MBA from the University of Southern California and was the first white officer to serve in Tuskegee's ROTC detachment. As such, he brought some definite ideas about how to help improve our student's performance. I welcomed his ideas but told him to put them on hold because as an HBCU graduate, I knew how to fix the performance challenge. I briefed the major and four captains on my plan for ROTC juniors (MSIII) who would be going to summer camp in 1981. I don't recall but don't believe that any of them was at the 1980 camp. I told them of Brigadier General Hutchinson's concerns about our student's performance both at ROTC camp and at the various branch schools and my plans for immediate improvement. I instructed that we would not teach from the ROTC standard curriculum for MSIII but would teach and test them on: map reading, marksmanship, drill and ceremonies (FM 22-5), current events (The Wall Street Journal), and on how to be assertive. I borrowed the Infantry axiom of "move, shoot, and communicate" to describe the task and assigned Capt. Elmer Polk, a hard-charging air defense artillery officer, as the primary MSIII instructor with the rest of us adding our expertise at the appropriate time. I led the assertive workshops by using situations encountered by students at the 1980 ROTC summer camp. Most situations had to do with the student's perceptions of race in their performance and evaluation of their assigned leadership role(s) at the camp. My goals were to coach them to (1) know what to do, (2) require others to do their part, and (3) ask what evaluation they were given and demand detailed explanations for any evaluation that were below average.

Brigadier General Hutchinson came to visit Tuskegee ROTC

Detachment early in the fall semester and was insistent on informing Dr. Foster about the poor performance of Tuskegee students at ROTC summer camp and at their branch schools. I advised against him making their performance an issue at his first meeting with Dr. Foster, but he felt strongly that his job was to inform university presidents when their students performed poorly. Prior to our meeting with the president, I alerted Ms. Punch, President Foster's secretary, of Hutchinson's primary message for the president. During the meeting, Foster brilliantly monopolized the conversation by listing the prestigious honors and awards Tuskegee students had earned in engineering and veterinary medicine while assuring Hutchinson that ROTC students would exceed prevailing ROTC standards under my leadership. He thanked us for coming and ushered us out of his office. Hutchinson was thoroughly impressed with Dr. Foster's ease, eloquence, and commanding presence.

Back in my office, Hutchinson wanted to know how I was going to improve Tuskegee students' ROTC performance. I said by teaching and testing assertiveness training, drill and ceremonies, map reading, and requiring them to read The Wall Street Journal. He was skeptical and asked how I thought those basic subjects would improve students' performance at summer camp. I used the evaluations of my students from the 1980 camp provided me by his staff. All the topics on my "move, shoot, and communicate" curriculum were the same ones used by the ROTC instructors to evaluate my students but in more detail. I pointed out to the general, the comments of, "below average performance in leadership positions" as the reasons I was teaching assertiveness training to our MSIII students. I also explained that The Wall Street Journal provided them current events for their use in casual conversations with others aspiring to be leaders in their chosen professions. Hutchinson was not happy that I was not following the standard ROTC curriculum but suggested that I should not ask for written permission to deviate from it. However, he was very pleased with his visit and repeated his admiration of Dr. Foster's demeanor and graciousness.

Tuskegee University was celebrating its hundredth anniversary, and we were doing our part to honor the graduates who had distinguished themselves in the US Army. The Hall of Fame centennial booklet listed all the ROTC graduates who achieved the rank of colonel or above. Capt. Elmer Polk, my stalwart instructor, also led the publication of the booklet.

My focus and routine on the myriad tasks we were pursuing was temporarily diverted by an unexpected call notifying me of my selection for promotion to colonel. The good news put to rest my concerns over Tuskegee University being my last assignment but did not alter my determination to improve the university's ROTC student performance. One month later, more unexpected good news came; this time I was notified of my selection for attendance at the Army War College. I thought hallelujah, but to preclude moving to Carlisle Barracks to attend the Army's War College in Pennsylvania, I requested and was granted approval to attend the Air War College in Montgomery, AL. Now I was really excited but even more motivated to see improvement in Tuskegee student performance at ROTC summer camp. The students were aware of my promotion and war college selection, and I used my advancement as evidence that using what they were learning in "move, shoot, and communicate" would also work for them in their life journey. My last official ROTC duty was as a company commander at ROTC summer camp at Fort Riley, KS. I think we had about thirty students attending summer camp, and they were distributed throughout the companies commanded by the PMS (lieutenant colonels and colonels) from colleges and universities in the south. I may have had one student from Tuskegee in my company, and the rest were from other colleges and universities in the south. Cadets were randomly chosen for leadership positions within the company and battalions and evaluated on their performance by a senior PMS officer in charge of evaluating and leading the cadets as they performed the leadership roles that made up the company organization from commander to first sergeant.

Each cadet also received peer evaluations. Evaluations were posted and made available to the PMS at mid-camp and at the end of summer camp. At mid-camp, Tuskegee had one cadet performing below average in leadership; the remainder were average or above. At the end of the camp, the below-average student voluntarily quit the ROTC program, and the rest were rated average or above average in all categories. We celebrated their accomplishments while at camp, and my joy was the look of confidence and pride individually and collectively on the faces of Tuskegee students.

Back on campus, Brigadier General Hutchinson called and congratulated me on my students' performance at summer camp.

He also told me that the prevalent comments among the evaluations were the observation that Tuskegee cadets were too aggressive; these observations were offered without further elaboration. I thanked him for the opportunity to be the PMS and learned that my successor had been named but wouldn't report until after school started in September. I left Tuskegee confident that the staff and my successor would have confident MSIV students to help prepare the new MSIII for a successful 1982 ROTC summer camp. I entered the Air War College grateful for the way things turned out at Tuskegee.

My worst scenario for my army career was replaced by the best chain of positive events that opened new advancement opportunities for me and my family. Jeffrey and Mel graduated from Robert E. Lee high school, and Betty had a good position at Maxwell AFB, where I would attend the nine-month Air War College. Life was good for us and promising for the boys. Jeff was a member of the National Guard and entered active duty for training at Fort McClellan, AL, and MeL entered Emporia State University in Kansas to major in business administration. Little Tous, Mel's best friend, gave up the fight to live after Mel left home for college. Tous spent his last days at Tuskegee's renowned veterinary clinic.

CHAPTER FOURTEEN

Germany: New Perspectives and Challenges

As a War College graduate and soon-to-be colonel, my new credentials vaulted me into a new and more challenging category of competitors for command selection. The most immediate sign of my competitive status was my selection as deputy inspector general, US Army Europe (USAREUR) with an assignment in Heidelberg, Germany. Lt. Gen. Richard "Dick" Trefry, the army inspector general, had first pick on newly selected colonels and War College graduates to carry out his new "systemic" approach to fixing army problems. His approach was endorsed by the chief of staff of the army and was seen as a better way to identify and fix problems versus the traditional compliance approach of former inspector generals.

All newly assigned inspector generals had to complete a five-week course in Washington, DC on "How the Army Runs." I not only received my graduation certificate from the new course but also was promoted to the rank of colonel by Lieutenant General Trefry and Major General Schwarzkopf and then assigned as the assistant deputy chief of staff, operations. The colonel's Eagle is an insignia that signals power from any perspective measured and was my "bull's eye" to reach a successful career. I returned from Washington to Heidelberg wearing the Eagles given to me in Fort Lewis by Chambers and Schwarzkopf and began observing the rituals of colonels aspiring to be on the command list at that level.

Col. Ralph Udick, the USAREUR inspector general, had completed his command at the level of colonel and was anxiously looking toward the release of the next brigadier general list. The investigations chief, one of two more colonels, had not made the list of his first eligibility and was waiting for the next one. Meanwhile, the chief of inspections, the remaining colonel, had made the list on his first eligibility and was waiting to take command. I think my being the most junior colonel and waiting on my first eligibility for command was the reason for my assignment as the deputy. Ralph was very helpful in coaching me on the issues and how to navigate through the USAREUR chief of staff, a major general, to get to the four-star commander in chief (CINC). As the USAREUR inspector general, Ralph appeared to know the colonels in command positions traditionally selected for promotion to brigadier general. I felt as if I were in the minors and being groomed for the majors with Ralph as my coach.

This was our first tour to Germany and could not have come at a better time with regard to time in service, seniority, and monetary exchange rates. Our waiting time for housing was reasonable; the space, including bedrooms, was more than ample for Betty and me, and one US dollar equaled three Dutch marks at the height of our tour. Betty was able to land a job, and we quickly established our sightseeing routine with weekend excursions through the wine growing region of western Germany on our way to Strasbourg, France. Life was good, and we were enjoying Germany as empty nesters. Lloyd, our oldest, was working in Washington, DC, Jeffrey was attending basic training at Fort McClellan, AL, and MEL was a freshman at Emporia State University, Emporia, KS. Jeff and MEL came to spend Christmas with us in 1982, and they too enjoyed the sights and sounds of Germany.

In early 1982, I received a call from Brig. Gen. John Foss (Gen. Retd.), whom I had never met and did not know, congratulating me on being selected for colonel command and assigned to a position in his command. I assumed that I had been selected to command a mechanized Infantry brigade and remember asking the designation of the brigade and its location. Foss, in a pleasant and conversational tone, explained that my command was part of the Seventh Army Training Command and that I would be the commander of the Maneuver Training Area at Hohenfels.

I finally got the message, was disappointed, but still upbeat because I was still on the command list. General Foss went on to explain that the two commands, Grafenwoehr Firing Center and Hohenfels Training Center, were added to the colonel command list because of their importance to maintaining the combat readiness of US combat units stationed in Germany. Because of the population density in Germany, these were the only two training areas in which the German government permitted firing of large caliber guns and the use of armored tracked vehicles.

Betty Is Reluctant to Leave Heidelberg

I was the first colonel chosen by a centralized selection board to command Hohenfels, the maneuvers training area for armored tracked vehicles. Previous commanders had been chosen locally and most regarded it as their last assignment before retirement. He went on to tell me that there were plenty of places for wives to shop in the Ober Falz and Bavaria and that my wife would like it. Betty had already told me she was not happy about leaving Heidelberg and that she was happy with her job and all that Heidelberg had to offer. I continued to follow orders, kept Betty informed about our moving dates, and knew that she would kick and scream all the way to the front gate of Hohenfels and then do what she could to help me in my command of the training area. I was still excited to be on the list and immediately shared my good news with my boss, Ralph Udick, who immediately told me to turn down the assignment. It was a "garrison command," he told me, and so far out of the mainstream that it was a dead end job. Despite his warning, I remained buoyant about the assignment and about being on the list and receiving the calls and messages of congratulations from friends and well-wishers.

Again, Betty was happy for me but not overjoyed about leaving Heidelberg for Hohenfels. She had been bombarded with the same reaction as Ralph Udick gave me by her own colleagues. At approximately 140 acres, the training area was large by German standards; however, the staff which included about twenty officers and less than a hundred enlisted soldiers was relatively small. The larger population was comprised of family members numbering about 200 and a German civilian workforce of about 125 persons. Most US soldiers and their families lived in the small communities of Hohenfels, Schmidmuhlen, Parsberg, and Emhof.

My first four months in 1983 were filled with recommended visits and courses to prepare me for the challenge of transitioning the training area from World War II targeting technology employing man-placed targets to electronically activated targets and systems for real-time feedback to commanders and troops. The army spared no expense to tailor courses that I thought would prepare me for the task ahead. All command selectees and wives attended the colonel command course at Fort Leavenworth, KS. Army senior managers recognized the value of including wives in the course as they played a vital role in helping us improve living and morale conditions for the families of our soldiers. I was very happy that Betty attended and felt that the experience would help me convince her to give up her lucrative position in the dynamic city of Heidelberg for the scenic rural beauty of Hohenfels and Bavaria. Ironically, she had an interesting and troubling experience in one of the orientation courses that achieved the opposite impression among some army wives from the one the course was designed to implement.

The wives' group was being briefed about the army's mission when the instructor made a comment about race and gender that crashed like a lead balloon. He emphasized to the group that the army was still white and male, raising the ire of the wives and especially the African American wives in the group. Brig. Gen. Colin Powell was assistant commandant at the time, and his wife, Alma, monitored the activities and instruction of the wives' group. She was not present at the briefing to hear the offensive comment, but heard about it. She singled Betty out at another event and asked her to relate the comment that had so upset the wives during the orientation session in question. After Betty shared the remarks with Alma, the commandant, Maj. Gen. (Gen. Retd.) Crosby "Butch" Saint appeared at the wives' group to emphasize the importance of army wives to the mission and success of the institution.

"Wake that Black Man Up!"

Meanwhile, we command selectees were briefed about the importance of our performance in the positions we were slated to perform by the four-star generals in charge of logistics, training, personnel, and acquisitions. Their presence was an unmistakable signal regarding the importance army senior leaders placed on the selection and command of colonel-level organizations. However, the briefing from Gen. Bernard Rogers, chief of staff of the army, was the most riveting of all. Rogers, an intense, no-nonsense leader, was lecturing on the importance of keeping our unit readiness indicators high when he abruptly shouted, "Wake that black man up!" There were five black colonels in the class, and each of us were scattered throughout the auditorium. The white officers around each of us immediately looked in our direction. Realizing that there was more than one black man in the room, the chief pointed to the one he accused of sleeping. A host of colonel instructors and aides to Rogers pounced on the startled colonel and escorted him out of the room. For the remainder of the afternoon, rumor had it that the targeted colonel had been taken off the command list and sent back to his duty station. Fortunately, the rumor was proven false when the colonel resumed the class and completed the requirements along with the rest of us.

I was also granted approval to visit the National Training Center (NTC), Fort Irwin, CA, to better understand how automated targets, opposing force, and impartial evaluators worked to improve the training effectiveness of participants. My thoughts were to adapt and replicate as much of the NTC at Hohenfels as German restrictions and senior commanders would permit. In the end, my hopes and prayers were answered in all respects. Betty agreed to accompany me to Hohenfels, and I was assuming command at the colonel level albeit a command that presented no significant advancement opportunity in the eyes of my peers. Betty and I journeyed to Graff to meet General and Mrs. Foss, and their gracious hospitality was an encouraging signal that they embraced and would do all in their power to help us be successful at Hohenfels. We had the opportunity to meet Col. Denny Rooney and his wife, Sally, the other couple also engaged in a journey of firsts. Denny was the first centralized command designee to command Grafenwoehr, and he, like me, was expecting a command under a combat division but was grateful for the opportunity to command.

At First Sight Hohenfels Confirms Betty's Worst Fears

Precommand preparations completed, Betty and I motored from Graff to Hohenfels on narrow highways through scenic Bavarian countryside and small German villages that still resembled life in the eighteenth century. We were in a festive mood, enjoying the idyllic setting and reminiscing about the journey we had traveled the past twenty years to experience the moment. The mood and conversation changed when we passed a sign welcoming us to Hohenfels Training Area (HTA). There were no buildings in sight, no trees, only clumps of small scrubs amidst irregular-shaped white rocks ranging in size from a beach ball to large igloos as far as the eye could see. Betty stopped talking, and I could only imagine her being assaulted by her worst fears as they became reality right before her eyes: a place with no stores, electric lights, running water, or television. At that moment, my own confidence evaporated, and even I no longer believed I could convince her otherwise.

We rode on in silence until we reached the main post headquarters. The headquarters had a commanding view of the major buildings that were the lifeblood of the community: the chapel, hospital, elementary school, the Post Exchange, Officers' Club, and the housing areas. Col. Ron Estep had commanded the post for the past five years and had assured me that all facilities and grounds were well maintained. He and his wife, Helga, had established a thriving and well-respected German American Friendship Program with the local communities that Betty and I would continue to emphasize during our tenure.

I went inside the headquarters, had a brief meeting with Col. Ron Estep, and traveled the short distance to the guest quarters in the large Officers' Club building less than hundred yards from the commander's house, which Ron and Helga would vacate the next morning in order to facilitate the change of command. The ceremony was well attended by local dignitaries that included mayors, business leaders, county administrators, senior US commanders with troops stationed at Hohenfels, and high-ranking German military officers. It was a large festive occasion mainly focused on the farewell of the Esteps, but many, if not most of the attendees, were also interested in meeting me and Betty, the first "Schwarz" (black) colonel and his wife to command the then thirty-year-old training area.

The change of command was a classic ceremony. It was held on the airstrip with almost all attached and assigned troops participating, German and American National Anthems played to open the ceremony, English and German language translators, and a motorized review of the troops in a restored World War II command jeep.

My First Speech in German Language Is Too Successful

All US commanders were required by the commander in chief of US Army Europe to give brief remarks in the German language as part of the command- wide efforts to improve American and German relationships throughout the country. With help from a

German translator, I gave my entire speech in the German language. My German translator had made a taped copy of my remarks in German, and I memorized the speech along with the appropriate phrasing and pauses as demonstrated by him. At the reception, many assumed that I was fluent in their language, wishing me well in German and showering me with other words and phrases that I didn't understand. Fortunately, Herr Scheurer, my translator, was by my side to interpret what they said so I could respond effectively. One irate businessman accosted me with a long angry- sounding message. I had no idea what he was saying, so I asked Herr Scheurer to interpret. As it turned out, the man was angry over the damage the American tanks and armored personnel carriers had caused to the highway that ran from the railhead to the training area and demanded that I stop those vehicles from using the highway. I assured him I would look into it, but from that moment on, I spoke English and let Mr. Scheurer translate for me.

My two-year command tour was characterized by the forces of change as well as the complacency of routine. It was staffed by professionals trained to implement the plans and programs designed at Seventh Army Training Command at Grafenwoehr. Hohenfels was largely run by about two hundred German supervisors and employees under my supervision with assistance from my deputy commander (major), operations officer (captain), and personnel officer (captain). The German workforce was proficient in running post facilities, maintaining the housing areas and training facilities.

Seventh Army Training staff scheduled the training rotations for combat brigades at Hohenfels and prepared and approved budgets for the operations of Hohenfels. The budget and operational policies that had been accepted by commanding generals from the commander in chief down to combat platoon leaders was to use Hohenfels maneuver space to develop and evaluate war fighting skills to repel an attack from East German and Soviet Armed Forces into the then Federal Republic of Germany. The mindset of US commanders in command of army forces in Germany was clear and uncompromising: always be ready to implement assigned ground defensive plans along the border with East Germany and the Soviet Union and make the most of training opportunities at Hohenfels and Grafenwoehr.

Promotion to colonel by Major General Schwarzkopf, assistant chief of staff operations, and Lt. Gen. Dick Trefry, army inspector general.

CHAPTER FIFTEEN

An Advocate for Change at Hohenfels

The commander of Hohenfels Maneuver Training Area meant that I had no role in how the units trained or their evaluation of training. General Foss and his successors expected me to play a more active role in the planning, budgeting, and execution of training at Hohenfels that would incorporate the best practices from the NTC at Fort Irwin, CA. My eagerness to participate was hampered by no announced policy to convert HTA to NTC standards. General Foss's chief of staff did not champion change, and my staff at HTA was not capable of developing a plan to integrate the two most effective tools from NTC into the training at HTA. A dedicated opposition force trained to apply Soviet tactics against the units during their training rotations, and a highly trained group of observers were there to evaluate commanders in all aspects of their maneuvers.

My approach was to advocate the above changes to my staff, the commanding general's chief of staff, visiting commanders, and anybody else that would listen. The chief of staff was the most difficult to sell because he defended the status quo on the basis of cost, personnel spaces, new facilities, new vehicles, and so on, and because he did not care for the proposed changes. He was one of the colonels whose name, according to the armchair pickers of the most likely candidates, was a sure bet to appear on the next brigadier general list. He had just completed commanding a forward deployed brigade and was a War College graduate, and I believe an operational research specialist with Pentagon staff experience on his resume. He had also been fortunate enough to land a coveted chief of staff position in a major army command.

The chief of staff controlled all my resources at HTA and knew all my plans for the training area before I briefed him or General

Foss. We maintained a cordial relationship despite our differences over the incorporation of the best NTC training practices at HTA. He was not selected on the next brigadier general promotion list and departed the chief of staff position, I believe for an assignment in Washington, DC. I don't recall the name of the new chief of staff but do recall that he was more receptive to my ideas for integrating effective NTC training concepts into HTA. The momentum of change really accelerated when Brig. Gen. Freddie Franks (Gen. Retd.) took over as commander of Seventh Army Training Command. Franks took ownership of the concept to integrate the best of NTC into HTA and did not hesitate to integrate me and my ideas into the planning and budgeting cycle that resulted in creation of the Maneuver Training Center at Hohenfels. I credit Franks for his laser-like vision and his director of resource management, Col. Jim Brayboy, for finding the resources to house, train, and maintain the CMTC. Hohenfels would now become similar to the army's automated national training center in California.

While I was dealing with the chief of staff over my proposed changes, I was also briefing my HTA staff, the German workforce, and visiting commanders (those who accepted my invitation) on the proposed changes. To my surprise, I was greeted by their perplexed looks and polite interest. The staff was supportive but doubtful while the German workforce was fearful of losing their jobs through automation. Nonetheless, I reassured them that we would retrain where we could and give them preference for the new jobs that were created. Ironically, the briefing and memos keeping them informed seemed only to exacerbate their fears as the talk of change gave way to planning and budgeting.

The senior officer in charge of the unit doing the training at HTA was invited to pay a courtesy visit before and after their session. Most did not avail themselves of the opportunity to visit my office, so I went to visit them to learn if HTA services were responsive to their training needs. To encourage their cooperation in maintaining the training and billeting facilities, I even advertised the award of a plaque to the commander who left the facilities and training site in a state of cleanliness. The plaques were hand carved with words that read: "KEYS TO EXCELLENCE-LEAD-COACH-TEACH- LEARN" and inscribed, "Presented to—Commander's Named for excellence at HTA." My operations sergeant had the motto boldly painted on the front of the operations building to encourage visiting commanders to help HTA and themselves to achieve and maintain excellence.

I have forgotten the names of all who responded to my challenge but recall awarding a plaque to Brigadier General Allen, commanding general, First Infantry Division (Forward), Maj. Gen. Charles Dyke, commanding general, Eight Infantry Division, and Brig. Gen. Ike Smith, ADC, First Armored Division. The awardees also received my briefing on the proposed change of adding a well-trained opposition force and controller evaluators to HTA. They generally were supportive but were more interested in the opportunity to select their own maneuver training needs at HTA rather than being evaluated by well- trained HTA cadre. I don't know how commanders reacted to the CMTC but believe that General Franks, a seasoned proponent of forward deployed forces, and his successors struck a balance in favor of the commander's training needs versus the controller or evaluator function.

With regard to the German workforce, I don't recall any German workers losing their positions during my tenure, and I don't believe that any lost their jobs during the implementation of the CMTC. The HTA staff was upgraded during my tenure with the addition of a lieutenant colonel as deputy commander, a major as operations officer, and a command sergeant major as the post CSM. A whole new command structure was added to operate the CMTC when it became operational. This was a successful example of change overcoming complacency and the right people showing up at the right time to accomplish what many felt was a dream.

Personal Tragedy, Faith, and Family

My command tour at Hohenfels was also characterized by personal tragedy that stretched our faith as a family and challenged my beliefs in self-confidence and determination. The murder of our oldest son was by far the greatest challenge I had to confront during my two-year command tour at Hohenfels. But there were other tough challenges as well. Among them were my orders to take command of all units between Hohenfels and the Czechoslovakia border and my search for my next advancement opportunity at the colonel command level. Commanders of military installations, and especially of training areas, are accustomed to the telephone ringing at their quarters late at night or in the early morning hours. When my phone rang early one morning in January 1984, I expected to hear the duty officer or NCO tell me about an accident that had occurred involving a soldier under my command. Instead, it was the voice of Priscilla, my sister-in-law, telling me that our oldest son had been killed in Seattle, WA. She was calling from her home in San Francisco. She herself had received an earlier call during which she was told by a detective in Seattle that Lloyd had been shot and killed, and she was calling to notify us. She was still in a state of shock and disbelief, mindful of the impact the news would have on Betty, and dreaded the fact that she had to make the call. She had no details beyond the bare facts, but provided me with the detective's name and number.

I turned immediately to Betty to fill her in on the details since she had already overheard some of them from my telephone conversation with Priscilla. At that point, I called my headquarters to contact Sarah, the army nurse at our hospital clinic, to come over and help to calm Betty's nerves. I, too, was in a state of shock but still managed to make a number of calls to learn as much as I could about Lloyd's death and to get the ball rolling for Betty, Jeffrey, and me to depart on emergency leave to get back to the USA where we could get some firsthand information as well as to make the necessary funeral arrangements.

Wade and his wife, Kathy, along with Hildegard, my secretary, arranged for our travel and got us to the Frankfort Airport, where we had no problem catching a flight for Saint Louis, MO. I think we had decided before leaving Germany that the funeral would be held in Hannibal at Betty's home church, and the burial would be in Bowling Green, MO, in a cemetery near his paternal grandfather's grave.

So we all gathered in Hannibal: MEL from Emporia State, KS; Cilia from San Francisco; Maurice from University of Minnesota; and Lawson, his biological father, from Silver Springs, MD. Everyone was still in a state of shock and wanted to know how such a terrible incident had happened. At the time, we could only piece together a mere sketch of what had actually transpired. It seems that Lloyd had taken a bus to Seattle to visit friends but by happenstance had run into an old friend who was the son of a lieutenant colonel and neighbor when we lived at Fort Lewis in the late 1970s. This chance meeting apparently took place within hours of Lloyd's arrival at the bus station. Subsequently, he and the friend stopped by a nightclub where the friend and the club doorman got into an argument. Lloyd intervened on his friend's behalf, and the argument escalated into a violent confrontation, resulting in the doorman shooting and killing him on the spot.

We shared this information with family and friends who were as shocked and heartbroken as we were. I made the arrangements for Lloyd's body to be flown back to Hannibal and for an autopsy to be performed by the local county coroner. Throughout the ordeal, I was also trying to be a calming influence and role model for Betty and our sons. I thought I was doing great until Chaplain (Col.) Paul Howard Easley, a family friend who had met Betty and the boys in Salina, KS, when I was in Vietnam, called to see how things were going and if we needed him to be there.

I remember thanking him for his offer to come while assuring him that he did not need to come since all the arrangements were made and Betty and the boys were doing as well as could be expected under the circumstances. I added that we would get through this, to which Paul replied, "I can tell by the tone of your voice that you are about to lose it. I am taking the next flight out, so pick me up at the airport." Paul came, participated in the funeral, and consoled those he knew as well as those he didn't know. In the end, he proved to be a great comfort to us all in our time of distress and sadness. He, along with our many friends and family, helped us to get through one day at a time.

After the funeral, Betty and I flew to Seattle to learn more about the shooting. We hired a lawyer, examined the investigation report, and gave our friends, John and Glenda Malloy (both deceased), power of attorney to pursue the case. Much to our chagrin and unhappiness, the county district attorney dismissed the case on the basis of eyewitness accounts that both the shooter and Lloyd were pointing weapons at each other, and under Seattle Law (and the code of the west), the homicide was ruled self-defense.

Back in Hohenfels, Betty and I managed to carry on with a lot of help and understanding from Jeffrey, close friends, and my boss. Jeff was a great source of comfort to both of us, but especially for Betty. She and Jeff both found jobs in Nurnberg, a ninety-mile drive round-trip from Hohenfels, and the job and road time helped her deal with the pain of Lloyd's death. I too was having difficulty reconciling being in Germany and worrying about MEL being so far from us in Emporia, KS.

The Eagle Insignia

A couple of weeks after returning from the funeral, I had not reengaged in the issues of commanding Hohenfels and was staring out the window in my office when Hildegard knocked on my door to tell me that General Foss was on the phone and wanted to talk to me. I answered, and General Foss said,

"Don, I know you have a lot on your mind now, and if you need to talk to me, I will either come to see you or send a helicopter to pick you up, but in the meantime, you have a post to command. If I can help, let me know." His concern and directness jolted me back to reality, and I started to get back in the swing of things with the command.

General Franks replaced Foss about halfway through my command tour, and in addition to taking ownership of my ideas to incorporate the best training practices from the National Training at Fort Irwin, CA, into Hohenfels and renaming it CMTC, he also pushed me to discover the power behind the insignia of the eagle worn on the shoulder of a colonel in the US Army. In the early 1980s, terrorist threats against American soldiers, their families, and installations in Germany were a real danger long before the September 11, 2001 attack in America. Near the end of my tour at Hohenfels, the four-star commander in chief of US Army Europe warned all commanders of a probable terrorist attack and directed that all commanders, down to and including small detachments operating independently, to take specific security steps and notify him within a twelve-hour window that the directive had been accomplished.

Franks relayed the directive to me and added that I would personally visit each of my subordinate commands to assure that the security measures were implemented. I immediately set out to visit my sites in Regensburg and a small refueling operation between Hohenfels and Regensburg. Satisfied that I had completed the task, I called Franks and reported that the mission had been accomplished. Franks asked why I did not include several intelligence and signal detachments located near the Czech border, and I said that they were not under my command, and I did not even know of their existence. "They are now," he said, "and I want you to personally check their compliance with the security directive of the CINC." I asked by what authority should I assume command of those installations. Franks simply replied, "By the colonel's eagles you are wearing on your shoulders." I flew to the locations, briefed the detachment commanders who appeared awed that a colonel had shown up to check their compliance with security, and reported mission accomplished to Franks. The immediate and unquestioned response from the commanders I met convinced me of the awesome power of the "Eagles" on my shoulders. I was certain that there was no colonel's position in the army that I could not perform and started my search for my next position.

About six months out from completing my command at HTA, I called Infantry Branch to ask where my next assignment would be. I was told that unless a general officer requested me by name—and none had to date—that I would have to find a high-visibility position (chief of staff or G3—operations officer—for a general officer) to remain competitive for promotion to brigadier general.

Earlier, I had talked to my mentor, Maj. Gen. Andy Chambers, commanding general, First Cavalry Division, in Germany who came to visit us at Hohenfels. Thanks to this encounter, I learned that he thought I was still competitive for selection to brigadier general. He strongly suggested that I should shave off my mustache because board members were critical of facial hair and often used it as a means of eliminating otherwise qualified contenders for promotion. I countered that my current boss Gen. Freddie Franks wore a mustache. He quickly shot back. "You're not Freddie Franks, West Point graduate with a Distinguished Service Cross and war hero from Vietnam." I got the message, shaved off my mustache, and started my search for a high- visibility colonel's position in Germany.

I checked with all the two- and three-star commands and learned that the commanders had already selected a colonel to fill the positions. Within two months of relinquishing my command, I had still not found highly competitive assignments and leveled my sights on finding an inspector general's position just to remain in Germany. From my contacts in the USAEUR inspector general's office, I learned that the VII Corps inspector general was completing his tour and the position would become vacant by the time I changed command in May 1985.

I knew that I was qualified and would receive approval by General Trefry, inspector general of the army, to fill the position, so I excitedly called the VII Corps personnel officer, a former Infantry Officer Advanced Course classmate, to inquire about the position. Günter told me that the incumbent was requesting an extension, but he would arrange for me to speak with the deputy corps commander, Maj. Gen. Joe Owens, and the approval authority within the corps for the position. General Owens essentially thanked me for my interest but was certain that the incumbent would be approved for his overseas tour extension and would remain in the position.

By this time I was getting desperate and called General Chambers for advice and help. When I told him about my dashed hopes with the VII Corps IG position, he chided me for giving up too easy and urged me to call Owens back to learn if the incumbent had been extended. Accustomed to following Chambers's suggestions, I called Owens, was greeted warmly, and informed that the incumbent's extension had been denied and that he would gladly accept me as the VII Corps IG. Several weeks later, a big headline in the Army Times Magazine announced that Chambers was to receive his third star and take command of VII Corps. Then I knew how all the pieces had fallen perfectly into place for my assignment as the VII Corps inspector general, just in time to relinquish command to my successor.

My change of command was a festive occasion. Betty, Jeffrey, MEL, and friends from all parts of Germany joined with the burgermeisters and dignitaries from the surrounding towns and villages to give us a grand farewell. I was especially touched to see Col. Bob Frix, major general retired (now deceased), and his wife,

Maureen "Mo," in attendance. Bob had been a close friend and ally on the post-training staff at Ft Lewis, WA, when I was trying to land a competitive position as brigade executive officer in the Ninth Infantry Division.

He, more than most outside of my family, shared my joy of completing a colonel designated command position. General Franks, Col. John Counts, and I reviewed the troops in the World War II command car as a prelude to passing the colors from me to John. I was familiar with passing the colors to John as he followed me in command of the Third Battalion Forty-Seventh Infantry at Ft Lewis, WA. This time I was not choked with emotion as I was at Fort Lewis because I was going to an assignment at Tuskegee that cast a shadow over my future. As a full colonel, I was certain to retire with thirty years of service and was headed for a job that I really wanted.

After the change of command, Betty and I followed the protocol established by my predecessor and left the reception for colonel counts. We already had our cars packed and waiting in front of our quarters, ready for the trip to Stuttgart. Betty and I were driven from the change of command to our house where a large group of German employees and several local bands had gathered to give us a hearty "Oberfaltz" or "Bavarian farewell." When I got out of the car, one of the German employees, holding a rope attached to a goat, came up to me, made a short speech in German, and gave the goat to me. The assembled crowd was in great spirits and laughed even louder when they saw the perplexed look on my face. "What do I do with the goat?" I asked the employee.

"It is your goat. You decide," he answered. My good friend and post fireman, Ludwig Kellermeier, came to my rescue and took the goat to the fire station. We left the post with the bands playing and friends waving and shouting words of friendship and farewell as we drove past the headquarters and through the countryside headed for the bright lights of Stuttgart and VII Corps Headquarters.

We had to move into temporary quarters because our assigned military house at Patch Barracks, Stuttgart, was undergoing repairs and wouldn't be available for a month or more. We were fortunate in that the housing officer leased us a large five-bedroom, furnished house as our temporary residence. We had not been in the house long, and I had not completed my orientation visits when a call from my sister came. She informed me that our mother had been hospitalized and she wanted me to come home. I knew exactly what that meant. In our phone conversations, I would always ask her how she was doing and if she needed me to come home, and she would always answer, "I'll let you know when I need you." Once again, the army personnel emergency leave system responded quickly and efficiently to get Betty, Jeff, MEL, and me on an airplane and to our St Louis destination. We made it to her bedside about seven hours before her death at 11:00 p.m., July 17, 1985 at St. Elizabeth's Hospital in Hannibal, MO. She left nothing to chance, included instructions in her will, and made me the executor of her estate. Plus, she had previously mailed me a letter in March of that year explaining about the money she had inherited from her sister, Lydia, and enumerating other monies that she had saved. "Just in case something happens, you will know where everything is—keep it under your hat," she had told me. I was sad but very thankful that she lived to see Betty and my marriage intact, our two sons doing well, and me being promoted to colonel. We returned to Stuttgart and resumed settling into our new quarters. General Chambers had assumed command of the corps during our absence, and he and his family's quarters was a block away from our own. Betty and Rita resumed their close relationship, and I received my marching orders from General Chambers.

Lloyd Phillip Lawson Scott Dec 1958–Jan 1984

CHAPTER SIXTEEN

"Is That the Best You Can Do?"

General Chambers was very concerned that VII Corps's accident and death rate was the highest in Europe, and he believed that commanders were not focusing enough attention on the enforcement of safety regulations pertaining to vehicles, weapons, and training. He gave me a warning order to mount a corps-wide inspection campaign that would focus commanders on reducing the number of accidents and improving the quality of training for all units under his command. VII Corps was the largest military organization in the US Army, totaling more than two hundred thousand soldiers, family members, US and German civilian employees, comprised of fourteen military communities and eleven major subordinate commands. As the corps inspector general, my meager staffing consisted of a total of about twenty-five personnel, including me, and was organized into two teams operating on an annual inspection plan that took eighteen months to inspect the military communities and major subordinate commands. When I briefed Chambers on my staffing and the fact that the inspection cycle took eighteen months to complete, he asked, "Is that the best you can do?"

But before I could respond, he said, "Don, I want every battalion- sized unit in the corps inspected within sixty days. Let me know how I can help. I know you can do it." With those marching orders and support, I revamped VII Corps IG inspection methodology from an annual general inspection cycle to an issue-focused systemic methodology. The issue was to focus commanders on safety and training through unannounced evaluation of their safety and training procedures based on their scheduled training activities. My two seasoned team leaders didn't believe initially that we could shift from the annual training schedule to the unannounced systemic methodology until I demanded implementation schedules that included our training and rehearsal periods. They met the scheduled deadlines, got excited when shown General Chambers's message announcing the new methodology, and took ownership of our implementation procedures.

General Chambers's message to all subordinate commanders in the corps left no doubt that he was serious about reducing the injury and death rate from accidents within VII Corps. As I recall, the message read: "Chambers Sends. Effectively on receipt of this message, all commanders are subject to unannounced inspector general evaluations focused on Safety, Evaluation and Training (SEAT) Procedures of scheduled training activities at the time of the IG's visit. Unsatisfactory evaluations will be briefed to the major subordinate commander who in turn will brief me on actions taken to correct the deficiency. Accidents resulting in serious injury or loss of life will be evaluated by the IG and reported to the major subordinate commander who in turn will brief me on actions taken to preclude similar or recurring accidents within the command. This message remains in effect until rescinded. General Chambers."

We started implementation around October 1985 and evaluated sixty- two battalions in a twenty-day period. I briefed the division commanders on the unsatisfactory findings within their command and received feedback from Maj. Gen. George Stotser that his session with General Chambers was helpful and enlightening for him and his subordinate commanders. General Chambers was so pleased with the results that he held an awards ceremony for the IG team members to recognize their outstanding contributions. About six months later, in writing my 1985 annual officer efficiency report, he bestowed glowing praise and stated in part, "He organized and implemented the most comprehensive safety program in the history of VII Corps and probably the army. In twenty days, he inspected sixty-two battalions, coaching brigade, and battalion commanders on developing and enforcing standards of safety, maintenance, training, leading, and caring. His innovative, creative, and expansive efforts have resulted in a 200 percent decrease in accidents (and the deaths and injuries that accompany them)." The results of the inspections brought about a favorable estimation of my talents and confirmed that I was one of General Chambers's most trusted advisors.

For the remainder of my tour as VII Corps IG, we applied our methodology and procedures to all military communities within VII Corps. I was gratified to witness the dedication and professionalism of IG team members who acted as personal representatives of General Chambers in carrying out the evaluation procedures. They were cheerful, upbeat, and in a coaching mode during the grueling pace of the twenty-day blitz to complete the inspections. My driver, Larry Furstenberg, was so dedicated that he, unbeknownst to me, cancelled his Christmas leave.

I knew that Larry had purchased his plane ticket to go visit his wife and children in Wisconsin and was scheduled to leave about a week before Christmas. My sergeant major had arranged for a replacement driver to cover Larry's absence the last two inspections before the start of the holiday season. I recall walking out to my van and there was Larry standing with the door open in his usual all business posture. I said, "Larry, what are you doing here?"

He said, "Well, sir, I wasn't sure that the new guy could check in with the teams, confirm your room confirmations, and get you where you needed to be on time, so I thought I had better do it." I thanked him for his concern and expressed my concern over the trouble he was likely to be in with his wife over cancelling his trip home. He explained that she understood because he was scheduled to go home in February or March and since he was not reenlisting, would not have to leave. Larry was the most dedicated and conscientious soldier I have ever known.

For the remainder of my tour, we settled into a routine, and Betty decided that she would go back to work. She had been asked by the VII Corps equal employment opportunity officer, Richard

Brown, a friend and fellow Lincoln University (MO) alum, to help out as his office administrator. Richard was highly motivated to perform well in support of General Chambers's directives and operational philosophy mandating that every employee should have the opportunity to succeed or fail on their own merit. Betty's knowledge and abilities coupled with her close relationship with General Chambers and Rita proved an invaluable asset to Richard and other principal staff members who were focused on making VII Corps great because of the trust and respect they had for General Chambers. Col. John Sherburne, G1, and Charlie Kent, G2, had worked for Chambers in the First Cavalry Division and, like me, were grateful for the opportunity he'd given us to serve in significant positions. We had all settled into a good working relationship, and Chambers's Corps was humming in all departments.

CHAPTER SEVENTEEN

An October to Remember

I was genuinely at peace with myself, enjoying my job, and had no grand expectations in my military career other than retiring at thirty years as a colonel. I felt that everything was going well in my job as the Corps IG and was accustomed to being summoned to General Chambers's office to give updates or receive new tasks. One September afternoon in 1985, "Mimi," my French secretary, told me that General Chambers wanted to see me. Enroute to his office, I mentally reviewed all the tasks he had given me to make sure none were outstanding. I recall entering his outer office and exchanging a glance with his aide, trying to glean a hint of what the meeting was about. However, he simply nodded as he instructed me to go on in because the general was waiting for me. I walked in, stood at my customary position of attention in front of his desk, and said something like, "Yes, sir, you wanted to see me."

Uncharacteristically, he did not motion me to take a seat but said in his best I've-got-news-for-you voice, "Don, the brigadier general list will be released later today, and you are on it." He then rose from his desk, came around, gave me a big hug, and said, "Congratulations, my man! You and Betty Jean have earned this!" I was happy, excited, and struggling to believe at the same time the reality of what I had just been told.

I asked to sit down so I could gain some semblance of composure and learn how all this would change our lives. He told me that I could only tell Betty after the list was released and spent the rest of the time sharing with me the names of other colonels stationed in Germany who had made the list, including a good friend of ours, Ernie Harrell, an engineer officer and the second African American on the list. I also learned that the reason he knew so much about who was on the list was because he was on the brigadier general selection board. He kept me in his office until I regained my composure, and I left his office to share the good news with Betty.

That night, Betty and I were invited down to General Chambers's quarters where he and Rita and their children celebrated our good fortune of making the brigadier general list. The festive occasion reminded me of the day and night he was notified of his selection for brigadier general at Fort Lewis, WA. Betty, our sons, and I were included and rejoiced over their good fortune as part of the extended family. It seemed that nothing had changed in our extended family relationship except that this time Betty and I were the ones who had to navigate the transition from field grade to general officer. The next several months in Germany were filled with announcements and celebrations that culminated with my frocking ceremony to brigadier general and departure to Fort Hood, TX, as the ADC, First Cavalry Division.

The first headline that helped me grasp the reality of my selection dawned as I gazed at a freshly minted copy of Stars and Stripes: "USAREUR Announces Six Colonels' Promotions!" Interestingly, five of the six of us newly selected for brigadier general rank were assigned at VII Corps. I learned some weeks later that our names were listed in the order approved by the board for promotion, which helped explain how I was selected by the chief of staff of the army to be the ADC, First Cavalry Division.

The August 26, 1986 letter from the General Officer Management Office (GOMO) welcomed me to the ranks of general officers and provided the details of promotions, assignments, and rules pertaining to the administration of general officers. Of immediate interest was the scheduled orientation of November 9–15, 1986 for all fifty-seven selectees and our wives. This and the announcement that General Wickham, army chief of staff, had approved my assignment to the First Cavalry Division with a reporting date in October was proof positive that our lives were headed in a direction approved and planned by the movers and shakers in the army power structure.

Thankfully, one of those was Andy Chambers, who had been our coach at every step along the way. He was very excited that I was assigned as ADC, First Cavalry Division, a post he himself had held before being selected to command the division. He also attempted to explain the dynamics of being assigned to III Corps Headquarter at Fort Hood, TX, with two divisions on the same post under its command. I got a glimpse of the command environment at Fort Hood in a congratulatory "For Your Eyes Only" message, dated September 10, 1986, from Lt. General Crosby "Butch" Saint that advised in part, "We are on a fast track with no red lights. Brush up on your hard core war fighting and training skills. No slack here."

After reviewing and reflecting on his message, my thoughts took me back to the real world. The excitement of the moment and receipt of Saint's message helped me merge my gratitude with a dose of reality and inspired me to think through my identity as a general officer before I left Germany for Fort Hood, TX.

The second public announcement was captured with an article accompanied by a picture General Chambers and Betty pinning on my star. The story appeared in the Greater Stuttgart Military Community Newspaper on Monday, October 27, 1986. The frocking meant that I would perform the duties of a brigadier general but would be paid as a colonel until I was promoted to brigadier general. The ceremony was well attended by friends from Hohenfels and throughout Germany. Jeffrey was able to attend as a private first class and driver for a good friend, Col. Johnny Wilson (Gen Ret), the commander of the First Armored Division Support Command. Prior to the pinning on ceremony, Jeff congratulated me on making brigadier general, and recognizing the emotional impact it was likely to have on my remarks, he said, "Dad, when you get up there to make your remarks, just remember that generals don't cry. They are supposed to twinkle not tinkle."

His advice came in very handy as I thought about how far we had come from Hunnewell and Hannibal and the family and friends who helped us along the way. And none had helped us more than the man and his wife who was pinning on my star. I came close to tinkling but with the grace of God managed to twinkle instead.

The farewell party was well organized by Col. John Sherburne and his wife, Linda, and was attended by the entire principal staff in a large tent setup near our house and attended by all our neighbors. Betty and I were touched by their warmth and good wishes, and I was comforted that General Chambers, Rita, and our neighbors would take good care of Betty while I was at Fort Hood.

The next day, October 22, 1986, General Chambers invited me to his office for my exit briefing and demonstrated the most awesome display of unconditional love I had ever experienced. He thanked me again for my contributions to VII Corps and used that opportunity to share his observations of my leadership that went far beyond the traits on the army's official performance evaluation report. His comments were penetrating and helpful. I had never considered my physical stature a factor of my performance until he explained how my size (6' 3" and 215 lbs) and no-nonsense manner could be an intimidating factor to some—he quickly added with a smile—but not to him because he was not easily intimidated. I knew that he was preparing me for my new position as ADC, First Calvary and III Corps, where I would be an unknown to my new bosses, Yeosock and Saint. Our meeting lasted for nearly two hours, and I felt privileged that General Chambers graciously showered me with his brilliant insights into human nature and especially his insights with regard to the general officer corps.

After my, come to Jesus, meeting with Chambers, I made the following entry into my "You're Gonna Be One" mock booklet (the gift from a friend in 1980 about becoming a general officer):

"I am a general officer in the US Army. I am entitled to and will demand when necessary all the rights and privileges due a general by law and custom. I will fully accept all responsibilities to carry out my duties under the law as well as those expected of me by superiors. I will make decisions on the basis of right versus personality. In gray areas, I will use my judgment versus a subordinate. I will not change my basic beliefs about humanity nor hide those social or ethnic mores that I enjoy as a native Black American."

I departed Germany on the October 23, 1986 en route to the First Calvary. I was finally leaving Germany after four years of trials, heartaches, and jubilation. I had arrived on the promotion list to colonel and was leaving as a "frocked" brigadier general. Thanks to a host of people, I was now "One."

Insights on the Germany Experience: The Good, the Sad, and the Miraculous

Sometimes life gives us a reset button that change our status and the way others see us. Being assigned to Germany as a promotable colonel and War College graduate significantly changed my career opportunities and the reception we received at the inspector general's office at USAEUR Headquarters in Heidelberg. The selection for command at HTA placed me in a more competitive status among my peers even though Hohenfels was not considered by them to be a competitive-level position. I knew that no prior incumbent of the position had been promoted to brigadier general but was optimistic about my chances because army senior leaders recognized its importance by adding it to the list of valued colonel-level command positions.

I think every profession has a career ladder that leads to advancement for the successful performer, and some may even have a "Hohenfels" that does not have a track record of incumbents rewarded with advancement. To me it is like gambling: if you don't invest, you won't win. However, if you invest in an enterprise where the odds are not in your favor, but keep you competitive to be a winner, you are foolish not to bet on yourself. Most colonels on the command list successfully complete their command tours but are not selected for promotion to brigadier general. It is impossible to identify the variables in the equation for the number selected each year, but the reward for those not selected is tangible and positive. Leading men and women entrusted to your care in the achievement of their assigned goals (and in the midst of their own personal struggles) is a satisfaction that lasts a lifetime.

Perhaps the most important benefit of having a reset button is that each individual must decide to activate their own button. I started work on my master's degree before knowing that I would be selected for colonel or the War College, an experience that equipped me with knowledge and abilities that would make me more marketable to an employer. Additional education is a sure way to achieve goals that lead to new and better career opportunities in our chosen or a new profession. So far I have spoken only of the good things that graced my life during my tour of duty in Germany. But the death of a loved one, whether old or young, is always a significant emotional event and lasting memory for those left to mourn and remember the departed. Both the death of our oldest son and of my mother happened during our Germany tour.

Lloyd's death at age twenty-five was a shock made even more painful by the inexplicable circumstances: a confrontation triggered by the impulse to intervene on behalf of a casual friend with an unknown detractor who took his life with a pistol. The details of his death remain unclear, but the pain of the incident and our loss remain fresh and unsettling. This has been the most difficult chapter for me to reconstruct and to share in this memoir. I am certain that our immediate family was only able to get through the pain of notification, burial, and resumption of our lives with the help of family, friends, and the kindness of coworkers and people in unexpected places.

I also learned that each person must handle grief in his or her own way. We can be present, pray, and provide physical assistance, but the spiritual healing must come from within. I think Jeffrey's presence was a big help for both of us, but especially for his mother. The prayers of our friends—especially our clergy and prayer warrior friends like Maria Alma Copeland, Paul Easley, and Mary Alice Heffner—were always with us, lifting us up in strength and faith. Their prayers and our efforts to resume our lives opened doors that helped us cope with Lloyd's death. Betty and Jeffrey found employment in Nurnberg, and I found solace in running two times a day which helped me to keep my mind focused on getting through the day.

It also helped to have a boss sensitive enough to offer companionship but realistic enough to know that I needed a gentle push to resume my responsibilities. Life goes on and those we lose to death live on in our memory. I loved him and knew that he loved me before he died because of our understanding of each other's efforts to become father and son early in his life and in my marriage to his mother. I think we forged a solid father– son relationship. I was further reassured of his love in a letter written to me just six months before his death. His letter is a reminder that a father–son relationship can only be based upon spending time together, accepting each other's shortcomings, and helping each other shoulder the burden of manhood. Lloyd was finding his own way when his life was cut short, and I often wonder if I could have helped him shoulder more of the burden in finding his own way.

By contrast, my mother died at eighty-eight years of age and lived a life of purpose focused on doing the best she could for the seven of us that she brought into this world. I was sad when she died but thankful that God had spared her to accomplish her life goals: to provide for Mary, her youngest daughter, and especially for Sis (Edith), her oldest daughter, who was unable to care for herself. She left a will that bequeathed the house and nearly all her savings (nearly $50,000) to her daughters. She gave the rest of us equal shares in two acres of land and a small sum of money from her remaining savings.

There was no grumbling or dissatisfaction voiced from my brother or sisters because we understood and supported Mom's goals. I like to think that my mother's interpretation of scripture in the way she treated her children worked well for us even though it differed from most interpretations: "To those whom much is given much is expected." Mom gave the most to those who needed the most and expected the rest of her children to take care of their own families and help those in need whenever they could. Her formula worked for us and accomplished the goal of providing for Mary and Sis until their deaths.

Again, my mother's death reaffirmed that each person must handle grief in his or her own way and resume life in the best manner possible. My mother's death also reinforced the need for me to specify in my own will the distribution of property and money so that those left behind have the resources to maintain their living standards after I am no longer here.

The decade of the 1980s ushered in the death of significant loved ones in our family which included my sister Essie in 1980; Momma Rose, Betty's mother in 1982; Lloyd, our oldest son in 1984; and my mother in 1985. It is amazing how we take for granted the presence in our lives of our closest loved ones until they die. Their deaths was a wake-up call for us to realize that there will be no more hugs, conversations, or interactions of any kind for the remainder of our earthly existence. We hear the call but struggle to develop a more loving relationship with those still living. We each have our own cherished memories of their smile, voice, and the contributions they made to our growth, development, and personhood but did not tell them how much they meant to us while they were here. We often put out of our memory those moments of disagreement that caused us to pass judgment, assign blame, and refrain from asking forgiveness. Had we been mindful of these things, we could have demonstrated the love for each other that never left our hearts. What I learned about the death of my loved ones in the 1980s helped me adjust to the deaths of my father-in-law, sisters, brother, and uncle. I am still working on expressions of unconditional love for my family and friends who remain above ground.

Here's a good one from my cache of life lessons: find a way to attract attention when no one is looking. The position of commander at HTA was not perceived as a competitive one by senior generals and my peers.

The lead-coach-teach-learn motto I established and made into a plaque attracted attention and helped to change my position from a keeper of facilities to an evaluator of leaders. All competitive professionals like to be recognized for their leadership prowess, and plaques and certificates are powerful tools to attract their attention.

Strong Leaders Grow Subordinates Who Excel

In real estate, location is everything. With regard to career enhancement, where and who you work for greatly influences your acceptance for career- advancing assignments. My being selected to command the only maneuver training facility in Germany did not enhance the importance of the facility in the minds of senior leaders nor did it elevate my professional standing or prove helpful in securing an assignment as a chief of staff or operations officer of a major command in Germany. The rejections strengthened my resolve and reinforced my perception that who you worked for and where you commanded made it easier to land a career-enhancing job as a division chief of staff or corps operations officer. My saving grace was nearing successful completion of a designated colonel-level command and the behind the scenes influence of General Chambers. Do what you can to remain competitive and be thankful for opportunities to display your talents no matter who your boss is or where the job may be located.

Leaders who make bold organizational decisions create opportunities for their subordinates to excel. Gens. Freddie Franks and Andy Chambers made it possible for me to grow, contribute to their vision, and earn their confidence. I think the focus of their resolve (the safety of soldiers and family members) was evident to their subordinate leaders and garnered their willful and loyal support. I approached implementation of their tasks from a perspective of helping each commander to fix their problems rather than reporting how badly their systems were broken. In that sense, most commanders or senior executives appreciate and reward subordinates who act as trusted advisors and cooperative allies rather than those who serve merely as reporters of broken systems and inefficient leaders.

Great mentors accentuate strengths, reward achievements, and help their students turn personal liabilities into professional assets. General Chambers was a masterful coach and demonstrator of unconditional love. He looked past my faults and always complimented me on the way I executed assigned tasks. However, during my exit interview with him on my way to Fort Hood, he deflated my bubble by sharing with me how my candor might intimidate my new general officer bosses at Fort Hood. He did not suggest that I change, only that I should beware that I was walking into a new environment. I was humbled that he had allowed me the freedom to express my ideas and implement his goals without coaching me on interactions with his generals or subordinates. I was even more grateful that he had shown unconditional love by accentuating my strengths while simultaneously looking past my faults to push for my promotion to brigadier general.

The Indispensable Role of Grace

For me, promotion to brigadier general was the icing on the cake. My career goal was to make full colonel. I worked hard to receive competitive assignments, did my best to excel in those assignments, and with the help of my wife and sons proudly wore the insignia of a full-bird colonel. After being selected to the colonel-level command list, I thought making brigadier general was possible but not probable. From listening to General Chambers's "war game" when we were at Fort Lewis, which sized up his own chances for making brigadier general, I began observing selection trends that related to my own window of opportunity. In doing so, I concluded that there were four factors for selection:

- demonstrating exceptional performance in career-enhancing positions at each rank
- having a champion on the board
- being at the right place and time
- having grace

The latter was responsible for the first three factors on my list. I don't minimize my efforts, family support, timely help from bosses and friends but believe that the combination of all above cannot equal the power of grace. Grace cannot be earned, purchased, or borrowed. It is a gift freely given unconditionally from God. It is not always recognized and is often confused with individual talent, intellect, or influential connections as the reasons for our exceptional achievement or success. I am exceptional because of grace being a constant unearned but welcome presence in my life.

Tough times and difficult moments in families often show the resilience of children. In the shadow of Lloyd's and my mother's death, I recall the joy and pride of seeing MEL, our youngest son, graduate from Emporia State University in 1985. He was the most self-disciplined of our sons and needed no prodding to complete his homework and assigned chores or to get up and get ready for school. I admired his decision to enter Emporia State because their admission policy championed enrollment of handicapped students, minorities, and diversity. He wanted to be at a place that prepared him for life in a diverse world and made the most of his experience. He earned good grades, pledged, became a member of Kappa Alpha Psi Fraternity, and met and married his wife and mother of our grandchildren, Taylor and Summer.

Mentoring opportunities sometimes come when you least expect them and under unpleasant circumstances. Darryl Hooks, a young African American second lieutenant, assigned to a maintenance company with a platoon attached to Hohenfels and came under my jurisdiction for violations and infractions of discipline. He was cited for driving under the influence of alcohol and had to give up his driving license for six months. This was about the same time we lost Lloyd, and with Jeff living with us and about the same age as Darryl, we developed close mentoring with Darryl that blossomed into a lifelong father– son relationship. I am in touch with the Rev. Darryl Hooks often and enjoy the satisfaction that comes from receiving feedback on the lessons he learned from interacting with Betty and me over the past thirty years.

CHAPTER EIGHTEEN

"It Only Takes One (Star) to Make You a General"

I left Germany in October 1986 as a newly minted "00B00"—the military occupational specialty awarded to general officers. The prophecy of Andy Chambers that it only takes one star to make you a general had come true. My promotion to brigadier general took Betty and me on a journey that could only be described as magical, the stuff of dreams and fairy tales. However, like all good fairy tales, we had our moments of disappointments and encounters with nonsupporters. And yet our rainbow-bright victory appeared at the end of our journey with my miraculous appointment to the rank of a one star or brigadier general. It was a high note of promise and expectation rather than one of disappointment and sadness.

I wore the one-star insignia for over five years—the first two years in a "frocked status," which meant carrying out the responsibilities of a brigadier general while still receiving the pay of a colonel. I was the ADC, First Cavalry Division, Fort Hood, TX, after which I became chief of staff, Second Army, Atlanta, GA. It was there that I decided to retire from the army to serve as chief of staff for the late Maynard Jackson, mayor of Atlanta, GA.

The GOMO gave me a choice assignment as the ADC, First Cavalry Division and scheduled me to attend the Center for Creative Leadership following the Brigadier Officer Orientation Conference for all fifty-seven selectees and our wives from November 9 to 15, 1986. My general officer tour started off with a bang, and I can truly say that the initial assignment and preparatory training promised a bright future for me with great promotion prospects for a second star as a general. So what happened?

The two-star selection board did not select me for promotion. That is the short and simple answer, and all that follows here is not intended to alibi or guess their reasons but to share the events that unfolded until my retirement from the army.

You play the hand that is dealt to you. I was dealt a great hand by GOMO, having been handed an assignment that was approved by the chief of staff, Army, and Gen. John Wickham in Washington, DC. This hand had to be played at Fort Hood, TX, where all the commanders had been basic branch armor before promotion to general. When I reported into III Corps Headquarters for my interview with Lt. Gen. "Butch" Saint, I was confident that as a basic branch Infantry officer I could perform my duties as ADC of the First Cavalry Division under his command. Saint's welcome emphasized that war fighting was his primary interest and advised that I had a steep hill to climb (to contribute to the training and evaluation of armored warfare). I assured him that I would quickly contribute to the First Cavalry's preparation for a successful rotation at the NTC, the premier evaluation of combat readiness for army divisions. Our brief meeting was cordial, but from my perspective, leery; he wasn't reassured by my statement, and I was uncertain of the standards he would use to evaluate my performance. I believe our perceptions of each other did not change during my two years with the First Cavalry. And as I recalled the personalities of this period, my thoughts about Saint were guided by my dad's guidance in my formative years: "If you can't say anything good about a person, don't say anything."

My welcome from the mayors of Killen, Harker Heights, and Copperas Cove, the towns surrounding Ft Hood, TX, was very warm and exceeded only by Maj. Gen. John Yeosock and the First Cavalry Division family (First Team). Maj. Gen. John Yeosock, commanding general of the First Cavalry and his wife, Betta, our good friends Col. Bob Frix, chief of staff, and his wife, Moe, one of Betty's dearest friends, made our new surroundings more comfortable and facilitated our housing assignment and reception by local community leaders.

My relationship with Yeosock was great during my eighteen-month tenure as his assistant commander, and my performance report included his recommendations for promotion to a second star and command of a division. Yeosock had been ADC under Andy Chambers and knew the First Calvary Division's organizational structure from top to bottom. He gave his brigade and separate battalion commanders the latitude to share in developing and implementing training goals and objectives. Collaboration and teamwork among commanders was a First Team legacy, and my role was to coach and assist.

During my tour as the ADC, the division successfully accomplished three major challenges and all the little ones thrown in: fielded and tested a new tactical communication system for the army, participated in REFORGER 87 (Return of US Forces to Germany in the event of a Soviet attack), and demonstrated tactical proficiency through force- on-force exercises at the army's NTC, Fort Irwin, CA.

The three events that played a significant role in shaping my experience as the ADC all occurred during training events away from Fort Hood, the Center for Creative Leadership, Return of Forces to Germany (REFORGER), and the NTC, Fort Irwin, CA.

My attendance at the Center for Creative Leadership, Greensboro, NC, during April 5–10, 1987 contributed to my self-discovery and helped me adjust to my role as ADC. I had been ADC for about five months, long enough for my direct reports to garner opinions about my leadership style. Their perceptions of my style were reported in a survey sponsored by the Center for Creative Leadership as part of their leadership assessment model.

The week-long course was interesting, well-executed, and provided useful insights about me that I was not aware of before. I was the only general officer among the twenty-three corporate executives that made up the course. As part of the center's assessment efforts, each of us was assigned to observe two fellow participants and render our assessment of their effectiveness in a group setting. Don from Burlington Industries and Bob from AT&T were my targets; they did not know the name of their student evaluator, and I was unaware of who was evaluating me. The course had the feel of a real spy setup and required us to closely observe each other's behavior.

A staff psychologist, who also observed each participant in group settings through a two-way mirror, gathered and analyzed the psychological tests and surveys from direct reports and supervisors. By the end of the course, they provided each of us with an assessment of our strengths and other traits that would improve our effectiveness as a leader in group settings. I was urged to be more patient with any subordinate whose understanding of problems or concepts did not equal mine and to be less dogmatic in my assessment of myself as being average.

I had stated to the class that I attributed my success in the army to being of average intelligence, hard work, and good luck. The psychologist countered with statistical data that showed a bell curve of lieutenants who entered the army when I did and the percentage who progressed to general officer. He showed me my IQ, told me that I was not a genius, and urged me to accept the practical implications for my leadership. He added that in matters involving complex problems, I got to the stoplight before a person with average intelligence. His example stuck, and I attempted to be more patient with briefings by subordinates back at Fort Hood and beyond. I also left the course with one exercise that was designed to help me identify who I could count on through good or bad times. The correct response was to write the name of a person who loves you no matter what you do or say. Betty, members of my immediate family, the Andy Chambers family, and Larry, my driver in VII Corps, are the first names that popped up when I went through the exercise. The names that pop up are your family.

My next major challenge was participation in REFORGER 1987. REFORGER exercises test more than strategic, tactical, and logistical concepts; personal communication and professional relationships are inevitably tested at all levels of command. The old saying of what comes around goes around aptly describes my observation of Brig. Gen. Oliver Dillard's interaction with a bold subordinate in 1974 during preparation for a REFORGER exercise in Germany. My REFORGER experience in 1988 caused me to recollect Dillard's experience that I recounted earlier in Chapter Eleven. Our shared African American racial identity coupled with the fact that we both held the position of ADC of an Armor Division made our situations comparable in that we both were faced with challenges from a strong-willed subordinate.

However, my situation differed from Dillard's in that it occurred at one of the major highlights of the REFORGER exercise—a river crossing where I was in command of the operation until two-thirds of the division made it across, at which point command reverted back to General Yeosock. The press corps was expected to cover the crossing, and like everything the First Cavalry did, we left nothing to chance. I rehearsed my ten-minute presentation to the media in which I planned to explain the salient point of the division's capability of moving sixty-ton tanks rapidly across the river. The exercise would serve to demonstrate the awesome technology and professional capability of the First Cavalry Division to perform this difficult and highly risky maneuver. General Yeosock approved my briefing, and our demonstration was set to go at the rehearsal site at the designated time.

Back at the division headquarters field site, information came from Saint that high-level dignitaries were expected to attend the demonstration and perhaps General Yeosock should do the briefing. Yeosock affirmed that we would stick with the plan that I would do the briefing and he would be at his forward location to assume command of the division when two-thirds had completed the river crossing.

We synchronized watches, confirmed launch coordinates and times, and headed to our respective locations. About one hour before launch time, I received a call from one of my subordinates, engineer commander, Lt. Col. Milton Hunter (African American), informing me that the demonstration had been moved up by one hour and that he was on the move. No one assigned to my small staff had received notification from the division G3, and we couldn't speak with the G3 because of radio listening silence. We moved directly to the crossing demonstration site and arrived before the press, Butch S, and his dignitaries. The briefing went well as rehearsed, the troops performed well as planned, and the dignitaries offered praise and expressed admiration over the demonstration along with my presentation. Butch S closed the demonstration by adding an overview of the "Phantom Warrior Corps," the nickname earned by III Corps during World War II, now rebranded by Butch S to reflect his concept for the use of armor under his command of III Corps.

Following the briefing, I immediately asked Lt. Col. Bill Nash, First Cavalry G3, why he did not notify me of the move up in good time. His response was straightforward as he explained that Saint had moved up the time. He went on to explain that the division was on radio listening silence, and road distance was too great to send a runner by vehicle to notify me of the change. He also volunteered that he was prepared to conduct the briefing had Yeosock or I not been able to make it to the demonstration site on time. Nash was one of Saint's mentees and enjoyed his complete confidence.

I completely understood the relationship and suspected that Nash was totally in sync with Saint's desires to replace me as the designated First Cavalry briefer. I had witnessed this scenario before, so I accepted Nash's version as the gospel and moved on. Several other high-profile events were similarly orchestrated without General Yeosock or me being in the approval chain. Recalling my observation of Brigadier General Dillard's interaction with a subordinate and my mental note about not allowing subordinates to usurp my authority, I was compelled to learn the advanced calculus of decision-making in the ranks of general officers. My understanding of basic military math was that four stars beat three, three beats two, and two beats one. I was also savvy enough to know that capable staff officers, as trusted agents of the general with the most stars, understands the math, the personalities involved, and how to stay out of the middle. I think Brigadier General Dillard, unlike me, might have discovered that lesson earlier in his career.

I spent a lot of time at the Army NTC, Fort Irwin, CA, as the senior officer in charge of the First Cavalry brigades being tested and evaluated by the NTC opposition force. This force was the best in the US Army at replicating Soviet tactics, and the evaluators were also considered the best evaluators of the competence and leadership of the tested unit's leaders. The brigadier general in command of the NTC, an armor officer, rigidly enforced rules to prevent tested units from learning the maneuver scenarios of their evaluation. As the ADC of the First Cavalry Division, I was not involved in the brigade's evaluation and considered myself an impartial observer of both the opposition force and the tested brigade.

The First Cavalry Brigade commanders were among the most professional officers and soldiers that I had ever met in my army career. Their professionalism and integrity were the strength of the division. Three of them were awarded their star and the 00B00 MOS during their career. Their approach to training at the NTC spoke volumes about their character, honesty, and professionalism. Like other visiting commanders to the NTC, they wanted to beat the NTC opposition force but not at the cost of spying on the opposition force or war-gaming the several scenarios of the opposition force. I completely shared their training philosophy and viewed my role as a general officer at the NTC as that of an impartial observer or trusted agent. I quickly learned from the brigadier general commanding the NTC at the time that there were no impartial observers or trusted agents allowed. I was flying over the training area in my assigned helicopter from the First Cavalry Division to observe the dispositions of both the opposition force and the brigade when my helicopter pilot, Chief Wuest, was ordered not to fly over the opposition force's area.

I questioned why this was so, and my pilot, who had flown my predecessor at NTC many times, did not know the answer. Upon landing, I asked Col. Bill West (Brig. Gen. Retd.), chief of the opposition force and senior controller at NTC, the reason for the change restricting me from flying over the opposition force. Bill and I were friends, but his explanation only fueled my anger at what I perceived to be a recent change in policy aimed at restricting my access to the opposition force and told him so. He, in turn, reported my reaction to his one-star boss, who called me on my tactical radio and threatened to report my refusal to follow his orders to Saint and that he would have me removed from the NTC.

I met with him and presented my view of being a trusted agent and general officer with a larger responsibility to evaluate readiness of army- training resources. The NTC commander countered by touting his experience and asserting that not every general saw it the way I did, so he established the restriction. I agreed to follow his no-fly rules but ran straight into another challenge to his rule by inviting friends to observe our First Cavalry training rotation at the NTC.

Outside visitors were permitted to observe training rotations of the unit being evaluated at NTC, and as the senior representative of the unit in training, I could invite two visitors. I invited Harvey Golf, a generous Dallas businessman and supporter of First Cavalry troopers, and longtime friend of every commanding general of the division since before Julius Becton, the first African American to command the First Cavalry. Harvey had successfully extended his privilege which allowed him access to the troops with Chambers and Yeosock. I had met Harvey through General Chambers at VII Corps in Germany and became one of his general officer contacts. He requested that I put him on the visitation list to honor his support to the troops, and I did so. The other visitor I placed on the list was Col. Jim Monroe, a friend from our Fort Lewis, WA, tour of duty, who had been selected to command a division support command.

I had followed NTC protocol before extending the invitations to my visitors and was surprised when told that the NTC commander wanted to talk to me about visiting privileges. He knew Harvey from his reputation as a staunch First Cavalry supporter as well as from reports of his previous visits at NTC.

Harvey was a warrant officer in the Texas National Guard but took liberties to go where his general officer host lived, dined, and visited. The NTC commander cautioned me to keep Harvey under control and having disposed of his concern over Harvey, went on to question my invitation to Monroe since he was not being assigned to the First Cavalry Division or III Corps. I answered that Monroe was a friend on the list to lead a division support command, and I wanted him to observe the rigors placed on units at the NTC. The experience would aid him in training his support command troops to perform their missions under the stress of a first-rate opposition force.

That ended the inquiry, and my visitors were treated courteously and enjoyed their visit. Ironically, Monroe became division support command commander in the Twenty-Fourth Infantry Division before the NTC commander assumed command of that division. I am sure that both used their knowledge of NTC training challenges to good effect in preparing their division for NTC rotations.

The First Team brigade commanders received excellent evaluations at the NTC, and I departed on good terms with the commander.

My tour as the ADC, First Cavalry Division, came to a close after eighteen months of fast-paced training events. Like all good things that draw to a close in the First Cavalry, pageantry, pomp, and ceremony are always the grand finale. I presided over John Yeosock's farewell and Maj. Gen. Bill Streeter's reception during the mounted review of division troops. All officers were mounted on the First Cavalry Division's stable of ceremonial horses, which made for a remarkable and picturesque scene.

The mayors of the surrounding communities and all local dignitaries were in attendance to witness the transfer of responsibility from Yeosock to Streeter. I was mounted on "old Bucky," seventeen hands tall, the oldest and most contrary mount in the division. "Bucky" moved every twenty to thirty seconds, and regardless of the sequence of events marking my position as commander of troops, "Bucky" and I modified the sequence to meet Bucky's movement patterns. We made it through the ceremony without the public noticing the deviations and the equestrians in attendance at the ceremony were complimentary of my "horsemanship." This division is the only division in the US Army that still retains the traditional horse cavalry formation to conduct the change of responsibility between commanders.

A month later, I was reassigned as the chief of staff, Second Army, outside of Atlanta, GA, and a mounted farewell ceremony was held for Betty and me. It capped the end of a magical experience for me as a career soldier and marked the beginning of what I suspected would be my last assignment in the army.

Atlanta, GA, had long been on my list of places to live, and now, courtesy of the US Army, we took up residence on Staff Row, the street where all army generals lived at Fort McPherson, GA. We were excited to be in Atlanta because I had relatives there, and many of our closest friends lived there, including our mentors, lieutenant general, and Mrs. Andy Chambers.

Lt. Gen. Orrin "Cotton" Whiddon, my new boss, and his wife, Harriett, welcomed us with a hearty reception and immediately included us in the circle of his trusted advisors. These included National Guard adjutant generals, US Army reserve and civilian aides to the secretary of the army from each of the thirteen southeastern states of the USA plus Puerto Rico and the US Virgin Islands under his command. I coordinated the approximately 450 military and civilian employees, who in turn coordinated the various programs between Second Army Headquarters and the assigned units. Lieutenant General Whiddon and Maj. Gen. Tom Tate, his deputy commander, travelled regularly throughout the command, leaving me in charge of the day-to-day operations of the headquarters.

Social opportunities throughout the command always included Betty and me, and we got to know the generals and civilian aides very well. Mayor T. Patton Adams of Columbia, SC, was one of the aides we got to know well. In fact, we spent a once in a lifetime weekend at a county fair in Columbia, SC, that featured country and western singer.

Lee Greenwood, who made "Proud to Be an American," a popular patriotic song in the 1980s. Betty and Harriett took pictures with him, and we joined in the singing along with a crowd of thousands in attendance at the event. I think we were probably the only African Americans among a crowd of thousands—but nobody seemed to notice that we were black.

CHAPTER NINETEEN

Gen. Colin Powell Causes a Sea Change

The biggest issue to confront General Whiddon during my tenure as his chief of staff was the National Guard's attempt to create a four-star command that would end their subordination to active army commanders. The politics of the issue appeared to favor the National Guard and was on the verge of being a done deal when Gen. Colin Powell assumed command of Forces Command (FORSCOM) in charge of all US Army, Army Reserves, and National Guard readiness training in the United States.

Whiddon had been one of Powell's division commanders in V Corps in Germany and quickly arranged for the Second Army commanders to meet with Powell on the issue. Whiddon shared with me the three- pronged approach General Powell put to good use in the meeting with the commanders to short circuit momentum and maintain the status quo. Although I had no role in that important issue, General Whiddon used it and every other opportunity he could to involve me in meetings with General Powell. In this regard, General Whiddon arranged several briefings and held a welcome reception for General and Mrs. Powell that gave Betty and me the opportunity to renew our acquaintance with them. More importantly, Atlanta corporate and community leaders went all out to welcome General and Mrs. Powell to Atlanta, which was a drastic departure from the low-key acknowledgment and reception given to his predecessors.

General Powell wisely used the fanfare to publicize the role of FORSCOM and arranged for all generals who lived on Staff Row at Fort McPherson to be included on the guest list for one of his grand receptions. To date, the black social elite of Atlanta had paid little attention to us black generals assigned to Fort McPherson prior to Powells' arrival. All that changed when the power couple came to town. I received several calls from black friends connected to the black business elite in Atlanta asking how they might be able to get invitations to attend the corporate receptions for the Powells. Betty and I attended the reception along with the other general officers and their wives on Staff Row and enjoyed the recognition accorded to us in the presence of the Powells.

During Powell's brief command of FORSCOM, I developed a casual and friendly relationship with the general. He lived two doors down from our quarters and spent time on weekends working on an old Volvo sedan in the alley behind our quarters. Coincidentally, I would be back there working on my old 1976 Cadillac. Betty and Alma had their own topics of conversation and continued their friendly relationship which had begun at Fort Leavenworth, KS, when Betty and I were attending the Colonel Command Course prior to our assignment at Hohenfels, Germany.

When General Powell left to become the chairman of the Joint Chiefs of Staff, the Atlanta business community went all out once more to honor him and Alma for their contributions to America. Betty and I were included as guests at most of their farewell events. It was in these gala surroundings that we met influential business leaders that would later help us to transition from military to civilian life. At one of these farewell functions, General Powell finished his remarks and was on his way back to his seat when he stopped by my table and said, "Don, I'm leaving all this to you. Don't call me because I will be busy."

Shortly after his departure, events galloped along at a rapid pace, prodding me to retire from the army to join Atlanta Mayor Maynard Jackson as his chief of staff. I was not selected for major general during my first year of eligibility and knew that I needed to start looking for civilian employment by March 1991 when I could still retire as a brigadier general. Felker Ward, a retired lieutenant colonel, successful lawyer, and well-connected businessman, was instrumental in connecting Betty and me to the black power elite in

Atlanta. I had recruited Felker for an appointment as civilian aide to the secretary of the army for Georgia, and amongst stiff competition, he was selected and became the first African American to represent the state as its civilian aide. I believe it was some time in 1990 that Felker called to invite Betty and me to dinner with him along with Jesse Hill, chairman of Atlanta Life Insurance Company, Herman Russell, the chairman and CEO of HJ Russell Construction Company, and their wives.

The formal announcement billed it as a get-acquainted dinner, and we gladly accepted, feeling that we were being evaluated for something more than mere friendship. The dinner was held at one of the exclusive restaurants in midtown Atlanta. It might have been Delmonico's Steak House. In any case, the atmosphere was very friendly and cheerful. I vividly recall a rush of anxiety on my part when the waiter asked for wine orders and Herman said, "Let's let the general select the wine."

Not being a connoisseur of wine but astute enough to see that the price ranged from $35 to $350 a bottle, I zeroed in on Oteia, Herman's wife, who appeared to be the rainmaker among the group and asked her preference. Oteia cut through the niceties and made her preference known, and everybody else agreed with her choice. The meal was great, the conversation lively, and Jesse Hill defused the mystery of the occasion by announcing that he wanted to introduce me to Maynard Jackson, mayor of Atlanta, because in his opinion the mayor could use the organizational skills of a general.

In my chief of staff role at Second Army, I presided over austere reductions in our civilian workforce. The reductions were a part of the army's goals to reduce personnel in military headquarters, and through a series of voluntary retirements and elimination of duplicate functions, we met our goals. The only bright spot in our lives was attendance at Super Bowl XXIV in New Orleans, LA. Betty's brother "MO" was the running back coach for the Denver Broncos, and her father joined us in Atlanta for the journey to

New Orleans.

The best part of the trip was spending time with the family and meeting John Elway and some of the Denver players. The Broncos were busted by Joe Montano and the San Francisco 49ers in a 55 to 10 rout.

The grand excitement of Atlanta winning the bid to host the 1996 Olympics was announced in September 1990 and lifted the spirits of everyone in Atlanta and probably in all of America. I remember reading the headline in the Atlanta Journal Constitution. "It's Atlanta!" the headline screamed in bold print. I caught the excitement and wished that I could be part of the effort to prepare the city for the Olympic Games. I had not heard anything from Jesse Hill about meeting with Maynard Jackson and speculated that the idea had died of impracticality. That an unknown general would be interviewed by the mayor who just landed the summer Olympic Games was not a likely scenario, and I forgot about it.

In the fall of 1990, the army was mobilizing reserve and National Guard units for possible duty in the Middle East, and I was deep into coordinating Second Army units for training and possible call-up. During this hectic time, Jesse Hill phoned to tell me that a meeting had been arranged for me with Mayor Maynard Jackson. I recall that the meeting was characterized as a thirty-minute meet and greet, so I prepared myself for a handshake and a few pleasantries.

To my surprise, the meeting lasted over ninety minutes, and Maynard offered me the job as chief of staff. I thanked him and told him that I would not be able to retire from the army as a brigadier general until March 3, 1991. He wrote a note to himself, and I returned home full of excitement about the job offer, but still not convinced that it was going to happen.

The army mobilization effort went into high gear over the Christmas holiday, and I was assigned to the NTC to assist in preparing the Georgia National Guard Forty-Eighth Infantry

Brigade for mobilization and duty in Iraq. The Forty-eighth Brigade trained exceptionally hard to become certified and achieved that distinction on the day the US troops defeated the Iraq Army. The officers and soldiers were excited over their accomplishment and a little disappointed that the war was over before they could get there.

On March 3, 1990, somewhere in the middle of the Mojave Desert, I received a note delivered by a sergeant major that Maynard Jackson had left a telephone message for me to call him. I looked at the note and was flabbergasted that Maynard remembered the date of my retirement eligibility as brigadier general. I hurriedly drove back to the office area of the NTC and called the number, and Maynard simply said, "General, it is time." Convinced of his sincerity, I told him I would submit my retirement papers when I returned to Fort McPherson and that we could work out the date that I would assume my duties as the chief of staff.

Betty was surprised and excited about the job confirmation. Likewise, Lieutenant General Crysel, my new boss, and General Ed Burba, FORSCOM commander, were also surprised but elated that one of their number had been elevated to a high-visibility position in the city that had just been awarded the 1996 Olympic Games. The newspaper headlines announced my appointment and the excitement among our neighbors on Staff Row was palpable. Brigadier and major generals retiring at Fort McPherson were normally not accorded a full retirement review, but General Burba made an exception for my retirement. And Mayor Maynard Jackson's involvement in our retirement ceremony as a guest of honor elevated the occasion and made a special day even more important to Betty and me.

The retirement ceremony was a great and symbolic way to end my military career that spanned thirty years, eight months, and seventeen days. Our sons, grandson, and daughter-in-law, my brother and his wife, sisters, Betty's brother, friends, military, and civilian came early and stayed late. Some like Brig. Gen. Julius

Johnson, the second graduate from Lincoln (MO) to be promoted to brigadier general, presented me a handsome clock to commemorate our connections: LU, same birth date, Kappa Alpha Psi and Andy Chambers. He too worked under Andy Chambers in Germany and earned his star in VII Corps.

I selected Col. "Jack" Holley, Second Army personnel director, to be the commander of troops. As he and I reviewed the line of troops, I fondly recalled the progress in race relations and equal opportunity during the more than thirty-year span from my days as a lieutenant in the 1960s to my retirement as a brigadier general in 1991. With each step Jack Holley and I made as we rounded the turn during my final review of the troops, I was thankful to God, Betty, family, and friends that we were born in the United States of America. And as the troops passed the reviewing stand, I was thankful that it only took one star to make you a general.

Insights Gleaned from General Officer Status

My insights from "It only takes one to make you a general" are intended to apply to any promotion that elevates one to a position where the perks, protocols, customs, and courtesies largely define the behavior of the incumbent and his or her response to subordinates. Entry into the general officer ranks visibly changes the status and expectations of those promoted to the one-star insignia or rank of a brigadier general in the US Army. Andy Chambers was right when he said it only takes one to make you a general even though a one star is at the bottom of the general officer rank structure. Without exception all are addressed as "general."

I did not want the accoutrements of rank and position to change my core values as an American of African descent and army officer dedicated to creating a military organization where both officers and soldiers could be all that they could be without regard to their race, color, or ethnicity. My thoughts on doing business as a general officer penned in my "You're Gonna Be One" mock booklet were prompted by my observations. I had witnessed firsthand situations in which general officers, black and white, had failed in their duty to address issues of inequality in promotions, assignments, and awards. The creed worked for me because of my strong belief that officers, and especially black officers, had a duty to address issues of racial bias. Moreover, they should actively help the commander to correct or expunge such inhibitors from the command. I attempted to help my commanders at Fort Hood and Fort Gillem establish an environment of fairness for soldiers, civilians, and family members.

Not receiving a second star was a big disappointment. When the two- star list was released in the spring of 1989 and my name was not on it, my mentor Andy Chambers and good friend Ernie Harrell, who was on the list, called and expressed their regrets. No one in my chain of command called or offered an explanation as to why I was not selected, and I accepted the nonselection as a signal to prepare for retirement as a brigadier general and to find a good-paying civilian job in Atlanta.

Lt. Gen. "Cotton" Whiddon's efforts to promote my talents paid handsome dividends in my civilian job search. Whiddon was a true champion of promoting my skills and abilities as his chief of staff to General Powell. Also, being included on the guest list with the other generals under Powell's command afforded us valuable exposure and introductions to influential businessmen that led to my appointment as Maynard Jackson's chief of staff for the city of Atlanta. There is a famous saying in the black church that "God never closes a door without leaving a window open."

I could not have penned a Hollywood script that would come close to the influential characters and sequence of events that made it possible for me to go from not being selected for a second star in the US Army to becoming chief of staff for the city of Atlanta, GA, the coveted site of the 1996 Summer Olympic Games.

I attribute the blueprint for that phenomenal turn of events to a steadfast belief that God had a purpose for my life and all I had to do was be faithful, do the best I could, and be open to new opportunities. Keeping the faith in the midst of unfolding events that give no hint or indication of what you are hoping and praying for is more difficult than it appears. There were days, weeks, and months without an encouraging word from General Officer Management Branch about promotion to a second star or from Jesse Hill and his companions about prospects of a job with Maynard Jackson and the city of Atlanta. I prayed while working on restoring a family-owned wooden icebox, stayed involved with my duties as chief of staff, accepted invitations to speak in the Atlanta community, and prayed some more.

My interview with Maynard Jackson came in October or November 1990 and was labeled a thirty-minute meet and greet affair by Jesse Hill. The ninety- minute meeting surprisingly ended with a job offer that led to my appointment as Maynard's chief of staff in April 1991. Faith, prayer, hard work, and trust are a prescription that I endorse for those disappointed over a lack of promotion opportunity and uncertain about their future employment opportunities.

My thirty years, eight months, and seventeen days in the US Army were commemorated by a full review of troops on the Fort McPherson parade field at Fort Mac. It was a glorious day, attended by our family, friends, and wellwishers. Jack Holley, my commander of troops, and I "trooped the line" together and brought to a glorious finish a full cycle of civil rights gains. I had gone from second lieutenant in a struggling, racially integrated army in 1960 with no African American generals on active military duty to being one of eighty African Americans promoted to general officer rank in the decades of the 1970s to the 1990s.

Army Retirement Parade Atlanta—Fort
McPherson, GA, 1991. Col. "Jack" Holley, commander of troops.

CHAPTER TWENTY

My Camelot Experience in Atlanta

My experience with Atlanta city government is best characterized by the word surprise. My arrival at city hall in April 1991 surprised most of the executives and city employees, and my departure in January 1993 caught everyone, including my wife, off guard. My time with Maynard Jackson, mayor of Atlanta, and Atlanta City government was exciting, challenging, and educational from beginning to end.

I went from chief of staff to chief operating officer in less than six months because of the accelerating pace of events surrounding preparations for the 1996 Olympic Games. Maynard was on his third term as Atlanta mayor and was a charismatic and dynamic leader. His leadership style was more that of "decide and announce" than to rely on study and recommendations from staff and executive advisors. I succeeded Cecilia Hunter as chief of staff and learned from her and John Reid, chief operating officer, that they were still looking for the money to pay my salary while my paperwork as a new city employee was being processed.

The positive benefit of Maynard's leadership style was a legacy of innovations for the city that would probably not have been realized through consensus and staff recommendations. They not only found the money for my salary but also found the funds to include me on an orientation trip to Spain, the site of the 1992 summer Olympics.

Leadership Style

As a professional army officer, I'd had lots of experience working for "decide and announce" leaders. Although unfamiliar with the political arena of Atlanta, I learned rapidly how to implement Maynard's "decide and announce" goals and objectives.

Maynard was a tremendous mentor and resource provider in my orientation to Atlanta history and politics. He was fiercely proud of his grandfather, John Wesley Dobbs, business man and leader in "Sweet Auburn," the black business district during the 1940s and 1950s, and gave me several windshield driving tours of Atlanta to show me how the city had progressed from racial segregation to the 1990s.

I soaked up his deep admiration for the "Atlanta Way" along with his progressive strategy of cooperation between African Americans and the white business community in order to prevent racial complaints and social unrest from escalating into riots or destruction of property. As the first black mayor of Atlanta, Maynard credited Mayor Allen Iverson with insight and action that created the "Atlanta Way," enabling him to build coalitions that made the city the crown jewel of the south. I also sensed Maynard's passion for leveling the economic playing field for minorities and especially African Americans, as he identified public places and businesses that discriminated against serving or hiring minorities. I also bore witness to his pride regarding the role that his alma mater, Morehouse College, had played alongside Spelman College, Morris Brown, and Clark Atlanta University in preparing black leaders to move Atlanta and America forward.

He was very fiercely proud and protective of Pashcal's Motel and Restaurant as the home of the Civil Rights Movement, and his praise for the wealth achieved by Atlanta Life Insurance Company as well as his admiration for Jesse Hill, chairman emeritus of that historic business, was enormous. Our windshield tours also included wealthy neighborhoods like Buckhead to impoverished areas like Vine City. He never failed to point out to me, as his new chief of staff, the central importance of maintaining contact with residents in all areas of the city. He also stressed the importance of city employees living within the city limits of Atlanta and was pleased that Betty and I purchased the former house of the president of Morehouse College in Southwest Atlanta on Flamingo Drive. His windshield tours were a great help to me during my visits with the eighteen-member Atlanta City Council. His mentoring skills and historical background on the city was a key factor in gaining their unanimous confirmation to serve as the mayor's chief of staff.

In my role as chief of staff, I supervised the legislative agenda with the council and county and state governmental agencies and Maynard's special staff that included public affairs, educational outreach, and special projects. I hired Eva Butler Jones, a city employee and a sergeant in the Army Reserves, to be my administrative assistant. Her familiarity with army protocols and leadership principles facilitated communication between Maynard's administrative assistants and my subordinates. I also recommended Col. John Holly, who was hired by Maynard to jumpstart his pride and joy, the Maynard Jackson Youth Foundation. John was totally dedicated to the foundation, often used his personal funds to cover expenses, and remained as the director for nearly twenty years.

Eve and John provided a bridge and successfully integrated my military leadership approach to improving the effectiveness of meetings at city hall. During one of my first "all hands" meeting with my staff, the biggest issue raised was a question regarding my preference for how I wanted to be addressed.

Following established protocols within the mayor's office where everyone called him Maynard, I said that they could call me by my first name or "general." All but one staff member said they were more comfortable with the title of "general." The lone dissenter, a veteran of the army, disdained using any titles that reminded him of his unpleasant experience in the military and opted to refer to me by my first name. I agreed and he seemed relieved.

My staff's advice and counsel helped me to navigate Maynard's rules of fairness and governance.

Minority Inclusion

My first lesson on Maynard's rules came from his request for me to review a contract proposal to construct a railway system between terminals at Hartsfield Atlanta Airport. This task was assigned during my first week on the job, and I was eager to prove my ability to synchronize the legal aspects of compliance with the city's contracting regulations.

I completed my review over a weekend, reported to Maynard that the contract met all requirements, and gave him the completed contract and a pen for him to sign it. He did not take the contract but asked how many African Americans were on the company's board of directors. Puzzled, my reply was that the city's contracting regulations did not require a bidding company to provide the identity of their board of directors.

Maynard responded that he required the information and instructed me to call Vernon Jordan, a native of Atlanta, former chairman of the National Urban League, and a lawyer well-connected to Fortune 500 companies. Jordan's role would be to provide assistance to the mayor's office in communicating the need for the company to have a minority on their board of directors in order to do business at the Atlanta Airport. Maynard's secretary found Vernon vacationing in the Mediterranean and arranged a phone connection. I introduced myself and the purpose of the call, passed the phone to Maynard, and listened as he gave his rationale for inclusion of African Americans on the company's board. He asked Jordan to convey that message to the chairman of the board. I was more than impressed. This was quintessential Maynard, acting heroically in the interest of fairness and equality away from the spotlight of public opinion.

I was even more impressed with his resolve to achieve inclusion of minorities on city contracts when the company sent him a letter promising to add a minority member to their board of directors. I hurriedly took the letter and the contract to him for signature only to be told, "I will need a name and a date of appointment before signing the contract." He added, "By the way, tell them that for this particular requirement, a female does not substitute for an African American." The requirement was met in record time, and Maynard signed the contract. My second steep-learning curve as chief of staff was being asked to create an office of Gay and Lesbian Outreach. Maynard saw the look on my face and asked if I had a problem with the task. I explained that the military culture had conditioned me to avoid the issue and requested a day to examine my thoughts on the matter. He granted me the time and then volunteered that he was not a champion of gay and lesbian sexual orientation, but as mayor of Atlanta, he was obligated to see that all citizens were treated fairly. He gave examples of how they were discriminated against and informed me that he had promised in his last election campaign to establish an office of Gay and Lesbian Outreach.

That night I mentioned the conversation to Betty and told her I had to think on it. Her immediate reply was, "You are no longer in the army. Maynard is your boss and has told you what he wants you to do." I agreed with Betty's logic, completely embraced Maynard's commitment to eradicate discrimination against all people regardless of their race, gender, or sexual orientation, and immediately set in motion the process to staff the new office.

The interviews for the position were interesting and, in one instance, challenging. One of the candidates, a lesbian, entered my office, looked at my military mementos, and began to interrogate me on my ability to be impartial to the gay or lesbian person hired to manage the office of Gay and Lesbian Outreach. She did not get the job but inadvertently helped me to establish questions for future candidates for the position that did not involve the candidate's sexual orientation. I established the first office of Gay and Lesbian Outreach, and Maynard was highly impressed with the quality and quantity of work accomplished by the office.

The chief of staff position afforded me many opportunities to meet important people in the city of Atlanta as well as others on the national stage. My introduction to the corporate executives of Atlanta was another example of the power Maynard Jackson exerted in the business community. The group was led by the late Roberto Goizueta, chairman and chief executive officer of Coca-Cola, who along with the CEOs of Georgia Power, Georgia Pacific, and about thirty other powerbrokers all filled the room to hear Maynard's update on the upcoming benefits to Atlanta as host of the 1996 Olympics. I was humbled at the warm reception I received as Maynard's new chief of staff and attributed their high regard for general officers to the stellar accomplishments of generals like Colin Powell, Norm Schwarzkopf, and their predecessors of World War II fame.

The most amazing dynamic among the leaders in the room was the deference shown to Goizueta by his colleagues, who, in turn, set the tone for Maynard to shine as the man of the hour. This feat was accomplished via their eloquent requests for all present to give their undivided attention and support to Atlanta's mayor. The exchange between them was like a well-rehearsed play with Maynard balancing his presentation with equal parts of solicitude and incentives offered to gain their participation.

Important Visitor

On another occasion, while walking through the mayor's reception room, I noticed a well-dressed man sitting erect and thumbing through magazines. I didn't think much of it until about forty-five minutes later when I noticed that he was still there. I introduced myself and asked the nature of his visit. He replied, "I am Bill Clinton, governor of Arkansas. I am running for president of the United States and just stopped by to see Mayor Jackson." His name did not ring a bell with me or the receptionist who had notified Maynard's secretary of Clinton's desire to see him. I excused myself, told Maynard about Clinton's long wait in his reception room, and learned that Maynard was not eager to meet with him because Clinton was looking for endorsements while Maynard was committed to the candidacy of Sen. Sam Nunn, who was also thinking of running for the presidency. Maynard told me to escort Clinton to his office, asked me to sit in, and after hearing Clinton's request for his support, politely encouraged his candidacy without promising to endorse him. Nunn did not run, and Maynard endorsed Clinton for president.

The novelty of having a retired general at city hall in Atlanta spread to Fulton County, where they hired Maj. Gen. John Stanford as the county manager. This was the first time in history that both the city and the county had two African American generals in senior leadership positions. John and I had never met until our paths crossed in Atlanta. We along with our wives, Betty and Patrica, became great friends during our journey of transitioning from the army into the politics of Atlanta. On the social and political fronts, Felker Ward, a military retiree with enormous stature as a successful businessman in Atlanta, and his wife, Mary, helped us to make a smooth transition into the exclusive circles of the city and county power elites.

I was getting comfortable in the chief of staff position when John Reid, an executive on loan from Coca-Cola, then serving as chief operating officer for the city, announced that he was returning to his position at Coca Cola in December 1991. Maynard asked if I was interested in the position, and I could barely hide my eagerness to take charge of the operational departments of the city. However, my enthusiasm about getting things done was met with challenges my military career had ill prepared me to handle. And like most overconfident executives, I did not see the showstoppers until the performance was well on its way.

My initial exposure to the world of managing the delivery of city services occurred when Maynard asked me to accompany him to a community town hall meeting. There were about fifty residents at the meeting, and before opening the floor for questions, Maynard introduced me as the new chief operating officer, made a point of emphasizing my background as a general in the army, and assured the audience that he had hired me to make the trains run on time at city hall. The complaints flowed one after another about the repeated requests to repair potholes in the streets, about garbage not being picked up on time, and about phone calls to city hall not being answered. Maynard said we would look into their complaints and asked me if I wanted to say anything. Eager to convince them of my sincerity, I vowed to use the city's resources to redress their grievances. I waxed eloquent and even promised that they would not only receive the requested services but also receive them in a timely manner.

On the way back to the city hall, Maynard explained that the residents of that community had never voted for him in the three times that he was elected mayor. I realized that I had made a big speech and promised more than I could prudently deliver and said as much. Maynard used the opportunity to emphasize an axiom of political life that remained constant: you always deliver for those who vote for you. On a humorous note, he also said that if I did manage to deliver, maybe they would vote for him if he chose to run for a fourth term or possibly for me if I decided to run for mayor. I assured him that I had no interest in running for political office and that I would make sure resources would always be used to support his voting constituents.

Challenges of the Democratic Process

The next no-brainer came on the heels of my assumption of chief operating officer duties when Maynard told me that a group of homeless people had built a makeshift community under the MLK Bridge and that their presence was delaying the start of construction work on the Georgia Dome. Again, I knew that my military background and leadership experience could resolve this issue within twenty-four hours. I called in Police Chief Eldrin Bell, a get-it-done leader, along with Michael Pack, chief of public works. A crisp order was issued for the immediate removal of the homeless community from under the bridge. As expected, Chief Bell assured me that they would be gone within twenty-four hours while Michael Pack raised so many legal issues that I had not considered that I sought the counsel of the city attorney. By the time the legal issues were identified, added to county and state interests, and the raised voices of advocates for the homeless, what I thought could be handled in twenty- four hours actually took more than thirty days to resolve.

The weekly meetings I chaired to discuss and develop an action plan to remove and relocate the homeless expanded to more than twenty-five interested parties and included the "mayor" of the homeless community. This thorny lesson in the democratic process modified my tendency to issue decisive orders before exploring cause and effect. The homeless community was successfully relocated, and the Atlanta Journal Constitution praised the mayor for the thoughtful and considerate approach taken to resolve the issue.

The least enjoyable task during my brief tenure as chief of staff and as chief operating officer was canvassing city council member votes on legislation of interest to Maynard that would be addressed at the Monday city council meetings. I spent whole weekends prior to those meetings attempting to contact council members and finally figured out that failure to call me back usually meant the council member was not supportive of Maynard's legislative agenda.

Even though I had good relations with Council President Marvin Arrington, Bill Campbell (former mayor), and Thomas Cuffie, Maynard's floor manager for legislation important to the mayor's agenda, my implementation of several decisions regarding the Atlanta Airport operations created friction between me and some council members. The first episode occurred within weeks of my appointment as the chief operating officer. The airport director, a former city council member, was implicated in illegal business dealings at the airport, and Maynard directed that I should fire him from the position without advance notice to him or the city council. The concern was that advance notice might give him opportunity to remove documents and evidence of his illegal transactions from the files in his possession. I coordinated his removal with the city attorney and security officials at the airport and made a surprise visit to the airport director's office. I read him his rights, supervised the removal of papers from his office files, changed the locks on doors to his office, and escorted him out of the building.

The council members were informed, and no issues were raised over my role in his removal. Maynard appointed an acting airport commissioner and approved the posting to hire a replacement for the position. A good number of candidates met the job qualifications, and I was in the process of scheduling interviews to select the best candidate for the position when Maynard was diagnosed with multiple blockages in his heart arteries. He was also scheduled to have immediate bypass surgery to remove the blockages.

However, prior to the surgery, Maynard agreed that I would proceed with the selection of an airport commissioner. Meanwhile, over the course of the next three weeks, I had narrowed the candidates to three, arranged for city council members on the airport committee to interview the three selected, and vetted them with Maynard's trusted advisors. A vocal outcry erupted from several city council members when they learned that I favored a white candidate and intended to nominate him to be the airport commissioner. I delayed further action until Maynard returned from sick leave.

Much to my surprise, on Maynard's first day back in the office, I passed by a glass-enclosed office and recognized Cuffie, Campbell, and Maynard in the room. Curious, I knocked on the door, stuck my head in, and asked if there was anything going on that I should know about. Maynard said that the two floor members were updating him on legislative issues that arose during his absence and that he would brief me later.

This was the first time I had been excluded from a meeting with the mayor's floor leaders, and I suspected that they were discussing my choice of candidate for airport commissioner. Since I had fully informed him of the candidate I proposed to nominate before sharing the information with the council members and shared with him the names of his advisors that knew or had interviewed and recommended the candidate for the position, I was disappointed when he suggested that we could extend the search and raise the salary to attract more qualified candidates. I understood and accepted that extending the search and raising the salary circumvented a vote on the candidate of my choice and paved the way for a candidate of their choice and color. The issue diminished my regard for some council member's objectivity in selecting candidates for city positions, but not my resolve to improve services to Atlanta residents.

The city's contracting process was one of those services that were perceived by some of Maynard's supporters to need changing. Sometime during the spring of 1992, Maynard came to my office to tell me of complaints he had received from some of his supporters. The allegation was that some business people who did not support his reelection were being awarded more contracts than his supporters, and he asked me to look into the bidding process. I had difficulty getting information from the contracting officer and decided to replace him. I appointed Joe Hall, retired army colonel, veteran city employee, former supervisor of taxi cab and vehicles for hire, and a trusted friend of many years. Joe left no issue unexamined and within a short time provided data that revealed that unsuccessful bidders were disqualified for their inability to meet the city's bonding requirements. Satisfied that contracting application procedures were fair to all applicants, I briefed Maynard on our findings, and he urged us to find a way to help applicants to meet the bonding requirements. We established seminars for applicants, identified ways to get around the bonding issue by partnering with bidders who met bonding requirements, and assisted in filling out applications. Unsuccessful bidders continued to complain to Maynard, and he continued to urge me to find a way to improve their chances to successfully compete for city contracts. We doubled our assistance programs, agreed to maintain the integrity of the contracting process, and even advocated partnerships with successful bidders. Nonetheless, the issue remained a source of tension for me and manifested itself in ways that I least expected.

In the fall of 1992, there were no burning issues or controversies at city hall or identified by the news media involving city government. So when my phone rang on a Sunday morning in November and Maynard asked if I could come down to meet with him at the office to talk about his plans for the future, I was not alarmed. Our grandson, Taylor, was visiting with us, and I told Betty that I was going down to meet with Maynard for a few hours. When I walked into Maynard's office, he looked relaxed, greeted me warmly, and said that he was thinking about running for a fourth term as mayor. Consequently, he wanted to go over a few changes he thought he should make to assure his success if he decided to run.

I listened as he explained the rigors of campaigning and the toll it would take on his administration and the governing process. My ears perked up, however, when he suggested that he needed to bring in a seasoned administrator to serve as chief operating officer during the campaign. He wanted my reaction to vacating the position so he could make that happen. My response was to ask if he was firing me, to which he quickly said no, that I was doing a good job and that I could move into the airport commissioner's position. Without hesitation, I heard myself saying that moving out of the chief operating officer's job would be unacceptable but that I would give him my resignation, leaving him free to organize his administration in way he chose as well as to run for reelection.

We talked about thirty minutes more, with him saying it was not his intention for me to leave his administration. My immediate response was to inform him that I had been contemplating starting a boot camp for youth and that resigning would give me the opportunity to do so. We agreed that my resignation would not be announced until the Christmas holiday season and would not be effective until January 1993. We concluded the conversation with a cordial exchange while I had yet to fully comprehend that I had terminated my employment.

Betty was shocked, absolutely flabbergasted, and couldn't believe her ears when I told her I had resigned from my position. I recounted the details of the meeting play by play, what Maynard said, what I said, but was unable to give her any satisfactory answer about how I was going to get a job or pay our bills. In fact, I had no idea what I was going to do. I was earning $90,000.00 a year as the chief operating officer but resigning meant giving that up to live on $60,000.00 in military retirement pay. Betty thought I had lost my mind. However, the money had never crossed my mind at the time of my decision; the only thing I had thought about was protecting my integrity and not being treated as an object of expediency to satisfy Maynard's reelection goals.

Betty expressed solemn disappointment with my decision, told me exactly how she felt, and continually reminded me that I was too old to start a boot camp. Still, I felt that I had made the right decision, factored in my discomfort with the pressure to help qualify applicants for city contracts who were unable to meet bonding requirements, and had no second thoughts.

Schwarzkopf visits Atlanta city hall. Left to right: me, Schwarzkopf, and Mayor Maynard Jackson.

CHAPTER TWENTY-ONE

Leaving City Hall:
Stepping Out on Faith

Immediately following my decision, I called an "all hands" meeting and, with Maynard at my side, announced my resignation, stating my desire to pursue other opportunities. Obviously, this was a euphemism that really meant I don't know what I am going to do, but I can't or won't stay in this job. Ironically, many of my colleagues, with a wink and a nod, said they understood and admired my decision to leave on my terms. Others by their silence or terse "Good luck!" appeared glad that I was leaving. The newspaper headlines emphasized that I was leaving to pursue other opportunities while speculating that my background as a retired brigadier general might not have been a good fit for the give and take of Atlanta politics.

My fortuitous arrival at city hall surprised many city employees, and my sudden departure surprised some but was predicted by others. The farewell party given for me by Maynard was subdued and not well attended. Nevertheless, it got the job done, and I went on my way with a cloud hanging over my head that suggested that Maynard and I had had a parting of the ways but agreed to remain civil about it. From my perspective, that represented a fair summation of our relationship.

January 1993 rolled around, and everyone except me went back to work. For the first time in my adult life, I was without a job. I established an office in my basement and busied myself exploring other employment opportunities in Atlanta. I quickly discovered that no one was eager to return my phone calls except for one contact who had volunteered to advise me when I first assumed my duties as Maynard's chief of staff. He was the late Dan Sweat, chief operating officer for the Carter Center and a former chief administrative officer for the city of Atlanta. Dan took me to lunch and schooled me on my job prospects in Atlanta following my resignation from the city. The CEOs of the major corporations in Atlanta perceived that Maynard and I had a falling out, so they would not risk hiring me and getting on the wrong side of him. Dan was interested in hiring me as his assistant at the Carter Center but passed for that reason.

Nonetheless, I appreciated his candor and decided to earnestly research and design a residential program to help young adults modify their behavior and complete high school. For about thirty days, I worked out of my house, interviewed law enforcement officials, visited boot camps for youth, and came face to face with the limitations of my military retirement pay. I finally swallowed my pride and visited the unemployment office. As soon as I walked through the door of the unemployment office, one of the clerks recognized me. The clerk was also kind enough to escort me to a private office where I could complete the application process.

Fortunately, the unemployment check made it possible for me to pay my travel and lunch expenses, and Felker Ward provided me office space in his well-appointed suite of offices on downtown Peachtree Street. Paul Easley,

John Stanford, Felker Ward, and Jesse Hill were all staunch supporters from the beginning and used their resources to help me to establish an office, form a board of directors, and find resources to implement the youth uplift program.

I designed the program to use retired military personnel as teachers and built the curriculum around classroom subjects and work projects to help students earn credits toward high school graduation and promote reliability and dependability. I named the program "Structured Training for Adolescent Reform" (STAR) and, with the help of Jesse Hill, briefed Pete McTier, chairman of the Coca-Cola Foundation, on the concept and resource needs. McTier thought the concept added the missing piece to a Georgia

State youth program the foundation had agreed to fund and counseled me to collaborate with Dr. George Napper Jr., newly hired director of the Georgia Department of Juvenile Justice.

But before I could arrange a meeting with Napper, I received a call from Ernie Harrell. The major general (retired) informed me that he had recommended me to a Korn/Ferry headhunter looking for a retired general to start a youth program for President Bill Clinton. A week or so later, Bill Tobin, then vice president of Korn/Ferry International, called to ask if I was interested in taking on the job of establishing the youth corps program for President Clinton. Tobin was in Florida when he called and asked if I could meet him there for the interview. I was already headed to Florida to visit a youth corps and agreed to meet him there.

The interview with Tobin was unusual in several respects. He had interviewed over twenty-five general officers and shared his frustration that the administration had not found one that met their qualifications. He explained the quasi-military requirements of the job, the short amount of time available to establish the program, and the fact that no one in the administration had military experience. I was uncharacteristically frank in telling him that I could do the job but would have to have complete authority to hire, design, and implement the program. Tobin inquired about my experience in designing and promoting the STAR Program and asked if I would leave it to accept the Clinton position if offered. I answered in the affirmative, and he promised to call me within a week.

True to his word, Tobin called and invited me to Washington, DC to interview with Catherine Milton, a representative of the Clinton team. Catherine emphasized that the start-up of the Civilian Community Corps (CCC) would be part of President Clinton's new AmeriCorps and that I would need to meet with Eli Segal, Clinton's campaign manager and newly appointed chief executive officer of the Corporation for National Service. I gave her my can-do speech with conditions of complete authority, and she eagerly arranged an interview for me with Eli and Shirley Sagawa, his primary assistant. The interview with Segal and Sagawa netted their approval, and I was offered the position.

Back in Atlanta, Maynard called to congratulate me on my new position and volunteered that he had given my leadership abilities high marks in his recommendation to President Clinton. I thanked him for his support, and from that moment until his death in 2003, we resumed cordial relations as if nothing had ever happened between us. Betty was extremely happy that I got the position, and we began planning for the move to Washington. I thanked all my supporters of the STAR program, suspended all pending arrangements, and concentrated on finalizing arrangements to leave Atlanta.

Insights: The Atlanta Experience

Atlanta holds a special place in my life because my appointment to the highest executive positions in Atlanta city government offered incredible opportunities. The emotional highs and lows inspired joyful exhilaration as well as profound introspection when searching for answers to difficult problems. My experience in that great city reaffirmed that friends could share the highs as well as help with building your dreams no matter how farfetched they may seem.

It is easy to be happy when you are among the elite, lavish with attention, and have all your materiel needs taken care of. My resignation drastically shifted our status away from the center of attention and being sought after to being on the outskirts of the mainstream and shunned. Most of what I cherish about life surfaced when I was down and out. It surged to the top like a lifeboat when I was struggling to hang on to my integrity and prove myself worthy in the eyes of my wife and close friends. Integrity and friends are the most important things after food, shelter, and clothing.

Using race or ethnicity as a factor in the hiring process is always wrong no matter the race or ethnicity of the user. Being challenged on my selection for the airport director on the basis of my race was an affront to me, and the first indicator that my sense of fair play was at odds with many members of the city council. In my view, a multiracial city should seek a highly qualified and diverse workforce to service the population it represents. Unfortunately, many on the city council justified the use of race as a factor in the hiring of the airport director on the basis that a color-blind hiring process could open the way for a downslide back to all white control of the city. I hope that view has given way to hiring a racially diverse and highly qualified staff in the city too busy to hate.

Giving orders that negatively impact the lives of others is easy when given from the safety of plush surroundings and out of view and hearing of those that will be the object of the order. Like a nail hitting a sledgehammer, my reality was restored when the "mayor" of the homeless community was present at the meeting to remove his community from their makeshift shelters under the Martin Luther King Bridge in Atlanta. The military's attempt to keep its leaders focused on the impact of decisions on those who must carry out their orders is reinforced by mandating that all officers must start as lieutenants and that sergeants must start out as privates. Perhaps all organizations—and especially the US Congress—should include a representative from the poor and disenfranchised when deliberating issues that will negatively impact them. An impromptu meeting called by your boss just for the two of you on a weekend should trigger your senses to sound a red alert. When Maynard called me that Sunday morning to meet him in the office around churchgoing time, I naively believed that I was part of the solution and not the problem. By asking me to respond to his proposal to vacate my position so that he could appoint someone else during his run for a fourth term triggered my ego rather than my survival instincts. The time tested and proven adage to not let your ego get in the way of your job did not occur to me at the time.

A different approach may have spared me and Betty the belt-tightening experience of living without the $90,000 salary I gave up when I resigned my position. My problem was failure to recognize the warning signs inherent in a meeting called on a Sunday and preparing myself for the possibility of an ambush. My advice is to stay on the alert for odd or unusual requests from your boss.

Friends don't beat you over the head for making what might appear to be a dumb or ill-advised decision; they use their influence to help you move on and prosper in a new direction. Paul Easley, Jesse Hill, John Standford, Felker Ward, and their wives stuck with us and used their considerable contacts in Atlanta to help me get support for my youth program concept. Friends like Ernie Harrell also volunteered their help rather than wait to be asked. Try not to make dumb mistakes, but choose friends wisely just in case you do.

Just as unlikely as my appointment as Maynard Jackson's chief of staff when I was looking to retire from the army was the call from the search firm, Korn/Ferry International, when I was looking to establish a youth development program. Some call it luck, others call it interesting, and I call it grace from God.

Korn/Ferry was nowhere in my consciousness, nor I in theirs until a friend, Ernie Harrell, on a chance meeting with Bill Tobin on an airplane learned of his organization's search for a retired general and mentioned my name. Serendipitous occurrences of such unlikely events have been chronicled throughout my memoir. Believe that you were born with a purpose in life and watch doors open to inexplicable opportunities at the times when they are most needed. It is called amazing grace for a reason.

CHAPTER TWENTY-TWO

NCCC Start-Up:
A Race against Time

My leadership in establishing the AmeriCorps NCCC is my greatest contribution to the American dream. Thousands of young men and women, eighteen and twenty-four years old, from all cultural and economic backgrounds of America have experienced the benefits of volunteering for a nine-month residential program; their work in national parks, urban and rural communities, and disaster relief operations builds better communities, restores the environment, and helps disaster-relief victims recover.

Those of us who started the program also lived the dream because we too were from diverse racial, economic, educational, and professional backgrounds and wanted to establish a national service program that was open to all American youth to do the kind of work and in the age group cited above.

Although most of us were military veterans, we had a strong contingent from the Peace Corps, nonprofit civic programs, and secondary education teachers. This group of passionate and dedicated founders was led by my army colonels and navy captains who embraced the vision of the founding legislatures, hired committed staff, and rigorously implemented my guidance to design and open the program at four campus location across the country. The leaders like Cols. Lew Heffner, Fred Peters, and Sarah Whitman (honorary colonel) at Washington, DC headquarters; Jo Ann Jolivet and Don Mathis (honorary colonel) at Aberdeen, MD; Jules Hampton at Denver; Naval Capt. Jeff Biel at Charleston; and Paul Johnson at San Diego embraced and modeled my five Cs: "communication, commitment, collaboration, compassion, and cooperation" that I wanted to guide our establishment of the program and influence corps members' behavior in the execution of their nine-month residential service program.

As of this writing the program and corps member behavior has not strayed from the five Cs in its twenty-year existence. Campus locations have changed, directors have come and gone, Federal Emergency Management Administration (FEMA) teams have joined NCCC, but continuity in some personnel still remains. Lequan Robeson started as a unit leader at Perry Point and continues as the campus director at Baltimore. Tom Bryant started as my lawyer and still does legal work for the Corporation of National and Community Service (CNCS). Charles Davenport started at Denver, moved to San Diego, was campus director at Washington, DC, has filled in wherever the need exists, and is still with CNCS. Kate Becker, one of my first hires, served as campus director at the DC campus and currently chairs the NCCC Advisory Board. She succeeded Gen. David Jones, former chairman of the Joint Chiefs of Staff, and Dick Carver, former mayor of Peoria and assistant secretary of the air force. Tony Perez, Milwaukee, WI, whom I appointed, continues on the board. Had I the vision to look beyond twenty years, I would have added "Continuity" to make six Cs, but my hindsight was corrected by these dedicated founders/leaders still with the program plus two of my first hires, Fred Peters and Merlene Mazyck, who served as national directors. Even more impressive in the ranks of "Continuity" is the complete list of 1st year pioneers still with the program at the end of this chapter.

My declaration of the NCCC being my greatest contribution to the American dream explains my reasons but not the herculean efforts to beat the clock and start the program. My approach did not consider failure or delay as an option.

As a Washington outsider, I approached the task with a determined attitude of doing whatever needed to be done to meet the deadline. Most Americans think of Washington, DC as the place where tax dollars go and get spent by elected officials out of touch with the rest of America. As a career military officer, I was well aware of the perception among my peers that Washington, DC was synonymous with the Pentagon and was a necessary assignment if one aspired to become a general officer. I found neither of these assumptions to be true. My acceptance of the position of director of the NCCC came after my retirement as an army brigadier general and was my first assignment to Washington, DC. I had no preconceived notions of how to get the job done.

The NCCC only existed on paper when I was recruited to become the program's director and chief architect. From day one, I made it known that yes, I would take on the formidable challenge of hammering out a blueprint, hiring senior staff, recruiting eligible candidates, and getting the organization up and running by the one-year deadline date, but that I would have to do it my way. The project began as a race against time since it was widely feared that the money for the massive federal undertaking would be diverted elsewhere if we did not move forward with deliberate speed. What was first called the CCC was initially the brainchild of sixteen bipartisan US senators and was considered to be the most inclusive program ever created by the federal government for sixteen- to twenty-four-year-old American youth. The program's legislative sponsors borrowed the best features from the US Military, the Civilian Conservation Corps of the 1930s, and the Peace Corps to create a hybrid civilian residential national service program.

I added the word "national" in front of the title in order to avoid confusion with President Franklin Roosevelt's CCC of the 1930s. Thereafter, the organization became known as the NCCC. The program's core mission would be to recruit youthful participants who would help to bolster undermanned projects in the areas of public safety, education, and the environment (working in local, state, and national parks) in communities across America. In return for their service, the participants would be housed on downsized or closed military bases, supervised and trained by a cadre of military veterans, and guided by former Peace Corps volunteers and community service professionals. They would receive a monthly stipend for their service. Moreover, at the completion of their ten-month tour, they would receive an education award of $4,725 or half of that amount as a cash award.

On December 7, 1992, the bipartisan senators successfully appealed to president elect Clinton to adopt the old CCC model as part of his National Service and Community Trust Act of 1993, and the money was carried over until the end of 1994. I was hired in the fall of 1993 to establish the aforementioned version of the CCC, and with the concurrence and recommendation of newly appointed CNCS CEO Eli Segal, President Bill Clinton appointed me as the director of the CCC. At the time of my hiring, we had one year to use the money or risk losing it to the treasury or other programs. The time crunch along with several other major challenges threatened the fledgling organization's viability before it even got off the launching pad. Ironically, it was the high hurdles facing us that made the start-up of the NCCC one of the most interesting and rewarding periods of my life.

One of the more intriguing aspects of my appointment as NCCC director was the move to Washington, DC itself. Betty and I had many military friends, some still on active duty and others retired, who helped us navigate the housing market and the city's transportation system. Knowledge of both areas was necessary to thrive in the DC area. Betty, as is her trademark, quickly established our residence and learned to navigate the I-95 corridor within weeks of her arrival. We found the city and area to be charming, full of historical and cultural sites to visit, and populated by people from all over the world. As a small town person, I marveled at how the DC melting pot blended people from all walks of life into a vibrant multicultural region. I wish more Americans had the opportunity to visit DC; I think they would come away with a greater appreciation for the cultural institutions that preserve and promote our heritage. An added bonus: entry into most of the city's historic institutions is free.

Getting things done in the many bureaucracies that make up Washington is often dependent upon titles and position within the three branches of government: legislative, executive, and judicial. My title of retired general coupled with my appointment as NCCC director by President Bill Clinton opened doors to needed resources in the executive and legislative branches that would have been closed otherwise. However, titles and appointments are no substitute for competence, knowledge, and courtesy in building relationships that are the real currency to get things done in Washington and elsewhere. Personally, I found that the people who carried important titles and performed the duties of high- level appointees were caring individuals wanting to make things better for the people who depended upon their services.

Among the top people I had the opportunity to meet and rely on for NCCC start-up support were Sen. Barbara Mikulski, Eli Segal, Sen. Harris Wofford, and assistant secretary of defense, Ed Dorn. It was these four that proved to be the most helpful and dependable. Senator Mikulski chaired the committee with oversight responsibility for national service and showed a genuine interest in providing the resources needed to support the participants of the NCCC and other AmeriCorps programs. She also showed an interest in holding us accountable for using the resources for their intended purpose. Eli and Harris as CEO and CNS, respectively, made certain that resources were distributed fairly and that NCCC received the administrative and logistical support to meet our goals. Ed Dorn provided a cadre of retirement eligible military officers to jump-start the project.

National Service Programs for American Youth

The NCCC was the first federal youth program that specifically targeted youth from disadvantaged backgrounds and across the full spectrum of race, gender, and economic status in America. In fact, 50 percent of the corps members were to come from disadvantaged backgrounds, which meant enrolling nonhigh school graduates within the age group sixteen to twenty-four. We scrupulously met all the specified enrollment requirements during the start-up, but eliminated the disadvantaged percentage as well as sixteen-year-olds and high school dropouts from eligibility after the first year. The evolving CNCS policy mandated that enrollment criteria be consistent for all AmeriCorps programs and that the NCCC be transitioned from a demonstration program into becoming AmeriCorps' residential program. I welcomed the adoption into AmeriCorps but not the exclusion of NCCC's original enrollment criteria.

Disadvantaged youth come from all regions of the country: small towns, rural areas, and the inner city. They all need to have the same avenues to gain skills, knowledge, and educational opportunities that are readily available to middle-class youth. The NCCC provided every element for their success; these included a job as a member of a team made up of high school and college graduates, a safe and professionally supervised place to live on a military base, and tutorial help to complete GED requirements for those without a high school diploma. In addition, the program, once completed, provided an educational award of $4,750 for college tuition or half of that amount as a cash award for those who did not elect college. However, the cash award was also dropped after start-up. I was disappointed to see this avenue closed for the sixteen- year-olds and disadvantaged youth. I also regretted that their absence from the campus denied college graduates from middle- and upper- class families the important lessons of life that can only be taught by those determined to escape from poverty and limited educational and employment opportunities.

During our first class, we witnessed many stories about the successful learning exchanges between corps members from diverse ethnic and educational backgrounds. One example that gained visibility throughout CNS and NCCC was a testimonial by an African American NCCC member and high school dropout from Chicago. He spoke stirringly to a White House audience—that included President Clinton—about the positive impact AmeriCorps had had on his life. Those present attested to the fact that there was not a dry eye in the audience. This young man's story serves to illustrate the life-changing impact of NCCC and AmeriCorps programs. I was also told that the corps member completed his GED by the end of his NCCC tour of duty. We need more opportunities for disadvantaged youth to work, learn, and develop in programs like NCCC.

Most middle-class Americans have little or no contact with poor families who earn or live below a median income. The term "economically disadvantaged" is rarely used in the media to describe poor families and the negative educational and developmental impact their economic status has on their children. The realities are that a significant number don't finish high school, are not qualified for decent jobs, and do not have a shot at a bright future. I believe that investing in programs like the NCCC is a better avenue for children from economically disadvantaged backgrounds because the benefits are mutually distributed to all. The disadvantaged volunteer completes high school while his fellow high school and college-educated peers learn from him as well. Moreover, the taxpayers receive services from volunteers that strengthen their communities and help residents. Overall, the volunteers learn the value of teamwork and cooperation as well as gain leadership skills in a gender, ethnic, and economically diverse environment.

Corps Members Comprising the NCCC

The willingness of young adults to volunteer for a new ten-month community service program designed to help build and strengthen American communities demonstrated amazing faith in their government to deliver what it promised. These young people taught each other tolerance and taught us to let them share in the responsibility for their own governance, safety, and welfare. Most were concerned about the social problems that plagued many communities and joined in to help fix them via projects targeting public safety, education, the environment, and those caused by natural disasters.

Over fifteen thousand Americans have completed a tour with the NCCC, and their contributions have helped thousands more recover from disasters and strengthen community programs to better serve their recipients. I marvel at the strength of NCCC participants, past and present, to volunteer to serve despite persistent threats to cut funding and end the program. I hope that the NCCC will still be around for the children and grandchildren of the first class to sign up for the program.

Diversity in Federally Funded Programs

The CCC legislation mandated diversity in staff selections and in corps member selections. We moved swiftly and purposefully to achieve that goal. Interestingly, my first three hires—Heffner, Harrell, and Peters, all African Americans—prompted questions about perceptions of fairness and cronyism rather than of their qualifications and suitability for the positions. Fortunately, the CEO accepted my argument that the US military's rigorous competitive promotion system—from enlisted men to officer ranks—selects individuals on the basis of performance regardless of race or gender. We used the same criteria and selected staff on the basis of competence, trust, and loyalty. The subject of fairness and cronyism never came up again in our hiring selections. Neither did race for that matter.

We were deliberate in targeting our mailing campaign and recruitment efforts to attract volunteers and create a diverse corps. Each campus started with a diverse group that closely approximated the ethnic and gender demographics in the United States at the time. Each campus had more females than males and had more high school and college graduates than high school dropouts. It was harder to convince potential volunteers from economically disadvantaged neighborhoods to join the program. Our recruiting window was about ninety days and mostly conducted through mailings and public service announcements.

Even given our shortcomings, we met the mandate specified in the enabling legislation.

NCCC CONTINUITY ROSTER

The names listed are individuals who were on staff during the first years of the program and who are currently on staff now:

Name	Position	Current Location	Location where NCCC Staff Service Began
Charles L. Davenport, Jr.	Director of Recruit- m e nt, S e l e c - tion and Place-ment	NCCC Headquarters	Denver, CO
Tom Bryant	General Counsel	NCCC Headquarters	NCCC Headquarters Washington, DC
Erma Hodge	Executive Assistant	NCCC Headquarters	NCCC Headquarters Washington, DC
Barbara Lane	Director of Projects and Partnerships	NCCC Headquarters	San Diego, CA
Katrina Mathis	Assistant Director for Recruitment and Partnerships	NCCC Headquarters	NCCC Headquarters Washington, DC
Sharon Morioka-Es-trada	Assessment Assistant	NCCC Headquarters	San Diego, CA

Michelle Royall	Assistant Director for Projects and Partnerships	NCCC Headquarters	Charleston, SC
Dot White	Project Manager for Operations	NCCC Headquarters	Charleston, SC

Nicholas Zefran	Senior Advisor for Member Development	NCCC Headquarters	NCCC Headquarters Washington, DC
Alann App	Deputy Region Director for Unit Leadership	Denver, CO	Denver, CO
Vaughn Cottman	Unit Leader	Denver, CO	Denver, CO
Kevin Rumery	Unit Leader	Denver, CO	Denver, CO
LaQuine, Roberson	Region Director	Baltimore, MD	Aberdeen, MD
Denise Jenkins	Deputy Region Director for Programming	Baltimore, MD	Charleston, SC
David Beach	Deputy Region Director for Unit Leadership	Baltimore, MD	Perry Point, MD
Amanda McCarty	Assistant Program Director	Baltimore, MD	Perry Point, MD

Jennifer Szeliga	Deputy Region Director for Programming	Sacramento, CA	San Diego, CA
Debbie Creamer	Counselor	Sacramento, CA	San Diego, CA
Jeanine Oien	Unit Leader	Sacramento, CA	San Diego, CA
Rich Smith	Deputy Region Director for Programming	Vicksburg, MS	Washington, DC
Jody Burns	Deputy Region Director for Programming	Vinton, IA	Charleston, SC
Angela Sarrels	Community Relations Specialist	Vinton, IA	Charleston, SC

CHAPTER TWENTY-THREE

NCCC Campuses Open:
A Sense of Joy and Accomplishment

We had earned every bit of it. We had fought our way through the tensions unleashed by hard-line differences in civilian and military leadership styles. We had swallowed tough compromises with regard to AmeriCorps policies that lopped off aspects of our program that we deeply valued. And with the clock ticking, we had made our deadline only by a hope and a prayer. Therefore, the sense of pride and accomplishment we felt as leaders and senior staff members when young recruits began reporting into the campuses was nothing short of pure joy.

The irrefutable evidence that we had made it was right in front of our eyes. We secretly felt we were witnessing a veritable miracle as we welcomed 275 eager corps members to their new home. They hailed from all over the USA, representing the racial, educational, gender, and economic diversity of our target group of sixteen- to twenty-four-year- old Americans. It was July 1994, and they were being welcomed and processed at our Aberdeen campus led by Jo Ann Jolivet. Just weeks later, on a warm and sunny day in early August, Jeff Biel welcomed 240 fresh recruits from the same cohort at Charleston Naval Training Center. In rapid succession, this lively and history-making scene continued to replicate itself as a cohort of 270 energetic corps members "in processed" at San Diego Naval Training Center in early September under the watchful eyes of Paul Johnson. Following on their heels—just three days later— Jules Hampton welcomed another 240 enthusiastic and diverse young service members being ushered into Denver's Lowry Air Force Base. Suddenly, the enormous challenge of managing and directing the positive energy visible on the faces of these youthful volunteers hit us, leaving no room for celebration. Our main focus would have to shift dramatically from recruitment and start- up maneuvers to fully operational campuses running at full throttle.

President Clinton Visits Aberdeen Corps Members

President Bill Clinton's visit to the Aberdeen campus generated tremendous excitement among the corps members. He stopped over at Havre de Grace, MD, in mid-September 1994 to observe their restoration work along the Chesapeake Bay. I believe the NCCC was the first AmeriCorps program the president toured, and he himself was visibly energized and excited about the discipline and skill exhibited by corps members as they engaged in a work project on the Chesapeake Bay. Eileen Rehrmann, Harford County executive, and Maj. Gen. Jim Monroe were also present and shared in the joy and excitement of Clinton's visit. The visit by the commander in chief of the USA was a fitting tribute to our efforts and signaled a triumph for the president's signature program.

Loosening the Reins of Top-Down, Decide- and-Announce Leadership Style

Many important changes to the NCCC happened during the two years after start-up that will not be covered in this memoir. Perhaps another effort or book will focus attention on those years as a fitting tribute to the cutting-edge contributions of AmeriCorps' residential jewel, the NCCC.

At the time, I viewed being the founding director of NCCC as the best job I'd managed to land since retiring from the US Army in 1991. In fact, I viewed it as a perfect fit for me since I was in the process of building a youth organization with a remarkably similar mission when I was offered the position. My three years as director provided much growth and many rewarding memories. As an organization, we were in fact growing up. We were retooling— making more democratic changes, adjustments, and upgrades in the

NCCC's command structure. The NCCC was becoming more inclusive of corps member participation in governance without sacrificing the authority of directors to make final decisions on significant matters of discipline and good order.

Susan Bates, ombudswoman, led the effort and did a magnificent job of influencing us to loosen our top-down, decide-and-announce military decision- making style. We began to include corps members in deliberations on matters of discipline and policy. Eli's and Shirley's insistence on CNS seniorexecutivesattending facilitative leadership (FL) also had a profound influence on my commitment to build a more inclusive decision-making structure from top to bottom within the NCCC. Happily, such changes did not impede the effectiveness of the corps.

On the contrary, consistent high praise for corps members during their work projects became a source of professional satisfaction. The Red Cross, FEMA, and Forest Service were champions of NCCC teams and relied on their rapid deployment capability and dependable competence to get the job done. Even the 1996 Olympic Committee was aware of AmeriCorps programs and especially of the NCCC's capabilities of providing support for their efforts. I was especially pleased with the prospect of going to the Atlanta Olympics, and up to that time, no thought of leaving the NCCC for another job ever entered my mind.

A Surprise Phone Call

Mary Sheridan, my executive assistant, said, "General, you have a call from a Gen. Tom Carney, deputy librarian of Congress." I told her I would take the call but was searching my brain and could only recall a Lt. Gen. Tom Carney who had been the deputy chief of staff for army personnel operations when I was on active duty. I didn't know him and certainly did not know that he was working at the Library of Congress. So when I said "Yes, sir!" the voice on the other end was cordial and direct. He explained that he was acting deputy librarian of Congress and that Gen. Colin Powell had recommended me to the librarian of Congress as a candidate to fill the deputy position. In response, he was calling to find out if I was interested in applying for the position. As intrigued and flabbergasted as I was about what I had just heard, I only remember saying how much I was enjoying my job as director of the NCCC and that I knew nothing about the Library of Congress. Wisely, General Carney chose to ignore my reply and invited me to have lunch at the library so he could tell me what the job was all about. I accepted the invitation without telling Mary or anyone else at the NCCC about the nature of the call.

Lunch with General Carney at the Library of Congress

We had a pleasant lunch on the top floor of the James Madison Building, where the executive suites are located. Plush carpets, deep- toned mahogany columns, and ample bookshelves framed the spacious rooms which were outfitted with richly appointed executive furniture everywhere you looked. Tom had lunch brought into the librarian's executive dining room with its broad window panels that spanned the entire length of the room. During our lunch, we could view the US Capitol and the other two Library of Congress buildings on the east side of Independence Avenue, southeast. It was an impressive view. At one point during the lunch, Tom walked to the window and dramatically pointed to the Jefferson and Adams buildings and said, "Your command would include a brigade-sized unit housed in these three magnificent buildings." Although I enjoyed the lunch and the physical layout of the buildings, I was not persuaded that I wanted to leave the NCCC for an unknown kingdom. I told Tom I would think about it.

Another Surprise Persuader

Between the months of April and June, I continued to focus on my NCCC duties and nearly forgot about Tom Carney's call about the Library of Congress job until Lt. Gen. Julius Becton called my home on a sunny weekend and urged me to apply for the deputy librarian position at the Library of Congress. General Becton, a mentor and friend in my post-military life and one of the first African Americans promoted to general in the 1970s, was his usual straight to the point self. Unbeknownst to me at the time was that Becton and Dr. Jim Billington, librarian of Congress, had graduated from the same school, lower Marion High School, Upper Marion, PA, where Becton had been a star athlete.

When General Becton called to persuade me to apply for the deputy librarian position, he spoke about his friendship with Dr. Billington and appealed to my sense of patriotism. He confided that the Library of Congress was undergoing a difficult organizational and operational period and was instrumental to the Congress, and the country needed me to help straighten it out. He also added for good measure that Gen. Colin Powell had recommended me to Dr. Billington for the position and in his genial but commanding way directed me to apply. I listened respectfully to his spiel but reiterated what had by now become my theme song: I love my NCCC job, and I am not interested in the Library of Congress position. His patience sorely tested, the general, with great insight, said, "Put your wife on the phone." He told Betty that the librarian of Congress wanted her husband's body, an artful and suggestive expression which caused her to recoil. He quickly rephrased the statement, explaining that the librarian wanted me to be his deputy and was willing to waive the dual compensation act so that I could receive both my retired military and Library of Congress salary. The conversation ended with Betty agreeing to persuade me to apply for the position.

I researched the job description, meditated on the advantages and disadvantages, and decided to apply for the position. I calculated that if the search team eliminated me from the list of candidates, Betty and the persuaders could not say that I didn't try. I met with members of the search team several times and realized that I was on the short list to interview with Dr. Jim Billington, librarian of Congress. The interview with Dr. Billington took place in the librarian's office in August 1996 and was conducted by a panel that included Billington, two members from the search team, the chief of staff and general counsel of the library. The interview was very formal and scripted; Billington read the instructions and asked questions that inquired about my management skills, leadership experience, and my experience in directing budgets for a large organization. The questions were asked exactly as written on the paper, and my answers were taken from my experience as chief of staff for the City of Atlanta, from Second Army, and from my role as director of the NCCC. The only give and take came after the formal interview when Dr. Billington asked a hypothetical question about how I would deal with a senior executive whose performance was below standard. My response was that I would begin with counseling and take more aggressive steps if the employee's performance did not improve and did not appear to meet his expectations. He pressed for more details, and when given the opportunity to ask questions, I continued the hypothetical discussion by asking Dr. Billington how he would respond if the senior executive was a friend of his who was terminated for incompetence. The interview ended on a cordial note, but the hypothetical give and take influenced my decision to decline the job if offered and to remain with the NCCC.

Betty was eager to hear how the interview went. I told her it went well but that I would decline the job if offered because of my uneasy exchange with Dr. Billington during the hypothetical give and take. I said something to the effect that working with the devil you know is better than casting your lot with the devil you don't know. I had barely finished my statement to Betty when the phone rang. It was Dr. Billington calling to tell me that he wanted us to have lunch in a more relaxed and private venue where the two of us could talk freely and clear up any questions that might not have been answered during the interview. I agreed to meet him, and we had lunch at a cozy downtown restaurant, by the end of which all my doubts about being able to work with him were completely erased. He stated that he had several more candidates to interview but that he would make his decision in a couple of weeks and the search firm would notify all candidates of his decision.

Time to Fish or Cut Bait

I had still told no one at the corporation or at NCCC about the interviews and carried out my NCCC responsibilities as if I had a lifetime appointment. Just before my interview with the Library of Congress, the corporation approved NCCC teams to support the Olympic Games in Atlanta. The teams, under the able leadership of Fred Peters as director of the Task Force, shortly became operational on site in Atlanta. I was visiting the team, talking to Fred, when Dr. Billington called on my cell phone. As soon as I heard the words "hold for Dr. Billington," I excused myself and left Fred's office to take the call. Dr. Billington went through the pleasantries and then offered me the job as deputy librarian with a report date of September 1996. He also confirmed the salary and waived the dual compensation provision so that I could draw my military retirement pay. I eagerly accepted the position and hung up the phone, dreading the fact of having to tell Harris Wofford, CEO of the CNCS, as well as Shirley Sagawa, managing director of the corporation, and the NCCC senior staff that I had accepted another position.

Fred knew me well enough to discern that the call was not an ordinary one and asked if everything was okay. I shared my good news about the job and also my apprehension at having to tell NCCC and CNS staff that I would be leaving. Fred, always the realist, suggested that I should call Harris rather than wait for a face-to-face meeting because bad news does not get better with age. Harris Wofford, as one of the bipartisan senators of the CCC, had taken over as CEO from Eli Segal and was a champion of the NCCC. I considered him a role model and knew that he would be disappointed about me leaving to take another job. I called, and he listened and lamented my departure. Point blank, he asked why

I was leaving. When I said to start receiving my military retirement pay and Library of Congress salary, he immediately offered to go to the president to waive the dual compensation rule so that I could start receiving my military pay. I told him Eli had attempted to get a waiver for me at least twice but was turned down each time. I also reminded him that a bird in the hand was worth two in the bush; I was taking the job. Harris was not a man to give up easily and attempted to persuade me to remain with the NCCC. He finally realized that I was committed to leaving and asked me if I knew a general officer who would be a good fit for the job.

Telling Harris I was leaving was dreadful enough, but announcing my departure to the NCCC staff was emotionally painful. We had depended on each other to do the impossible, and despite the fact that I was trying to put a good face on my reason for leaving, the eyes looking back at me revealed sadness and disappointment. I understood their somber mood, thanked them for their support, wished them well, and told them of my confidence in their abilities to take care of the NCCC. As I suspected, Harris and Lt. Gen. Andy Chambers, my mentor and friend, hit it off from the start, and Andy was hired as the director of NCCC. Andy's selection and the unforgettable farewell from Harris, Shirley, and the CNS staff, the NCCC family of staff, campus directors, and young corps members capped the end of an incredible opportunity to render service to others along my life's journey.

Insights: Unique Qualities of Military Veterans and Powell's Influence

Military veterans bring instant cohesion to civilian projects needing a sense of urgency for on-time completion and within budget constraints. The NCCC was completed by a dedicated group of army, navy, marine corps, air force, and coast guard veterans. I doubt seriously that the project would have been completed without the culture of teamwork, respect for the chain of command, and duty-first attitude fostered by the uniformed military services. I am deeply grateful for the efforts of the military, DOD civilians, and returned Peace Corps volunteers who followed the lead of the retired army colonels and navy captains to open the NCCC campuses described above. Our work was so effective that the NCCC still attracts volunteers and FEMA resources AmeriCorps NCCC to train and deploy teams dedicated to disaster-relief operations. More importantly, NCCC testimonials continue to applaud the contributions received from service in the corps and relate the accolades received from community leaders for the work they perform throughout the United States.

I was both humbled and surprised when told that Gen. Colin Powell had given my name to Dr. Jim Billington as a candidate to become his deputy librarian of Congress. Dr. Billington and a host of world leaders regard General Powell as a premier leader whose personal attributes match his stellar performance in the highest positions of trust and responsibility in America. I received closer and more serious consideration for the position because of the general's unsolicited endorsement.

We first met General and Mrs. Powell at Fort Leavenworth, KS; he was assistant commanding general, CGSC, and I was attending the precommand course in preparation to assume command of Hohenfels Maneuver Training Center in Germany. His wife, Alma, was monitoring a course for our spouses when one of the male instructors made a comment that drew the ire of Betty and a few other African American spouses in attendance. That was the start of Betty and Alma's mutual friendship.

My first professional encounter with General Powell was as inspector general, VII US Corps, in Stuttgart, Germany. Gen. "Andy" Chambers, commander, VII US Corps, championed my work as his inspector general when General Powell was conducting orientation visits as the newly appointed commander of V Corps in Germany. I briefed him on the significant decrease in training accidents and traffic deaths as a result of the safety and training evaluations we conducted throughout the corps area. My next and closet professional contact with General Powell was as chief of staff, Second US Army, Fort Gillem, GA (Atlanta). General Powell was the commanding general of all army troops in the United States (US Forces Command) and lived two houses down from us on Staff Row, Fort McPherson, GA. We often chatted on weekends while working on our vintage automobiles on the garage street behind our quarters. My boss at the time, Lt. Gen. Orion "Cotton" Whiddon, reported directly to General Powell and regularly briefed him on the National Guard and US Army Reserve issues within our thirteen states region. General Whiddon championed my contributions to his efforts and used every opportunity to include me in meetings with General Powell. Betty and I were also included on the guest list of farewell parties held in honor of the Powells when they left Atlanta for his appointment as chairman of the Joint Chiefs of Staff.

I was humbled and surprised because General Powell noticed me and Betty's contributions to the military and followed our post-military career to the extent of recommending me for deputy librarian of Congress. Betty and I are grateful to the Powells for their trust and investment. And as a takeaway from General Powell's endorsement, I offer the following unsolicited advice: Do every job as if God is watching and evaluating how you treat others in the performance of your duties and responsibilities. Work hard to cultivate and exhibit personal attributes that show in your behavior and relationships with others; your rank and worth is reflected in your speech, posture, and dress.

Likewise, always remember that someone above your position may take notice of your contributions in the position you occupy and, as a result, may endorse you for an important position. For sure, immediate subordinates under your supervision will notice and judge your fitness for the position you occupy.

President Bill Clinton visits NCCC.
Me shaking Clinton's hand and others like Eileen Rehrmann, Harford County executive, MD; Maj. Gen. Jim Monroe, new commander, Aberdeen Proving Ground, MD; and Maj.
Gen. Dick Trageman, outgoing commander Aberdeen.>>

CHAPTER TWENTY-FOUR

Library of Congress: Challenge, Change, and Celebration

Generals fix broken stuff. And according to the 1995 Booze, Allen, and Price Waterhouse Government Accounting Office (GAO) report, Library of Congress managers had a lot of broken stuff in 1995. Dr. James H. Billington, librarian of Congress, was looking for help—and this was not the first time library management had required outside help to fix a major problem. The annals of the library's history record that the Congress appointed a general to fix a major problem with the library as far back as 1888.

The US Congress appointed Brig. Gen. Thomas Casey, chief of US Army Corps of Engineers, to complete construction of the Thomas Jefferson Building because of significant problems with the civilian architecture firm contracted to erect the building. The general completed the most beautiful building in Washington, DC on time and under budget and exceeded construction standards. One hundred plus years later, the Congress took an active interest in closely monitoring the efforts of library managers to fix the eight critical operational systems identified in the aforementioned report that were negatively impacting the library's performance of its mission.

On October 1, 1996, I was sworn into my new position as deputy librarian of Congress by Dr. James H. Billington and confirmed by Sen. John Warner (R-VA), chairman, Joint Committee on the Library, to manage the day- today operations of the facility. My explicit task was to fix the operating systems and systematize library management. This chapter of my memoirs will cover my introduction to the library as well as the highlights of those assignments which I considered to be the most challenging and interesting during my ten-year tenure.

I received a warm welcome in a festive atmosphere from Dr. Billington and the members of the powerful Executive Committee (EC). The mood of each EC member was cordial and upbeat, affording me the opportunity to record my first impressions of those whom I would develop a close working relationship during my time at the library. Winston Tabb, associate librarian and head of the largest department, appeared formal in approach and always talked and moved with a purpose. Director Dan Mulhollan, Congressional Research Service (CRS), also walked fast and spoke rapidly. Jo Ann Jenkins, chief of staff, spoke thoughtfully and chose her words carefully. Acting Deputy Tom Carney, though observant, spoke little. By contrast, Dr. Billington commanded a rich vocabulary and spoke fluently about the library as well as his expectations of me as the new addition to the EC. His manner left no doubt that he was in charge. I also met Mary Beth Peters, director of Copyrights, and Dr. Rubens Medina, director of the Law Library, at the small reception and noted that they spoke little and were not members of the EC.

Mrs. Marjorie Billington was also present and warmly welcomed Betty and me to the library family. Betty held the Bible while Dr. Billington conducted my oath of office in his large executive conference room. The Bible came from the library's rare book collection and was the first English language Bible published in the United States. The small reception after the ceremony left me with the impression that all were genuine in their welcome and that the GAO report citing the need for a major overhaul had not dampened the spirit of the executive leadership.

Sobering Words of Welcome

Dr. Billington and Gen. Tom Carney scheduled receptions for managers and employees to come to the sixth floor to meet me, thereby satisfying a strong need of library workers to know their leaders. They also scheduled me to visit the service units and administrative support units in order to acquaint me with the diversity of work encompassed by the Library of Congress.

The library had over four thousand employees distributed through four service units as well as administrative and logistical support staff. Long lines of employees streamed from the hallways into the librarian's reception office to shake hands and offer welcoming comments. The reception took the better part of a week, and it seemed to me as if all the employees in the library took advantage of the opportunity. Any notion of celebrity was completely destroyed by an African American female employee from human resources. She paused, looked up at me, and stated somberly, "We really need you. I don't know how long you are going to be here, but I am praying for you." Her comment caused me to wonder how many of her fellow employees shared her hopes and concerns about my ability to right the ship and survive.

My visits to the various units of the library helped me understand the work and challenges faced by the managers and employees. The visits reminded me of a similar orientation I experienced as the ADC of the First Cavalry Division with one major exception. I was familiar with the roles and purposes of the units that made up the cavalry. With the exception of the administrative and support functions, I had no clue about the roles and purposes of the functional units that made up the library. I was looking to assess the morale of the employees, and by the end of my visits, I concluded that the majority of the employees loved their jobs, were proud to work for the library, and wanted the library to do well. The leaders I met appeared unaware of the negative impacts in nine critical areas that the GAO report said they were having in their units.

Straight with no Chaser

My orientation visit was capped off with a scheduled meeting by Dr.

Billington and I with Sen. John Warner (R-VA), who was then chairman of the Joint Committee of the Library. I recall that the meeting was late in the day, and Senator Warner, though expecting us, took a pause from the stack of documents in front of him to greet us. Dr. Billington was gracious in his introduction of me to Senator Warner, who warmly welcomed me to the library and minced no words telling me and Dr. Billington what he expected of us. He firmly stated to Dr. Billington, "Jim, you continue to lead the Library of Congress as the librarian." To me he stated, "General, you are responsible and accountable to the Congress for the day-to-day operations of the Library of Congress." He offered his continued support, wished us the best, and returned to his work.

I left his office knowing that we both shared the hot seat and that Dr. Billington and I had to work as if we were joined at the hip in order to resolve the library's daunting challenges. I reviewed the congressional legislation that specified my duties and began thinking about how I could fix the day-to-day problems and help Dr. Billington to exercise command of the library's defining vision and resources.

Breakfast with Billington

At the end of my first week at the library, Dr. Billington suggested that we could have breakfast together in his dining room. We seated ourselves and were served our cereal by Tina, a library cafeteria employee who excused herself after warmly welcoming us to breakfast. Dr. Billington looked at me and said, "I don't have an agenda. I just wanted us to get to know each other. Do you have anything you want to talk about?" I suggested that we start by giving thanks for all that had transpired in our lives to bring us together at this point. We each gave our short prayer of thanksgiving and talked about working together to manage the library.

His desire for me to take the lead in fixing broken systems was convincing and reassuring. Through that first meeting, we established a routine that lasted the duration of my time at the library. I believe that prayer is a force multiplier and that through these meetings we developed mutual trust and respect for each other that withstood the strains of crisis and dissension within our chain of command.

Dr. Billington had served in the military, respected the experience, and held me and other career military veterans in high regard. He downplayed his being drafted as a private with a Ph.D. and completing Infantry OCS, followed by service as an aide to Allen Dulles, the head of the CIA in the 1950s. OCS in the 1950s was physically and mentally very demanding, with little tolerance for mistakes. Dr. Billington's respect for the military service ethic proved a helpful bridge to our trust in each other.

It was at our breakfast meetings that I observed Dr. Billington's formidable communication skills which were reinforced by his gift of extraordinary intelligence. I recall one morning our discussion centered on books that inspired us, and I admitted my difficulty with The Confessions of St. Augustine. Dr. Billington said that he had read it a long time ago and asked me how far I had gotten, and I said, "Only to chapter 3." He began telling me the context of the historical times of Augustine, spoke of the writer's family background, and explained the spiritual journey that led Augustine to Christianity, the main reason he wrote the book. I recall that as Dr. Billington spoke, his word pictures had a mesmerizing effect on me. He appeared to be a witness to all that he spoke about, and I visualized the scenes as if I were present.

On occasion, he would invite others to have breakfast with us. Dr. John Hope Franklin, noted historian and prize-winning author and recipient of the library's John W. Kluge prize, dined with us several times. At one of those meetings, I was grappling with an invitation to attend and speak to my forty-fifth anniversary high school graduating class. I mentioned my reluctance to attend because I was a graduating senior in the first class of African

American students to integrate the school and still harbored resentment because of my exclusion from after- school social activities. Dr. Franklin listened and asked, "Do they know how you feel?" When I said no, he said, "Then you must go because if you don't tell them your view of that year, they will go to their graves believing something that was not accurate." His advice, insight, and wisdom were like medicine for my debilitating thoughts and food for my understanding. The privilege of dining and listening to two great historians and men of character was a priceless opportunity. The other great product of our prayer breakfast meetings was the opportunity to address concerns about the library, our families, and our country that only a divine creator could fix. We always resolved to do our part and leave the rest to providence.

Library Management

After our meeting with Senator Warner, I relied on my military training and experience to assess the library's mission. Once I was crystal clear on its concept of operation, I could best determine how I could influence the dayto-day operations. The library's organizational chart showed the Office of the Librarian at the top with four department heads reporting directly to Dr.

Billington. The chief of staff and office of the deputy librarian were also within the office of the librarian and reported to Dr. Billington. The various support and administrative units reported to the deputy and the chief of staff.

From all that I had read or heard, the four department heads, chief of staff, and a few special staff officers relished their direct reporting status to the librarian and could make decisions without the deputy being in the loop. This was unacceptable to me because Senator Warner's words, deeply etched into my survival lobe, inspired me to insert myself ahead of all department heads. I borrowed from my experience as an ADC, and with Dr. Billington's concurrence and delegated authority, I changed the organizational chart to show that we shared authority to make library-wide decisions. We redrew library organizational charts to show him as the librarian and me as the deputy in the top block with all senior leaders reporting directly to us. The changes were implemented quickly and communicated through meetings with senior executives and those who reported directly to me and Dr. Billington.

This approach was new to senior executives accustomed to reporting to Dr. Billington; it was also new to the three executive secretaries for Dr. Billington, Joann, and me. We all worked together and adjusted to my authority to issue library-wide policies and decisions. Such authority had previously been exclusively the domain of the librarian. The primary reason this approach worked was because Dr. Billington agreed early in my tenure that there would be no secrets between him and me. Telling him was like telling me and vice versa. Many tested our bond of trust over the ten years and learned that we were faithful in our commitment to support each other.

Meetings

Prior to my first EC meeting, Gen. Tom Carney, acting deputy and consultant to the librarian, told me that meetings tended to last for hours without reaching resolutions. In addition, I had read the GAO's scathing critique of the library's management and infrastructure but decided to announce my intention of making no changes in the way business meetings were conducted until I had observed them for ninety days. My good intentions lasted all of two hours.

Even though Dr. Billington assured me that he was comfortable with me chairing the EC meetings, I was cautious in my opening remarks and drew on my experience as a trained facilitator to defer to him as the ultimate decisionmaker for the institution. Winston, Dan, and Dr. Billington dominated the discussion which lasted over ninety minutes, and ended when Dan and Winston excused themselves and departed for another meeting. Though I had promised in my opening remarks not to make major changes in the prevailing order of conducting library business prior to an extended period of observation and evaluation, I knew at the end of that meeting that I would renege on my promise. The meeting format would have to be changed immediately in order to gain control of the agenda and maximize effective outcomes.

I met with Dr. Billington immediately afterward to explain my frustration with the meeting and told him I wanted to introduce FL which would provide an effective structure for EC meetings that would produce results and improve relationships. Fortunately, he too was weary of long meetings which did not contribute to solving the problems at hand. I extolled the virtues of the FL format and its effectiveness in achieving results. However, I think my most convincing argument with Dr. Billington was sharing with him my experience in applying the built-in decision-making features of FL at AmeriCorps. There the technique kept me in charge of the decision-making process. My point was that it could accomplish the same results for the LOC by keeping him and me in charge. He agreed to support my decision to make FL the library's official meeting format, and I wasted no time preparing my staff to get abreast of the new meeting structure.

The use of the FL system involved five levels of decision-making: deciding and announcing, gathering input from individuals and deciding, gathering input from teams and deciding, consensus, and delegating with constraints. I opted to decide and announce in order to initiate the change. My rationale to make FL mandatory for all managers in the library was based on my belief that discipline, structure, and focus in meetings best accomplish desired results. My primary concern was focusing all the leaders on fixing the GAO recommendations, which were known within the library as the management improvement plan. I instructed Karen and Lucy, my direct subordinates, on the rudiments of preparing and conducting meetings using FL principles and tools. They in turn drafted the agenda for the conduct of our next and future meetings and sent it to EC members. The two desired outcomes of the meeting were (1) to instruct EC members on how to prepare for and participate in future EC meetings and (2) to announce that all 550 managers at the library would be trained in FL. Both goals were presented in a "decide and announce" style by me with Dr. Billington's strong support.

My second EC meeting followed the prepared agenda provided to members in advance and allowed me to experience the formidable questioning powers of Dan and Winston. In turn, they experienced my determination to fix problems and to hold managers accountable by using FL as a structured meeting approach. The major concerns of the two principle budget holders, Dan and Winston, were the costs of FL training sessions and leaving employees without supervisors. Their questions were appropriate and, I thought, fell into the need-to-know category. I arranged for the owner of Interaction Associates, teachers of FL, to answer cost, time, and other implementation questions. I also pointed out the key differences in the consensus approach to decision- making and "decide and announce." The first method allowed room for modifications, compromises, and adjustments to the boss's directives; however, the "decide and announce" method simply meant following orders. The meeting ended within the allotted time and achieved the desired results. Marianne Hughes, the cofounder of Interaction Associates, attended a later meeting and presented the features of FL to senior library executives and the content and conduct of the five-day course to train all 550 library managers. Dan and Winston agreed to find new funds to cover the training costs. All department heads wanted a pilot to help Interaction Associates conduct the course and reduce costs. I agreed, the pilot was conducted, and all 550 managers were trained at the Holiday Inn during March 1997.

The second group of senior executives and decision-makers within the library was the Senior Management Reporting Group

(SMRG). The SMRG, as its name implied, was a large unwieldy group of about twenty senior leaders and department heads who managed financial, administrative, and logistical services and who reported directly to the deputy librarian. My first take on this state of affairs was that the group as constituted was unmanageable. I sensed the apparent tension between executives of major service departments because only two of them, Dan, and Winston, served on the EC while others could only get their department's interests heard through the SMRG. I also observed and heard anxiety in the questions from service unit department executives about their access and input with regard to EC decisions. I sensed that relationships between service and support executives were strained because they believed EC members frequently made library- wide decisions without consulting them.

The SMRG meeting took place within a week of my announcement of FL for all managers. I also had a second meeting with this large group to explain FL and how I would perform day-to-day operations at the library. The prepared notes of that meeting revealed not only the tensions between executives but also the culture that library executives had grown comfortable with. During that meeting, I observed the tensions between EC members and support staff in the primacy of decision-making within the library. I spent a lot of time clarifying roles between Dr. Billington and myself; between Jo Ann, chief of staff, and myself; and between Dr. Billington, members of the EC, and myself.

Although the focus of the agenda was organizing the SMRG to better resolve the issues under their purview through cooperation with each other and other appropriate stakeholders, I sensed resistance in the form of their need to know more. I also gained the impression that EC members and special staff saw me as a barrier to their direct access to Dr. Billington on issues of primary concern to him. I emphasized that it was imperative to inform Dr. Billington directly on issues of central concern to him in particular and to inform me immediately afterward.

The minutes of that meeting showed that there was a good deal of one-way communication in the meeting but allowed me to identify individual department heads with their peculiar areas of expertise, their primary concerns, and points of tension with me and other library leaders. Most importantly, as a group, the SMRG members gave the overall impression of wanting to work cooperatively and within the FL guidelines that I had established. Nonetheless, I decided that I would not use the SMRG as a governing or decision-making body but rather as a liaison to inform and disseminate EC decisions and information to subordinates. The mandatory training of library managers in FL was the first major announcement to the SMRG. We gradually phased out the SMRG meeting altogether in favor of creating the Operations Committee which proved more effective in implementing EC decisions.

Personal Accountability

My first forty-five days left me with the uneasy feeling that library managers were not focused on the resolution of GAO improvement issues. I learned from my subordinates that performance evaluations were required by library regulations but not enforced. I shared my concerns with Dr. Billington about the neglect of library performance evaluations as a performance management tool, and he agreed to support my application of performance evaluations to focus the library staff on completing specific goals on an annual basis. The use of performance evaluations to hold subordinates accountable—and especially EC members—bolstered my confidence that we could resolve the critical issues underscored in the GAO report.

My 1997 report, coming ninety days after taking on the job as deputy librarian, received Dr. Billington's enthusiastic approval and encouragement. He commented: "It is very encouraging to me—and invigorating to all of us here—to be beginning a new year with such a vigorous and focused associate as you have already proven to be in such a short time. Many thanks and Godspeed for 1997."

My report proved to be the clarion call that catapulted us on a successful path to inspire managers to focus on and achieve library-wide goals and objectives for each of the ten years I was at the library. I do not use the word "inspire" lightly because when I learned that performance evaluations carried monetary awards based on merit-based ratings, I had one simple rule: managers who failed to achieve my or the librarian's goals and objectives would not be awarded a satisfactory rating; hence, no added money.

Dr. Billington's written response to my performance plan was very encouraging and useful; he was fully supportive of efforts to tighten up the performance evaluation system. He also effectively targeted what he called our leading deficiency: the lack of proactive and self-generated initiatives. He also seized the opportunity to add two areas for library- wide special initiatives: (1) developing new ways (or improving and enhancing old ones) of serving the Congress with the entire resources of the library and (2) treating the National Digital Library (NDL) as a library-wide institutional priority for 1997. He, therefore, mandated, "NDL must receive increased support throughout the library in the coming year if we are to meet our promises to the Congress. In particular, we must make a major effort to find and begin digitizing materiel that is much more broadly interesting—especially in our K-12 target audience— so that we can compile and package more compelling resource materials that will command the attention of Congress and private sector supporters."

Dr. Billington consistently focused attention on using library resources to serve Congress, the American people, and the world throughout my tenure at the library. And at times, he pushed us to exceed accepted norms by delivering more than our skills, resources, and level of cooperation led us to believe that we were capable of delivering. His inspired vision motivated me to work with library leaders and to bring in new leaders with the expertise and experience to achieve his projections.

CHAPTER TWENTY-FIVE

Conflicts, Challenges, and Accomplishments

I approached the job of confronting challenges at the library the same as I did in the military by using authority over others to resolve issues, strengthen the team, and develop leaders. My efforts to resolve major management issues at the library involved what I label as battles or skirmishes with senior leaders that added yet another layer of complexity to the broken systems. The internal dynamics of the EC battles were accentuated by Dr. Billington's leadership style, which was accessible, interesting, and responsive. Many such skirmishes were also fueled by factors beyond his control. The congressional budget clerks and the library's governing hierarchy created powerful challenges to Dr. Billington's leadership over the library's budget processes. The House budget clerk, in some ways, usurped Dr. Billington's authority over library managers. I was shocked during my first year to learn that the clerk handed down an order that all senior library managers could not be away from the library two weeks before the library's budget hearing in case he had questions that needed answers. I was advised by EC members and by the budget officer not to challenge his authority. I heeded their advice.

At my first meeting with the clerk, I was made privy to a litany of past mismanagement practices by library managers as a justification for his strong intervention policies. He stated his intention was to keep the pressure on until he saw a change. I accepted his challenge and assured him that we would fix past mismanagement practices and earn his trust. After my first year, he stopped giving orders to library managers but continued to insist that John Webster, the library's chief financial officer, was his trusted agent and the only library contact he would meet with on budget issues. This often put John in an awkward position, but it was the hand he had been dealt. Winston Tabb was also in an awkward position as the head of library services and a member of the EC. He sometimes had to defend his large department against library- wide administrative and support units that were also funded in the same overall Library of Congress budget. Dan Mulhollan had separate budget authority, occupied space, used infrastructure services provided by library administrative and support services, and often argued that his budget resources could be used only in direct support of the Congress. Dan consistently championed the needs of his own department though they often conflicted with the needs of other parts of the library.

With a five-member EC, the numbers favored Dr. Billington, Joann, and me. However, the crafty dynamics of the board coupled with Dan's and Winston's habits of promoting their points of view with Dr. Billington before meetings made the outcomes always predictable. I increased the board membership to seven, which helped to balance points of view but did not change the dynamics of decision-making for me or Dr. Billington.

My Greatest Challenge

My greatest internal battle at the library was implementing the automated selection and hiring system. If there were battle streamers to identify internal wars within the ranks, this would be the largest, most complex, and most beneficial of all the battles I had fought at the library. The issues had fermented among library managers and African American employees for more than twenty years and frayed sensitive nerves on both sides. All library managers, including me during my first three years, tiptoed around the subject because of its volatility. Racial discrimination, perceived racial favoritism, intrigue, and coercion were all bound in one package known as the "Cook Case."

The library's human resources system had been hovering under a cloud of incompetence which cried out for redress long before my arrival in October 1996.

The thorniest issue involved claims of racial discrimination against African American employees in the library's hiring process. In 1975, Howard Cook and a group of African American employees filed an administrative grievance alleging racist practices within the library hierarchy. The issue lingered without redress until around 1986 when Dr. Tommy Shaw, a statistician in HR, filed a lawsuit against the library alleging that the library's hiring procedure discriminated against African Americans. The superior district judge integrated Shaw's complaint with Howard Cook's allegations to form a class action suit named after Howard Cook.

Superior District Court Judge Norma Holloway ruled in favor of library employees in 1995 and placed the library's hiring procedures under court supervision until the library could prove to the satisfaction of the court that its hiring system did not discriminate against African American employees. As a result, concerned members of the Congressional Black Caucus asserted their prerogatives to push the library to change the hiring system and increase the number of African American leaders in the senior and middle manager grades. When I arrived in October 1996, most of the senior leadership positions in HR were filled by African American employees who were also members of the Cook class action lawsuit. Members of the Congressional Black Caucus leaned hard on library managers to promote African Americans to senior-level positions. A prevailing view among African American employees was that library managers resented the pressure and made life harder for those appointed to senior leadership positions. Rumors floated around that the African American deputy librarian who preceded me was a victim of such resentment and as a result remained in the position for less than a year. In the library as a whole, ten African Americans were serving in senior leadership positions by the time of my arrival, and most were in staff positions directly under the chief of staff and deputy librarian. Only three were in library services, the largest service unit; the congressional research service had one, while the copyright and the law library had none.

District Court Oversight of HR

The affirmative action reviews conducted by HR employees used a court-approved formula to determine if African American employees considered for positions were treated fairly by library managers. The reviews were complex, time-consuming, and contentious. Most EC members did not believe that library managers discriminated in choosing the best-qualified candidates and offered little assistance in changing the system used to select new hires. A secondary complaint against HR was the length of time—about 120 days— that it took to fill library vacancies. This anomaly was coupled with a critical concern that the library's aging workforce could see a hasty exit of retirees in the year 2000 without a speedy and efficient HR to replace them.

In 1998, I proposed, and the EC unanimously agreed to a study that we called "HR 21." The probe would examine the impact of the aging workforce and what would be needed to speed up the hiring process in the event of mass retirement in the year 2000. We hired an outside personnel consulting firm to complete a study of the library's hiring process. They recommended contracting with a well-known personnel automation system to fix our hiring problems. However, their recommendations did not factor in the court's oversight and mandate of affirmative action reviews.

Cook's class action attorneys increasingly complained to the court that the library's hiring system continued to discriminate against African American employees and that we were not serious about changing the system. At one point, the plaintiffs and their attorney petitioned the judge to place the library under receivership, and the judge was actually considering the petition. Simultaneous with the legal complaints, some library employees who were members of the class action initiative sent updates to members of the Congressional Black Caucus that provoked some members to send blistering letters criticizing Dr.

Billington for his intransigence.

Moved to Action

Members of the EC were generally informed of the latest motion or ruling in the Cook case by Elizabeth Pugh, general counsel, and Gerry Otremba, director of congressional liaison; this also included congressional letter complaints. During my first three years, the usual response from EC members was to criticize HR's incompetence while preparing talking points for inclusion in the response prepared for Dr. Billington's signature. Joann would usually coordinate the office of personnel, general counsel, and congressional liaison's response for Dr. Billington, and I had accepted these four as being the appropriate staff to handle Cook-related issues for the library.

Events in 1999 compelled me to tackle the HR and Cook Case hiring problems. My involvement was triggered by heated discussions at EC meetings and questions about library management's capability to prioritize the National Academy of Science (NAS) report commissioned by Dr. Billington. At one EC meeting in late 1999, Gerry Otremba read a letter from a member of the Congressional Black Caucus strongly accusing Dr. Billington of taking no action to end discrimination against African Americans in the library's hiring process. At another EC meeting within the same month, Elizabeth Pugh, general counsel, read a letter from the Cook Class Action attorney threatening to file a motion to place the library's hiring and selection procedures in receivership of the court.

During each instance, the absurdity of EC members giving advice to Dr. Billington, the general counsel, and the chief of congressional liaison as if they were merely consultants hit me full force. It became crystal clear to me that Dan and Winston, the two senior members of the EC responsible for two-thirds of the selection and hiring process in the library, also shared responsibility for fixing the problem. I said as much, and they both essentially agreed that they were not discriminating in their hiring procedures and alleged that the court's finding of discrimination against African American employees was questionable. I accepted their opinion but firmly stated that from that moment forward the EC as a body would take responsibility for resolving the HR and Cook problems.

The second most compelling factor resulted from a National Academy Study that Dr. Billington commissioned to assess the library's rapidly expanding use of digital technology. The NAS concluded its study in September 2000 by recommending that the library launch a national digital preservation program. But it also stated bluntly that the library's HR was crippled by the Cook Case. The report used clear and descriptive language that questioned senior management's ability to use technology effectively without resolving the HR/ Cook issues. The report also touched a raw nerve when it identified that the EC itself was conflicted in representing the library as a whole because of the competing organizational interests of Library Services and CRS. We had cleaned up the GAO management issues, and I now felt like I could no longer tiptoe around the HR/Cook issue. The battle had to be waged.

My Change Agents

Terri Smith, Elizabeth Pugh, and Linda Rix of Avue Technologies launched our automated selection and hiring system in August 2000. This team, augmented by Marsha Byrd, Tom Bryant, and their assistants, proved to be my strongest allies during the toughest challenges of automated system implementation. Terri was hired with the expectation that she could lead HR's highly skeptical employees and gain the trust of doubting library managers. The resulting mandate would enable her to build a fully functioning human resources organization to meet the library's requirements. Terri, Elizabeth Pugh, and Marcia Byrd, Pugh's assistant, would be the point persons who would successfully navigate library managers through the intertwined Cook Case, observe personnel mandates, and initiate functional changes in human resources. The three relatively new hires were not intimidated by the long history of the Cook case or the formidable challenges of gaining EC approval to change operating systems and policies.

Implementation of the HR automated system forced every unit in the library to examine job descriptions and analyze the knowledge, skills, and abilities required to do the job. That process and other implementation features slowed the hiring of needed employees, frustrated managers, and caused some to cast the blame for the implementation problems on Terri and HR and on me for my championing of Avue Technologies.

The showdown came in 2001. I was on vacation with Betty and our grandson, Taylor, when I received a call from Tom Bryant telling me that Dan and Winston had gone to see Dr. Billington, asking him to abort the Avue implementation project. I immediately called Dr. Billington, who assured me that he supported me and asked me to continue my vacation. Later in the fall, during the library's budget hearing with the senate, I was called to testify during CRS's budget testimony, a rarity, since Dan was usually the only one from the library to speak on CRS budget issues.

Sen. Bob Bennett (R-Utah) asked me why CRS was having difficulty hiring and replacing employees. I called Dan to sit beside me and inquired if he wanted to answer, and he uncharacteristically deferred to me. I told the senator that the library's hiring and selection process was encumbered by a long-standing court order targeting racial discrimination against African Americans that hampered our implementation process. I offered to provide the details for the record and indicated that the technical problems would be resolved. The senator said, "General, I trust you to fix the system," and that ended covert efforts to get rid of me or to abort the implementation of Avue. The Avue automated hiring system was implemented, and the district court ceased oversight of the library's selection and hiring system. The Equal Opportunity Office's discrimination case backlog was the last bastion of Cookdominated issues. Gilbert Sandate, EEO officer, spoke softly but got results as he successfully navigated his way through the backlog of cases that numbered in the hundreds. This action removed stopgaps and dramatically facilitated the retirements of eligible employees all within one year. Subsequently, with the help of Jesse James, assistant general counsel, and Charles Carron of Labor Management Relations, a new and more efficient process was established to adjudicate and resolve the library's discrimination complaints.

I credit library leaders for working through implementation difficulties and for making knowledge, skills, and abilities the basis for selecting the best candidate for job vacancies in the library. Terri Smith, Elizabeth Pugh, Marsha Byrd, Gil Sandate, Charles Carron, Tom Bryant, and Jim Billington all deserve medals of valor for their intelligence and perseverance in bringing about this hard-won and important victory. All senior executives hired after 2003 were selected by the new system, and several, as of this writing, are still serving at the library.

Terrorist Threats

The dynamic forces that shape events at the library never take a vacation or a coffee break. The 9/11 attack against the Pentagon, contaminated mail sent through Capitol mail distribution systems, and a visitor wounding a capitol police officer with a gun required the library to improve its emergency management procedures to enhance the safety of employees on Capitol Hill. Under my direction, Linda Washington, chief of support services, and

Kenneth Lopez, director of security, established a highly effective emergency management team that responded to all terrorist or emergency-related incidents. The greatest change in security was the merger of the Library of Congress police with the Capitol Hill police.

The library's police department was a fully accredited law enforcement department with its own police union. The police exercised full policing powers on library premises and more importantly, inspected bags and briefcases of library employees and visitors as a precaution against theft of library property. The terrorist threat to Capitol Hill buildings also caused the senate and House members to view the entire Capitol Hill complex as one entity and to merge the small library police with the much larger Capitol Hill police force. Dr.

Billington's first concern with the merger was the retention of physical security measures by Capitol Hill police to protect library treasures from theft, vandalism, and mutilation.

I worked very closely with Chief of Police Terry Gainer to insure that Capitol Hill police understood the importance of protecting the collections and to make certain that eligible library police officers did not lose seniority, rank, or retirement benefits because of the merger. Protecting books was not a part of the Capitol police mindset, and Chief Gainer accepted the responsibility after being presented with Dr. Billington's statutory authority and accountability to the Congress for the protection of the library's collection.

I regarded library police officers as my troops and was disappointed that we could not work out a better compromise for older police officers whose age or time in service made them ineligible for retirement within the Capitol Hill police system. Chief Gainer was a man of his word and accommodated most of our requests in support of library police officers. Ken Lopez also went the extra mile to retain some of our older officers in security-related duties.

I regarded the merger as the end of an era. No longer would the LOC employ a totally independent police force on Capitol Hill. Therefore, the merger inaugurated and established a seamlessly integrated security network under the direction of the US Capitol police. The threat and technology issues justified the merger and came as a fitting challenge to my interests, knowledge, and abilities as the deputy librarian. Tensions ran high within the ranks of both police forces. Meanwhile, both forces had strong justifications for and against the merger, and in the end, the order to merge was not an option for the library. I fully concurred with the need for the merger order and believe I helped all concerned to implement it in the spirit of cooperation and compromise.

King Solomon said that the end of a thing is better than its beginning. Therefore, I have chosen to detail the two accomplishments that were the most challenging and the most beneficial to the library, its employees, the Congress, and the American people. The other accomplishments, which I think of as battle streamers, also meant a great deal to the mission of the library and the success of its employees. Following is a list of the "battle streamers" or library management accomplishments during 1996–2006:

- resolved BA/PW/GAO management improvement recommendations
- introduced FL and mandated the training of all 550 library managers
- placed all employees on one e-mail system
- made the library a smoke-free workplace
- expanded EC membership and added law library, copyright, and strategic initiatives
- established Operations Committee
- supervised implementation of integrated library system

- instituted copyright electronic registration, recordation, and deposit systems
- initiated global legal information system
- brought up all library systems to the year 2000 compliance.
- completed Fort Mead book storage modules
- completed Packard Audio Visual Center, Culpepper, VA
- directed establishment of the Veterans History Project
- hired and mentored senior executives
- established an automated selection and hiring system
- established program, management, and budget execution systems
- merged library police with Capitol Hill police

A Defining Moment of Faith: From Personal Crisis to Unexpected Blessing

Prior to my battles with the HR/Cook Case, Betty suffered a heart attack and underwent a six-hour quadruple bypass surgery. The operation was conducted at Walter Reed Army Hospital and is included here because of the unexpected outcome of the surgery in addition to other related cause-andeffect factors.

Betty had complained of acid indigestion for several weeks during April 1999, would not go to the doctor, and insisted on treating herself. My futile attempts to get her to seek medical help finally caused me to deceive her into thinking that we were going to church on a Sunday morning, but instead, I drove her straight to Walter Reed's emergency room. The emergency room doctor diagnosed Betty as having a heart attack and admitted her to the hospital. The next morning, the chief surgeon told me that tests confirmed that Betty had five blockages in her heart valves and that he had assigned his best surgeon, Dr. (Major) Corcoran, to remove the blockages. The surgery was scheduled for that afternoon, and I asked if my sons and Betty's family members should be notified to be by her side after the surgery. He said that it was my option but that open heart surgery was pretty routine and he expected everything to go smoothly. He estimated that the procedure would take about three or four hours.

Four hours passed, and there was no word from the doctor about Betty's progress. The chief surgeon came in with a grim look on his face and told me that there had been complications with bleeding and that perhaps I wanted to notify my family members. I recall going to the chapel and praying to God to spare Betty's life. During my prayer request, an inner voice asked me what I would do for her that I had not done in thirty-seven years of marriage. I answered, "Support her ministry." Meanwhile, the doctor was able to stop the bleeding and placed her in intensive care where she experienced a minor stroke.

She managed to survive that one, but during recovery at home, she suffered another stroke. A trip back to the hospital and more tests revealed that she had a blocked carotid artery, which meant yet another surgery to fix the problem.

After the surgery, Betty returned home for recovery and called me at the office to tell me that she just learned about a class action lawsuit against a company that sold diet pills believed to be the cause of heart problems in people that took them. She had taken the pills and wanted to know what I thought about her joining the lawsuit. I was about to say it would probably be a waste of time but remembered my prayer to support her and quickly said, "Yes, you don't have anything to lose." She hired a lawyer, joined the suit, and added her name to the list.

Betty Recovers and Accompanies Me to Brazil

Dr. Billington was closely monitoring Betty's medical ordeal and suggested that I should visit one of the library's acquisition offices and take Betty with me.

At the time, the library had acquisition offices in Rio de Janeiro, Brazil; Nairobi, Kenya; Islamabad, Pakistan; New Delhi, India; and Jakarta, Indonesia. I chose Rio, and the library's office director there included Sao Paulo, Brasilia, and Bahia. It was a wonderful trip in all respects. I gained a greater understanding of the relationship between the library's acquisition offices and the US State Department's support. I was also impressed with the multicultural makeup of Brazil's population and especially the apparent African influence in their cultural identity. I was especially attracted to the openness and hospitality of the people we met in Bahia. I felt at home in Bahia as if I had been there before. The trip lifted Betty's spirits and I believe helped her regain her vibrant personality that the surgery and strokes had dampened. I was thankful that she was able to make the trip and for Dr. Billington's support and understanding that made it all possible. We returned home and resumed our routine of work, Sunday worship services, and socializing with friends.

In the spring of 2000, I received a jolting phone call from Betty. Her lawyer told her that a check from the company that made the diet pills was ready for her to pick up, and she wanted me to go with her to pick it up. A little surprised and excited, we arrived, and she was handed the envelope. As she opened it, her mouth flew open. She handed it to me. I saw more zeros on that one check than I had ever seen before. The amount of the check was more than my annual library salary and military retirement pay combined! We were excited, happy, and shocked.

True to what I call her ministry—generosity to others—Betty wrote checks to family members, friends, churches, and charities and paid off some of our bills. The unexpected settlement money also provided a down payment on a condominium in Virginia Beach and significantly improved our financial retirement portfolio. Her surgery had taken us to the brink of sorrow and fear of her death to the comfort of a more secure retirement portfolio. Her return to reasonably good health, our financial ability to share with family and friends, and the knowledge that God provided for all our needs proved to be major assets in my battles at the Library of Congress.

CHAPTER TWENTY-SIX

The Glamorous Side of My Duties at the Library of Congress

The fun part of being the deputy librarian included travel to some of the most exciting countries in the world, alongside some of the most influential people in the United States, and socializing with the powerful, the rich, and the famous in the most glamorous building in Washington, DC. Getting paid to do it was the icing on the cake.

Presidents, members of Congress, distinguished members of the arts and humanities community, and the corporate community frequently host their important events in the magnificent Thomas Jefferson Building. Dr. Billington and Marjorie, the official host and hostess of these events, commissioned Betty and me to assist in welcoming guests to the library. The events were exciting opportunities to chat with the distinguished guests and have photographs taken for unbelieving friends and relatives. Our photo albums include photographs with Presidents Bill Clinton, George W. Bush, George H. W. Bush and their wives, and a host of other distinguished guests at the library.

Among the most spectacular events hosted at the library were the gala evenings sponsored by the James Madison Council. Dr. Billington and the late John Kluge, founding chairman of the council, recruited private sector benefactors to serve as an advisory board to the librarian. Members make annual gifts in support of the library's outreach programs. My most memorable event was a gala in honor of John Kluge's enormous gift to the library held at the Jefferson Building. Popular singer Tony Bennet and renowned actor James Earl Jones were featured performers, and the guests included General and Mrs. Colin Powell, other generals, and a host of congressional representatives. It was a gala to be remembered.

Travels with the Madison Council to legendary European capitals were among our most treasured journeys. The librarian arranged visits with cultural institutions in host countries, and Betty and I were included to share host responsibilities with Dr. Billington and Marjorie on two Madison Council cultural visits. Our trip to Russia in 2002 included visits to St. Petersburg and Moscow. My most vivid recollection on that tour was chatting with Jerry Jones, owner of the Dallas Cowboys, as we perched on a railed overlook of the Peter Hof Palace, eighteenth-century summer palace of Peter the Great, prior to entering the palace for a catered dinner. The opportunity to dine in the palace and learn about the history associated with Peter the Great gave me a keen appreciation and respect for the Library of Congress as the library of the United States of America. I am certain that the generous flow of Russian spirits added to the glow of the evening.

Our second cultural tour with the Madison Council, in September 2004, was even more spectacular as we visited the places Thomas Jefferson, John Adams, and Benjamin Franklin lived and worked during America's quest for independence. David McCulloh, noted author and biographer of John Adams, along with his lovely wife, Rosa Lee, provided a colorful narrative detailing the work and social contact of these illustrious founding fathers in Amsterdam, Paris, and London. It was a truly remarkable tour and learning experience for all! The tour began in Amsterdam, where I had the unexpected opportunity to represent Dr. Billington as spokesperson at the home of the American ambassador, the Hague and other sites on the itinerary. I was never so happy to turn over the protocol duties as I was when Dr. Billington assumed those duties for the remainder of the tour.

Every memorable trip boasts some unusual occurrence that becomes the subject of good-natured humor. In this case, I lost Betty and Joyce Miller, the late wife of Madison Council member Ed Miller. The group minus Betty and Joyce was attending a private dinner in the Le Grand Vefour, one of Paris's most attractive restaurants, because of its eighteenth-century decor. Betty and Joyce arrived over an hour late and announced that they had been locked inside one of the shops on the plaza where the entire group had toured prior to dinner. No one missed them. Luckily for them, a night watchman discovered the mishap and released them. Unflattering for me was the chiding I received for not being able to account for my troops. Some even accused me of attempting to have a solo night out in Paris. Betty and Joyce failed to see the humor in the affair no matter how it was explained.

The Madison Council tours provided lifetime memories and associations that made my tenure at the Library of Congress the most informative, interesting, and enjoyable job of my working career. The opportunity to meet presidents, foreign dignitaries, members of Congress, actors, entertainers, musicians, and authors in the incomparable beauty and architecture of the great hall, the Members' Room, and Coolidge Auditorium in the Thomas Jefferson Building was a blessing beyond my grandest expectations. But as grand an experience as these events were for me, the duties of the deputy librarian as well as Dr. Billington's expectations required that I promote the library on all occasions. My ears and eyes were always attuned to the reception accorded by the security and library escorts to visitors as they entered the building. The sound system was also a constant concern because acoustics of the grand space was difficult to moderate for voice and music. John, the soundman, and I were on great speaking terms when the sound worked well. Fortunately, we were on good speaking terms most of the time.

Refresh, Renew, and Retire

My goal from the beginning of my tour at the library was to help improve operating systems and develop leaders able to sustain them as well as leaders capable of meeting new challenges. Around the time that we were facing one hurdle after another in implementing the HR automation system, I made a commitment to Dr. Billington that I would remain at the library until we developed competent leaders who could lead as well as follow. My statement was prompted by the departure of Winston Tabb, a long-time senior staffer and trusted leader, who decided to retire at that time. New leaders had been hired to lead library services, human resources, equal opportunity, inspector general, and financial services. The expanded EC was working well as a team, and the Operations Committee was coordinating and implementing library-wide decisions under my guidance.

The Congressional Chief Administrative Officer's Council of which I was a member and the Congressional Budget Committees were pleased with the library's management of allocated resources. Dr. Billington was comfortable with promoting Joann to perform as a chief operating officer and to carry out his vision and goals. Additionally, I measured the library's operating efficiency by the results of outside audit reports and how well Dr. Billington and my subordinates accomplished their annual performance goals. We received a clean audit report from an outside auditor nine of the ten years I was at the library. Our support staff also accomplished their performance goals and kept the library out of negative media coverage for most of that time. I also wanted to travel, write my memoirs, and enjoy my senior years while in reasonably good health, and the year 2006 marked ten years at the library.

The Retirement Party

It is a rare boss who throws a retirement party for a subordinate tailor made to the retiree's own specifications. Dr. Billington and Marjorie exceeded my expectations and gave Betty and me a party to remember in the Members' Room of the Thomas Jefferson Building. Our guests included close friends from the military, a former boss from AmeriCorps, a distinguished and good friend from the Madison Council, and my trusted colleagues. It was a special honor to have three former US Army Corps commanders and their wives present as our special guests; Gen. Colin Powell had commanded V Corps before becoming the chairman of the Joint Chiefs of Staff, and Lt. Gens. Julius Becton and Andy Chambers, respectively, had commanded VII Corps. Their presence was even more special because, along with their wives, they had helped me and Betty to achieve the goals that had led to our fantastic journey ending in retirement from the Library of Congress.

Harris Wofford, former CEO of AmeriCorps, was also a special mentor. Also Jay Kislak, Madison Council member and generous benefactor to the library's collections, developed a close relationship with us, and his presence made us feel valued beyond being an employee at the library. But the most treasured guests at the party were Sandy Bryant, widow of our dear friend and fellow library associate Tom, who died in 2003; George and Rose Hudgins, whom we met at the CGSC, Fort Leavenworth, KS, in 1975; and Paul Easley, who met Betty and our sons at Shilling Manor during my first tour in Vietnam in 1969.

Dr. Billington's acknowledgment of my contributions to the library and expressions of friendship for Betty and me capped off the end of the best job that I had held in my forty-six-year career. The 1996 Rich Ahern drawing of the Thomas Jefferson Building is a treasured gift from Dr. Billington and the library staff—an ever joyful reminder of the challenges and fulfillment we experienced at the Library of Congress. I thank the good Lord for saving the best for last!

Insights

The insights gained from my tenure at the Library of Congress provide me with a unique platform to talk about the institution, leadership strategies, and operational techniques that worked for me during my appointment. I am certain that the issues addressed will confront leaders at the library and other public institutions for the next ten years (until the generation of leaders developed by the World War II work ethic are no longer in the twenty-first century workforce). I also attempt to tell my multiracial grandchildren that they will struggle with equality in America from a class or economic point of view as I struggled with equality from a racial point of view.

One of Kind Leadership Requirements

The library is a unique cultural institution that requires a balanced leadership approach. Scholars have historically been appointed to be the librarian because the position demands the depth and understanding of the knowledge that only scholars attain through years of study, research, writing, and teaching. Dr. Billington's passion for the acquisition and preservation of all forms of knowledge continues to serve the library well. Until my appointment, the deputy had been chosen from the ranks within the library and lacked the knowledge and experience of using the latest management tools to lead large complex organizations. I think Dr. Billington's and my knowledge, skill sets, and leadership strengths perfectly balanced the unique requirements of the institution.

Scholars should continue to lead the library's mission of securing, preserving knowledge, and making the library's collections available to the Congress and the American public. Scholars protect freedom of expression and business leaders look to cut waste and streamline operations to meet budget allocations. The scholar in Dr. Billington made the necessary move to cut acquisitions as well as to safeguard the collections only as decisions of last resort.

Future deputy librarians and senior leaders should be graduates of the Senior Executive Course conducted by the Executive Branch of government or from other reputable universities that teach the most effective management tools and their application to operating systems. Cultural institutions, and especially the Library of Congress, have a history of promoting from within and thereby risk falling behind in the use of technology or other innovative techniques.

The Art of Leadership

The military teaches that leadership is an art and that the first principle of the art is to know yourself and to seek self-improvement. Dr. Billington's decision to conduct a search for a leader to manage the day-to-day operations of the library and to confer upon the selected candidate the authority necessary to do the job was a mark of good leadership. His unflinching support of my leadership efforts marked him as an outstanding leader in my book. He adopted my decisions as his own, and in turn, I never made a decision without his prior knowledge or consent. My sole agenda was to fix the broken operating systems and to keep Billington in charge of the library. The object lesson is that good leaders must also be good followers and trust direct subordinates to carry out assigned goals and objectives. Don't hire anyone you don't trust to carry out your goals and objectives with your best interests in mind.

Organizational Change and Change Agents

I was hired to change the library's dysfunctional operating systems and discovered the hardest part of organizational change was the stranglehold the library culture imposed on leaders who needed to make changes. I attribute this culture of resistance to change to two reasons. The average tenure of a library employee was close to twenty- five years, and most employees had a mindset of entitlement with regard to the positions they held. Leaders were promoted from within without receiving formal executive leadership training to develop their knowledge and abilities in application of the best practices for leading an effective workforce. This phenomenon created a culture of leaders who sometimes desired change but who lacked the skill sets or forcefulness to root out the operational systems and dysfunctional practices they had created.

Change agents are developed in organizations that train leaders to excel in competitive work environments where excellence is rewarded and teamwork is a highly rated attribute on performance evaluations. As a career army officer, competition, achievement, and teamwork must be demonstrated in every assignment and repeated at each level of rank you are fortunate enough to be achieve. Promotion to brigadier general imposes an even greater demand to achieve organizational goals because of the mandatory retirement requirement if you are not promoted to the next rank within two years after reaching thirty years of service.

The Library of Congress was the first place I worked where leaders did not fear being fired for incompetence and library managers found it easier to move incompetent employees to other positions rather than accumulate the mountain of paperwork to document termination of an unproductive employee. I took a two pronged approach to bring about change at the library. I used the performance evaluation to confront and aid subordinates in achieving assigned goals and tasks. Some support staff members chose to retire rather than put up with my "coaching" to help them achieve their assigned goals or objectives. A few were reassigned to positions more in sync with their skills and abilities.

My most successful approach was to hire knowledgeable leaders from outside of the library who were accustomed to achieving performance standards as the basis for retaining their position. Everyone I hired came from a competitive work environment like the military, and all were eager to prove their abilities to fix or improve dysfunctional operating systems. Terri Smith, HR director, bore the brunt of the most difficult change to fix the HR/Cook automation system. She, like all successful change agents, was confident in her ability to lead skeptical followers and doubtful colleagues through the most challenging and unforeseen problems that are characteristic of new automation systems. The retraining of employees is usually the culprit and also the answer as was the case in the library's implementation effort. Linda Rix, co-owner of the system we were installing, proved to be a valued ally since her expert knowledge of the personnel classification system was more than sufficient to answer the "why" and "how" inherent in the task of fixing the exasperating problems.

The other essential ingredient of an effective change agent is to "coach" nonbelievers past their skepticism and give them the credit for making the new system part of the organization's new way of doing business. Employees feel good about themselves when they have accomplished a difficult task. Likewise, library employees had a new bounce in their step after they trained all of us "leaders" how to use the new hiring and selection system.

The most important thing to look for in a change agent is what drives them to take on the tough challenges. I believe it is their motivation to develop their teams' capabilities to deliver services or support and to build good working relationships up and down the chain of command. I know that is what drove me to compete for the position of deputy librarian, and I think the same is true of the change agents that led the installation of the HR/Cook automation hiring and selection system. I am grateful for their dedication and perseverance.

Raising the Productivity Bar

Most meetings are unproductive and waste the time of participants. I introduced FL to library managers because meetings were unproductive and too many important issues were not being addressed or resolved. FL principles and practices also helped library managers to employ a common language to communicate and choose appropriate levels of decision-making to resolve issues. Words like "desired outcomes," "stake holders," "and levels of decision-making" became an integral part of library managers' vocabulary. The highly sensitive HR/Cook issue was made more manageable because FL provided the tools to communicate and achieve our desired outcomes. I am a devout advocate of FL and even use its principles and practices in my communication with family and friends. I am told that library managers continue to use FL in their meetings, and I hope the practice has now become institutionalized.

The Peculiarities of Decision-Making in the US Congress

The legislative branch of the federal government is a large bureaucracy that conducts business and makes decisions by way of committees. Committee chairs are selected based on seniority of the political party in power and are staffed by individuals whom they appoint to manage the day-to-day business operations of the committee. The chairs and members of their committees, all elected representatives, are so busy with other responsibilities—running their offices and taking care of constituents in their district, serving on other committees, and fund- raising activities—that they delegate enormous power and authority to their clerks in the running of legislative branch agencies like the Library of Congress.

Strangely, it was the congressional clerk who had the first and last word about our budget or other management issues. Even though Dr. Billington was highly respected by the committee chairman and legislative branch members, the clerks had to be convinced that the numbers and rationale for any business we placed on the table were solid and viable. Fortunately, my credibility as a "fixer" of broken systems was enhanced by the respect and admiration members and their staff held for retired generals and admirals. Together, Dr. Billington and I were successful in gaining the respect and support of the clerks to support the library's budget submissions. Even in lean years when the Congress imposed across the board cuts on all legislative branch agencies, the library fared better than other agencies.

The Invaluable Role of Senate Icons

Rarely did a member of Congress have enough individual power to influence committee members, regardless of party affiliation, to insert money in an agency's budget based on his credibility alone. The late Sen. Ted Stevens (R-AK) was a rare exception. He had nearly a billion dollars over five years inserted into the library's budget to ensure that the library developed the capacity to handle and process digital data. His motive was simply to keep the congressional library relevant in the digital era.

During my tenure at the library, senators in addition to Stevens, whose influence could move committees to compromise or fund needed innovations, were Senators Byrd (D-WVA), Daniel Inoyue (D-HI), Ted Kennedy (D-MA), and John Warner (R-VA). These senators have all passed on except Warner, and it is our sad loss. The United States as a great democratic nation is less effective without senators of strong credentials and great credibility who put America's interests before the interests of their party or themselves.

Race and Equality in America

The Howard Cook case at the Library of Congress was symptomatic of racial attitudes held by African Americans and white Americans in twentieth-century America. Most of the library employees who filed the racial discrimination suit against the library managers targeted by their complaint grew up in a racially segregated society that prohibited African Americans from holding positions of responsibility over white employees. The gist of the case is that library managers resisted the complaints and the court decided the issue in favor of the employees after seventeen years of deliberations. It then took another seven years for library managers to implement a fair and impartial hiring system to end the court's oversight role. These unfortunate events remain a testament to the lingering nature of racial tensions in America.

Civil rights laws and others that reinforce equal opportunity by prohibiting discrimination based on race, gender, and sexual orientation require leaders to enforce such laws. I felt compelled to change the hiring and selection criteria for library employees because, in my opinion, it was morally the right thing to do. Dr. Billington also felt strongly about ending the perceptions of racial discrimination against African American employees and staunchly supported the implementation of the HR automation hiring and selection system.

Sadly, there are individuals in our American society who use race and ethnicity for political and economic gain. Fortunately, I don't believe that most Americans are racists or engage in activities that promote discrimination in the workplace, community, or place of worship. However, most Americans have a high tolerance for those who do discriminate, and unless directly affected by such activities, will not oppose the overt acts of discrimination. The surest way to ensure equality for all in twenty-first-century America is for the majority of Americans to take a stand against those who use race and ethnicity for political gain whenever and wherever it occurs.

Betty's and my parents challenged individuals who attempted to demean or disrespect us as persons of worth even though segregation laws assigned us to the status of second-class citizens. We challenged those who attempted to disrespect or discriminate against our sons even after segregation laws had been overturned and civil rights laws had been enacted to end racial discrimination in America. My point is that laws alone are not enough; individuals in positions of authority must enforce the laws. But even more importantly, each individual must stand up for his or her own rights and demand to be treated fairly under the laws set forth in the US Constitution.

Divine Spirit in My Life

I am aware that talking about God is a sensitive subject to many and especially in relation to the issues one must confront in the workplace. Nonetheless, I feel compelled to talk about my faith and the role it has played in my actions at the Library of Congress. I feel compelled to credit God, my Creator, with the positive results that helped others at the library. My spiritual beliefs evolved way before I came to the library and have sustained me through bad as well as good times. The three statements about God and prayer that guide my beliefs, behavior, and actions are the pillars of my simple faith about God: God is a spirit and must be worshiped in spirit and in truth (John 4:24). God made us in His image and gave us the gift to choose. And we know that all things work together for good to them that love God, to them who are called according to His purpose (Rom. 8:28).

My precarious path from Hunnewell, MO, to the Library of Congress is only comprehensible to me because of the greater force in my life that opened doors where none existed. My appointment as the deputy librarian is but one of many "miracles" that have happened in my life. I choose to share it with my readers as the first of many extraordinary outcomes during my ten-year sojourn at the library. When first contacted about working at the Library of Congress, I had no idea of even where it was located, what its mission was, or who ran it. I learned from the search firm in charge of screening applicants that I was the only nonlibrary professional among the candidates. After researching the mission and problems at the library, I decided that I wanted the position, went to the Thomas Jefferson Building, stood on the portico facing the Capitol, and essentially said the following prayer: "Lord, if it is your purpose for me to be the deputy librarian of Congress, I will accept the good with the bad and be submissive to your purposes." Five years later, during the implementation of the HR/Cook automation hiring and selection system, I remembered my commitment and prayed consistently for guidance. At one point of exasperation, I asked God to move whoever was the stumbling block to the implementation, including me, and was bolstered by Dr. Billington's support during a moment of crisis.

My prayers during Betty's quadruple heart bypass were singly focused on her survival and the restoration of her health. Her recovery from the strokes without any side effects was also a remarkable outcome that we attributed to God's grace and purpose. The unexpected payment received from the manufacturer of the diets pills was also a remarkable blessing that greatly improved our financial status and retirement options. We have also learned that God's generosity rewards those who are also generous with the blessings she provides. Betty is also a believer in prayer and in the power of the Holy Spirit to intervene in the lives of each member of our family and friends. We have a long list of preachers and devout believers in God and the power of prayer whose prayers helped us through our experiences at the Library of Congress.

I share these insights because Betty and I believe that God guides and intervenes in our lives. I also share this because any good that we accomplished for library employees and leaders, members of the legislative branch, and Madison Council members belongs to our Creator. In turn, we give praise to God for all in the aforementioned group who helped us during our journey at the library.

An Exemplary Philanthropist

Madison Council members support the library's acquisition efforts through their generous gifts and service as advisors to Dr. Billington. The most remarkable part of the organization is the background of the two men responsible for its existence. They are Dr. Billington and the late John Kluge, founding chairman of the council, a man who epitomizes the best in unselfish ambition, exemplary accomplishment, and humility. John Kluge came to America as a young man with only a small wood carving of a horse and became a billionaire through his investments in the television and entertainment industry. He donated $60 million dollars to the library as a gift to fund the Kluge prize, a one-million- dollar prize to be awarded to scholars who distinguish themselves in the sciences and humanities. Dr. Billington, on the other hand, grew up in a lower middle-class family in Philadelphia and distinguished himself as a Rhodes Scholar in history. It was he who ignited Mr. Kluge's desire to financially reward scholars for their unselfish research and study in the advancement of science and the humanities. I believe Dr. Billington's passion for knowledge, honesty, and tireless effort to make the library's collections available to the American people and the world are the reasons Madison Council members are so generous with their gifts and time.

It was a great honor and privilege to be included as guests in Madison Council members' homes and to observe individuals of wealth use their discretionary income to support the Library of Congress.

The Power of Mentoring

Organizations where senior leaders mentor their support staff build strong leaders. The US military leaders have always passed on the tricks of the trade or lessons learned to their subordinates. Most of what I learned from senior military leaders was through observation of their leadership by example and practice. Gen. Richard E. Cavazos left an indelible impression on how he used his position as commanding general, Ninth Infantry Division, to develop training programs that strengthened the bonds of teamwork between all units within the division. In every job I held after my tour of duty with Cavazos, I used his example to inform my actions and goals. Such is the power of an outstanding mentor.

Likewise, I attempted to mentor my direct subordinates at the Library of Congress on how to "lead," "coach," "teach," and "learn," the four activities leaders must perform to be successful. I learned these principles from watching and interviewing commanders who employed them to train their soldiers at the Maneuver Training Center at Hohenfels, Germany. I think the "coaching" activity was the most effective tool at the library because my subordinates were experts in their respective professional areas but had limited exposure and experience to the broader application of leadership outside of the library.

My leadership experience in the military, with the Atlanta city government, and with AmeriCorps provided a treasure trove of useful suggestions and recommendations to support the goals I envisioned for the library. During my last four years at the library, senior leaders demonstrated an excellent understanding of these principles, and I saw evidence that they were mentoring their own support staff. I only hope that my example as the deputy librarian of Congress still informs the actions and goals of library leaders.

My Last Hoorah

My retirement from the Library of Congress marked the completion of fifty years in the workforce and was a joyous occasion for Betty and me. I have recounted some of the blessings we experienced during this appointment and have afforded a glimpse of the powerful people who attended our farewell dinner party. For those like my grandchildren who may not read this until they are old and gray, here are the reasons we use the word "special" to describe the people and the place. The Members' Room in the Thomas Jefferson Building at the library—the site of our formal farewell party—can only be used by members of Congress or by individuals who are granted permission by the librarian with approval of the Speaker of the House's office. The thirteenth librarian of Congress, appointed by President Ronald Regan, and his wife hosted the party and our guests. Among our guests and friends were African American generals who were among the first to be promoted to the rank of brigadier general in the early 1970s and the first to command at the highest levels within the Department of Defense.

This special place and these special people made history because many black and white leaders—among them Presidents Harry Truman, John Kennedy, and Lyndon Johnson, along with Thurgood Marshall and Martin Luther King Jr.—made it possible for African Americans to compete and be rewarded on the basis of skill, knowledge, and competence. It is my hope and prayer that the Members' Room in the Thomas Jefferson Building will continue to be available to host special people who dedicate themselves to serving an America that values competence, skill, and knowledge regardless of ethnicity, gender, or sexual orientation. This was my last job and what a ride for me and Betty to remember in our retirement years.

Library of Congress retirement picture, the Great Hall, Thomas Jefferson Building.

Gallery of Significant Relationships and Places

CHAPTER TWENTY-SEVEN

The Power of Choice and Relationships

"Time, circumstance, preparation, and chance continue to bring young people into
the world dependent upon someone to help them to be successful in life. Caring parents and teachers, champions of equality, and the cultivation of faith in a God that loves unconditionally-and wants us to love each other- hold out to them a strong chance for success. This combination of human development tools helped me to succeed during the tests of war, economic disasters, and social unrest during my early years. It is still my firm belief that the tools represent the best hope of those who would embrace and employ them to help our young people achieve success in the twenty-

first century."

- The above quote, Chapter Two, Lincoln University
and Insight on

My Early Years, focused on helping young people because at the time I believed that helping a young adult make good choices was the best assurance against the pitfalls of disappointment, failure, and broken relationships. However, Choice and Relationships are important to adults throughout their lives. This chapter focuses on adults of all ages because every choice has consequences, and each relationship has the potential of pain or pleasure in human behavior at all stages of life. So, What's God got to do with it?

God the creator gave humans a choice and then warns Adam of dire consequences if he disregarded His warning and ate from the tree of life and knowledge. Gen 2:15-18.

Choice and free will are the greatest gift to humans and the source of much happiness and sorrow. God promised Adam that his life would be plagued with hardship and death because of disobedience and God has delivered on that promise through each generation. Jesus promised an abundant life on earth and life after death for those who accept Him and His teachings and practice his commandments in which He collapsed the ten into two: "Love the Lord your God with all your heart and with all your soul and with all your mind. This is the first and greatest commandment. And the second is like it:'Love your neighbor as yourself.' All the Law and the Prophets hang on these two commandments." (Mat 22:37-40 NIV).

The third force between human choice, relationship and consequence is the 'Holy Spirit that comes with acceptance of Jesus Christ. This spirit can influence predictable outcomes from bad choices into favorable outcomes without a trace of evidence of why, who, or how the outcome occurred.

God and the teaching of Jesus Christ are the best and most practical approach to a successful life. Humans must adjust to the rhythm of nature and disruptive choices of other humans. God the creator of the universe and humanity gives a prescription for making Choices that help navigate life through good and bad times and emphasizes the establishment of relationships that work for our individual and common good.

My life story is an example of how God, Jesus and the Holy Spirit affected my choices and life outcomes. My timid acceptance of God and Jesus Christ as a teenager, the choices I and others made for me in my adult life were influenced by the Holy Spirit (unexplainable results) that sustained me through disappointments and triumphs of my life. As you read the summary of my choices below, think of your story and your choices.

As a teenager I obeyed the suggestion of my mother and joined the church in Hunnewell and was baptized in a pond near Labelle MO, signaling that I accepted God and Jesus Christ in my life; as a high school graduate, the Choice to enroll me in college was made by a committee of family members lead by my brother-in-law who took me and his son to Lincoln University and enrolled us in the university; at Lincoln, I choose to enroll in ROTC because I needed the monthly stipend of $37.50 to help pay my living expenses. Betty and I choose to marry each other, and I choose to remain in the army and accept a culture that demanded obedience to living standards based on rank, customs and courtesies rather than on personal freedoms, cultural, racial, religious or political norms; at Fort Benning, I choose to challenge racial discrimination in housing in Columbus, GA and the Commanding General choose to provide housing for my family on Fort Benning, and challenged the city of Columbus to end the discriminatory practice; at Tuskegee, I choose to challenge the army's policy of assigning black officers to Historical Black Colleges and white officers to white colleges in the southern United States in the early 1970s, and after 14 months, Infantry Assignments Branch choose to reassign me from Tuskegee University back to Vietnam; there, I choose to appeal my assignment to a combat area on the basis of equity (I had combat duty my first tour-other Infantry Officers; white and graduates of the prestigious Command and General Staff College; I had not been selected) available with no combat duty and received coveted assignments in non-combat areas; and the senior director of army personnel in the region choose to reassign me to a non- combat position; at Fort Lewis, WA, I refused an assignment to Turkey under threat of career ending consequences, voluntarily returned to Tuskegee University as Professor of Military Science, a position from which no incumbent had been promoted or offered another assignment, and within two months at Tuskegee an army selection board of senior officers choose me to attend the US Air Force War College and for promotion to the rank of Colonel; in Germany, successfully- ending command as a Colonel and seeking a position to remain competitive for consideration and selection to general officer, and was told that all Colonel vacancies had been filled with exception of one that was pending approval by headquarters in Washington, D.C., advised by my mentor, General Chambers that I continue calling the commander with the vacancy pending approval of extension. I followed his advice and was chosen for the position. The next day, I learned in the newspaper that General Chambers had been appointed to command that organization; at Stuttgart, I reported directly to General Chambers, a pleasant personality with exceptionally high standards, exceeded his goals and was selected for promotion to Brigadier General. Chambers was on the selection panel that chose me for promotion to Brigadier General and was influential in my assignment to the First Cavalry Division an assignment that historically saw the incumbent promoted for a second star; at Fort Gillian GA and within months of my eligibility for consideration of selection for a second star or mandatory retirement from the army, a group of influential black business entrepreneurs in Atlanta GA arranged a meeting for me with the mayor of Atlanta who offered me a job as his Chief of Staff on the first day of my eligibility to retire from the army; as Chief Operating Officer, I choose to resign from the City of Atlanta for reasons of ego, decided to start a 'bootcamp type program for youth, was struggling to make ends meet and on recommendation from a friend, received an offer from a search firm looking to fill a position to launch AmeriCorps residential program under President Bill Clinton- chosen for the position and completed the task; at AmeriCorps, received an unsolicited offer to add my name to a search firm to hire a Deputy Librarian of Congress- declined the invitation and urged by friends of the Librarian of Congress who contacted Betty to convince me to apply because General Colin

Powell had recommended me for the position. I was chosen for the position and served as Deputy Librarian and Chief Operating Officer for ten years.

These series of Choices all involved relationships, prayers, and good fortune that I attribute to the power of the Holy Spirit that intervenes in the affairs of humans and circumstances we create. I'm certain your choices and story also have challenges, triumphs and disappointments as did mine. Was God and the Holy Spirit among my choices?

My list of significant life choices above doesn't emphasize my communication with God prior to making the choice. As a matter of routine my prayers were the Lord's Prayer at church and bedtime and to bless the food at mealtimes. I only prayed for help after being told I was going to Vietnam, or going to Tuskegee the first time, or at the threat of going to Turkey, and after our son, Lloyd's death, and after Betty's quadruple heart by- pass and a stroke. These personal disappointments and moments of sorrow and fear gradually changed my prayer routines. It is important to pray and meditate with God daily before choices are made as well as after unexpected events thrust choices upon you. The choice to pray to God is the first and most significant choice in the spirit realm of which you do your part, Jesus, and the Holy Spirit do their part. This interaction offers no guarantees that your prayers will be answered, the only guarantee is the presence of God, Jesus and the Holy Spirit with you no matter what happens. And best of all, the guarantee of eternal life. Eternal life may be a debatable topic with you. Relationships on the other hand, are inevitably the source of pain, pleasure or a little of both? Are you happy with your relationships and are your relationships happy with you?

My list of choices above also does not go into detail about the relationships and individuals who made the choices that were not to my liking, or the choices that were favorable and taught me the lessons that align with the teachings of Jesus, Holy Spirit and God. Those outcomes contributed to my development.

There were many individuals in my circle of influence above with whom I had relationships that ranged from great to good. Among supervisors, General Chambers and Dr. Billington were the two supervisors who rank in the great category. Their demeanor and regard for the well-being of others taught me that demanding high expectations with kindness and encouragement fit perfectly with the teachings of Jesus and the Holy Spirit.; they both commended others for effort, rewarded accomplishment and shared in failure resulting from unforeseen circumstances. I worked for Dr Billington ten years the longest in my 45-year career and was in a mentoring relationship with General Chambers for ten years before working under his direct supervision for eighteen months. He remained my mentor and friend until his death in 2017. These two, the Powells, Sister Chuck, Betty and Mel and the axioms and purpose of William Glasser's Choice Theory augment the teachings of Jesus Christ and helped me offer what I believe to be the best approach to establish relationships that achieve mutual happiness in life's journey.

However, before sharing that approach to mutual happiness in relationships, I think it important to explain how I came to know about Glasser. I learned about Glasser in my pursuit of a master's degree in Counseling and Human Development at Troy State University, Montgomery, AL; that was the year after I turned down the Turkey assignment in 1981, and was preparing for a civilian career in Alabama. As noted earlier, the eminence of my retirement did not occur and the thought of Glasser's Reality Therapy did not cross my mind again until updating *Recipient of Grace Continued* in 2022! The only reason I can give for thinking about Reality Therapy and Glasser was my realization that in writing *American Racism and What You Can Do About It* in 2020, my reality of the difficulties of race in America was not the reality of white America. When I looked up Reality Therapy, I learned that the theory had evolved into a list of axioms that influenced Glasser to change the name to Choice Theory- a way to teach people how to get along well with the people they want to get along well with. Although I am not certified to teach the program my understanding of the basic premise of his theory and three of his ten axioms supports my approach to establishing mutual and happy relationships with and among your circles of influence. I am humbled and privileged to share **what** I believe is the best approach to establishing mutual and productive relationships with and among your circles of influence :

1. Choose to submit to a comprehensive relationship with God and his precepts under the stewardship of Jesus and the Holy Spirit in all you think, do, and say. Being human, you will not always live up to this commitment and when necessary, ask for mercy and grace and renew your commitment. (Kingdom Men Rising, Devotional, Dr. Tony Evan, 2021.)

2. Set high standards for self and others, commend effort, and reward accomplishments.
   "God has given us each the ability to do certain things well. So, if God has given you the ability to prophesy, speak out when you have faith that God is speaking through you. If your gift is that of serving others, serve them well. If you are a teacher, do a good job of teaching. If your gift is to encourage others, do it! If you have money, share it generously. If God has given you leadership ability, take the responsibility seriously. And if you have a gift for showing kindness to others, do it gladly." (Romans 12:6-8 NLT).

3. The only person's behavior we can control is our own (Glasser).

This self-evident truth was revealed during my relationship and role as husband and father. When first married, I was expected to control Betty and my sons behavior in accordance with army regulations governing family behavior and conduct. As we grew older in our relationships the circumstances of my military deployments made us aware that I had to rely on Betty to provide for our sons and take care of bills and other interests. We both came to trust each other and our sons to behave in each other's best interest. i.e., the volunteer submission of personal freedom in support of our shared goal and best interests. **How do you see your relationships when it involves giving others freedom or control over your life?**

Number 3 above is the first of ten axioms that Glasser believes affect the happiness and well-being of humans, his remaining 9 are provided for your reflection and awareness:

2. All we can give or get from each other is information- how we deal with information is our choice,

3. All long-lasting psychological problems are relationship problems,

4. The problem relationship is always a part of our present lives,

5. What happens in the past has a great deal to do with what we are today, but revisiting this painful past has little or nothing to do with what we need to do now,

6. We are driven by 5 genetic needs; love and belonging, power, freedom, survival, and fun- we can only satisfy our own needs,

7. We can only satisfy these needs by satisfying pictures in our quality world,

8. All we can do from birth to death is behave. All behavior is total behavior and is made up of 4 inseparable components; acting, thinking, feeling, and physiology,

9. All behavior is total behavior designated by verbs, usually gerunds, and named by the component that is most recognizable, for example, named by the formation that I am

too depressed or am depressing-instead of I am suffering from depression or am depressed. This language denotes choice,

10.　　　All total behavior is chosen. We have direct control over the acting and thinking components. We can indirectly control feelings and physiology. (Choice Theory, William Glasser Audio Book, Harper Collins, 2013.

4. Recognize that we seek relationships that validate who we want to be, and we join or associate with people and organizations that behave, think, and support what we admire or aspire to become. Humans have a strong need to belong to a tribe, organization, or culture but have difficulty identifying with individuals across tribal or cultural groups based on behavioral acts of kindness, goodness, humility, or compassion. Glassers Axioms 6-8 and 10 are compelling forces that influence our relationships.

5. Strive to be comfortable in your own skin. God made us humans in His image and commanded us to love one another. In the presence of groups of a different racial, cultural, gender, or economic status be kind, patient, and humble. General Powell received this compliment at his televised funeral service. I endorsed the sentiment and believe we should all strive for this trait.

6. Recognize that Control in relationships should be to safeguard the freedoms of the participants in the pursuit of common goals that support their interests and well-being. This applies to personal relationships, public safety, community relationships, civic and religious relationships, etc.

My six recommendations to nurture good and productive relationships require daily attention to those in your circle of relationships: God, family, friends, at home, the workplace, community, and public and private gatherings. The six are essential to pursue in America's multicultural democracy where race and skin color are often used as criteria for acceptance in opportunities that lead to health, wealth, and wellbeing. Attitude, belief, behavior and compatibility must become the basis of acceptance in relationships rather than race, religion or skin color.

In summary, this chapter is about the power of choice and relationships. God has the power and gives it to each of us with the caveat of choice. Our choice is to exercise His choice and accept the strength and help from Jesus and the Holy Spirit to have life abundant on earth and eternal life after death. His prescription of how to live with one another is not difficult to understand and only requires submission to a comprehensive relationship with the teachings of His Son and acceptance of the Holy Spirit as we go about making choices in our lives. You don't have to be perfect, smart, rich, tall, short, or perfect height and weight, good-looking, of a particular race or color, male or female. **You just have to submit to His creation like all other forms of life and matter that conforms to His purpose**. You are fearfully and wonderfully made and can choose to be powerful in your Choices and Relationships in this life.

I am thankful for the significant six who were influenced by the power of God, Jesus and the Holy Spirit in their lives. Their death and contribution to my life gave me the courage to share this chapter with you. I pray you use your power to influence those you love and care about in your circles of relationships.

CHAPTER TWENTY- EIGHT

Different Perspectives and Shared Goals

Different perspectives and shared goals are about our beliefs in the Declaration of Independence and the US Constitution; whether we believe it applies to all Americans equally or some more than others. Different perspectives is also about what we Americans believe is our national purpose as a country, our identity as Americans, and who is responsible for what we think is wrong with America. At present, national polls agree that Americans are divided in their beliefs into all those perspectives with no political party, elected, or popular personality earning the trust of the majority to unite the country towards a common purpose. We are left to figure out for ourselves answers to the above questions. Before Betty, my wife of 57 years died, I believed that the self-evident truth that we are all created equal and endowed by our creator with the rights of life, liberty, and the pursuit of happiness was a shared belief for most Americans. I believed this despite my ancestors being enslaved and myself having to live through racial segregation and limited opportunities in my youth and mid-thirties. Since Betty's death and the significant divisiveness referenced above, I have closely examined my journey through America's past in my attempt to discover why Americans are so divided.

Betty died in April 2019 and after her funeral, my grief was so great that I revisited our life together reflecting on our challenges as black children navigating a racially segregated Missouri until the 1954 school desegregation decision; as newly married adults in 1962 embarking on a career in the US Army, and being among the first Negroes (the term African Americans didn't gain acceptance until the 1980s) to assume career-enhancing leadership positions at each level of command from the grade of Captain to General Officer in 1985 and in our post military accomplishments until her death. We had endured a lot and accomplished much. I was proud of our success and attributed our success to the sacrifices of black soldiers, civil rights leaders, and white allies who had made our journey possible. In fact, my reflections led me to examine the American treatment of enslaved Africans from 1619 up through 2020 and concluded that American Racism was so deeply embedded in all facets of American life that racism was still the most divisive issue in America. My book, *American Racism and What You*

Can Do About It was inspired by grief and my desire to help end racism in America. As I was writing, *American Racism and What You Can Do About It,* in the summer of 2020, I became aware and alarmed that President Trump was not carrying the torch of multicultural democracy forward but was encouraging white nationalists to pursue their interest in racial superiority. I noticed that military color guards that had purposefully been racially integrated over past decades were increasingly made up of all white servicemembers at public celebrations and at burial honors for veterans at Arlington National Cemetery. I was so concerned about American democracy being at risk under Trump that I directed my comments in *American Racism and What You Can Do About It* to white voters urging them to vote for a President who would support the Declaration of Independence and the US Constitution and not to vote for Trump. I had concluded that Trump was seeking autocratic rule and using white nationalists' groups as a wedge to entice white voters to choose a candidate (Trump) who would insure white political domination regardless of whites becoming a racial minority in America. I was glad that Biden won the Presidency but concerned however, that Trump received 50% of the white vote, and even more alarmed in 2021 over Trump's attempts to overturn the election results. The January 6, 2021, attack against the US Capitol by white nationalists' groups and Make America Great Again (MAGA) supporters was the greatest domestic threat to American democracy since the US Civil War. However, I continued to think that embedded racism fueled Trump's and his followers' motives but found it hard to believe that 50 per cent of white voters wanted to destroy American democracy and the greatest example of self-government in the history of the world. My doubts about racism being the major issue of the Trump-MAGA threat caused me to examine the racial issue from my personal perspective -the racially restricted opportunities and overt violence against black Americans in the 1940s-1975 era, and the post-civil rights era from 1980s – to the present when greater opportunities and less overt violence against black Americans occurred.

Being a witness to history has its advantages especially when it pertains to firsthand experience with the official racial segregation laws of the 1940s-1970s against black Americans in the south and border states of Delaware, Kentucky, Maryland, Missouri, and west Virginia in the areas of schools, employment, housing, and places of amusement and entertainment. I am also a witness to the positive changes in opportunity that reflects a more multicultural America that is paralyzed by divisiveness since 2017-present. To compare the two eras and the evidence of racism in both eras I selected four headings to compare the racial sentiment of black and white Americans as a factor in America's image abroad and the response of leaders and the media to the racial issue in America:

- **National Purpose** (the issues that unite the country)
- **White Sentiment Towards Black Americans** (Attitude towards racial segregation, violence and reaction to equality towards Black Americans),
- **National Leaders- Political and Public** (moral courage to improve racial equality and keep the country united to achieve our National Purpose) and
- **The Role of Media** (a help or hinderance with the sentiment of racial equality in America during the 1940s-1975 era and 2017-present era.

1940s-1975: Resistance to the Politics of Freedom*

(*Enforcing US Constitutional Laws to include the disenfranchised and protect their individual rights and Opportunities)

My first-hand experience with the racial segregation experience during this period was characteristic of African Americans in small towns and rural areas in the Mid-west and border states in America until my graduation from Lincoln University; and my experience as an adult and career army officer was typical of black Americans of my generation who were among the first to integrate in their chosen profession. We complied with the racial segregation laws and practices because that was the best choice available to live and hope for better options. The better option came with the desegregation of the military by President Harry Truman, the legal arguments of Thurgood Marshall and the National Association and Advancement of Colored People (NAACP), and the peaceful protests lead by Martin Luther King Jr., and others. The resentment and resistance of white citizens across the south and some northern cities were identified as racism by sociologist and eventually acknowledged and addressed by Presidents Eisenhower, Kennedy, Johnson and appointed leaders. While the story of the Civil Rights movements is widely replayed during Black History month, those without firsthand experience may not focus on the importance of the explanations and arguments that explained the "why" behind the resentment and resistance of integration as I am attempting to highlight below.

National Purpose. The victory over Germany and Japan and America's total support of the war effort united all Americans no matter the political tensions over domestic issues. Every American family regardless of race or economic status shared the risk of providing soldiers or volunteers to the military and or civilian effort in support of the war; this heartfelt contribution united Americans under Democrat and Republican administrations well into the 1970s.

Racial Policies and White Sentiment. The rigorously enforced segregation policies by state and local authorities were deeply entrenched in all aspects of life from birth to death in the southern and border states. Negroes had fought as service members in racially segregated military units and volunteered as civilian workers in support of the war effort (The term African American did not gain popular acceptance until the 1980s). Racial violence against negro soldiers returning from the war increased along with civil rights efforts to end racial discrimination in America. However, racial laws and policies were complied with by negroes and supported by the white majority until federal enforcement of civil rights laws were initiated by President Truman in 1948 that opened the Civil Rights movement in the 1950s. The chronological peaceful protests by Negroes to end the separate and unequal treatment by whites began with the bus boycott in 1955, followed by the freedom riders, negro, and white students to end segregated seating on interstate buses in 1961, then sit-ins to gain service at counters in restaurants rather than be served in the back or refused service. All these peaceful efforts were often met with violence and sometimes the death of the protesters. The 1954 Supreme Court decision to end racial segregation in public schools in the south and border states was fiercely resisted in the southern states. Southern governors and white citizens' councils were formed to resist compliance with the law. The integration of Little Rock High School in 1957, the University of Mississippi in 1962, and the University of Alabama in 1963 generated large groups of white protesters and violence that required the use of federal troops to compel the admission of black students. The bombing of the 16th Street Baptist Church in Birminhmam, AL September 15, 1963, by four Ku Klux Klan terrorists, killed four young Negro girls and wounded 22 others. Another significant reaction against racial integration were the assassination of Medgar Evers by a Ku Klux Klan terrorist also in Mississippi in 1963. The march for voting rights across the Edmund Pettis Bridge in Selma in 1965 resulted in Alabama state Troopers attacking the marchers with dogs and beating them with clubs to deter them from voting. The scene was so horrible that media reporters named it "bloody Sunday". As an example of the danger to blacks traveling in the south, in 1969, I was assigned to Fort Benning, Ga with my family and felt that the sentiment against Negroes in the south was so strong that we drove from Hannibal, MO non-stop to Fort Benning (765 miles). We did not want to risk an overnight stay in a motel or hotel in the south. I covered that incident in Chapter Seven to emphasize the racial inequalities of Negroes in the military stationed at Fort Benning and Columbus, GA in 1969. The 1960s can easily be declared the decade of resistance and resentment that broke the stranglehold of racial segregation in the southern states of America.

National Leaders. True to the definition of exceptional, only a few national leaders used their influence to address the toughest issue during this era. The gallery of leaders identified below is exceptional in at least two ways; the white leaders had the courage and integrity to tell people who looked like them that equality under the law in America was guaranteed under the US Constitution and would be enforced by the federal government; Negro leaders had the courage to demand equal rights through peaceful protests, and to publicly disagree with people who looked like them who demanded equality by any means necessary. These leaders were chosen by me based on their willingness to use the power of their influence and office to enforce the law or to risk their lives through peaceful demonstrations in the face of hostile police, or white protesters and armed white nationalists' groups. President Harry Truman leads this gallery and ranks with Abraham Lincoln in vision, courage, and integrity, as a champion of humanity in his circle of responsibility as President of the United States.

President Harry Truman

President Harry Truman, the Thirty-Third President of the United States stands alone in his successful efforts to end racial segregation in the United States Military and employment in the Federal Government in Washington, D.C. As Vice President, Truman was thrust into the Presidency when President Roosevelt died in April 1945. President Truman successfully ended the war with Germany, in May 1945 and with the Japanese, in September 1945. America was thrust into the world leadership position and the title of the leader of the free world. President Harry S. Truman stands alone in his willingness to lead members of his race to end discrimination in the United State Military and in the US Federal Government. In July 1948, President Truman signed Executive Order 9980 which ended 166 years of all-white military forces to defend American domestic and international interests. There were no large Civil Rights protesters marching in the streets demanding integration, although there had been a long and steady stream of negro protesting racial segregation in every war since the end of the US Civil War and creation of all black units to prevent integrating the US military forces. Additionally, President Truman did not have the support of admirals, generals, or the secretaries of the military departments to desegregate the military; to the contrary, the flag and general officers- many of them promoted to a fifth star for their exceptional war-time service, and the civilian leaders strongly advised President Truman not to risk the readiness of the services by desegregating the military forces. So why did Truman sign the order? The best answer is found in the book, *Unexampled Courage, The Blinding of Sgt. Isaac Woodard and the Awakening of President Harry S. Truman and Judge J. Waties Waring* by Judge Richard Gergel. I think Truman signed the order because it was the right thing to do (humanitarian reason). President Truman was also exceptional in that he won most of the southern states in his bid for the Presidency over Thomas E. Dewey even though the southern democrats split from the Democratic Party and voted for Strom

Thurmond (SC). Even more amazing, the racial sentiment throughout the country was against accepting the negro as equal citizens. President Truman, unlike the leaders who followed him in the Civil Rights struggles, was without strong supporters in his administration. He was the driving force behind appointing an integrated commission on Civil Rights and prosecuting the police officer who blinded Sgt Isaac Woodard in South Carolina. 2023 marks the 75th anniversary of Truman desegregating the US Military and the event will focus on his wisdom, vision, and courage as an ordinary human blessed with the extraordinary gift to respect the humanity of others in his circle of responsibility.

President Truman's significant accomplishments in moving America towards a more equal and just democracy in 1948 did not however, erase the anxiety or racial discrimination experienced by Negro citizens in America.

Returning veterans of all races had experienced war-torn countries and minority servicemembers had been exposed to better treatment by Europeans than white Americans in the US. All servicemembers returned home eager to get an education, and jobs, resume marriages, or marry and start families. Minority servicemembers and especially Negro and Asian veterans, believed that they had shared the same risk as white soldiers and resented the inequality. The entrenched separate and unequal practices against Negro veterans resumed increasing hostility over the advantages white veterans received in homeownership loans, jobs, and business ownerships that were not offered to minority veterans. Racial tensions increased and only a few exceptional leaders at the national level (President Harry Truman and Branch Rickey, Brooklyn Dodgers desegregating baseball with Jackie Robinson) saw the need to address the issue in the 1940s. President Truman's desegregation of the military was an unpredictable act that opened the door to possibilities of equal rights for all Americans. Negroes began to earnestly believe that segregated public schools could be integrated and white southern governors began planning to preserve segregation in public schools no matter the cost or by any means necessary.

In the 1950s America and the world learned that the anchor of white sentiment about Negro equality was fastened to the legal ruling of "separate but equal" and rested on the sanctity of white children being educated separately from negro children. The showdown over the stranglehold of racism in America took place in the early 1950s at the Supreme Court of the United States of America. I was 14 years old in 1952, was in the 9th grade, and bussed 70 miles round trip to attend Douglas High School, Hannibal, MO the regional high school for negro children in northeast Missouri. I was aware that negroes in the southern and border states were forced to attend separate schools and could only attend Historically Black Colleges. I was generally aware that the NAACP and Thurgood Marshall were using the courts to make the Negro schools equal to white schools in terms of buildings, teachers, and teaching materials. I sensed that the "separate but equal" school issue was based on the belief that Negroes were inferior to whites and the comments of southern governors during that period confirmed my intuition. The governors and politicians from the south and most white politicians embraced the 1896 Supreme Court ruling Plessy v. Ferguson that confirmed that separate facilities for Negroes were Constitutional as long as they were equal. That ruling was the law of the land for fifty-eight years and would have survived longer had it not been for Thurgood Marshall, NAACP legal attorney, J. Waties Waring. US District Judge in South Carolina where Marshall argued that separate schools for black children were unconstitutional, the sudden death of Supreme Court Justice Fred Vinson, **Earl Warren,** Vinson's successor, and Herbert Brownell, Jr., US Attorney General for President Dwight Eisenhower, Truman's successor as US President. Each official played a unique role representing their individual perspective about the law as it pertained to race, equality, and justice in America. Their collective effort changed America **but**

Earl Warren, by example and persuasion stands because of his moral persuasion and leadership. He influenced the eight associate justices to act on the basis that the power of the law resides in the person appointed or elected to apply the law to the people the law governs.

Thurgood Marshall

Thurgood Marshall was one of a few Negro Lawyers in America with the qualification to practice law and represent the Constitutional Rights of Negro Citizens in Virginia, Kansas, South Carolina, and the District of Columbia the states selected by the NAACP to challenge the constitutionality of Plessey v Ferguson commonly known as the "separate but equal" doctrine. The doctrine was applied to public accommodations and living areas in towns and cities to enforce Jim Crow laws throughout the southern and border states in America.

Thurgood was the Director of the NAACP'S Legal Defense Fund, and the chief architect of the school desegregation cases. He selected Clarendon School District Number 22, Clarendon County, South Carolina as the most glaring inequality of schools between white and negro students. The county had 6,725 Negro students taught in 22 delipidated and poorly resourced structures as compared to 225 white students taught in 12 well-maintained and resourced structures in the same county. The case was Briggs v. Elliott, May 1952 and Marshall was eager to represent Harry and Liza Briggs lead complainants against the state. It was obvious to Marshall that the great disparity in the buildings alone would be sufficient to prove the inequality and challenges that the state was in violation of the Fourteenth Amendment. However, a tip and suggestion from **Judge J. Waties Waring, District Judge Eastern South Carolina** compelled Marshall to change his strategy. Waring advised Marshall that the Governor wanted to preserve racially segregated schools and was submitting a $75 million dollar bond to make the negro schools equal to the white schools in the county. He further advised Marshall to make his primary argument about the psychological damage suffered by negro children by being made to feel inferior to white children because of separate schools-violates equal treatment of the law under the Fourteenth Amendment. Waring further explained that the case would be heard by a three-panel court, and he would be one of the judges hearing the case and under the rules of the federal court system that any case challenging the Constitutionality of a state's action, if one judge dissents, the case automatically gets a hearing at the Supreme Court.

Waring advised Marshall to notify the complainants of the change in strategy and the risks of retaliation for filing the suit against the school board before the start of the trial. The Briggs were undeterred and urged Marshall to proceed with vigor.

During the trial, Marshall attacked the facilities but also emphasized the psychological harm to Negro children by being treated as inferior to white children. The state attorney dismissed the psychological impacts on Negro children and relied on the state of South Carolina's willingness to upgrade their facilities as the winning formula for the state and for the Supreme Court should the case appear before that body. Two members of the three-judge panel ruled in favor of the state and Waring dissented writing that segregation was unconstitutional. The case was forwarded to the Supreme Court and placed on the docket to be heard by the justices. The white power structure of the state and Clarendon County punished the Negro population for exercising their rights for equality of education for their children. Reverend Joseph DeLaine was a member of the NAACP and a teacher at the negro school- he, his wife, daughter, and two nieces, all teachers, were fired by the all-white Clarendon County school board. Harry and Eliza Briggs, lead plaintiffs in the case also suffered for their involvement in the case. Harry, a navy veteran and service station attendant was fired from his job, and Eliza, a maid at a motel was fired from her job. Negro farmers in the county were denied loans to plant their crops, and other Negroes who had loans were forced to pay them off. Despite their loss, the negro residents had the highest regard for Marshall and regarded their sacrifice as a win for themselves and equality for Negroes throughout America.

The case was sent to the Supreme Court in 1952 and over the period of the next four years, Thurgood Marshall would remain the most courageous voice for equality in America and the only African American to lead the legal challenge against "separate but equal" that began the most significant progress in American Civil Rights. The following major significant events assured the unanimous decision that resulted in the desegregation of public schools in the southern and border states of America:

The December 1952 case was heard by the Supreme Court under Chief Justice Fred Vinson. The justices in a closed session after the hearing decided not to take a vote but agreed to have the case reargued in 1953 to give the Eisenhower administration and especially the attorney general the opportunity to submit a brief on the merits of the case. **President Eisenhower** was concerned over the attorney general, **Herbert G. Brownell Jr's**, submission of a brief to the court. Eisenhower told Brownell of his concerns over his participation and asked Brownell his view of the case. Brownell explained that he believed that Plessy was wrongly decided and should be overturned. Eisenhower accepted his answer and insisted that he make it clear that it was his personal view. Eisenhower was keenly aware of the discomfort of the southern governors over the NAACP's challenge to the constitutionality of the "separate but equal" doctrine of segregated schools and he had assured Governor Byrnes, South Carolina that regardless of the outcome of the case the justice department would defer to the local control of the state's responsibility over local issues.

*Examination of the personal papers of the associate justices under Vinson the justices would have voted 5-4 or 6-3 to retain "separate but equal" under Plessy.

Death Changes the Outcome

In early March 1953, the Eisenhower administration was having difficulty finding a Solicitor General to represent the administration at the Supreme Court and asked Earl Warren, three-time consecutive Governor of California if he was interested in the position. Warren had supported Eisenhower during his campaign for president and Eisenhower had mentioned a possible appointment to the court if a vacancy became available. Warren and Brownell set up a code to indicate when a firm offer was made for him to fill the position. Brownell sent the coded message and Warren accepted the position September 3, 1953, as the Solicitor General of the Supreme Court.

September 8, 1953, Chief Justice Fred Vinson died in his sleep from a heart attack. He was 63 years of age and not known to be in ill health. Eisenhower had to scramble to develop a list of qualifications he desired the new Chief Justice to have. In a letter to his brother, Milton, after Vinson's funeral, he listed these qualities: a man of known and recognizable integrity, wide experience in government, of competence in law, national stature in reputation to help in my effort to restore the court to the high position of prestige it once enjoyed.

Brownell had Eisenhower's full confidence in handling issues of the court including the selection of the Chief Justice of the Supreme Court. Brownell and Warren met at McClellan Air Force in Sacramento, CA where Warren's political views were questioned and determined to be compatible with Eisenhower's middle-of-the-road Republican values. Brownell reported to the President that he thought Warren was the top man for the job as Chief Justice of the Supreme Court. Eisenhower appointed Warren and was present at the small but dignified ceremony at the Supreme Court when Warren took the oath of office on October 5, 1953. On the same day a Washington Post reporter wrote that American prestige abroad had been damaged because of the racial problems and the impact a court decision on school desegregation could have on the problem. The reporter quoted Brownell's awareness of the concerns and of the President's commitment to equality and states' rights more than any President in modern times.

Brownell submits a 188-page brief on the segregation cases stating that the United States Supreme Court had both the authority and duty to end racial segregation in schools. He found the history of the Fourteenth Amendment "inconclusive" on the issue. He argued that the framers of the amendment established a broad constitutional principle of full and complete equality of all persons under the law and forbade legal distinctions based on race or color. He concluded that the amendment, "compels a state to grant the benefits of public education to all its people equally without regard to differences of race or color." And Brownell ended with a recommendation that a court decree abolishing school segregation permit a reasonable length of time for the integration of the white and black school systems. *Eisenhower vs Warren: The Battle for Civil Rights and Liberties, James F. Simon, pg 142.*

Earl Warren

On his first day as Chief Justice, **Earl Warren** used his leadership and political skills to earn the trust of the justices and to meet them on their turf-the chambers of each associate justice. Warren visited the senior associate justice, Hugo Black in his chambers and asked him to introduce him to each justice and chair meetings until he felt comfortable with the protocols of the court. At his meetings he listened to each justice's concerns rather than share his views or philosophies about leadership or expectations as Chief Justice. By the end of his meetings, Warren had a good sense of each justice's views on the court's role in deciding legal opinions argued before the court.

December 7, 1953, Chief Justice Warren and the eight associate justices began three days of argument of the school segregation cases. All 300 seats were filled with black and white citizens eager to hear the cases. The South Carolina case of Briggs v. Elliott was the case of interest to the press and most of the visitors. Thurgood Marshall confidently opened his argument challenging the justices to end the vestige of slavery by ending the "separate but equal" doctrine that harmed the self-image of Negro Children for life. Chief Justice Warren only interrupted Marshall to ask, **"what is the power in the Fourteenth Amendment that allows the court to end "separate but equal"?** Marshall asked, **"the power"?** and made no attempt to answer the question. He continued pointing to the deplorable facilities in the Negro schools as compared to the well-built and maintained white schools. Davis, the eloquent lawyer representing South Carolina hammered on the fact that "separate but equal" had been challenged nine times and was proven to be constitutional nine times. He concluded that the Negro schools in South Carolina will be equal to the white schools and would be the model for all Negro schools in southern and border states schools. He ended his argument and the justices retired to decide the case.

Warren announces his views of the case, asks the justices to present their views without voting, and influences them to realize they are the "power" over the Fourteenth Amendment. Warren's words are so profound that they merit being recorded for posterity and passed to succeeding generations. He stated in the conference with justices December 12, 1953:

"I can't escape the feeling that no matter how much the Court wants to avoid it, it must decide the issue of whether segregation is allowable in public schools." He spoke about the legitimate concerns the states raised about overturning Plessy and continued to share his deeply held beliefs. **"But the more I've heard and thought, the more I've come to conclude that the basis of segregation and "separate but equal" rests upon a**

concept of the inherent inferiority of the colored race. I don't see how Plessy and the cases following it can be sustained on any other theory. If we are to sustain segregation, we also must do it upon that basis." After laying down that gauntlet Warren added "I don't see how in this day and age we can set any group apart from the rest and say that they are not entitled to the same treatment as all others. To do so would be contrary to the Thirteenth, Fourteenth, and Fifteenth Amendments. They were intended to make the slaves equal with all others. Personally, I can't see how today we can justify segregation based solely on race." Even though he had made no exceptions in his castigation of segregation he knew that some states would have greater difficulty ending segregated schools and concluded his view of crafting the decision in a thoughtful and pragmatic way. "It would be unfortunate if we had to take precipitous action that would inflame more than necessary" He was not too concerned of a desegregation order on Kansas and border states but knew that southern states were different. "But it's not the same in the deep south. It will take all the wisdom of this court to dispose of the matter with a minimum of emotion and strife. How we do it is important." He ended by saying, "My instincts and feelings lead me to say that in these cases we should abolish the practice of segregation in the public schools—but in a tolerant way." *Eisenhower vs Warren: The Battle for Civil Rights and Liberties,* James F. Simon, pages 146-150

Each associate judge in order of seniority provided his view of the case. Each associate started his statement with an acknowledgment that he did not believe God made any race of people inferior to the others. Justices Reed (KY) and Jackson (NY) and Clark (TX) thought that there was enough law to support Plessey but indicated a. willingness to hear how a desegregation order could be done without causing more harm than good. **Warren made a concerted effort to visit and establish a personal relationship with each justice, listening to their concerns and explaining his unequivocal beliefs of fairness in the application and interpretation of laws governing Americans**. With his statesman-like approach, denouncing the practice but not the politicians supporting "separate but equal", Warren earned the willful support and opinion of each associate justice to end Plessey and desegregation in public schools in America. The unanimous decision to end racial segregation in public schools was heralded as the most significant ruling in America since the 1857 Dred Scott that former slaves could never become citizens of the United States. The New York Times, Time Magazine, Negro Press heralded the decision as a major event that would change the lives of millions of families in America. And so, it did! Succeeding Presidents would continue the leadership of racially integrating American institutions to give meaning to equality and justice for all.

Dr. Martin Luther King, Jr., Presidents John F. Kennedy and Lyndon B. Johnson

The desegregation of the University of Mississippi and the University of Alabama dominated headlines that reflected American sentiment about race relations during the 1960s. Martin Luther King Jr., John F. Kennedy, and Lyndon B. Johnson were the national leaders who provided the leadership that helped the country bridge the turmoil to reach a state of relative harmony and acceptance of African American presence in public and corporate institutions in America by the 1980s.

- **Dr. Martin Luther King,** Jr. more than any preacher or religious leader in America confronted black and white Americans to change based on the teachings of Jesus Christ. He had the courage to preach and model non-violent protests to increase the attention of the world on the injustice of inequality towards African Americans by white Americans perseverance of institutional racism. Malcolm X was the chief critic against non-violent approach to end the violent attacks on white police and white supremacist groups to intimidate African Americans from demanding their Civil Rights as citizens of the United States. King's courage to lead non-violent protesters in the presence of police armed with guns, clubs, electronic shock sticks and attack-trained dogs was oblivious and his repeated marches throughout the south and Chicago challenged Christian leaders and political leaders who professed to believe in the teachings of Jesus Christ and the creed that Americans were created equal and had the right to pursue life, liberty and the pursuit of happiness. King's March on Washington Speech is regarded by many as the most inspiring in American history and ranks in importance with Abraham Lincoln's Gettysburg address.

- **John F. Kennedy,** Thirty-Fifth President of the United States. I had just entered the US Army as a Second Lieutenant (1960) and was inspired by Kennedy's speech and promising support of equal rights for African Americans. The Army was still using daily personnel forms ('morning report') to account for personnel strength of individuals assigned to units by race, rank, gender and status of everyone assigned to that unit. The report was segregated to show whites on one page and blacks on a separate page. I was the commanding officer and accounted for on the Negro page even though I verified that the report was accurate for the entire unit.. The Kennedy administration ceased the segregated format in his first year in office. I viewed the abolishment of that requirement as one of the first signals that Kennedy was continuing the eradication of racism in America. However, his use of federal troops to force the university of Mississippi to enroll James Meredith and the University of Alabama to enroll Vivian Malone and James Hood was a clear message to southern governors and those across America who shared their resentment that the US Constitution applied equally to all and would be enforced.

- **Lyndon Johnson, Thirty-Sixth President's** legislative powers and strong support of voting rights further moved the arc of equality towards the multi-cultural America of 2022. Johnson's televised speech March 15, 1965, delivered to a joint session of congress and the American people on the need to provide constitutional rights to African Americans was regarded by some as the sincerest effort of any president to champion equal rights for black Americans. The New York Times editorial, capturing the historical perspective of the speech, wrote, "No other American president had so completely identified himself with the cause of the Negro. No other President had made the issue of equality for Negroes so frankly a moral cause to himself and all Americans." The American ideal of one nation, under God with liberty and justice for all, would not have been achieved without the leadership, courage and commitment of the national leaders above. Racism was enabled and enforced by laws before Truman, Thurgood Marshall, Earl Warren, Eisenhower, Martin Luther King, Jr., Kennedy, and Johnson stood up to overturn those laws and used federal force to enforce the laws. The racial sentiment of whites that tolerated overt violence against African Americans is no longer visible. Those of us who remember the violence and practice of that era are declining in numbers and not anxious to see a repeat of that sordid past.

The Role of Media

In the 1940s thru the early 1950s most Americans received news from newspapers, radio and movie theaters. Even in Hunnewell during WWII I remember going to the opera house (the "Colored" section was in the back of the balcony) to see cowboy movies after the latest showing of the war effort in Europe and the Pacific. Weekly and national newspapers carried stories about locals serving in the military as well as reporting on local events identifying negroes by name who died, got arrested, or had social activities in the town's Negro community. Newspapers in the southern and border states were supportive of the "separate but equal" status and rarely reported both sides of racial violence against Negroes. The Negro newspapers, The Kansas City Call, Chicago Defender, Pittsburg Courier, St. Louis Argus, Atlanta

Daily World, to name a few, were the principal sources of providing Negroes news about Civil Rights progress, violence against Negroes and updates on NAACP issues like Thurgood Marshall's efforts to end "separate but equal" schools. White politicians paid little attention to the Negro press because majority sentiment was not concerned about Negro equality. The popularity of television in the 1950s and beyond changed political interest in Negro inequality because of America's role as the leaders of the free world and champion of democracy.

A picture is truly more descriptive than a thousand words. The camera transports images in real-time all around the world and the images of police beating peaceful citizens marching to gain the right to vote, have decent schools and housing is at the heart of what a democratic country is supposed to provide. The picture or image transmitted is explained by a professional journalist taught to present the facts that described the scene being shown to anyone watching. This television phenomenon awakened millions of white Americans to the brutality imposed by the elected officials they voted and supported for who were leading the violence against peaceful protesters demanding equality as American citizens. The image of "bloody Sunday" that captured Martin Luther King, Jr., and the late Congressman, John Lewis being beaten by police as they marched for their rights across the Edmond Pettis Bridge in Selma, Alabama, …. awakened many around the world as to America's commitment to freedom around the world at the time freedom was denied to American citizens in their own country.

The national media and particularly, television, played a significant role of exposing the harsh realities of racial inequality against negroes in America and slowly but assuredly prompted national elected officials to support the changes mentioned above. The professionalism and courage of journalist to risk their personal safety to report both sides of the story were a significant ally to America's racial minority quest for equal rights in the 1950s-1980s era. The majority racial sentiment against negroes was captured on television and racism was overtly violent. The "separate but equal" and Jim Crow law enforcement practices were exposed, compelling, and in most cases, forcing southern elected officials to accept equality under the law for negro citizens. Over time, the death of white supremacist like former Governor of Alabama, George Wallace and teaching negro and white children as classmates in public schools, and becoming teammates at athletic events produced a new normal among succeeding generations of Americans that continues into the Twenty First Century.

2000-2022:   The Terrorist Attack of 9/11/2001 and the Beginning of American Divisiveness

My firsthand experience with racism during this period was typical of African Americans who achieved success in their professions as senior executives responsible for directing and achieving organizational goals. The overt racial discrimination of African Americans that took place in the 1940s-1970s era were rare in the beginning of the Twenty-First Century. Racial discrimination embedded in institutional practices of hiring, promotions and equality were the norm during this era. Nevertheless, my asessment of **National Purpose, White Sentiment Towards Black Americans, National Leaders and The Role of Media** shows a deterioration of each element and highlights the growing fear among a large segment of voters who rallied behind former President Trump and his MAGA movement. The MAGA influence clearly attracts white supremacist groups and contributes to some of the divisiveness among Americans but other factors beyond racism also contributed to the slide into our current disunity beginning at the start of the Twenty-first Century.

America and the world had successfully prepared computers and electronic devices to begin the Twenty-First century without a catastrophe in the myriad automated tasks governments, corporations, community and civic organizations relied on to perform their essential mission and functions. I was the Chief Operating Officer for the Library of Congress and successfully coordinated the library's systems to merge with the Legislative Branch of the federal government. On the international front, America had successfully led a 35-nation coalition to remove Iraq from Kuwait and won a clear military victory for the first time since WWII. American forces were also reducing military strength in Germany because of the fall of the Berlin Wall in 1989 and the end of the Cold War with Russia and the former Soviet Union. In all, Americans were feeling good about our place in the world and was focused on domestic issues with newly elected President Bill Clinton. The country was making noticeable progress in racial equality as judged by the appointment of African Americans to cabinet level positions and executive positions in both the Executive and Legislative branches of government. I had been appointed by President Clinton to form the residential program of AmeriCorps National Civilian Community Corps and later by the Librarian of Congress with US Senate approval to serve as the Deputy Librarian and Chief Operations Officer. The issue of racial discrimination against African Americans at the Library was a longstanding issue, and continued to be a concern in American public, private and corporate sectors across the country. However, I'm comfortable in stating that African Americans were generally pleased with President Clinton's efforts to champion equality during his eight years in office. The beginning of the Twenty-First Century and the terrorist attack on September 11, 2001, was a day that changed America and erased the sense of security and protection against foreign and domestic threats to Americans. It was a day that shattered the good feelings Americans had about our national purpose and a day that thrust our national and elected leaders into the spotlight to explain, act, comfort and rally Americans to bond together to defeat the threat and continue to live without fear and intimidation. President George W. Bush did his part and was followed by Presidents Obama, Trump and Biden. The divisiveness among Americans increased with the election of President Obama because of his being the first African American President of the US and worsened under President Trump who purposedly questioned Obama's American citizenship status and developed the slogan to "Make America Great Again" that appealed to white nationalist and white supremacist groups. The goal of this comparison seeks to identify how much of the divisiveness is attributed to racism and/or other factors that keep Americans from coming together for the common good of democracy.

National Purpose. Americans continue to believe that we are the protectors of freedom and democracy around the world. That legacy was earned by the men, women and families who sacrificed and won the Victory of WWII. The current generation of Americans accept the rewards of that legacy left by our ancestors, nearly all died out now, who left us government and military institutions that they built and maintained into the Twenty-First Century. Nearly every President of the US born in the twentieth century served in WWII, and according to the United States Senate website over 115 senators had WWII service. Eight of the most influential senators with WWII experience served into the Twenty-First Century. They were influential because they bridged the gap between following orders as servicemen and making policy as senators. They also had status and stature with Presidents, Cabinet Officers and General and Admirals in the Uniformed Services. Their names were: Daniel K. Akaka, D-HI, Jesse Helms, R-NC, Fritz Hollings, D-SC, Daniel K. Inouye, D-HI, Frank Lautenberg, D-NJ, William N. Roth, Jr., D-NJ, Ted Stevens, R-AK, Strom Thurmond, RSC and John W. Warner, R-VA. These eight senators along with notable US Senators and Vietnam veterans John McCain, R-AZ and John Kerry, D-MA, provided the extra dimensions of voluntarily giving up personal freedom to serve the common good of American democracy. There are no US Senators serving in this time period with comparable military and/or legislative experience. The domestic and foreign threats of the Twenty-First Century provide Americans with candidates for elective office who are strong on words and lacking in experience of serving our country and missing the knowledge of teamwork in the operation of military systems that project power to deter potential enemies and enforce our policies. Currently, I can think of no threat or issue to our American way of life that would motivate sixty percent (60%) of adults, 21 and above, who would volunteer their time and risk their life to defeat a threat to American freedoms, physical safety or personal liberty. The polarization between race, wealth, lifestyle choice, geographical region and religious beliefs, and political preference is so deeply embedded in personal rights that community welfare has little influence on national purpose. The 2022 mid-term elections voted the Republicans to lead the US House of representatives with a very narrow majority. The 2022 election results did not heal the divide. The aftermath of the January 6, 2021, insurrection and former President Trump's influence over the Republican party signal a continuation of the divide leading into the Presidential election of 2024.

The national purpose continues to require elected officials to protect America and Americans against all enemies, foreign and domestic. The political, racial, and economic divide between Americans make it more difficult to gain consensus on a national purpose for America.

White Sentiment (Attitude towards racial segregation, violence against African Americans and other minorities). White sentiment towards African Americans and minorities is generally accepting in all modes of interstate travels and accommodations. Equal employment, housing, education and health opportunities have improved but lag white Americans. The greatest and most visible white sentiment against African Americans is in the application of equal protection of the laws by state and federal agencies. During the Obama administration Senator Mitch McConnel and the Republican party refused to vote on the

President's nomination to fill a supreme court vacancy. The Trevon Martin killing in Florida by George Zimmerman sparked white sentiment in support of the shooter's right to act as a vigilante; in New York, the arrest and death of Eric Garner by a choke hold administered by a policeman sparked national outrage by African Americans in the injustice to African Americans in the custody of law enforcement officers. The trend of police injustice continued under the administration of Donald Trump. The deaths of George Floyd, Breonna Taylor, and Ahmaud Arbery generated the Black Lives Matter movement that was supported by white and minority Americans. The Black Lives Matter protesters were confronted by the Washington D.C. Police, and President Trump's disparaging remarks towards their purpose inspired MAGA followers to oppose the march. The MAGA followers sought to dilute the support of African American and white supporters of the BLM movement; they attempted to blame Black Lives Matter protesters as influencing anti -police marchers in Oregon, Wisconsin and other urban cities.

White sentiment against African Americans in predominantly white cities and counties in western states cannot be accurately assessed. However, most residents in those areas vote Republican and most support Donald Trump. I think fear of not seeing people who look like them in states with large urban populations and in federal elected positions is among the factors that divide America. Nearly 90 per cent of the Republican party was made up of non-Hispanic white Americans in 2013. That number has probably not changed, and current party leaders and candidates spend enormous sums of money promoting issues that divide Americans. White sentiment remains a factor in all aspects of American governance because of the historical significance of the founding of America.

National Leaders- Political and Public (Moral courage to improve racial or gender equality to keep the country united under the Constitution of the United States in pursuit of our national purpose.)

The current divide among Americans was accelerated by the 9/11 terrorist attack. In 2001, shortly after the terrorist crashed planes into the twin towers in New York, at the Pentagon in Washington, D.C. and crashed the hijacked plane into the ground near Shanksville, PA., various national polls showed most Americans (nearly 70%) favored retaliation and a willingness to risk life and limb to bring the attackers to justice. President George W. Bush, responded to the attack and his successors, Presidents Barack Obama, Donald Trump and Joe Biden, followed or amended Bush's policies that resulted in the longest war in US history.

The Bush administration identified that the attack was organized and carried out by Al Qaeda a terrorist organization founded by Osama ben Laden and affiliated with the Taliban, a fundamental Islamic Group primarily madeup of the Pashtun tribe in Afghanistan. The 19 terrorist who hijacked and flew the planes into the buildings were from Saudi Arabi (15), Egypt (2) and Lebanon (2). Bush began bombing in Afghanistan in October 2001 and within weeks sent ground troops to search and destroy al Qaeda believed to be operating in caves in the mountains between Pakistan and Afghanistan. Progress was slow but effective pressure was being applied against al Qaeda. In 2003 the Bush administration made the case through the CIA that Saddam Hussein and Iraq possessed weapons of mass destruction, was connected to the 9/11 attack and posed a threat to America and the world. Bush diverted military resources from Afghanistan and ordered an attack against Iraq. The attack was successful and was over in three weeks. On March 1, 2003, the Bush administration captured Khalid Sheik Mohammed, mastermind behind the 9/11 terrorist attacks. When Bush leaves office in 2008 Troops are still in Iraq and Afghanistan.

Obama assumed the role of Commander-in-Chief in 2008 and sent more troops to support efforts in Iraq and Afghanistan. The strength total of US forces in Afghanistan would rise to 100,000 thousand during Obama's term. One of the highlights of Obama's administration was the killing of Osama bin Laden in Pakistan on May 2, 2011. Obama and his Secretary of Defense, Republican, Robert Gates, agreed to announce a troop withdrawal schedule to signal to the Afghan President that his army needed to protect the country as US forces transferred security functions and returned to the US. The administration withdrew 30,000 thousand troops in 2012 with a projected plan to have all troops out by 2016. For various reasons there were about 16,000 troops in Afghanistan and 5,000 in Iraq when Obama left office in 2017. **Trump became Commander-in-Chief in 2017** and cautioned against a hasty withdrawal of the remaining troops in Afghanistan. He hastily removed all troops from Iraq and left contractor support to the Iraqi Government. In 2019 Trump cancelled peace talks between the US-Taliban and Afghan Government after a car bomb exploded by the Taliban claimed the lives of 12 Afghans and one American. The next year Trump negotiated with the Taliban to withdraw all 13,000 thousand US Troops by May 1, 2021, in exchange with their ties to al Qaeda and no attacks against US forces. The Trump administration ended their term in office believing the Taliban would honor their agreement and the Afghanistan government forces were strong enough to maintain control of their country.

Biden as Vice President under Obama was the best prepared of the Commander-in-Chief's to pick up Trump's agreement to end America'solvement in Afghanistan. His administration accepted Trump's withdrawal of troops by May 2021 and because of pressure from military veterans with close friendships of Afghan interpreters the administration agreed to and began relocating loyal Afghan supporters of US troops and moved to have the troops and supporters out by August 31. During the tension filled evacuation of troops, the Taliban regained additional terriority and the Afghan military forces collapsed. The President of Afghanistan fled the country and the Taliban established control of the country. Americans had grown weary of the war, agreed with ending US involvement and divided over the success or failures of the 20-year war.

None of the four Presidents could boast of eliminating the terrorist threats from Iraq and Afghanistan nor could they claim to have brought Americans closer together on divisive domestic issues such as: Gun control and massacres in schools, churches/synagogues and shopping malls; border control and illegal immigrants and police brutality against African Americans. Obama did improve health care but with little support from Republicans. The COVOID 19 pandemic was the most devastating virus since smallpox and affected each country's operating systems to care for their people. Trump purposefully minimized the seriousness of the virus to keep business and markets open. Many of his followers refused to comply with the Center for Disease Control precautions that resulted in many more deaths and crisis for hospitals and health care providers nationwide. Biden's leadership and aggressive production of antivirus vaccines helped reduce the spread of the virus and a return to somewhat normal life in America and the world. He is also using the Presidential Office to defend American democracy and calling out Republican members who are attempting to overturn election results and attacked the US Capitol January 6, 2021. And although **President Biden** is not among the 49 Americans who have given important speeches in the 21st Century he is doing more than any other elected, public or private person to protect America's democracy.

American Rhetoric.com list 49 Important Speeches in 21st Century America and only Bush and Obama are among the Presidents listed above. Bush spoke from the Oval Office on the night of September 11, 2001. His words of reassurance and of America's resolve and promise to find and punish the attackers were issued with calm and confidence. Bush's other three speeches were 9/11 Address to a Joint Session of Congress, 2002 State of the Union Address and Israel-Palestine Two-State Solution, 24 June

2002. Obama's four speeches on the list were not about the terrorist attack and were entitled: 2004 Democratic National Convention, Keynote Address, 27 July 2004, Boston, MA; Commencement Address at Knox College, 4 June 2005, Galesburg, IL. "A More Perfect Union", 18 March 2008, Philadelphia, PA, and Speech at the "Together We Thrive: Tucson and America' Memorial, McKale Memorial Center, University of Arizona, Tucson Arizona, 12 January 2011. None of the speeches by Bush or Obama resulted in an expression of commitment to a policy that changed America or achieved a legacy towards the ideals of America. The list of leaders in the 21st Century with public trust of the American people is short. Other than President Biden, I know of no other public or civic leader who has shown moral courage and leadership to resolve any of the domestic or foreign threats that divide Americans. On the other side of courage is fear, and Donald Trump is the leading protagonist stroking the behavior of divisiveness among the Republicans. Where truth and honesty are the bedrock of democracy; lies and deceit are the lifelines of fear. The Republican party make no effort to recruit African Americans and minorities into the party. The few minorities who identify as Republicans don't champion equal rights and are only visible in photo and television opportunities that support party issues. I believe that the MAGA followers are afraid that as white Americans become the minority racial group their control of governing institutions will decline and so will their power and prestige. This is the motivating factor Republicans are attempting to change the rules of counting election ballots to make certain that the right candidate wins the election. The battle between fear and courage will depend on individuals who chose to make choices that benefit themselves without penalizing their neighbor.

Perhaps the void in leaders with moral courage results from a lack of example of service in our homes, schools, communities or governments. We have produced generations of youth more concerned with self- gratification than helping others. The results of most of our elected leaders reflect self-interest over common interest and shared responsibilities. America has done better when leaders who believe in democracy, family, church, the environment, etc take center stage and champion their cause for the benefit of the next generation of Americans.

The Role of Media. (A help or hinderance with the sentiment of racial equality in America during the above era).

I was in my early 60s and at the Library of Congress when the internet and use of email was a novelty. In fact, it was difficult to get the older workforce to use the email as a quick and reliable means of communicating. In a relatively short period of time the print and television media have been replaced by social media platforms that allow individuals to transmit whatever is on their mind 24/7. Donald Trump used social media platforms to win the 2016 election over Hillary Clinton. That platform has no editor, fact checker, or monitor and is the most popular among Americans of all age groups. Lies, half- truths, and wild opinion can be transmitted around the globe in seconds! I believe social media is the primary reason Americans are divided on the major domestic issues. Social media is not a reliable means to transmit important personal or official information, knowledge or instructions.

Parents and teachers are not able to control their children's access to topics on any subject on social media. This information enabler is simultaneously an advantage and a threat to democracy. It is a worldwide resource that misinforms as much as it informs. The best hope is to educate children on the difference between information, facts, and knowledge. America has done better when a champion of freedom of the press uses available platforms to expose truths that threaten the varied forms of freedoms, individual, religion, assembly, etc.

Comparison: American Racism of 1940s-1970s vs American's Racial Divide in the Twenty-First Century:

I am blessed to have lived through the 1940s to the present (2023) and share my observations and experience as an American of African descent. I boldly and gratefully proclaim that "The overt racism of the 1940s-1970ss in the southern and border states is not visible in America in the Twenty First Century." That is a great achievement because of past champions of enforcing American democratic ideals.

Courageous black and white leaders of the 1940s-1970s rose above the entrenched racial segregation practices of their generation to establish a more inclusive and equitable America. That observation and truth does not alter the influence of race in the politics, economics and status of Americans today.

White Americans continue to be the dominant political, economic and cultural force in the country. The dominant members of their racial group have historically struggled with the inclusion of minorities and women as equals in the self-evident truths of the US Declaration of Independence and the Constitution and always found a way to restrict the opportunities accorded to women and minorities. The two political party system has historically attracted whites who championed freedom for minorities or limited government and strong business interests. The Republicans in the 1860s championed freedom and Democrats favored business including the retention of slavery and free labor. After the Civil War both parties pursued their political interests without jeopardizing the unity of white dominance of the political and economic process. In my view, white democrats begin the drift towards the Republican Party when Harry Truman, a Democrat, began to practice what I identify as the **politics of freedom -enacting and enforcing laws to grant minorities and women equal rights to the freedoms and opportunities granted all citizens of the United States, redressing injustices to minorities because of their race or**

conditions of servitude; using the force of the federal government to grant minorities equal justice and rights of the US Constitution, and appointing qualified individuals to all levels in the Executive, Legislative and Judicial branches of governance. These are the practices of politics that strengthens the fabric of society, encourages the poor and uneducated to improve their status in life, and rewards individuals based on excellence and accomplishment regardless of race, ethnicity, gender or sexual orientation. The process requires politicians to become allies with minority members and as was the case in the 1950s and 1960s to use the power of the federal government to force the states to comply with the constitutional rights of minority citizens. One of the most heartwarming stories I read about the power of freedom to change attitude and perspective came from Chief Justice Earl Warren's conversation with Associate Justice Tom Clark of Texas. Prior to reaching a unanimous decision on overturning the "separate but equal" law Warren asked Clark for his opinion of the case. Clark stated that he was inclined to vote against overturning the law because the evidence presented to show psychological damage to black children was not convincing. Warren's unequivocal belief that black people were not inferior to white people prompted Clark to reassess his opinion of black people. After reflecting on the obstacles and conditions overcame by black people in his native Texas, he told Warren that their progress in a short period of time was astonishing and on that basis he could support ending "separate but equal". The freedom to examine personal bias and beliefs in a non-threatening manner offers hope and opportunity for change. **Change has been the most significant accomplishment of the politics of freedom.**

Since the 1940s minorities have chosen to become members of the Democratic Party because of the opportunities. The practical results of the politics of freedom are reflected in the multiracial members of the party. Even though their diversity compels them to argue, agree, and disagree on behalf of their constituents over the party's governing priorities they feel connected and valued as citizens of the United States. The Democrats politics of freedom, as my life story attests, has done more to advance the self-evident truths of America than the Republicans who practice the politics of fear.

With the exception of Abraham Lincoln and Ulysses Grant in the 1860s and Dwight Eisenhower in 1954-57, **the Republican party has practiced what I call the politics of fear- limiting government support of personal assistance in health care, welfare assistance and ending abortion rights; restricting opportunities for equal access to jobs, education, housing; providing tax incentives for the wealthy; providing incentives for entrepreneurs to grow business and create jobs; reducing gun control regulations; reducing minority immigration; and reducing federal support of large cities and metropolitan areas.** The party does not recruit minorities and only welcomes wealthy or high-profile individuals who become spokespersons for reducing or ending government health care, social security, or welfare programs. Their fear of crime encourages access to guns, fear of losing power encourages redistricting voter districts, and fear of becoming a racial minority encourages stricter border controls and sending illegal immigrants out of America. Since Donald Trump has taken over the party the fear of liberal multi-racial Americans taking over the country has resulted in the assault on the US Capitol to stop the congress from certifying the 2020 election of President Joe Biden. The politics of fear under Trump is the primary reason for the divide between Americans. Fear and ignorance in the Republican Party is the primary threat to our democracy.

Different Perspectives and Shared Goals for America Leave Me Troubled but Thankful

I started this chapter looking for someone to blame for the divisiveness of Americans and questioning if race was still the dominant force that influence the voting decisions of white Americans. Although I blamed Trump for the divide in America, I believe the fear of becoming a racial minority rather than racism is a dominant factor among white voters who support Trump. A second factor among all voters is the lack of an obligation for 18 to 24 year old youth to serve the country for a short period in a national service organization. However, I am ending the chapter giving thanks and praise to God for my parents and for being born in America in 1938. The exceptional men and women whose courage and humanity gave me and millions of Americans the opportunities provided through their **politics of freedom** and commitment to the self-evident truths of the Declaration of Independence and Constitution of the United States. Harry Truman, Thurgood Marshall, Earl Warren, Martin Luther King, Jr., and others who passed and enforced the laws that made the self-evident truths a reality for my and future generations of Americans. Except for Thurgood Marshall and the other African Americans leading the efforts in the politics of freedom, the white officials rose above the racial sentiment of their peers and family to accomplish a moral good for all Americans. Their courage was matched by the courage of Martin Luther King Jr., and the black protesters who marched and died to exercise their civil rights for me and future generations of Americans. Their good works and opportunities are now being threatened by a current group of Americans who share the same or similar racial sentiments against a multi-racial democracy as did their ancestors in the 1940s-1970ss. They also share the fear of losing what they believe to be their birthright as white Americans to remain in control of the election process regardless of the outcome of the popular or electoral votes. I am troubled by their racial ideology, criminal behavior, and antidemocracy example but not enough to lose faith in the American people and the **politics of freedom**.

The politics of freedom is not a democrat or republican ideology. It is a morally based way of life that encompasses the

Christian principles of loving your neighbor, forgiving, and recognizing that the self-evident truths are bestowed on us by our common creator. Nationally famous Americans like Abraham Lincoln, Harry Truman, a republican and democrat, both flawed human beings like the rest of us, practiced the politics of freedom. The practice was made in America because of our unique and flawed history in search of a more perfect union. I am confident that the divide will not be repaired between election cycles but the better angels among us will prevail. **The politics of freedom is battle tested, gender inclusive, race neutral with no limitations on age. This winning formula molds perspectives to embrace the realities of the self-evident truths for all Americans. It is the pathway to group Americans by behavior and accomplishment rather than by race and stereotype.**

CHAPTER TWENTY-NINE

Black Repositories of Freedom: New Philadephia, IL and Lincoln University Missouri

Mainstream American institutions were founded by white Americans and embrace the self-evident truths in the Declaration of Independence as a foundational basis of American freedom and success of those institutions. Rare are the American institutions founded by African Americans before and after the American Civil War that made the self-evident truths work for their interests with the alliance of like-minded white Americans who believe that the self-evident truths apply to all Americans. Free Frank McWorter the founder of New Philadelphia, IL in 1836, and the former slaves and Civil War soldiers of the 62nd and 65th Colored Infantries and their white officer, founded Lincoln University, Jefferson City, MO in 1866. These two institutions, one – New Philadelphia -exists in memory and on the original town site that was designated a US National Park site by the United Congress in December 2022, -and Lincoln University MO has been in continuous operation since 1866. Both are repositories of making the self-evident truths work for like-minded Americans in a government that excluded minorities and women from the rights of the US Constitution at the time of their founding. **The purpose of this chapter is to emphasize the collective importance of like-minded Americans who believe that the self-evident truths apply to all Americans; and that Americans should build institutions that help others pursue their passions, goals and aspirations based on common interests and willing behavior to accept human diversity as an essential part of the American experience.** My abbreviated account of the founders and their ally's' accomplishments are intended to show that the best antidote against government or individual attempts to exclude minorities and women from the US Constitution is like-minded Americans working together to secure their God given rights against those in opposition to those truths. New Philadelphia and Lincoln University Missouri are repositories of these truths.

Free Frank McWorter and New Philadelphia

American founders denied enslaved Africans from using their skills and abilities to live as free men and women, with few exceptions, until the end of the Civil War and passage of the thirteenth, fourteenth, and fifteenth amendments to the US Constitution. Free Frank McWorter was an exceptional individual; born in 1777 the son of an enslaved West African mother and the property of his white slave owner father in South Carolina. Frank was enslaved in South Carolina and Kentucky for over 40 years of his life. He married an enslaved woman named Lucy in Kentucky and fathered four enslaved children, the property of Lucy's slave owner. He purchased Lucy's freedom when she was pregnant with his fifth child who would be born free in Kentucky. At the age of 45, Frank purchased his own freedom from his half brothers and sister who inherited his ownership rights from their deceased father. Frank remained in Kentucky on acreage he purchased from profits from a saltpeter cave (used to make gunpowder) he owned in Kentucky. Frank and Lucy had two more free born children in Kentucky before their oldest enslaved son, Frank Jr., 22, escaped to Canada on the underground railroad. Frank simultaneously negotiated with his son's owner to purchase Frank Jr's freedom while communicating with his son through the underground railroad to return to Kentucky. Frank traded his saltpeter operation for his son's freedom paper in 1830 and at about the same time frame, sold his land in Pulaski County Kentucky and purchased 160 acres from a white doctor in Kentucky, sight unseen in the state of Illinois. At the time many whites were leaving the states of

Kentucky and Tennessee to settle lands in Illinois and start a new life. Settlers with slaves were permitted to bring them to Illinois but free persons of color were required to have their freedom papers, letters attesting to their good reputation from twenty or more white people and a bond or funds to pay living expenses.

At the age of 53, Frank, Lucy, and their free children- Frank Jr., Squire, Commodore and Lucy Ann left their enslaved children in Pulaski County, KY enroute to Pike County, IL to begin a new life with necessary documentation as free persons of color. The. 500-mile journey usually took three months but an early winter in 1830 delayed their arrival in IL to spring 1831. In the short span of 24 years as a free person of color in Pike County, Illinois Frank's accomplishments rivals the most ingenious, responsible and courage pioneer in America's settlement in the 1830s. In chronological order:

- The first man (law stipulated ownership of land be a white man) to establish ownership in Hadley Township in Pike County, IL. He added 500 more acres to the 160 he initially purchased.

- At the age of 58, returned to Kentucky and purchased his son, Solomon, age 20.

- At 59 years old, platted 43 acres of his land into town lots for the establishment of a Town he named New Philadelphia. He sold the lots to anyone who could afford to purchase a lot and New Philadelphia became the first town platted by an African American in America that was multi- racial. Every person in the community knew that Frank was selling the lots to purchase the freedom of his enslaved children in Kentucky.

- At the age of 60, influential white neighbors successfully petitioned the Illinois State Legislature to pass a bill to legalize Frank and Lucy by performing a marriage ceremony and adding McWorter as their and the children's last name.

Up to that time they had simply been known as Free Frank and Free Lucy.

- At 66, Frank returned to Kentucky and purchased his daughter, Sarah's freedom for $950.00

- At the age of 69, Frank made a will that divided the land to his sons and established funds to purchase the freedom of his last enslaved daughter and grandchildren who remained enslaved.

- At 73 years of age, Frank returned to Kentucky and purchased the freedom of his oldest daughter, Juda enslaved for 50 years and named after his West African mother.

- Frank died in 1854 at the age of 77 just six years before the start of the Civil War. **A few of his grandchildren and children of residents of New Philadelphia would attend Lincoln University MO in the 1890s.**

New Philadelphia continued to prosper under the leadership of Solomon, Frank's second oldest son until a new railroad track by-passed the town isolating it and making it more difficult ship farm crops and goods to markets in Hannibal, MO and Pikesville, IL. The townsite was abandoned by the late 1940s and buildings collapsed/removed, and the land returned to agricultural use. However, Free Frank's descendants, former residents, and descendants of white neighbors kept his memory and accomplishments from being lost to history. Family members and descendants of former neighbors and friends have formed a New Philadelphia Association to keep the site and memory alive. The site is on the Register of National Historic Places, and became a National Parks site in December 2022. As of this writing, the original town site has been preserved with kiosks explaining the location of original buildings and abbreviated history of New Philadelphia. For those interested in more information or details of Frank's life, accomplishments, and times the following resources are recommended: *https://www.newphiladelphiall. org,* New

Philadelphia: Julia E.K. Walker, Professor of History, University of Texas, Austin, great-great granddaughter of Free Frank and Lucy McWorter, Free Frank: A Black Pioneer on the Antebellum Frontier, 1983, University of Kentucky Press, New Philadelphia: An Archaeology of Race in the Heartland, Paul A. Shackel, University of California Press, 2011, New Philadelphia, Gerald A McWorter and Kate Williams McWorter, for the New Philadelphia Association Free Franks achievements provides universal and timeless lessons.

- Seek alliance with individuals who share your belief that all humans are endowed with self-evident truths

- Learn how to communicate effectively with those who do not share your belief

- Keep promises and commitments. The spoken and written word require committed persons to make them a reality

- Humility and putting the interests of others first builds trust and strengthens the organization

- Inclusion based on shared goals, mutual effort, and mutual respect are the primary values that build a strong America

Free Frank and the New Philadelphia story merits the recognition of a National Historic Site, a State of Illinois State Historic site and A National Parks Service site. I am grateful to be a member of the New Philadelphia Association and to introduce the site to readers not familiar with the story. In addition to the universal lessons above, the story is a tribute to faith, family, freedom and friendship in the struggle to build America as one nation, under God with Liberty and Justice for All. Several of Free Frank's grandchildren and residents from New Philadelphia attended Lincoln University MO in the 1890s making the connection a bridge to the exceptional achievement of the founders of both Black Repositories of Freedom.

Lincoln University Missouri was Founded by Black Soldiers of the 62nd and 65th Colored Infantry Regiments and 1st Lieutenant Richard Baxter Foster, Adjutant, 62nd Regiment

The book of Ecclesiastes records, "that the end of a thing is better than it's beginning, and patience is better than pride." (Ecc 7:8-9 NIV). Lincoln University Missouri has been in continuous operation since 1866 and was started to specifically educate newly freed enslaved Africans in the state of Missouri. The university is clearly a repository of American History from an African American perspective. As a Historically Black College (HBC) in the state of Missouri, Lincoln Institute evolved from a basic elementary school to a four-year accredited university designated as a comprehensive land-grant institution serving a diverse clientele. The history of every American institution started in the "new birth of freedom" after the Civil War and survived the major impediments of inclusion for all (Reconstruction, "Jim Crow Laws", "separate but equal" and the 1960s Civil Rights protests) in the journey towards equal rights for all, survived because of the influence of one or more individuals at a critical period in the institution's existence. Lincoln University Missouri is among the survivors. My focus in this section is to identify the individuals who I believe influenced the development of Lincoln University to survive and become the unique HBC that serves the primarily black residential students and white commuter students to date.

The Beginning 1865-1900

Great accomplishments are great because of the monumental obstacles created by individuals to oppose the establishment of the project, institution, or idea. At the close of the Civil War the 11 states of the confederacy clearly opposed the idea that newly freed African Americans should be included as having rights under the US Constitution. Missouri, while not a confederate state, had half of its white population in agreement with the southerners that the self-evident truths did not apply to the newly freed enslaved Africans. The black men and members of the 62nd and 65th Colored Infantries and their white officers were keenly aware of the white sentiment in Missouri as they sat around the campfire in Texas to find a solution for their relatives and future generations.

- **Soldiers of the 62nd and 65th Colored Infantry** -among their numbers were **Samuel Sexton** who contributed $100.00 dollars, nearly one years pay and **Logan Bennet** whose life-long support of the Institute merited a dormitory named in his honor. Raising $6,000.00 dollars was the most impactful action available to the black soldiers. There were few black educated people in Missouri or America that could take on the task of starting a school for blacks in Missouri. **Their dream inspired action and example.**

Richard Baxter Foster, educated at Dartmouth College, Hanover, New Hampshire, an abolitionist, and former US Army Officer, volunteered to take on the task of starting Lincoln Institute in Missouri. A Missouri state board of trustees was formed to advise and help to raise additional money for the school. The governor and state superintendent of schools were members of the board along with other influential St. Louis businessmen. Foster experienced opposition in St. Louis and Jefferson City to his efforts to start Lincoln. He was rejected by Methodist clergy in St. Louis because the students would be black and in Jefferson City because he was white and the students were black. The Missouri state legislature offered little help even though the state legislature had passed a bill for negro education without funds. And Foster's startup as a private school at the dilapidated "Hobo" Hill location was funded by donations from the Federal Governments Freedmen's bureau and in-state philanthropic agencies. Foster devoted 5 years to the start of Lincoln Institute and was instrumental in moving the idea forward using the funds from the soldiers, the Freedman's Bureau and other philanthropic sources. Foster is one of the essential persons in the founding of Lincoln Institute. His contribution is grist for the theory that "one person can make a difference". Foster's image is included on the Soldiers Monument sculptured by Ed Dwight. There used to be a male dormitory named for Foster when I was a student at Lincoln University in 1956-1960.

- **Inman E. Page** first President of Lincoln Institute 1880-1898. With the deeding of its property to the state in 1789, Lincoln Institute formally became a state Institution. **Lincoln institute became a land-grant institution under the second Morrill Act of 1890. The federal funds were not appropriated to states that discriminated based on race or color in the admissions of students; funds were distributed to states for the establishment of separate institutions for blacks.** Page was born in slavery and his father purchased the freedom for his entire family. He attended Howard University, transferred to Brown University and was voted the class orator at graduation in 1877. Page had amazing success getting funds from the Missouri State Legislature, $10 thousand dollars for an Industrial Arts building, $9 thousand for machinery and tools, and $ 1 thousand dollars to build a residence for the President. Later in 1895 the legislature appropriated $40 thousand dollars to build Memorial Hall in honor of the soldiers. President Page also improved teacher training at the Institute and added courses to the college curriculum. The first and current Inman E. Page Library honors his name.

1920-1940

The Governor and Board of Curators continued to manage Lincoln Institute from their white majority perspective as primarily a black teacher training institute with a college department for black Missourians, native Americans and blacks from other states. Staff and teaching positions at Lincoln were heavily populated by politically connected in the early 1900s.

- In 1920 the black voters in St. Louis elected the first black state representative to the Missouri legislature. **Walthall**

Moore, Howard University educated came to the legislature with a bill to make Lincoln a university and change its status to a four-year college. His bill also recommended the governor change the Lincoln Board of Curators membership to eight appointed members, 4 white and 4 black members from across the state, and to appoint the state Superintendent of Schools as an ex-officio member. The bill was passed with the exception that the governor could appoint members for four-year terms and Curators could be of the same political party unlike Curators at white Missouri State colleges where terms were six years and members could not be of the same political party. **Walthall More** would exercise considerable influence in the affairs of Lincoln University for several years. He is honored with the Walthall Moore Small Animal Research Center named in his honor.

- At the time Moore's bill was passed the Curators rehired **Inman Page** who was in his 70s and accused of using his influence to support a political candidate. The President of Curators at Lincoln wanted "a much younger man than Page with character and ability" to become Lincoln's President and to lead the effort to convert Lincoln from an Institute to a four-year college. **Nathan B. Young** moved Lincoln University to become a four-year college and first-class institution of higher learning in the Middle West. Young's credentials were equal to the challenge: he earned his bachelor's and master's degrees from Oberlin College in 1892, had been a Principal in Birmingham, AL for four years, was head of the Tuskegee Institute Academic department for four years and served as President of Florida Agricultural and Mechanical University (FAMU) for twenty-one years. Upon Young's arrival as President in August 1923, Lincoln was not recognized as a quality institution of higher learning. It was unaccredited and better known as a poorly organized institution governed by politics and personalities. He immediately organized the university into departments; upgraded physical facilities; and raised the qualifications for college teaching. In his relatively short tenure, 1923-1927 and 1929-1931, Young built the foundation that his successors followed that produced a stellar faculty of PhD notables in the 1950s that other highly ranked HBCU's referred to Lincoln University MO as the "Harvard of the Mid-West". Young's ally, **Dr. Joseph Ellif,** professor at Missouri University and a member of Lincoln's Board of Curator was also a man of character and ability. The Board of Curators voted to terminate young's successor, President **Charles Florence** after six years of continuing to strengthen Lincoln as a first-class college. Ellif submitted his resignation and charged that the underlying cause of the termination was politics and that such action would cause Lincoln to lose its accreditation. The North Central Association of which Ellif was a member also threatened to place Lincoln on probation if the state did not correct the matter of political meddling. Elliff's resignation was effective as the Governor adopted the same rules for appointing curators and honoring their autonomy as was the custom with the University of Missouri. Young Hall is named in honor of Nathan B. Young and Elliff hall honors the contribution of Joseph Elliff.

Lloyd Gaines and Lucille Bluford are included for their activism that impacted Lincoln University's development and opportunities to strengthen educational opportunities for black students in Missouri. Gaines graduated from Lincoln in 1935 and applied for admission to the University of Missouri Law School. Denied by the University, Gaines sued the Registrar of the University to gain admission to the Law School. The Registrar denied admission and invoked the provision that the state of MO would pay for black students to attend university classes in a border state that was not offered at Lincoln. The Missouri State Supreme Court upheld the answer of the registrar and Gaines petitioned the US Supreme Court who ruled that the University of MO either had to admit Gaines or the state had to fund Lincoln University to open a Law School. The Lincoln University Law School opened in St. Louis in 1939. Gaines did not apply and mysteriously disappeared and was never heard from again. The Law school closed in 1955.

Lucille Bluford, a graduate of the University of Kansas in 1939, applied for admission to the University of Missouri graduate school of Journalism. The graduate school accepted her transcripts, but the officials turned her away in the registration line because she was black. She was denied eleven times. She petitioned the US Supreme Court and the court ruled that either the University of Missouri Journalism School admit her or the state appropriate money for Lincoln University MO to establish a School of Journalism. Lincoln University opened the Journalism School in 1942 on the campus in Jefferson City. The state appropriation did not cover the necessary courses and another student, Edith Massey, sued the University of Missouri to make available the professors to teach the courses at Lincoln University in Jefferson City. They provided the instructors until the state appropriated the necessary funds to Lincoln University to staff the Journalism School with the necessary professors. To avoid further lawsuits against the University of Missouri the Missouri General Assembly, through the Taylor Bill of 1939, mandated Lincoln University to establish graduate programs. Master of Arts degree in Education and in History were begun because of the mandate. The Board of Curators at Missouri colleges and the Missouri General Assembly were protecting the status quo of "separate but equal" at the time in history.

1950-1970 Diversity, Inclusion and Identity

In September 1956 President **Earl Edgar Dawson** inherited the reins of a well-managed, respected and successful Lincoln University with highly regarded professors with PhDs from the most prestigious colleges and universities in America. Athletic teams were winners, the student population came from the upper third of their high schools and adjusted to the high academic standards expected of caring and demanding professors. Campus life was orderly with curfews for women, civility and courtesy by men towards women and respect towards each other. The relationship between Lincoln black students and Jefferson City was strained because of the racial restrictions denying service to blacks in restaurants and other public facilities that prohibited black access. The 1954 Supreme Court decision to integrate public schools in southern and border states immediately propelled Lincoln on a course of racial inclusion that would challenge the leadership of future Presidents and their administrations. President Dawson, senior faculty and staff were launched into the journey of racial inclusion from the perspective of a minority race accepting a majority race. From the moment of the announcement of the US Supreme Court's decision to integrate public schools in 1954 into the late 1960s the inclusion of white students was smooth and the interaction with Jefferson City officials and community began improving. Missouri Attorney General John M. Dalton immediately set the tone of acceptance of the 1954 decision by publicly stating shortly after the court's announcement in May 1954 that Missouri segregation laws were null and void. The Lincoln University Board of Curators also unanimously agreed to enroll white students at Lincoln. Shortly after the announcement the Jefferson City School Board also announced the integration of black students from grades 9-12 into the white high school and hotels and restaurants opened to blacks in Jefferson City. The quick progress to implement racial integration at Lincoln prompted Ebony Magazine in March 1958 to run a picture of an attractive black and white female student at

Lincoln MO on the cover with a headline that read, "Lincoln University The School Too Good to Die ". The article stressed that white students did not see Lincoln as a 'Negro' university-it is a good local school they proudly attend." President Dawson took full advantage of the opportunity to expand the university: Added a 3,000-seat auditorium, a new 1900 seat gymnasium with classrooms and offices for the Department of Health and Physical education.

- The signs of racial progress between the white community and Lincoln University continued well into the mid-1960s when the clouds of unrest among the on -campus black student population disturbed the peace through protests and destruction of campus and business owned property in Jefferson City. The unrest began in 1967 and ended in 1969 and the retirement of President Dawson. The details of the cause, response and effect are thoroughly explained in *The Soldiers' Dream Continued: A Pictorial History of Lincoln University of Missouri,* by Antonio F. Holland with Timothy R. Roberts, Dennis White and edited by Rosemary Hearn, 1991. The essence of the issues involved the perception of some on-campus black student population that the administration was not providing adequate food service, maintaining dormitories sufficiently, too restrictive in on campus dress and too much deference towards accommodating white commuter students and the Jefferson City community. The 1967 unrest began as a mild protest over the quality of food service and minor issues during the spring semester that were considered resolved by the university and student government only to erupt more forcefully in the fall semester. The 1968 unrest centered around the Jefferson City Tribune's uncomplimentary remarks about Martin Luther King Jr's character and reputation the day before and the day after his funeral. Student activists rallied to protest and demand a retraction of the editorials that got out of control and resulted in looting and damages to downtown Jefferson City merchants. The 1969 unrest was a major confrontation between the administration and on-campus black student population that resulted in students taking control of the student center, setting fire to the center, Memorial Hall, and Page Library, and firing shots at law enforcement officials. The Jefferson City Police, Missouri Highway Patrol and Missouri National Guard posted over 400 personnel on Lincoln's campus to help the administration restore order. The president and faculty each adopted different approaches to resolving the crisis with the President's solution to expel the "committee representatives" and spokespersons for the students being the outcome. The damage to Lincoln University was the image of "The School Too Good to Die" that had been thoughtfully and willfully developed since its founding in 1866 and the damage done to the good relations that had been forged with Jefferson City since the Missouri Attorney General announced the death of racial segregation in 1954.

- **Dr Walter C. Daniel** accepted the Presidency of Lincoln University when many withdrew their application because of the on-campus student protests of 1967-1969. When asked why he accepted the position he reportedly said, "The position is a challenge and there is a job to do here- putting the campus back together as a working unit". (Note 2., Chapter IV Notes, The Soldiers' Dream cited earlier). Dr. Daniel, BS in English, Johnson C. Smith University, M.S. South Dakota State University and Ph.D. Bowling Green State University, Ohio. In three short years not only did Dr Daniels put the campus back together through his campaign of signs around the campus and throughout Jefferson City that read, "Mighty Proud of Lincoln", he also added 14 new doctorates in 1971. His brick and-mortar accomplishments include repairing and reopening the Scruggs Student Center, which was partially destroyed by fire, a new football stadium that was named after the beloved Dwight T. Reed in 1984, a women's dormitory, renamed in honor of President Dawson, built a FM Radio Station, KLUM-FM in a house owned by the university on Dunklin Street that broadcasts within a 75-mile radius of Jefferson City. Dr. Daniel surprised many in the LU family by resigning as President in October 1972, to accept a position as Vice Chancellor of the University of Missouri -Columbia, at that time the highest position held by a black person at the university..

1982-1986: The Near Fatal Threat to the Soldiers' Dream

When in the course of human events the convergence of everything that could go wrong does go wrong to protect that which we value most, it takes more than a miracle to save what we value most. In **1984-1986 A determined effort by** the Missouri Coordinating Board for Higher Education (CBHE) nearly passed legislation to change Lincoln University to become a state Regional University serving the higher educational needs of residents in a ten-county area surrounding Jefferson City. The surprise attack began under interim **President John Chavis** (1982-1984) in 1984 and continued under President **Thomas Miller Jenkins**, (1984-1986). The early salvo from the CBHE came in December 1984 when the board voted to recommend the elimination of graduate programs in agriculture at Lincoln University and to change the University's statewide university governing board to a regional one. The CBHE rationale, interpretation of facts and figures to support the change was cobbled into House Bill 515 sponsored by a state representative from a 98 per cent white district near Herman, MO. The announcement of the bill and particulars caught the university by surprise and rallied the university faculty, administration, and national alumni association in a unity of effort that discredited the CBHE's facts, interpretation of enrollment data, and more importantly, highlighted that the new ten county regional Lincoln University would exclude the black students from Kansas City, St Louis and the Missouri Bootheel counties that Lincoln was formed to serve and had served since 1866. In the vernacular of language used on the quadrangle (the gathering place in front of Schweich Hall and the cafeteria back in the 1950s-1960s)', "President Jenkin's team took 'em to school and sent 'em packing with an apple and a funny book". The CBHE and misinformed sponsor of HB #515, withdrew the legislation in the fall of 1985. However, in June 1986, a greater crisis was uncovered and publicly announced by the director of CBHE. Lincoln university had a deficit of $600 thousand dollars and was directed to take all necessary actions to enter a financial restricting under bankruptcy laws. **The crisis would be the worst threat to the university in its storied history**. After a series of alarms, outcries and recommendations the university's fate was placed in Governor John Ashcroft's hands. Recommendations to Governor Ashcroft included: close the university temporarily; make Lincoln a fifth campus of the University of Missouri or allow the newly appointed Lincoln Board of Curators to continue the progress in fiscal accountability and continue its mission. Thankfully, Governor Ashcroft's approved the newly reconstituted LU Board of Curators (his appointments included the Plant Manager of Westinghouse in Jefferson City, an Investment Banker; an AT&T Attorney; an Attorney from Ralston Purina in St. Louis, and later, a veteran Missouri school official from Russellville.) recommendation. And because of his decision thousands of students continue to attend, become educated, and exposed to the most culturally diverse college of higher education in Missouri. Because the CBHE generated crisis (HB # 515 to make Lincoln University a regional college) and the financial deficit crisis that nearly ended Lincoln University as a Historical Black College - comprehensive land-grant institution, serving a diverse clientele, contains essential arguments all appointed officials should be required to read the outcome of this crisis. Additionally, the generational and sociological changes of the past could inform the university and alumni leaders of how to remain abreast of future changes that may impact Lincoln's HBCU status. Dr. Antonio Holland's, Chapter V, the 1980's: Catastrophe and a New Beginning, *The Soldiers 'Dream Continued: A Pictorial History of Lincoln University of Missouri, 1991, Should* be mandatory reading by university and alumni leaders. The document is well written and researched.

- Lincoln's reputation suffered a major blow during the deficit crisis. The state's major newspapers lambasted the university and the administration for mismanagement. The American Association of University Professors defined the term 'financial exigency' -the equivalent of a business filing for reorganization under bankruptcy laws- as "an imminent financial crisis, which threatens the survival of the institution as a whole and which cannot be alleviated by less drastic means." The director of the CBHE, whose attempt to make Lincoln a regional state college failed, now directed the university to begin financial exigency actions. The director of CBHE was supported by the state auditor who joined the chorus of alarm because Lincoln University was the first in the history of the state to adopt such an emergency declaration. The university's claim that arbitrary funding cuts in prior years before the deficit contributed to the problem is a probable cause. However, the voluntary resignations of five members of the board of curators, two budget officers and President Jenkins along with the termination of some administrative staff were the necessary actions towards a solution that looked to be the end of Lincoln University Missouri. However, the behind the scenes hiring of the budget officers and President Jenkins as consultants by the newly constituted board and with the knowledge of the CBHE helped to straighten out the accounting mess that likely resulted from the three major reorganization of the staff and faculty in a ten-year span. The negative aspect of the deficit that may have influenced the Governor's decision to allow Lincoln to fix its deficit problems could have been a public statement by a University of Missouri Executive. When asked about the possibility of the state placing Lincoln under MU, the executive stated that MU had no interest in taking over any responsibility for Lincoln's operation. Finally, the new board's hiring **of Dr Givens, President**, Harris Stowe State Teachers College, St. Louis as "Chief Executive Administrator" for six months in 1987 and followed by the hiring **of Dr. Norman Auburn** and **Dr. Luther Foster**, Academy for Educational Development to serve as acting President and as Vice President part time respectively to help the board select a new president proved to be a collective act of wisdom to save Lincoln University. Dr. Auburn was President Emeritus of the University of Akron, Ohio, had served as acting president of several schools and served as acting President of Lincoln on a full-time basis. Dr. Luther Foster had distinguished himself as President of Tuskegee Institute (University) for nearly thirty years served as Vice President of Lincoln on a part-time basis. These two professionals bolstered the confidence of the CBHE and the governor and helped the board of curators find a new president. **Presidents Chavis, Jenkins and Vice President Carl Smith, Lincoln University Alumni Association** are credited with marshalling the support that helped save our beloved university.

- **President Wendell G. Rayburn, Sr.,** (1988-1986) restored Lincoln's fiscal image and increased the enrollment every year of his tenure. The curators with the help of the management team chose Dr. Rayburn, former President, Savannah State College, from more than ninety applications. His leadership and accomplishments during his tenure reaffirmed that he was the best choice for the position at this critical time in the university's history. Just months after his inauguration the director, CBHE proposed that Lincoln become part of a Missouri state university system combining it with Central Missouri State University, Warrensburg; Southeast Missouri University, Cape Girardeau; and Northwest Missouri State University, Marysville. The new system would operate under a statewide governing board. Even more significant, Lincoln would give up its 1890 Land Grant status to Harris Stowe Teachers College in St. Louis. **Dr. Rayburn opposed this scheme as being harmful to Lincoln and his written response left no doubt of the importance of the 1890 Land Grant status in conjunction with the Missouri Attorney General's 1954 statement of Lincoln University mission and purpose to the state and America. In the first instance Lincoln would lose $10 million dollars annually in grant and research programs in agriculture related opportunities by giving up the land grant status and secondly, the state of Missouri does not have the authority to transfer 1890 land grant dollars, and thirdly Dr. Rayburn stated the suggestion of transferring the land grant status to Harris Stowe because most of the students there were black would be a return to the separate but equal status for black schools. He concluded his statement by emphasizing that both the 1890 land grant and 1954 Missouri Attorney General's statements emphasized access to all and that Lincoln was known for peaceful integration and its cultural diversity.** The director, CBHE dropped the issue. Lincoln's enrollment continued to soar from Dr. Rayburn's hiring of full-time recruiters; one to focus on Missouri urban and out-of state areas and the other to focus on Mid-Missouri. However, his most significant accomplishment was the unanimous board decision to remove the financial exigency that signaled

Lincoln's financial management systems were under control and producing the desired results. The university also had a million-dollar surplus, and Dr. Rayburn credited **Earl Wilson,** a 1957 alum and retired senior executive from IBM who Dr. Rayburn called "the million-dollar man". Dr. Rayburn left Lincoln in 1996 to become vice president-secretary-treasurer and senior associate of the American Association of State Colleges and Universities in Washington, D.C.

1997-2012: The Soldiers Monument and Memorial Plaza

Dr. David Henson (1997-2005)was a fierce advocate for Lincoln University's founding legacy and retention as a Historical Black College. He proposed the creation of the monument and plaza as an image that would be a daily reminder that Lincoln was founded by the 62nd and 65th Colored Infantry Regiment and their white officer, Lt Richard Baxter Foster. After the death of Dr. Henson and appointment **of Dr. Carolyn Mahoney (2005-2012),** one of her first acts was to continue the project. I was appointed to the fundraising committee, and we successfully dedicated the monument in 2008. The monument surpassed the dreams of Henson and Mahoney by not only becoming a popular campus site for recognition of Lincoln's founders and purpose in Jefferson City, but also nationally through the popular televised program of Good Morning America.

2022 – Dr John Moseley

As I close this chapter in November 2022, Lincoln University Missouri continues to be a Repository of Freedom with an African American perspective under the leadership of **President John B, Moseley** the first white president since the college became a university in 1921. I attended Moseley's inauguration in September

2022 as the 21st President and was impressed by his vision and passion to grow the university. Some black alumni question his suitability to lead Lincoln University as a Historical Black College considering past attempts by some in the Missouri legislature to make Lincoln a regional state university or become a satellite under the University of Missouri system. I recognize the threat to Lincoln's HBC status but believe Moseley is committed to the importance of the 1890 land-grant annual funds to Lincoln and the purpose of the Morrill Act recognizing the educational needs specific to black Americans. Lincoln's identity has been strongly identified with serving the needs of black Americans since it's founding in 1866 and reinforced by the 1890 Morrill Act. Those needs have not changed even with the passage of the 1954 Supreme Court decision and African American opportunities to attend universities of choice in America. There continues to be large populations of black Americans disadvantaged by poverty and race where aspiring youth have limited opportunities to attend state or other institutions of higher learning. Dr. Moseley's 10/23/2022 letter to alumni addresses this concern and announced his hiring of five full time regional recruiters to work in urban areas in the state of Missouri and in urban areas of other states that send black students to Lincoln. Additionally, Moseley established an on campus tutoring program to retain students to develop and graduate from Lincoln. This early initiative is not a predictor of President Moseley's success but in my opinion, he is off to a good start and on the right path to retain Lincoln's HBCU status while embracing the collegiate aspirations of commuter students. His actions also identify with past Lincoln Presidents above who understood the importance of holding on to Lincoln's identity as an 1890 land-grant institution, seeking to increase the enrollment and retention of black students in Missouri while simultaneously providing a welcoming environment to educate white and minority commuter students. President Moseley will be required to make many tough decisions in his tenure that will determine how well or how poorly Lincoln

University educates students to meet their life challenges. Although I have confidence in Moseley's leadership, a capable and responsible board of curators and alumni association officers are the other legs of the stool needed to accomplish Lincoln's mission. Both are appointed or filled by a political process beyond the University President's control but not his ability to influence. I encourage and support the three entities to work together to prepare Lincoln University students to meet their life challenges at the university and in their chosen field of work after graduation. While no one can know the future, university presidents and faculty can prepare students to apply the knowledge they teach and help them adjust to the changing environment and circumstances they will experience in the world of work. Lincoln's trademark has always been to prepare her students to excel in their chosen field. Moseley's grade card will be evaluated by the students who excelled in their life challenges thirty years from now. President Dawson and faculty during my years at Lincoln receive very high marks.

I share with you below my recall of the campus environment and the faculty at Lincoln University that prepared me and my generation to apply the knowledge they taught to prepare us for the world of change and challenge.

1956-1960: Lincoln University Faculty and Preparation of Students

I attended Lincoln University from 1956-1960 and summarize below the societal setting of the university, the qualifications and role of professors, and in broad terms, how well my LU experience prepared me to meet my life challenges:

- Lincoln was a well-managed small black college with an enrollment of approximately 1400 black students and less than 100 white students during the day. The 1954 Supreme Court decision was being implemented as reported under President Dawson's tenure above.

- The faculty and professors were 98 percent black and highly qualified. Many Ph.D. professors had over 30 years' experience with solid academic work in their specialty; among them were: Doctors Greene and Sherman

- Savage, history; Hardiman, Latin, Spanish, and French; Talbot, Physics.

- C.B. Taylor, Industrial Education; Pullam, Biology and Mr. Cecil Blue, MA, Harvard, English. Those with 20 to 8 years teaching experience were, Doctors Seeney, education; Pawley, Speech and Theatre; Pride, Journalism.

- Hoard, education and Dean of Students; Byrd, Chemistry; Fuller, Music and first African American to receive a Ph.D. in music, and Oliver Cox, author of Caste, Class, and Race: A Study in Social Dynamics, 1948; Sociologist; Ruth Muse, mathematics; and Hazel McDaniel Teabeau, English,

- I majored in Graphic Arts and minored in Industrial Education. My major interest was in Army ROTC. I had no white academic instructors and all ROTC instructors were black except the white supply sergeant.

- The professors were very much aware of their responsibility to prepare us for jobs within the black community and for jobs in our profession that were opening to blacks because of the efforts of civil rights organizations. When speaking about racial prejudice in the workforce they emphasized the acquisition of knowledge as the most effective tool to defeat racial prejudice. • Many LU grads in my generation were the tip of the spear integrating public, corporate and military institutions and in a short span of 30 years became senior executives of those organizations. The resume of our accomplishments speaks well for Lincoln University professors preparing graduates in the 1950-1980 era to meet professional challenges.

I pray that President Moseley and faculty will receive high marks for teaching their students how to acquire, apply and use knowledge in their ever-changing world and life circumstances from alums thirty years from now. My knowledge and character development at Lincoln not only enabled me to acquire additional skills and competitive qualifications with other college graduates but also helped me discover the importance of institutions founded by African Americans in cooperation with white allies. That is why Lincoln University MO is a repository of America with an African American perspective and must remain open to a diverse college population.

Lincoln University MO and New Philadelphia, IL: Repositories of Freedom that Merit Support and Exceptional Leaders

Lincoln University Missouri and New Philadelphia, IL are two of a few institutions in America founded during the era of slavery by African Americans in cooperation with like-minded white Americans. Both are a repository of freedom with an African American perspective that demonstrate the application of the self-evident truths by black and white citizens in a government divided by custom or laws that denied equal rights and opportunity based on race, color, gender or national origin at the time of their founding. They continue to exist because of leaders and supporters who cherish the rights of liberty and justice for all based on behavior and achievement and not race, gender or other personal preferences. We can learn much about the role that faith, family, freedom and friends played in the establishment of these two repositories of freedom and continues to play in the protection of their existence. I am grateful to be affiliated with both New Philadelphia Association and Lincoln University Missouri. I am inspired by the amazing accomplishments of Free Frank McWorter and humbled by the opportunity Lincoln University Missouri gave me to live a life of adventure and service from Hunnewell, Missouri to distant corners of the world as a soldier and as a Senior Government Executive in Atlanta, GA and Washington, D.C. with the city of Atlanta, AmeriCorps and the Library of Congress respectively. Thanks for keeping New Philadelphia and Lincoln University American repositories of freedom with an African American perspective.

MY RETIREMENT YEARS

Visiting family and friends and mourning the loss of loved ones are the activities that usually occupy a retiree's time. Betty and I are no exception. My brother, two sisters, and many close friends have passed since my retirement. And learning to be a caregiver and a receiver of care has also been a part of this season of my life. But through it all, grace continues to smile and open doors of understanding for me about the cause and effect of racial discrimination in America. I was too busy during my working years to connect the dots of our shared past and to see how blacks and whites can commemorate the end of the Civil War for different reasons.

My volunteer activities, with one exception, have been with organizations that preserve local and national historic events associated with African American contributions to the event. My volunteer efforts with the sesquicentennial observance of the Civil War have been gratifying and informative. And the exception was helping President Obama become president of the United States in 2008. It was an eye- opening experience for me and Betty. The election campaign was a national survey of racial attitudes among all Americans, but especially of black and white Americans.

The Obama campaign experience came early in my retirement and was filled with moments of pride offset by disbelief at some of the reactions against candidate Obama. The campaign got into high gear in 2007 and coincided with my search for something worthwhile to do. Betty and I were spending the winter and spring in Nevada, and Betty, eager to get involved, jumped right into volunteering at Obama's campaign office not far from our home in Henderson, NV.

The excitement and prospects for electing our first African American president of the United States was contagious. I had never been involved in political campaigns because of the legal prohibitions against government employees campaigning for candidates for state or national office. But I was now on my own time, free to express my rights as an American citizen, and so I volunteered to help elect Obama as president of the USA. Betty and I worked the phones, canvassed neighborhoods for support, and served as precinct captains in our voting district.

The campaign brought out the best and worst in our country's racial attitudes and showed that race continued to be a factor among the electorate we contacted in our district. On several occasions, someone took our "Obama for President" yard signs down, prompting me to complain to the local police. My call received what I considered to be a frivolous response. When I asked if

I could shoot anybody I caught trespassing on my property or attempting to take down my Obama sign, the officer or representative suddenly woke up. The serious consequences that could result from such unlawful actions became evident, and shortly thereafter, public service announcements began airing a warning that removal of yard signs was a prosecutable offense.

On another occasion, while engaged in door-to-door canvassing for Obama support in our neighborhood, I rang the doorbell of a man who opened the door, took one look at the material I had in my hand, and said, "You are in the wrong neighborhood" and closed the door. I can't say that I was surprised at his reaction because most residents in our housing area had McCain signs in their yard. I felt no animosity against those who preferred McCain over Obama, but I did resent the disdain many expressed against candidate Obama. Nonetheless, I was still excited about Obama's candidacy and even relished the opportunity to be included among the retired generals and flag officers invited to meet with Obama on June 18, 2008, in Washington, DC.

There were about sixty flag and general officers representing all branches of the military and holding the ranks of one to four stars. I was one of fifteen African American generals and felt that Obama understood the processes to fund the military and maintain a strong defense to meet potential threats against American security interests. He also appeared to know when to impose his authority over those generals who had a tendency to dominate the conversation. He proved adept at smoothly changing the topic to one of interest to him.

I was so impressed that I accepted his request to use my influence on his behalf in communities where we were influential. I wrote an editorial in response to a letter opposing Obama by a reader of the Monroe City Gazette, the small town in MO where I had worked as a young adult and graduated from high school. I was also the grand marshal of Monroe City's sesquicentennial parade, and during private conversations with my former high school classmates, I championed his fitness to be the president of the USA. I detected by their silence that he was not high on their list.

We were in Nevada when the electoral votes were counted, and President Barack Obama became the forty-fourth president and the first person of multiracial heritage to hold that office. We were ecstatic, freaked out, and emotional! At the time, I thought that the majority of Americans demonstrated that we had finally reached a point in the country's race relations where skin color and ethnicity were no longer disqualifying factors for the highest elective office in America. For a brief moment, I thought that Martin Luther King Jr.'s dream of "character over color" had become a reality and that American political, civic, and business leaders had buried racism alongside Jim Crow. The jury is still out on that issue. However, my participation on volunteer boards gives me hope that the current generation of Americans will bury racism in America for good. Useful answers and persuasion can be found at the historical sites that preserve the stories that helped to establish the cherished freedoms in our constitution. Some of those stories can provide unexpected discoveries behind our troubled race relations past. The Cass County (MO) museum's Civil War exhibit was such a setting for Betty and me.

The exhibit showed pictures of the entire populations of Jackson, Bates, Cass, and parts of Vernon counties, MO, being evicted from their homes by a union general officer during the Civil War. Pictures of families walking alongside wagons loaded with their belongings and headed east looking for a place to settle. I was surprised to learn that many relocated to northeastern Missouri and settled in Hannibal, Palmyra, and Mexico, not far from my home in Hunnewell. I understood for the first time in my life how those evicted residents could bring their hatred of all things union to their new communities and rigidly enforce racial segregation practices against me and other black residents in the community. Had I not been a member of the Freedom's Frontier National Historic Area Board and invited to the museum's Civil War exhibit as a member of the board, I doubt that I would have ever gone to Cass County. My discovery put to rest a nagging question I had growing up in that area as to what could have caused some whites to dislike or hate black people so much. That exhibit and other pictorial accounts of historical events preserved at the organizations I worked with since retirement don't excuse or justify hatred; they expose the harsh treatment that causes people to hate.

The organizations I volunteered with below are staffed by talented men and women whose passion for preserving the fruits of freedoms are contagious. They fueled my desire to volunteer and share observations about the historical interpretation preserved at those sites. Some are troubling and others are a call for awareness and involvement. All my comments and observations are driven by the vision of an America created by the founding fathers and restated by Martin Luther King Jr. Grace, the unseen mover for the good of mankind, played a key role in my involvement with the American Folk Life Center (AFC), the Missouri State Parks Foundation (MSPF), Freedoms Frontier National Historical Area (FFNHA), Hannibal's African American Life and History Project (HAALHP), and Mission Readiness, retired flag officers for a strong military defense. Each organization is unique and so is my reason for becoming involved.

The AFC was created by congress as the American Folk life Preservation Act and made it a part of the Library of Congress. The act recognizes that building a strong nation does not require the sacrifice of cultural differences and that American culture has a fundamental influence on the desires, beliefs, values, and character of the American people, and that it appropriates for congress to support the AFC to preserve, support, revitalize, and disseminate American folk life traditions and arts. When I retired from the Library of Congress in 2007, Dr. James Billington, the librarian of Congress, asked if there was anything he could do that would suit my interests in retirement. I immediately stated, "An appointment to the AFC's board of trustees." I am on my second appointment and still believe the AFC to be the most important cultural institution for the preservation of American music, ethnic cultural events, and American folklore. Among the AFC's prize collections are Slave Narratives obtained by volunteers who interviewed former slaves during the WPA of President Franklin D. Roosevelt's administration (Henry Dant, my great-grandfather's story is included in the collection); the US Civil Rights Exhibit, a joint collection of documents and information in partnership with the Smithsonian Institution that covers African American struggles to gain the freedoms under the US Constitution from the Civil War to the Voting Rights Act of 1965; and the Veterans History Project, established by the US Congress and implemented under my guidance as the deputy librarian of Congress in 2000. Many Americans are unaware of the AFC and its interesting collection of American cultural history. If you want to know more about the AFC, visit www. loc.gov/folklife.

The MSPF raises money to support the maintenance of parks and historical sites for Missouri residents. My involvement with the MSPF was totally unexpected. I was in Nevada in 2008 when my phone rang, and I was asked if I would serve on the MSPF to champion the establishment of a memorial in honor of the first African American soldiers who fought in the Civil War at a site called Island Mound, Bates County, near Butler, MO. The caller was John Riddick, a member of MSPF who had gotten my name from the daughter of one of Betty's friends living in Washington, DC. I was initially skeptical because I had never heard of the battle but agreed to become an MSPF member and champion the cause. The facts proved to be correct because the Kansas First Colored Volunteer Infantry were recruited, outfitted, and trained by Jim Lane, a US senator from Kansas.

Senator Lane was appointed by President Abraham Lincoln to raise regiments of Union Forces to fight in the Civil War. Without Lincoln's approval, Lane's black soldiers fought against a well-armed group of Missouri Confederate Bushwhackers on October 22, 1863, and won. Their successful battle was reported in Harper's Weekly Magazine and momentarily laid to rest the notion that African Americans lacked fighting capability.

As the only African American member on the MSPF board, I credit Pamela Boatwright, the organization's former executive director, Jim Denny,

Missouri Civil War historian; Dr. Doug Eiken, former director, Missouri State Parks (MSP); and Bill Bryan, director MSP, for doing the heavy lifting and making Island Mound a state historical site in 2012. My role as the champion of the Kansas First Colored Volunteer Infantry historical site gave me the opportunity to address the members of Missouri Governor Jay Nixon's Sesquicentennial Civil War Commission to recommend goals for the observance of the numerous Civil War battles fought in Missouri. My main suggestion was to use the observances to educate visitors on the ideological conflicts between the 1776 Declaration of Independence and the US Constitution of 1787 that fueled each side to fight for their respective beliefs.

Missouri as a border state remained in the union but had as many confederate sympathizers as it did union loyalists. The abolitionist and northern supporters of the Civil War believed that the ideals expressed in the declaration pertained to all Americans, including slaves; the confederate and southern supporters believed that the US Constitution gave them the right to protect their property, including their slaves. The issues are still debatable.

The board included my recommendation to use the battle sites to educate visitors without including the specifics of the constitution versus the declaration. I was okay with their decision but continued to highlight the ideological differences between the documents in my briefings and discussions about Island Mound and Civil War battles. For more info on MSPF check out: www. missouristateparksfoundation. org.

FFNHA consists of the twelve western Missouri counties and twenty- nine eastern Kansas counties where the Civil War and Civil Rights battles took place and mark the places that led to the freedoms we cherish in the constitution. FFNHA was designated a heritage area by the US Congress and signed into law by President George W. Bush in 2004. It is partially administered by the National Park Service and a joint board of MO and KS residents . . .

I was invited to be on the board by John Dillingham, former board chair, after he had heard my presentation at the inaugural of Island Mound. I welcomed the opportunity to serve on the FFNHA because of the important Civil War and Civil Rights battles that occurred in the FFNHA.

My visits to some of the battle sites informed my understanding of why there is still anger and mistrust between the offspring of our ancestors who participated or were deeply affected by the emotional scars from those battles. Some (African Americans, whites, Native Americans), on both sides of the issues, still harbor ill feelings for the way their ancestors were treated long after the issues had been settled on paper and the participants had rotted in their graves. The three battles in the Missouri–Kansas wars to illustrate how the chain of memory continues to carry the scars for some are the battle of Island Mound, the Lawrence Kansas massacre, and the mass evacuation of Jackson, Bates, Cass, and parts of Vernon counties in Missouri. Although I used the mass eviction to open the chapter earlier, the chain of events is better understood in the context of their occurrence.

Black soldiers armed and trained in Leavenworth, KS, marched into the confederate stronghold of Island Mound, near Butler, MO, dressed in union uniforms and carrying rifles. They killed several bushwhackers, established a fort, and named it Fort Africa. The sight of former slaves dressed in uniforms and carrying guns was an affront to the bushwhackers and was considered another antagonistic act of Kansans against Missourians. About one year later, in August 1863, the raid by Quantrill on Lawrence, KS, targeted and killed over 150 men and boys for no reasons other than being from Kansas and supporting the abolitionist movement. The chain of memory is still coloring the way some interpret the events 150 years later.

African American struggles for civil and equal rights after the Civil War continued, and the state of Kansas was one of the sites that bore the name of the most significant supreme court ruling that ended racial segregation in public schools in America: Brown versus Topeka Board of Education. More importantly, the 1954 supreme court decision struck down the "separate but equal" segregation law established under the landmark case of Plessy versus Ferguson handed down in 1896. This case was the basis for denying blacks access to public accommodations throughout the south and border states. Monroe School, one of the original schools for blacks in Topeka, is now a national historic site run by the National Park Services. The site houses a complete chronicle of African American civil and equal rights struggles in America. Moreover, it is one of the premier locations within the FFNHA and helps explain the importance of this geographical region to the establishment of the freedoms that characterize our identity as Americans. That is the good news; the sad part is that these freedoms were won by the blood, sweat, and tears of our ancestors—and far too many Americans take them for granted. I am encouraged by the number of white Americans who support and champion the preservation of these hard-won freedoms. At the same time, I am disappointed by the few African Americans who are involved in the preservation and interpretation of these significant achievements in the evolving creation of American democracy. No group of Americans have shed more tears, lost more blood, or poured out more sweat than our African American ancestors. For more information on FFNHA visit: www. freedomsfrontier.org.

HAALHP exhibits the contributions of Hannibal's African American residents before, during, and after slavery up to the integration of public schools in Hannibal and Northeast, MO. Faye Dant, founding director of HAALHP, is the wife of my first cousin, Joel. Hannibal is Betty's hometown, and her sister still lives there. I attended high school there for three years. And in addition to Joel and Faye returning to live there, his two sisters—Bobby and Tysa— have also relocated there. But the most compelling reason to get involved was the opportunity to preserve and display African American contributions to the geographical area of our birth and the investments our ancestors made on our behalf so that we could have better opportunities than they had. If we don't tell their story or preserve African American contributions to our communities, we run the risk of the stories not being included or being marginalized by others. Faye's commitment to inclusion inspired us to volunteer our time and resources to serve on her board and to help achieve her worthwhile and commendable goals.

When Joel and Faye relocated to Hannibal in 2008, there was no trace of the vibrant black community that had evolved during racial segregation. This lively community was still visible when they left to pursue their successful professional careers in human resources in 1970. The black business sections, black schools, and black entertainment venues had been demolished, and most of the black teachers and entrepreneurs had died. No memorials or museums had been established to show the contributions of black residents to Hannibal. Hannibal was famous as the birthplace of America's most popular writer, Samuel Clemens aka Mark Twain, and had a museum that exhibited the history of the town's historic past minus any reference to the African American presence in the city.

Faye observed what was happening, was moved to action, and inspired Joel, Betty, me, and several locally prominent interracial residents to join her. These included James O'Donnell, owner of O'Donnell Funeral Home, and Jane and Joe Miller and Phillip Smith, our high school classmates, who volunteered to serve on the HAALHP board of directors. The exhibit opened in September 2010 and was displayed as part of the Hannibal Museum, in the heart of the Mark Twain tourist district. The exhibit displayed the contributions of black business, educational, and civic leaders to the African American community in Hannibal before slavery up through the 1954 supreme court decision that integrated public schools in northeast Missouri in 1955.

The exhibit drew support from all sectors of Hannibal and especially from African American churches. Faye expanded her focus from displaying pictures, articles, and artifacts of black Hannibal natives during the exhibit period to include the real-life identity of Twain's character "Jim," a slave on his uncle's farm in Florida, MO, who lived in Hannibal after emancipation. This notable figure was little known or mentioned as an integral part of Hannibal's African American past. She discovered that the exhibit opened lines of communication between black and white Hannibal residents. This dialogue was sparked by adding the real-life identity of Daniel Quarrels, fictionalized as "Jim" in Mark Twain's Adventures of Huckleberry Finn, and drew the attention and participation of Twain scholars from far and wide.

As chairman and board members, we helped Faye stage a grand opening of "The Huck Finn Freedom Center: Jim's Journey" on September 21, 2013, in a stand-alone historical building built by slaves during the Civil War. The event drew a large crowd that included the mayor, local educators, business and civic leaders, and a Mark Twain scholar, Dr. Shelley Fisher Fishkin, Stanford University, Joseph S. Atha, professor of humanities, professor of English, and director of American studies. Fishkin, author of, Lighting Out for the Territories, has taken an active interest in the project.

Hannibal, MO, is typical of most small towns experiencing an aging population coupled with dwindling job opportunities for high school graduates while simultaneously struggling to embrace the inevitability of a multiracial majority in America. The plight of African Americans in those communities is dire as there is no bench strength to carry forward African American cultural, civic, and religious institutions that flourished during the era of racial segregation. Such institutions are slowly dying because of a dwindling black population. Contemporary leaders have not yet found ways to make local institutions equally attractive to whites and multiracial groups, a development which would insure their vitality as viable community, religious, and civic organizations. I think Faye's model is the best available approach to promote better community relations through the use of Mark Twain's stories about race in historical Hannibal. Doors could open that may help preserve Hannibal's African American churches and civic institutions. These grace-infused portals may well provide needed support to such institutions in their evolutionary journey to become full-fledged community organization while preserving their historical past. Visit www.jimsjourney.org for an interesting glimpse of Mark Twain's Hannibal, MO.

Mission: Readiness: This nonpartisan national security organization of five hundred retired admirals, generals, and other retired senior military leaders advocates for smart investment in American children. I was asked and agreed to help convince members of Congress and the general public on the need to invest in smart educational programs. My most interesting involvement was in Las Vegas, NV, during the summer of 2013. I along with Major General Bath of the US Air Force was asked to brief Senate Majority Leader Harry Reid, NV, on the educational crisis and its devastating impact on military recruitment. Our mission was to secure Senator Reid's support of early childhood education as a federal and state partnership aimed at redressing the issue. Bath, a longtime associate of Senator Reid, told me to mention my appointment as Maynard Jackson's chief operating officer in Atlanta, GA, as the surest way to grab the senator's interest. It worked, and Senator Reid enthusiastically agreed to put the issue on his agenda. I doubt that the issue will rise to the top of his agenda given the strength of the Republicans in the senate. It is a sad fact of American politics that any issue President Obama supports— including a federal and state partnership to bolster the skills proficiency of American youth— Republicans in Congress are likely to oppose. For more information on Mission Readiness visit www. missionreadiness.org.

My participation on the volunteer boards has done more than give me something to do. I have learned that there are still Americans who donate their time to preserve our cultural history and in so doing, are protecting the American dream. As I said in the introduction, my story is about the American dream. And as long as there are reminders that American freedoms are etched in the hearts, hopes, dreams, and aspirations of our citizens, the dream will never die. I say that even in the midst of the current national outrage over the police killings of black men in Ferguson, MO, New York, NY, and Cleveland, OH. The demonstrators who are protesting the injustice are black, white, Latino, Asian, and multiracial. The use of dogs, nightsticks, and fire hoses did not stop black people from demanding equal justice during the Civil Rights Movements of the

1950s; current demonstrators will not be stopped until the police and the citizen they are sworn to protect honor the pact that makes us Americans: the belief that all men (people) are created equal and endowed by their creator with the rights of liberty, justice, and the pursuit of happiness, and community laws are equally enforced.

I know from personal experience that it required an Eleanor Roosevelt,

Harry Truman, Thurgood Marshall, John Kennedy, Lyndon Johnson, and Martin Luther King Jr. to bring about the change that helped my generation achieve the American dream. And I'm grateful and also a bit worried.

I don't see an emergent leader among the current generation with the courage of our past heroes to keep the dream alive for the rich to prosper while making opportunity for the poor and disenfranchised to rise to the middle class and beyond.

My faith in the unseen mover for the good of mankind tells me that an emergent leader will come forth because America and the American dream is her cherished project. How else do you explain a poor black kid from Hunnewell navigating through racially segregated institutions and earning his way through evolving multiracial educational and employment organizations to become a brigadier general in the US Army, chief operating officer, city of Atlanta, GA, founding national director, AmeriCorps' NCCC, and deputy librarian/chief operating officer, Library of Congress.

The enduring inspiration of the founding declaration and those who preserve its freedoms will always be the ladder of escape from disadvantaged circumstances in America. I am a witness that for those who believe and act, Grace will help you tell her incredible story.

MY GOVERNING VALUES

Spiritual: Jesus Christ introduced me to God, and I enjoy the privilege of being His adopted son. As Christ's ambassador, I am learning to be obedient to His word so that I can join Him in doing His kingdom work on earth as He has done in heaven. I get orders from Christ through bible study, prayer, circumstances, and members of the body of Christ. The Holy Spirit is my advocate in all circumstances, and together, we are greater than Satan who is in the world.

Ego Check: "For I say, through the grace given unto me, to every man that is among you, not to think of himself more highly than he ought to think; but to think soberly, according as God hath dealt to every man the measure of faith." Romans 12:3 (KJV)

Working Relationships: "Love one another with brotherly affection. Outdo one another in showing honor, Do not be slothful in zeal, be fervent in spirit, serve the Lord. Rejoice in hope, be patient in tribulation, be constant in prayer. Contribute to the needs of the saints and seek to show hospitality." Romans 12:10-14 (ESV)

Social Relationships: "Be of the same mind one toward another. Mind not high things but condescend to men of low estate. Be not wise in your own conceits. Recompense to no man evil for evil. Provide things honest in the sight of all men. If it be possible, as much as lieth in you, live peaceably with all men." Romans 12:16-18 (KJV)

Understanding: "Trust in the Lord with all thine heart; and lean not unto thine own understanding. In all thy ways acknowledge him, and he shall direct thy paths. Be not wise in thine own eyes; fear the Lord and depart from evil." Proverbs 3:2,5-7(ESV)

Rhyme or Reason of Life
"Racial Identity and Birth are no Predictors of Humanity and Worth"

I was clear in my purpose for updating Recipient of Grace Continued and gave it my best effort to deliver what I promised. I had intended to use this space to hammer home the importance of Power of Choice and Relationships in our lives and the importance of an American perspective vs a racial, privileged, or self-centered perspective in the discussion of Different Perspectives and Shared Goals as Americans. However, in reviewing my notes, outlines, and pages of the original and added chapters of *Recipient of Grace Continued* the whole of my life got me thinking if there is a rhyme or reason for the purpose of life? My reflection on the stories of New Philadelphia and Lincoln University Missouri gave me an answer that explains Free Frank and the founders of Lincoln University and my life experiences.

There is a rhyme and a reason for human existence and that logical reason is: Use your God given rights and talents to help yourself and others achieve their God given rights and talents. The rhyme above explains the absurdity of using race, wealth or any other predictor of power and success to value human worth based on a person's racial identity. A person's worth to humanity is based on her/his willingness to use personal influence or office to empower others to enjoy equal rights and opportunities afforded others under the covenant of The Declaration of Independence and US Constitution as amended. In that regard, being an American is special when individuals respect the rights of others as accorded to themselves. **The Declaration of Independence and Constitution is what makes America special in the world of nations.** That is why the actions of Harry Truman, Thurgood Marshall, Earl Warren and others in chapter Twenty-Nine are highlighted as examples of their courage to use their influence for the equal rights and opportunities for African Americans and disenfranchised citizens of Americans. **This is what it means to be an American. I suggest that all Americans wean ourselves from racial bias and strive to evaluate, accept, and choose our relationships based on behavior, belief, attitude, accomplishment and compatibility, and leave race out of the evaluation. This is particularly suggested in choosing our elected political leaders and representatives.**

The founders of New Philadelphia and Lincoln University Missouri teach the most fascinating lesson about humanity and the power to overcome evil with good. The founders of each place did not allow their enslavement to stop them from using what they had to achieve their aspirations and dreams for themselves and others. Their willingness to invest all that they had- time, resources and energy- attracted allies with influence to help them in the common cause of freedom; to care for family, friends and neighbors in pursuit of life, liberty and happiness; a pursuit that does not subordinate the rights of individuals based on race, gender, or other inalienable gifts from God. These nuggets of humanity are powerful because New Philadelphia and Lincoln University Missouri are still visible and reinforcing those lessons of humanity daily. The Lincoln University Missouri example is even more vivid because hundreds of thousands have been prepared to pursue their educational goals and life challenges at the institute that evolved into a university. Thousands of racially diverse students continue to be educated at the university yearly. They and we alums are the recipient of the founders' exercise of their courage to start a school in Missouri for black Americans against odds too great to calculate in 1866.

The update of Recipient of Grace Continued satisfied my need to share my thoughts and hopefully, encourage you to reflect on your relationships, perspective as an American, and your purpose in life. The update challenged me to clarify my perspectives for your evaluation of my ideas and thoughts about Americans and America solely based on your rights as an American and fellow human. I'm grateful to the understanding and help from The Holy Spirit, Anne Lopez, Steve Lofton, Jack Windom, Sonja Scott Woods, Gailya McElroy Scott, Summer Scott, Clotele Palmer and Dorothy Butler Gilliam. Most of all I'm proud to be a recipient of God's Grace and to be an American.

This is a wrap. Until next time and please remember that:

Racial Identity and Birth are no Predictors of Humanity and Worth

K

N

Q

R

153, 186,

199–200, 223, 225, 259, 267,
277, 281, 284
Roosevelt, Franklin D., 2,
4, 284 Russell, Harold, 5,
91, 110

S

Saint, Crosby "Butch," 154, 177–78,
186, 189–91
San Diego (city in California),
222, 229–30 scholars, 268–69,
276
Schwarzkopf, Norman, 135, 138–39,
141, 151, 214
Scott, Merrill Edward LaVern, ix, xvii, 54–55, 65, 68,
124–25, 128, 132,
143, 152, 163, 165, 167–68, 184
Seabrook (lieutenant colonel), 110–11, 113–14
Seattle (city in Washington), 144, 163–64
Segal, Eli, 217, 223, 225, 233, 237,
258–59 sepa-
ration, 1, 105,
132 Shilling
Manor, 68,
268

Simko (lieutenant colo-
nel), 87–88, 92 slavery,
1–2, 13, 26, 288–89
slaves, 2, 19, 286, 289

Smith, Ike, 162
Smith, Renzo, 5, 12, 15–16, 57, 68
South Vietnam, 93, 114

Vietnam, 61, 64–65, 68, 74, 76, 87, 92–93, 96, 99–106, 110–16, 118–21, 132, 164, 166, 268
Vietnamese Army, 117

W

Walker (general), 95–97 Wall Street Journal, 147–48
Warner, Mark, 243, 246
Washington, DC (capital of the United States of America), xvi, 2, 100, 110, 114, 117, 119, 134, 151–52, 161, 186, 217, 222–24, 229–30, 241
Washington Colored School, 4, 6, 10–11, 15
Weekly, Ralph, 64, 285
Westervelt, John, 131, 134–35
West Point, 34, 58–59, 63, 70–71, 89, 108, 127–28, 141, 166
Whiddon, Orion "Cotton," 193, 195, 200, 239
White, Edna, 5, 15
Whitman, Sarah, 221
Williams, Roy, 5, 15, 229
Wofford, Harris, 128, 141, 224–25, 237, 267
women, 49, 68–71, 179, 221, 284

Wright, Bob, 10, 17–20, 92, 103, 134, 141, 167, 186–87, 258, 288 Wright, Rose, 10, 19

Y

www.ingramcontent.com/pod-product-compliance
Lightning Source LLC
Chambersburg PA
CBHW050312160726
48002CB00001B/6